The Triumph of Conservatism

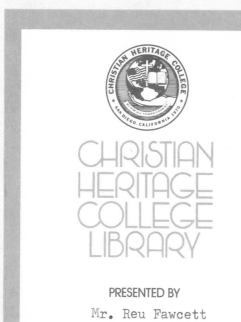

The Triumph

of Conservatism

A REINTERPRETATION

OF AMERICAN HISTORY, 1900-1916

Gabriel Kolko

THE FREE PRESS
A Division of Macmillan Publishing Co., Inc.
NEW YORK

Collier Macmillan Publishers
LONDON

The Free Press
A Division of Macmillan Publishing Co., Inc.
866 Third Avenue, New York, N.Y. 10022

Collier Macmillan Canada, Ltd.

First Free Press Paperback Edition 1977

Library of Congress Catalog Card Number: 63-16588

Printed in the United States of America

printing number
1 2 3 4 5 6 7 8 9 10

ISBN-0-02-916650-0

To my parents

ACKNOWLEDGMENTS

EVERY RESEARCHER owes debts to library workers and archivists that can only be acknowledged but never repaid. This book would be far poorer were it not for the splendid assistance given by the staff of the various sections of the National Archives, and especially the Business Economics Branch. I am also grateful for the cooperation given by the staffs of the Manuscript Division of the Library of Congress, the University of Virginia Library, the Columbia University Library, and the Williams College Library. The various Harvard University Libraries provided not only admirable working facilities but also a congenial climate and stimulating friends.

All references to Federal Trade Commission materials in the National Archives, or manuscripts in the F.T.C. Building, are based on the commission's kind permission to allow me to examine their hitherto closed records. Needless to say, neither the commission nor any other agency is in any way responsible for my use and interpretation of materials under their jurisdiction.

Readers will notice that I do not discuss railroads in my history. Such a consideration will be the topic of a more specialized volume, *Railroads and Regulation,* to be published in the near future. Suffice it to say, the history of railroads and government regulation in the period 1877–1916 reinforces the more general theme developed in this book.

GABRIEL KOLKO

CONTENTS

INTRODUCTION

THIS IS A BOOK that is motivated by a concern with the seemingly nonacademic question of "what might have been." All men speculate or dream as they choose, but the value of the speculation depends on the questions asked and on the way they are answered. Speculation of the type prompting this volume has its value only if it leads to the re-examination of what happened—what *really* happened—in the past.

The political or economic history of a single nation, especially during a specific, critical period which has a determining influence on the decades that follow, should be examined with provocative questions in mind. And there is no more provocative question than: Could the American political experience in the twentieth century, and the nature of our economic institutions, have been radically different? Every society has its Pangloss who will reply in the negative. But to suggest that such a reply is mere apologetics would be a fruitless, inaccurate oversimplification. Predominantly, the great political and sociological theorists of this century have pessimistically described and predicted an inexorable trend toward centralization, conformity, bureaucracy—toward a variety of totalitarianism—and yet they have frequently been personally repelled by such a future.

Unless one believes in an invisible, transcendent destiny in American history, the study of men and institutions becomes the prerequisite for discovering how one's question should be answered. The nature of the questions in this study demands that history be more than a re-interpretation of what is already known, in large part because what is known is insufficient, but also because histories of America from the turn of the century onwards have all too frequently been obsessed by effects rather than causes. Theories and generalizations based on such an approach have ignored concrete actions and intentions, and for this reason the study of consequences and effects has also been deficient.

Assuming that the burden of proof is ultimately on the writer, I contend that the period from approximately 1900 until the United States' intervention in the war, labeled the "progressive" era by virtually all historians, was really an era of conservatism. Moreover, the triumph of conservatism that I will describe in detail throughout this book was the result not of any impersonal, mechanistic necessity but of the conscious needs and decisions of specific men and institutions.

There were any number of options involving government and economics abstractly available to national political leaders during the period 1900-1916, and in virtually every case they chose those solutions to problems advocated by the representatives of concerned business and financial interests. Such proposals were usually motivated by the needs of the interested businesses, and political intervention into the economy was frequently merely a response to the demands of particular businessmen. In brief, conservative solutions to the emerging problems of an industrial society were almost uniformly applied. The result was a conservative triumph in the sense that there was an effort to preserve the basic social and economic relations essential to a capitalist society, an effort that was frequently consciously as well as functionally conservative.

I use the attempt to preserve existing power and social relationships as the criterion for conservatism because none other has any practical meaning. Only if we mechanistically assume that government intervention in the economy, and a departure from orthodox laissez faire, automatically benefits the general welfare can we say that government economic regulation by its very nature is also progressive in the common meaning of that term. Each measure must be investigated for its intentions and consequences in altering the existing power arrangements, a task historians have largely neglected.

I shall state my basic proposition as baldly as possible so that my essential theme can be kept in mind, and reservations and intricacies will be developed in the course of the book. For the sake of communicatior I will use the term *progressive* and *progressivism,* but not, as have most historians, in their commonsense meanings.

Progressivism was initially a movement for the political rationalization of business and industrial conditions, a movement that operated on the assumption that the general welfare of the community could be best served by satisfying the concrete needs of business. But the regulation itself was invariably controlled by leaders of the regulated industry, and directed toward ends they deemed acceptable or desirable. In part this came about because the regulatory movements were usually initiated by the dominant businesses to be regulated, but it also resulted from the nearly universal belief among political leaders in the basic justice of private property relations as they essentially existed, a belief that set the ultimate limits on the leaders' possible actions.

It is business control over politics (and by "business" I mean the major economic interests) rather than political regulation of the economy that is the significant phenomenon of the Progressive Era. Such domination was direct and indirect, but significant only insofar as it provided means for achieving a greater end—political capitalism. *Political capitalism* is the utilization of political outlets to attain conditions of stability, predictability, and security—to attain rationalization —in the economy. *Stability* is the elimination of internecine competition and erratic fluctuations in the economy. *Predictability* is the ability, on the basis of politically stabilized and secured means, to plan future economic action on the basis of fairly calculable expectations. By *security* I mean protection from the political attacks latent in any formally democratic political structure. I do not give to *rationalization* its frequent definition as the improvement of efficiency, output, or internal organization of a company; I mean by the term, rather, the organization of the economy and the larger political and social spheres in a manner that will allow corporations to function in a predictable and secure environment permitting reasonable profits over the long run. My contention in this volume is not that all of these objectives were attained by World War I, but that important and significant legislative steps in these directions were taken, and that these steps include most of the distinctive legislative measures of what has commonly been called the Progressive Period.

Political capitalism, as I have defined it, was a term unheard of in the Progressive Period. Big business did not always have a coherent theory of economic goals and their relationship to immediate actions, although certain individuals did think through explicit ideas in this connection. The advocacy of specific measures was frequently opportunistic, but many individuals with similar interests tended to prescribe roughly the same solution to each concrete problem, and to operationally construct an economic program. It was never a question of regulation or no regulation, of state control or laissez faire; there were, rather, the questions of what kind of regulation and by whom. The fundamental proposition that political solutions were to be applied freely, if not for some other industry's problems then at least for one's own, was never seriously questioned in practice. My focus is on the dominant trends, and on the assumptions behind these trends as to the desirable distribution of power and the type of social relations one wished to create or preserve. And I am concerned with the implementation and administration of a political capitalism, and with the political and economic context in which it flourished.

Why did economic interests require and demand political intervention by the *federal* government and a reincarnation of the Hamiltonian unity of politics and economics?

In part the answer is that the federal government was *always*. involved in the economy in various crucial ways, and that laissez faire never existed in an economy where local and federal governments financed the construction of a significant part of the railroad system, and provided lucrative means of obtaining fortunes. This has been known to historians for decades, and need not be belabored. But the significant reason for many businessmen welcoming and working to increase federal intervention into their affairs has been virtually ignored by historians and economists. This oversight was due to the illusion that American industry was centralized and monopolized to such an extent that it could rationalize the activity in its various branches voluntarily. Quite the opposite was true.

Despite the large number of mergers, and the growth in the absolute size of many corporations, the dominant tendency in the American economy at the beginning of this century was toward growing competition. Competition was unacceptable to many key business and financial interests, and the merger movement was to a large extent a reflection of voluntary, unsuccessful business efforts to bring irresistible competitive trends under control. Although profit was always a consideration, rationalization of the market was frequently a necessary prerequisite for maintaining long-term profits. As new competitors sprang up, and as economic power was diffused throughout an expanding nation, it became apparent to many important businessmen that only the national government could rationalize the economy. Although specific conditions varied from industry to industry, internal problems that could be solved only by political means were the common denominator in those industries whose leaders advocated greater federal regulation. Ironically, contrary to the consensus of historians, it was not the existence of monopoly that caused the federal government to intervene in the economy, but the lack of it.

There are really two methods, both valid, of examining the political control of the economy during the period 1900-1916. One way would be to examine the effects of legislation insofar as it aided or hurt industries irrespective of those industries' attitude toward a measure when it was first proposed. The other approach is to examine the extent to which business advocated some measure before it was enacted, and the nature of the final law. Both procedures will be used in this study. The second is the more significant, however, since it points up the needs and nature of the economy, and focuses more clearly on the disparity between the conventional interpretation of progressivism and the informal realities. Moreover, it illustrates the fact that many key businessmen articulated a conscious policy favoring the intervention of the national government into the economy. Because of such a policy there was a consensus on key legislation regulating business that has been overlooked by historians. Important businessmen did not, on the whole, regard politics as a necessary evil, but as an important part of their larger position in society. Because of their positive theory of the state, key business elements managed to define the basic form and content of the major federal legislation that was enacted. They provided direction to existing opinion for regulation, but in a number of crucial cases they were the first to initiate that sentiment. They were able to define such sentiment because, in the last analysis, the major political leaders of the Progressive Era—Roosevelt, Taft, and Wilson—were sufficiently conservative to respond to their initiatives.

Although the main view in the business community was for a rationalization of the conditions of the economy through political means, advocates of such intervention, the J. P. Morgan interests being the most notable, were occasionally prepared to exploit the government in an irregular manner that was advantageous as well. The desire for a larger industrial stability did not exclude an occasional foray into government property, or the utilization of the government to sanction a business arrangement of questionable legality. Such side actions, however, did not alter the basic pattern. In addition, business advocacy of *federal* regulation was motivated by more than a desire to stabilize industries that had moved beyond state boundaries. The needs of the economy were such, of course, as to demand federal as opposed to random state economic regulation. But a crucial factor was the bulwark which essentially conservative national regulation provided against state regulations that were either haphazard or, what is more important, far more responsible to more radical, genuinely progressive local communities. National progressivism, then, becomes the defense of business against the democratic ferment that was nascent in the states.

Federal economic regulation took two crucial forms. The first was a series of informal détentes and agreements between various businesses and the federal government, a means especially favored by Theodore Roosevelt. The second and more significant approach was outright regulation and the creation of administrative commissions intended to maintain continuous supervision over phases of the economy. We shall examine both forms from the viewpoint of their origins, intent, and consequences; we shall examine, too, a number of movements for regulation that failed to find legislative fulfilment of any sort but that provide insight into the problems and needs of the economy in the Progressive Era.

If business did not always obtain its legislative ends in the precise shape it wanted them, its goals and means were nevertheless clear. In the long run, key business leaders realized, they had no vested interest in a chaotic industry and economy in which not only their profits but their very existence might be challenged.

The questions of whether industrialism imposes narrow limits on the economic and political organization of a society, or on the freedom of men to alter the status quo in some decisive way, have been relatively settled ones for the large majority of social scientists. Max Weber, perhaps more than any social theorist of the past century, articulated a comprehensive framework which has profoundly influenced Western social science to answer such questions in the positive. The bureaucratic nature of the modern state and of modern industry, to Weber, restricted all possibilities for changing the basic structure of modern society. The tendency toward centralization in politics and industry, toward a mechanical impersonality designed to maximize efficiency, seemed to Weber to be the dominant theme in Western society, and the Weberian analysis has sunk deep roots into academic discussions of the problem. The systematic economics of Karl Marx—as opposed to that of "Marxists"—also sustained the argument that the basic trend in capitalist development was toward the centralization of industry. Indeed, such centralization was an indispensable aspect of Western industrialism, and could not be circumvented. Both Marx and Weber, one an opponent of capitalism and the other indifferent to it, suggested that industrialism and capitalism, as they saw both develop, were part of the unalterable march of history.

The relevance of the American experience to the systematic theories of both Weber and Marx will be explored in greater detail in the conclusion, my argument being that neither of the two men, for all their sensitivity and insight, offered much that is of value to understanding the development of capitalism and industrialism in the United States. Indeed, the American experience, I shall try to contend, offers much to disprove the formal theories of probably the two greatest social theorists of the past century. It is perhaps unfair to Marx, who based his case on the conditions existing in England and Western Europe in the mid-nineteenth century, to burden him with American history at the beginning of the twentieth, but he was not terribly modest about its applicability, and any respectable theory should have the predictive value its author ascribes to it. Weber, on the other hand, frequently stated that the United States was the prime example of modern capitalism in the twentieth century, if not the best proof of his theory.

American historians, with some notable exceptions, have tended, without relying on comprehensive theoretical systems of the Weberian or Marxist variety, also to regard the development of the economy as largely an impersonal, inevitable phenomenon. All too frequently they have assumed that concentration and the elimination of competition—business giantism or monopoly—was the dominant tendency in the economy. The relationship between the growth of new competition and new centers of economic power and the legislative enactments of the Progressive Era has been virtually ignored. On the contrary, federal legislation to most historians has appeared to be a reaction against the power of the giant monopoly, or a negative response to the very process of industrialism itself by a threatened middle-class being uprooted from its secure world by corporate capitalism. A centralized economy, historians have asserted, required a centralized federal power to prevent it from damaging the public interest, and the conventional political image of the Progressive Era is of the federal government as a neutral, if not humane, shield between the public and the Morgans, Rockefellers, and Harrimans. Progressivism has been portrayed as essentially a middle-class defense against the status pretensions of the new industrialists, a defense of human values against acquisitive habits, a reassertion of the older tradition of rural individualism.

Recent historians have, for the most part, assumed monopoly was an economic reality concomitant with maximum efficiency even where, as I shall show, it was little more than a political slogan. For it is one thing to say that there was a growth of vast accumulations of corporate power, quite another to claim that there existed a largely monopolistic control over the various economic sectors. Power may be concentrated, as it was, but the extent of that concentration is crucial. Historians of the period have too often confused the power of corporate concentration with total monopoly. The distinction is not merely important to American economic history, it is vital for the understanding of the political history of the period. And to the extent that historians have accepted the consensus among contemporaries as to the inevitable growth of monopoly at the turn of the century, they have failed to appreciate the dynamic interrelationship between politics and economics in the Progressive Era.

I shall be accused of oversimplifying what historians have written about the Progressive Era, and with some justice. But I believe it can be stated that although there are important and significant monographic works or histories of specific phases of progressivism which provide evidence to disprove aspects of such a comprehensive interpretation, no other theory of the nature of the Progressive Era has, in fact, yet been offered. And even most of the critical historians have accepted the traditional view of progressivism as a whole. No synthesis of the specific studies disproving what is, for better or worse, the conventionally accepted interpretation among historians of the Progressive Period has been attempted. Nor has there really been a serious effort to re-examine the structural conditions and problems of the economy during the period and to relate them to the political and especially the detailed legislative history of the era. And it is here, more than any other place, that a new synthesis and a new interpretation is required.

Yet the exceptional historical works that have raised doubts about specific phases of the larger image of progressivism are suggestive in that they indicate that the time for reinterpreting the Progressive Era and the nature, character, and purpose of progressivism, is opportune. The work of the Handlins, Louis Hartz, and Carter Goodrich, to name only a few, in showing the *dependence* of business on politics for government aid and support until the Civil War suggests that the unity of business and politics was still a relatively fresh memory by the end of the nineteenth century. Sidney Fine has pointed out how many businessmen treated laissez faire and Social Darwinian doctrine gingerly when it was to their interest to have the government aid them. William Miller has shown that the background and origins, and hence the status, of the triumphant industrialists was respectable and at least well-to-do, implicitly raising questions about the status conflict between the allegedly old elite and the new. John Morton Blum has expressed doubts as to the radicalism of Theodore Roosevelt, whom he has portrayed as a progressive conservative, but ultimately a conservative. And, perhaps more than anyone else, Arthur S. Link has critically dissected the history of the Wilson Administration in a manner that forces the historian to doubt whether the conventional usage of the term "progressive" really describes the New Freedom.

Although other monographs and studies can be cited, there are still too many loose ends in the traditional view of the Progressive Period, and no synthesis. More important, there has been no effort to study the entire period as an integrated whole. The very best work, such as Link's, deals with presidential periods, but the movements for legislative enactments ran through nearly all the administrations, and can only be really understood in that context. For without such a comprehensive view, the origins and motives behind the legislative components of the Progressive Period cannot be fully comprehended, assuming that there is some correlation between intentions or purposes and results. And although historians have increasingly been puzzled by the growing incompatibility of the specific studies with the larger interpretation, they have not been able to reconcile or explain the disparities. The Progressive Era has been treated as a series of episodes, unrelated to one another in some integrated manner, with growing enigmas as the quantity of new research into the period increases. The Progressive Party was one incident, the Food and Drug Act another, the conservation movement yet one more event.

In this study I shall attempt to treat the Progressive Era as an interrelated and, I hope, explicable whole, set in the context of the nature and tendencies of the economy. Ultimately, the analysis that follows is of interest only if it throws light on the broader theoretical issues concerning the extent to which a larger industrial necessity imposed limits on the political structure, and the manner in which politics shaped the economic system.

CHAPTER ONE

MONOPOLIES AND
MERGERS:
PREDICTIONS AND
PROMISES

NOT MERELY PRESENT-DAY HISTORIANS but also contemporary observers of the growth of big business were virtually unanimous in believing that the concentration of economic power and the growth of "monopoly" and the "trust" was an inevitable result of the modern capitalist *and* industrial process. This unanimity was shared not only by the conventional celebrators of the status quo—the businessmen, conservative journalists, and intellectuals—but also by the critics of capitalism. Indeed, at the turn of the twentieth century a belief in the necessity, if not the desirability, of big business was one of the nearly universal tenets of American thought.

It is to be expected, of course, that the large majority of the important businessmen who contemplated and wrote about the growth of big business were ideologically receptive to a rationale of it. The similarity of economic values held by both small and big businessmen was

sufficiently great to undermine the serious possibility of the sort of social analysis capable of challenging the big businessman's belief in the
necessity and desirability of the economic world as he saw it evolving.
This agreement on fundamentals, needless to say, has never meant
there could not be very substantial disagreement among businessmen
on particular issues of specific importance to one type of industry, or
to a business of a certain size. But the signal fact of American business
history is the consensus among businessmen, of varying degrees of importance and in different industries, that the capitalist system is worth
maintaining in one form or another; this has resulted in a general attitude that has not necessarily been opposed to decisive innovation in
the economic sphere, but which has opposed radical economic programs that might, in the process of altering the concentration of economic power, also undermine the stability, if not the very existence,
of the status quo. If the small businessman has at times joined antimonopoly crusades, the least that can be said is that he has never
pursued his beliefs to the point where his own stake in the existing
economic order has been endangered.

But, even granting the belief of so many historians in the existence
of small businessmen who have challenged the supremacy of the great
business enterprises, the evidence indicates that the vast majority accepted the inevitability of the monopoly movement in the economy
even if they believed it undesirable. The prevalent nonacademic analysis at the turn of the century was that the cold, hard facts of industrial
life and technology favored the growth of big business, and that little
could be done to change the limitations these facts placed on political
programs for economic change. Such assumptions, based on a few
years' experience with the merger movement, were as much wish-
fulfilment as descriptions of reality. By 1907 many big businessmen
were aware that their world was more complicated, and their utterances were increasingly to become celebrations of a situation they
hoped to attain rather than of the world they actually lived in.

The Inevitable
Monopoly

Important businessmen and their lawyers in the first years of this
century were convinced that big business was necessary, inevitable,

and desirable as a prerequisite to rationally organizing economic life. And the destructiveness of competition and the alleged technical superiority of consolidated firms were the catalytic agents of change which made industrial cooperation and concentration a part of the "march of civilization," as S. C. T. Dodd, Standard Oil's lawyer, phrased it. Although there was a formal commitment to varieties of laissez faire economic theory in most of the academic world, big businessmen developed their own functional doctrine very much opposed to competition as either a desirable mechanism or as a goal. ". . . the 'trust,' " wrote James J. Hill in 1901, "came into being as the result of an effort to obviate ruinous competition." "Competition is industrial war," wrote James Logan, manager of the U.S. Envelope Company in the same year. "Ignorant, unrestricted competition, carried to its logical conclusion, means death to some of the combatants and injury for all. Even the victor does not soon recover from the wounds received in the conflict."[1] The instinct of survival made combination inevitable, for combination was "caused primarily by the desire to obviate the effects of competition"—or at least this was the dominant contemporary view of the matter.[2]

At the same time, combinations were the logical outcome of technological considerations, according to big business opinion. The larger the output the smaller the cost of production, suggested Charles M. Schwab of United States Steel, and this meant lower supervision costs, better goods, and lower prices.

The validity of the notion that corporate consolidation leads to industrial efficiency will be examined later. But a belief in this proposition was shared by virtually all of the important businessmen who wrote or commented on the matter in the pre-World War I period, and it is this belief which became the operational basis of their actions. Buttressed by this conviction, men such as Schwab, Elbert H. Gary, John D. Rockefeller, and John D. Archbold were certain that their economic behavior was "inevitably" preordained. This synthesis of the doctrines of the efficiency of consolidations and the destructiveness of competition is echoed again and again in the later part of this period. Even when the big business community developed an involved and often shifting set of political goals it never ceased to view itself as making the technologically efficient and inevitable response to the evils of unrestricted competition. "Unrestricted competition had been tried out to a conclusion," an American Tobacco Company executive wrote in 1912, "with the result that the industrial fabric of the nation was confronted with an almost tragic condition of impending bankruptcy. Unrestricted competition had proven a deceptive mirage, and its victims were struggling on every hand to find some means of escape from the perils of their environment. In this trying situation, it was perfectly natural that the idea of rational co-operation in lieu of cut-throat competition should suggest itself."[3]

At least a decade before his younger brothers embarked on that grey, pessimistic intellectual discourse which now has a classic place in American intellectual history, Charles Francis Adams, Jr., president of the Union Pacific Railroad from 1884-1890, was announcing that "the principle of consolidation . . . is a necessity—a natural law of growth. You may not like it: you will have to reconcile yourselves to it." "The modern world does its work through vast aggregations of men and capital. . . . This is a sort of latter-day manifest destiny." Periods of intense competition were perpetually followed by combinations and monopolies, according to Adams. "The law is invariable. It knows no exceptions."[4] But, ignoring the fact that the essence of Brooks and Henry Adams' generalizations on the role of the corporation in modern life can be found expressed with great clarity in the earlier writings of their older brother, what is significant is that the widespread belief among important businessmen in the inevitability, if not the desirability, of the concentration of economic power was shared by most contemporary intellectuals and journalists. And although many intellectuals and journalists were critical of the functions or even the nature of the massive corporation, most, like Charles Francis Adams, Jr., resigned themselves to their necessity and shared the consensus on the character and future of the American economy.

Academic economists of the historical school were less concerned about the classical preoccupation with the nature and conditions of competition than they were with fostering a positive attitude toward minimal government regulation of the economy. It was this tacit acceptance of a theory directed toward redressing the existing balance of social and economic power via political means that meant that, on an analytical basis at least, the probably most sophisticated group of American economic thinkers accepted the same fundamental premises on the nature of the industrial structure as most major businessmen. The variations on the businessman's essential theme are as diverse as academic minds are subtle, but a clear pattern can be distinguished. Richard T. Ely, for example, maintained that large-scale business was inevitable, but that, save for certain types of services, monopolies in the pure sense were not preordained; the burden of his writing was concerned with the desirability of government regulation of "artificial" monopolies that had sprung up rather than with regulation as a means for restoring purely competitive conditions. Henry C. Adams, one of the founders of the American Economic Association, saw in monopoly, which was "natural" only in railroads, the possibility of "cheapness and efficiency," and was attracted by its advantages—provided it was controlled by minimal government regulations. By and large, historical economists such as E. Benjamin Andrews, Arthur T. Hadley, Edwin R. A. Seligman, and Simon N. Patten were ready to "accept," with little empirical analysis, the existence of a trend toward monopoly as a starting point on which to provide proof of their theories on the desirable relation of economics to government. And virtually all assumed that, whether monopolistic or not, combined capital avoided the waste of small-scale production.

It is to be expected, of course, that the movement toward corporate concentration had less sophisticated supporters in the academic world as well. S. A. Martin, president of Wilson College, told the Civic Federation of Chicago's Trust Conference in September, 1899, ". . . trusts are here and here to stay as the result of the inevitable laws of industrial development."[5] Less detached defenses of the alleged monopoly movement were as common as big business' interest in cultivating a rationale for its existence. George Gunton, popular economist who spent a number of his years as editor of *Gunton's Magazine* while on an annual retainer of $15,000 from Standard Oil of New Jersey, defended the necessity and desirability of big business. John Moody, whose data-gathering service probably gave him more factual insights into the workings of business than any of his contemporaries, was convinced that "The modern Trust is the natural outcome or evolution of societary conditions and ethical standards which are recognized and established among men to-day as being necessary elements in the development of civilization."[6]

But even among the critics of business there was a general acceptance of the inevitability, and often the ultimate desirability of the "trust." Ray Stannard Baker and John B. Walker, for example, thought monopoly to be progressive. Hardboiled Lincoln Steffens, who main-

tained that business was the source of political corruption, was nevertheless convinced that business concentration was inevitable. Only a
small minority of the muckrakers were concerned with the causes
rather than the consequences of the alleged business debauching of
politics, and most of them assumed that there were always certain
constants in American society, among which were "the trusts."

It is ironic that the greatest celebrators of the alleged trend toward
corporate monopolies could be found among that element in American politics with attitudes sufficiently critical of the status quo to suggest programmatic alternatives to the growth of monopoly—the socialists. After the demise of the Populist movement, only the socialists
were in a position to explicitly reject a policy of economic change limited, as in the case of the advocates of laissez faire, by a conservative
fear of undermining the fundamental institution of private control of
the economy in the process of attempting to restore competition. But
American socialists were Marxists, and Frederick Engels, with characteristic sharpness, had made it clear that "the progressive evolution of
production and exchange nevertheless brings us with necessity to the
present capitalist mode of production, to the monopolisation of the
means of production and the means of subsistence in the hands of the
one, numerically small, class. . . ." Thus armed, American socialists
shared the general belief in the inevitability of corporate concentration
and monopoly, even after key business leaders began realizing it no
longer fitted the facts.

". . . one cannot but acknowledge the natural development of the
successive steps of this [Standard Oil] monopoly," the Social Democratic Party's *Campaign Book of 1900* declared. "No better way could
be invented by which the natural resources may be made available for
the world's need. The lesson of the trust, how to secure the greatest
satisfaction for the least expenditure of human energy, is too good to
be lost." W. J. Ghent, a socialist writer, saw "an irresistible movement—now almost at its culmination—toward great combinations in
specific trades . . . ," and these combinations would dictate the terms
of existence for the small business permitted to survive. Even Henry
Demarest Lloyd, who was not a Marxist but eventually joined the
Socialist Party, gave up his vagueness on the possible alternatives to
monopoly expressed in *Wealth against Commonwealth* and concluded
"centralisation [was] . . . one of the tendencies of the age."

But the resignation of the socialists to inevitable monopoly was not merely a passive commitment to an article of faith. It stimulated many of them to a personal admiration of big businessmen unequalled by most paid eulogists. Indeed, big businessmen were the vehicles of progress and the guarantors of socialism, and worth defending from personal attacks for the parts they played in an impersonal industrial process. For the socialists "are not making the Revolution," *The Worker* declared in April, 1901. "It would be nearer the truth to say that Morgan and Rockefeller are making it." When Ida Tarbell's *History of Standard Oil* appeared, Gaylord Wilshire, publisher of the mass circulation socialist *Wilshire's Magazine,* criticized her for not being more sympathetic to Rockefeller as an individual. The system was predestined and "Mr. Rockefeller was forced by unavoidable circumstances to pursue his path of consolidation. . . . The fault exists not in the individual but in the system." When J. P. Morgan died in 1914, the Socialist *Call* wrote "if Morgan is remembered at all, it will be for the part he played in making it [socialism] possible and assisting, though unconsciously, in its realization."[7]

Although crucial aspects of the intellectual consensus on the role of big business in the American economy were challenged now and again, and a Louis Brandeis might question the necessary relationship between size and efficiency or an Edward Dana Durand could suggest that monopoly was not inevitable and competition was somehow attainable, the significant fact is the pervasiveness of the proposition that economic concentration, if not monopoly, is inevitable and is the price to be paid for maximum industrial efficiency.

Mergers and Promoters

At the turn of the century the vast majority of the businessmen who defended monopoly and corporate concentration believed in it as a goal, and often strove to attain it, but their beliefs were based on a very limited experience which they thought would extend into the future. Monopoly, however, was the exceptional and not the routine characteristic of most industries, and the use of the term "monopoly" or "trust" by defenders of the status quo was based more on wish-fulfilment than on economic reality. (By "trust" I mean effective control of an industry by one firm or a working alliance of firms. Contemporary usage of the term usually equated it with mere large size or concentration, without any specific reference to the extent of market control but with the implicit assumption that large size could be equated with control.)

Many big businessmen, such as Elbert H. Gary, knew that monopoly and the total concentration of economic power did not exist even as they defended it as inevitable. What they were defending was concentration and their monopolistic aspirations, aspirations that never materialized despite their enthusiastic efforts. These key businessmen believed concentration and combination led to efficiency and lower costs, and therefore worked for them energetically. And although we might find this inconsistency natural among the militantly unreflective, it can be suggested that what these men were defending was the status quo, their past actions and consolidation, their future actions and, hopefully, industrial domination.[8]

Certainly it can be said that there was a revolution in the American business structure from about 1897 on—a revolution caused by the sudden rise of a merger movement and the capitalization of new combinations on an unprecedented scale. But the revolution was abortive, whereas the intellectual conclusions based upon it were projected into the future and survived long after the revolution's death. Indeed, the preoccupation with monopoly, which seemed imminent at the turn of the century, led to general intellectual confusion as to the important distinction between monopoly and concentration, and this confusion has seriously interfered with subsequent efforts for a proper understanding of the nature of the American economy and politics in the Progressive Era.

In 1895 only 43 firms disappeared as a result of mergers, and merger capitalizations were $41 million. In 1898, 303 firms disappeared, and merger capitalization was $651 million; and in 1899 the peak was reached when 1,208 firms disappeared as a result of mergers, and merger capitalizations soared to $2,263 million. In 1900 the movement declined precipitously to 340 firm disappearances, and a capitalization of $442 million, and in 1901 the last great merger movement, largely centered about the formation of United States Steel, occurred when 423 firms disappeared, and capitalization amounted to $2,053 million. But the merger movement declined sharply after 1901, despite the permanent impact it had on the modern American intellectual tradition. During 1895-1904 there was an annual average firm disappearance of 301 companies and a total annual average capitalization of $691 million. During 1905-1914 an average of only 100 firms disappeared each year, and average capitalization was $221 million. More important, from 1895 to 1920 only eight industries accounted for 77 per cent of the merger capitalizations and 68 per cent of the net firm disappearances. In effect, the merger movement was largely restricted to a minority of the dominant American industries, and that for only a few years.

The merger movement was caused primarily by the growth of a capital market for industrial stocks after the return of economic prosperity in late 1897. The railroad industry, which was the main preoccupation of European investors who had plunged $3.0 billion into the United States by 1890, was overexpanded and unprofitable. Capital invested in manufacturing increased 121 per cent from 1880 to 1890, and despite the depression of 1893-1897 increased 51 per cent over the next decade. In this context of shifting economic interests, the history of the 1890's is one of sharpening and extending the existing institutional structures for raising capital, and thereby creating movements for mergers, concentration, and, hopefully, monopoly in the American industrial structure.

The stock exchanges of the major financial centers had specialized in railroads until the 1890's, although the Boston Stock Exchange had a copper mine section in the early 1850's which helped establish that city's domination over the American copper industry until the end of the century. Boston, in addition to textiles, was also to dominate the capital market for the electrical and telephone industries until the turn of the century. In 1890 no more than ten industrial stock issues were quoted regularly in the financial journals. By 1893 the number increased to about thirty, and by 1897 to over two hundred.

Industrial capital until the late 1890's came mainly from short-term loans and self-financing out of profits, aiding instability and bankruptcies during the periods of economic decline or depressions. By the 1890's industrial shares became widely available as a result of the creation of new issues from mergers and the reconversion of many trusts, in the literal sense, into unified corporations. And many industrial leaders, ready to retire or diversify their fortunes—Andrew Carnegie is the most notable example—were anxious to develop outlets for their shares. Each new wave of mergers created new sources of capital in a sort of multiplier fashion, and, quite ironically, the very creation of mergers and new industrial combinations led to the availability of funds in the hands of capitalists which often ended, as we shall see, in the creation of competing firms.

The director and coordinator of this industrial metamorphosis was the promoter. To the extent that the dominant stimulus for the promoter was watered stock and his charge for the transaction, the economic concentration which took place at the turn of the century was based on factors other than technological elements inherent in any advanced industrial society. But even if not interested in the transaction fees per se, the promoter was invariably motivated by concern for his own profit position and financial standing, and merely regarded promotion as the means of maintaining or re-establishing it.

Promoters included in their ranks both members of firms being merged and outsiders seeking to stimulate consolidations in order to obtain a share of the profits of the merger. In a number of spectacular instances the insiders of a group of firms sought to interest outside promoters capable of financing or organizing the merger. Quantifications of the nature and source of all or a significant number of promotions do not exist, but some of the more important variations can be illustrated.

William H. Moore and his brother, James H. Moore, were among the three or four most significant promoters. It would be difficult to regard them as anything more than brilliant gamblers. In 1898 William H. Moore organized, at the request of a committee of manufacturers, the American Tin Plate Company out of a group of thirty-five to forty plants. He took options on the component companies and obtained loans to pay for them and provide working expenses. After choosing all officers and directors, he sold $18 million in preferred and $28 million in common stock to bankers and capitalists. Out of this sum he awarded himself $10 million. The Moore brothers were not always so fortunate, however. In 1899 they gave Andrew Carnegie $1 million for an option to try to raise $350 million from bankers to float the sale of Carnegie Steel. They failed, and Carnegie pocketed the money. Similar failures in 1896 forced the Moore brothers into insolvency.

Not infrequently a single manufacturer would turn promoter in order to try to eliminate competition or instability. John W. Gates successfully proved in a law suit that he earned less than $400,000 through underwriting profits and the exchange of shares in the promotion of American Steel and Wire Company in 1899. His only substantial profits were on his component properties that he turned over to the new firm. In the case of the Amalgamated Copper Company, formed in 1899 to gain effective control over the copper industry, outsiders and insiders united. Thomas Lawson, Henry H. Rogers, and William Rockefeller, none of whom had any special competence in the copper industry, cooperated with Anaconda Copper. J. P. Morgan, the largest single industrial promoter and the dominating figure in railroad mergers, resorted to nearly every variation of insider and outsider promotions. Morgan, the Moore brothers, John R. Dos Passos, Moore and Schley, and Charles R. Flint collectively probably accounted for a minority of the total mergers and less than half of the value of all mergers; in addition, there were innumerable single individuals and investment bankers involved in the merger movement.

If the merger movement as organized by promoters was the result of "inevitable" impulses within the capitalist economy, as well as technological imperatives to maximum efficiency, we should determine whether the organization of these new corporations was arranged in such a manner as to: (1) make the competitive entry of new firms increasingly difficult, and (2) avoid the accusation of being organized primarily to create the profits of promotion. It is understood that unless the merger of firms within an industry obtained control of a crucial raw material, patents, or trade advantage, it would have to maintain a reasonable price and profit level or else run the risk of attracting new competitors or allowing existing ones to grow, the risk being scaled to the capital requirements of successful entry. Overcapitalization of the stock of a merged firm, therefore, is an indication of the extent to which a merger was executed to obtain maximum industrial efficiency, control over the competitive annoyances of the industry, or the profits of promotion and speculation. Watered stock meant higher prices in order to pay dividends, and higher prices opened possibilities of new competitive entries.

It is significant, of course, that the heyday of the merger movement was restricted to a few years, and ended almost as abruptly as it began. There are now few academic defenders of the thesis that the merger movement was primarily the outcome of industrial rationality or a desire for control of economic conditions. Charles R. Flint, one of the more important promoters and organizer of twenty-four consolidations, naturally claimed that mergers were intended mainly to attack the evils of competition, and that the profits of promoters were greatly exaggerated by critics. Capitalization, he maintained, was not overinflated, and Flint published data showing that the average return on the *market value* of the stock of forty-seven merged firms was 13.6 per cent.[9]

The evidence is overwhelming, however, to indicate that the watering and overcapitalization of the securities of merged companies was the general rule. This fact was widely acknowledged at the time by economists, by most promoters, and by many businessmen. It was simply not generalized upon or related to contemporary theories on the necessity and inevitability of the trust. Indeed, the incompatibility between the obvious ulterior motives behind the merger movement and social theory was ignored even by those attacking the evils of watered stock. J. P. Morgan's lawyer, Francis Lynde Stetson, frankly admitted that he opposed any scheme for limiting overcapitalization that risked "taking away from men of enterprise their paramount motive for corporate organization. . . ."[10]

A government study in 1900 of 183 industrial combinations shows that stocks and bonds valued at $3,085,000,000 were issued for plants with a total capital worth of $1,459,000,000. The Department of Labor, in the same year, claimed that a substantial group of combinations they studied issued stocks valued at twice the cost of reproducing active plants. Arthur S. Dewing, in a study of fourteen mergers, found that the average overcapitalization was well in excess of 50 per cent of the assets. The large majority of mergers clearly capitalized their firms on the basis of preferred stock representing the cost of the real property or assets and common stock representing the costs of promotion, the expenses of amalgamation, and the expectations of future earnings as a result of the merger. John W. Gates, Henry O. Havemeyer, and John R. Dos Passos freely admitted that common stock represented the promoter's estimate of the potential earning power of consolidations. The profits of underwriters, in many instances, came exclusively from the sale of securities, not anticipated dividends, and this fact alone placed a premium on overcapitalization.

Seven of the combined firms that later entered the United States Steel merger paid out $63 million in stock as commissions to promoters, excluding bonuses and other forms of commission. The tangible assets and property of United States Steel on April 1, 1901, were worth $676 million, and the average market value of the shares it acquired was $793 million in 1899-1901. The total capitalization of the firm was $1,403 million, and the cost of promotion and underwriting consumed over $150 million of this amount. United States Rubber, in much the same way, based its capitalization on 50 per cent watered stock, the common shares representing "the increased earning capacity by reason of the consolidation. . . ."[11]

Promotion, with its premium on speculation to maximize its profits, soon extended its heady gambling mentality to the general stock market. Brokers emphasized the more profitable speculative stock orders rather than investment buying, and they directed their customers to the speculative issues. The commission rates on speculative orders made investment orders less profitable, and by no later than 1904-1907 the volume of transactions on the stock market far exceeded investment demand. This trend alarmed a number of more conservative capitalists primarily concerned with the means, not the ends, of the merger movement, and led to dire predictions, most of which were realized by 1932. Russell Sage wrote in 1901 that watered stock "has also . . . produced a feeling of unrest and disquiet, industrial and political, that threatens, sooner or later, to bring serious results." Henry Clews, the banker, was less restrained.

Many of these [combinations] have been organized in disregard and defiance of legitimate finance, and have exposed the stock market and all the monetary interests depending upon them to risks and disastrous disturbances inseparable from organizations whose foundations rest largely on wind and water. . . .[12]

J. P. Morgan persistently overcapitalized his promotion schemes whenever he was able to do so. His greatest triumph was United States Steel, but when the merger initiative came from insiders, as in the case of International Harvester, Morgan restricted himself to more limited, yet amply lucrative profits. In every case, however, Morgan sought to obtain substantial, if not total, managerial control or board representation.

Morgan's efforts were generally marked by success, and had he avoided managerial responsibilities his fortunes might have been larger and his reputation would certainly have been better. In the case of the formation of the International Mercantile Marine Company, Morgan became deeply involved in a grossly overextended venture. His firm initially received $5.5 million in preferred and common stock at par, and a share of the $22 million paid to bond underwriters. An additional $6 million went to shipper-promoters, and the new firm was burdened with a total of $34 million in merger fees on a preferred and common stock issuance of $120 million and $50 million in cash. But the company was poorly conceived and poorly managed: in the end the Morgan firm lost about $2 million, and International Mercantile Marine went out of business after World War I. In the case of American Telephone and Telegraph, Morgan fought for effective control of the board, which he managed to obtain in 1907. As part of an over-all effort to replace New England management and financial connections, a Morgan-led syndicate obtained a $100 million bond flotation, but was able to dispose of only $10 million before giving up the effort in 1908. Although Morgan's philosophy of trying to obtain managerial control along with the profits of promotion was, on the whole, profitable, it is questionable whether he increased managerial or industrial efficiency. The primary goal of promotions was, as Francis Lynde Stetson admitted, profits. Insofar as Morgan's profits were not immediate or short-range, but tied to the managerial and profit performance of the new company, Morgan tended to do relatively poorly. And in several spectacular instances Morgan either lost money or, as in the railroad industry, bankrupted companies.

To the extent that promotions and mergers were organized among competing firms, the dominant causal factor behind the merger and consolidation movement can be said to have been the existence of internecine competition. A market for industrial securities did not exist in any significant form before 1897, but it most certainly continued after the decline of the merger movement in 1901, and the history of the movement must be explained by more than a market for securities. In the period 1897-1901 the merger movement was the unique result of the rise of a market for securities and an impetus to eliminate competition, and the success of outside promoters was dependent on both factors. But the decline of mergers was due to the collapse of the promises of stability, profits, and industrial co-operation. Save for the outside promoter who took his profit immediately and then broke his ties with the consolidation, the larger part of the mergers brought neither greater profits nor less competition. Quite the opposite occurred. There was *more* competition, and profits, if anything, declined. Most contemporary economists and many smaller businessmen failed to appreciate this fact, and historians have probably failed to recognize it altogether. This phenomenon, I maintain, is a vital key to understanding the political history of the period of reform preceding World War I.

Most important businessmen did not comprehend the general demise of the merger and consolidation movement save in their own industry, and were unable to understand the larger economic context in which they operated. Businessmen, as a group, are not prone to reflection, much less theoretical generalization, but they did act to ameliorate their own illnesses. Now and again, however, a business journal commented on the failure of the merger movement and on the real trends, as opposed to commonly accepted mythology, in the American economy as a whole. In late 1900 *The Iron Age* lamented:

Experience has shown that very few of the promises of the promoters of consolidations have materialized. That some of them are satisfactorily profitable is undoubtedly true. . . . Others are less so; some are con-spicuously unprofitable; some have dissolved, and more will have to dissolve within the next two or three years. Before another wave of the consolidation movement overtakes us, if it ever does, the experiment will have proved itself by the test of time.[18]

CHAPTER TWO

COMPETITION AND
DECENTRALIZATION:
THE FAILURE TO
RATIONALIZE
INDUSTRY

THE FIRST DECADES of this century were years of intense and growing competition. They were also years of economic expansion and, in a number of industries, greater internal concentration of capital and output. But neither of these phenomena was incompatible with increased competition. From 1899 to 1904 the number of manufacturing firms in the United States increased 4.2 per cent, and from 1904 to 1909 they increased 24.2 per cent—a growth of 29.4 per cent for the entire decade. Of the nine manufacturing industries with a product value of $500 million and up in 1909, only one, the iron and steel industry, had less than 1,000 establishments, and the exception had 446. In the thirty-nine industries with products valued at $100-500 million, only three had less than one hundred establishments.[1] The numbers of business failures from 1890 on followed the classic pattern of being high in depressions and low in periods of prosperity, and there is no evidence whatsoever that failures due to competition were any more numerous in 1900 than in 1925.

The new mergers, with their size, efficiency, and capitalization, were unable to stem the tide of competitive growth. Quite the contrary! They were more likely than not unable to compete successfully or hold on to their share of the market, and this fact became one of utmost political importance. The very motives behind the merger movement, and the concern with promotion of enterprises irrespective of the health of the component firms or the advantages of combination, led to an immediate apprehension among well-informed businessmen. "One question of great interest in relation to our new industrial combinations is whether a proper readjustment of their hugely inflated capital and excessive charges will place them permanently in a condition of efficiency, productiveness, solvency, and prosperity, or whether they will ultimately drift, one by one, into the hands of receivers . . ." said Henry Clews at the opening of the century.[2]

This skepticism was more than justified by subsequent events, since the promises of the promoters were, by all criteria, mirages. Forty-eight pre-World War I manufacturing mergers studied by the National Industrial Conference Board had a nominal return on their net worth in 1903-1910 averaging 5.8 per cent—no greater than the average to other firms. Arthur S. Dewing, studying thirty-five mergers of five or more firms in existence at least ten years before 1914, discovered that the steep fixed interest charges and contingent preferred stock dividends imposed by promoters led to a radical deflation of promoters' promises. The earnings of the pre-merger firms were about one-fifth greater than the ten-year average profits of the new consolidation. Promoter estimates of expected ten-year earning turned out to be about twice the actual performance. Another study by Dewing reveals that heavy fixed charges on the basis of expected earnings, administrative difficulties, and continued competition caused ten mergers to earn an average of 65 per cent of their pre-consolidation profits. Shaw Livermore, in a study seeking to defend the success of 328 mergers formed during 1888-1905, nevertheless was forced to conclude that only 49 per cent were "successes" in the sense that their rate of earnings compared favorably after 1918 to other companies in their field. Forty per cent failed altogether, and 11 per cent limped along at lower than average profit levels. He judged the main causes of failures to be poor judgment by promoters, dishonesty, and the decline of the industries.

The inescapable conclusion is that mergers were not particularly formidable and successful, and surely were incapable of exerting control over competitors within their own industries. "Mere bulk, whether of capital or of production, is not, *per se,* an element of strength," *The Iron Age* commented in 1900. "Some of the new plants are better equipped, carry less dead weight of unproductive assets and can produce more cheaply per unit of output than the consolidations can. So far as can be judged, the great industrial aggregations, instead of discouraging competition, have rather encouraged it."[3] Most of the new mergers started out with less than monopoly control, and virtually all lost their initial share of the market. This failure, discussed in detail later in the chapter, was due to the rise of important new competitors and the significant economies of size attainable at lower production levels. Thirteen consolidations studied by Dewing controlled an average of only 54 per cent of the output of their industries upon organization, and the U.S. Industrial Commission studied a sample with an average market share of 71 per cent. Of seventy-two mergers listed by Ralph L. Nelson, twenty-one controlled 42.5 to 62.5 per cent of their markets upon formation, twenty-five controlled 62.5 to 82.5 per cent, sixteen controlled over 82.5 per cent, and ten controlled "large" portions.

There is also data to suggest that very large corporations as a whole did poorly—and many of these were recent mergers. Alfred L. Bernheim studied the 109 corporations with a capitalization of $10 million and up in 1903. Sixteen of these failed before 1914 and were dropped from the list, leaving ninety-three. Only twenty-two of the remainder paid common stock dividends of over 5 per cent during 1900-1914, and twenty-four paid nothing. Their average dividend on common stock over the period was 4.3 per cent. The market value of the common stock of forty-eight of the companies declined over 1900-1914, and rose in only forty-five instances.

In the light of such mediocre profit records it should not surprise one to discover that the mobility of giant firms out of the ranks of the largest hundred industrial corporations was high. Of the fifty largest companies in 1909, seven could not be found in the ranks of the top hundred in 1919, and twenty could not be found there in 1929; for the top hundred corporations in 1909 the figures are forty-seven drop-outs by 1919 and sixty-one by 1929. By comparison, of the top one hundred industrials in 1937, only twenty-eight could not be found in that category in 1957. Bernheim studied the fate of the ninety-nine largest industrials of 1909 by 1924, and found that forty-seven of them could not be found among the largest two hundred corporations of every type. Of this forty-seven, seven had dissolved, three had written down their capital to realistic proportions and were disqualified, nine had become unable even to pay their preferred dividends in full, two had paid no common dividends, ten had merged or reorganized without loss, and sixteen had failed to grow fast enough after 1909.[4]

Many large corporations soon found their overcentralization unprofitable, and tried to reduce plant sizes and distribute plants more widely throughout the nation. In the case of United States Steel, as we shall see, the organizational structure was centralized only at the very highest policy level, and autonomous operating units and specialized staffs have been a general trend in the large corporate structure since the turn of the century. To the extent that Joseph A. Schumpeter was correct in holding that each significant new innovation was embodied in a new firm and the leadership of new men in a still dynamic capitalism—and that firms that do not innovate die—it can also be said that important competitive trends were inherent in the economic structure. The growth in the number of individual patents issued until the peak year of 1916 indicates that innovation was very much a part of the American economy and technology until World War I. Even if organized corporate and government research and development now dominates the field, and many private patents are purchased just to be suppressed, or are infringed merely because most private inventors are economically helpless, enough individuals were able to break into established fields, or to create entirely new ones, to make a significant economic difference.[5] For all of these reasons *The New York Financier,* in opposition to the vast majority of contemporary writers and modern historians, was correct when it observed in June, 1900, that "The most serious problem that confronts trust combinations today is competition from independent sources. . . . In iron and steel, in paper and in constructive processes of large magnitude the sources of production are being multiplied, with a resultant decrease in profits. . . . When the papers speak of a cessation of operation in certain trust industries, they fail to mention the awakening of new life in independent plants. . . ."[6]

This "awakening of new life" in the economy is the subject of the case studies that follow. The examples are significant not only because of their economic role, but also because of their political roles. Moreover, although these typologies reflect a trend, they also involve industries which most historians have been inclined to think proved the conventionally accepted thesis that the tendency in industrial life at the beginning of this century was toward economic concentration and monopoly. They are the "classic" examples of the "trust"—steel, oil, telephones, meat, and a number of others. And in all of these cases we find a fluidity of economic circumstances and radical changes generally slighted by the historian. The shifting markets and resources, the loss of relative power by the dominant companies, the specific failure of the merger movement in attaining either stability or economic control—these are the significant features that emerge from our case studies.

The Iron and
Steel Industry

In 1889 there were 719 companies in the blast furnace, steel work, or rolling mill industry.[7] Many of these firms produced a whole range of steel and iron products, from wire to tinplate, and the steel and iron industry is best characterized as being highly competitive at the time. Since the capital requirement for the consolidation of any important segment of the industry was too high, and since there was no means of preventing the sufficiently powerful firms specializing in one branch of the industry from diversifying into others, the history of the steel industry in the late 1880's and 1890's is one of voluntary efforts to arrange a variety of pools and price and marketing agreements. These, as we shall see, were almost universally failures, and did not solve any of the basic problems inherent in a competitive market structure. The result was a series of mammoth mergers and consolidations which ultimately led to the formation of United States Steel, which also failed to attain stability and control of the market.

The price of most steel goods declined more or less regularly until 1894-1895, and although prices generally rose in subsequent years, there was continual insecurity within the industry as to what each competitor might do next. The apprehension was later justified. The dozens of attempts at voluntary pools in various sections of the steel industry took place after periods of intense price competition, and the pools were in effect agreements to recuperate before more internecine wars. The Bessemer Pig Iron Association and the Bessemer Steel Association were formed in the mid-1890's and failed to control either prices or excess output. The steel billet pool failed, as did the wire and wire-nail pools. No sooner was an agreement made than a single firm would decide to violate some phase of it and eventually bring the whole structure down. Only the steel rail pool, among the many tried, was moderately successful. Its unique position was due to the small number of competing firms, their willingness to accept low profit levels, and the fact that the pool handed 53 per cent of the market over to the major pool buster, Andrew Carnegie. The *Addyston Pipe* decision by the Supreme Court in December, 1899, ended the possibility of lawfully resurrecting the pool system by declaring illegal the division of markets and price-fixing.

The voluntary pool period, having failed to attain its aims, was followed by a period of mergers between competitive firms which came little short of failure as well. The Moore brothers organized the American Can, American Steel Hoop, National Steel, and American Tin Plate companies. In 1898 Morgan formed the Federal Steel Corporation with a capitalization of $200 million, the largest of the twenty-one major iron and steel consolidations during 1898-1900. In 1899 John W. Gates merged seventeen wire companies into the American Steel and Wire Company. Despite the ample amounts of watered stock available for new mergers and the gargantuan efforts of Morgan, Gates, and the Moores, the steel industry in 1899 remained competitive. Although the number of firms with blast furnaces declined 27 per cent from 1889 to 1899, there were still 223 establishments left. And the number of steel work and rolling mill companies increased 7 per cent over the same period, to 445.

With the merger movement at least temporarily failing to attain stability and control within the industry, the ten or more large and powerful new consolidations confronted each other in an uneasy armed neutrality. The crisis came in the spring of 1900 when Carnegie decided to build a large tube plant at Conneaut, Ohio, his first in that field, thereby threatening J. P. Morgan's new promotion, the National Tube Company, and shattering the general agreement within the industry not to diversify into competitive areas. National Tube withdrew its contracts with Carnegie and proceeded to plan its own steel works. In June, 1900, American Steel and Wire decided to begin producing its own steel and canceled its contract with Carnegie. The American Bridge Company followed suit, National Steel began preparing for its own production, and Federal Steel indicated its interest in beginning to produce wire goods. American Steel Hoop cut its steel orders with Carnegie and prepared to enter the wire, rods, and nail business. The working, informal détente between the Morgan, Gates, and Carnegie empires collapsed amid threatening diversification and price competition that promised to drive the overcapitalized steel mergers to bankruptcy and ruin.

Carnegie and Gates were clearly dangerous nuisances to Morgan, especially since Carnegie probably had the lowest steel costs in the nation and could be especially formidable in any competitive struggle. Moreover, Carnegie was threatening Morgan on another front.

In 1899 Alexander J. Cassatt became president of the Pennsylvania Railroad and moved to end a long-standing rebate agreement established by Carnegie and Thomas Scott, former Pennsylvania president. The agreement had allowed Carnegie to receive rates equivalent to what he would have charged himself had he built his own railroad, often cutting rates by one-half. Carnegie decided to retaliate against Cassatt by making an agreement with George Gould, son of Jay Gould, to build a railroad to Baltimore parallel with the Pennsylvania Railroad for much of the way, thereby threatening the entire Eastern railroad system. With Gates calling for renewed competition and Carnegie endangering the Morgan steel and railroad empire, it was inevitable that attempts at permanent reconciliation via a merger be made.

By the end of 1900 both Gates and Carnegie were having sober second thoughts about the desirability of a full-scale conflict with the Morgan steel companies. In addition, since 1898 Carnegie had been undergoing a series of internal company disputes with Henry Clay

Frick which eventually led to a total break and a reorganization of the company. The old man was tired, and the idea of retiring must have appealed to him. Carnegie authorized Charles M. Schwab to hint at a banquet in New York in December, 1900, at which Morgan was present, that the integration and specialization of the entire steel industry was a desirable goal. Within a month Schwab, Gates, Morgan, and Carnegie completed all negotiations, and the United States Steel Corporation was officially organized in New Jersey on February 23, 1901. But the integration of the steel industry was not the primary goal of the merger, since the company started with substantial competition left in the field. The goal was to eliminate the two most important and irrational steel producers in the industry, and, hopefully, to introduce stability, not control, over the steel market. Approximately 40 per cent of the steel industry was left outside the merger. Instead of making an effort to extend control over it, Morgan chose to capitalize United States Steel with over 50 per cent water and to filter over $150 million of U.S. Steel's $1,403 million capital to the promoters and underwriters.

United States Steel consisted of what had once been 138 different companies. Some of these, such as Carnegie, were highly efficient industrial units run with probably maximum economy. American Steel and Wire, on the other hand, closed down approximately two-fifths of the plants it acquired in 1899 as antiquated or unnecessary. All, however, were absorbed by U.S. Steel. Had the motive behind the formation of United States Steel been efficiency and integration, weaker combinations would have been excluded. Thus it is clear that the merger was directed at minimizing potentially devastating competition.

The organizational structure of the new company reflected this fact as well. United States Steel was not an operating company but essentially a security-holding company with a board of directors and finance committee which controlled the power in the last instance, but often had great difficulty in establishing hegemony over each of the ten great divisions within the corporation. Each of these components had its own president and board and practical jurisdiction over its own operations and labor policy. Judge Gary, chairman of U.S. Steel's board, freely admitted that this decentralization policy was the most efficient method of management.

In the process of constructing the organizational hierarchy for the new corporation, the tensions between the executives with back-grounds in steel-making (especially those from Carnegie Steel) and the new financial controllers led to immediate conflicts which undercut the assertion that the corporation was the inevitable outcome of industrial technology. Charles Schwab, who had worked his way up the Carnegie ranks, became the first president of U.S. Steel, and immediately clashed with Judge Elbert Gary, chairman of the executive committee and Morgan's representative. By July, 1901, Schwab was threatening to resign because of the new financiers "who do not understand the whole steel situation."[8] Schwab later complained that the outsiders on U.S. Steel's board, especially Marshall Field and H. H. Rogers, were trying to exploit the corporation for their own purposes by selling it assorted companies or schemes. Over the next few years the power in the firm was shifted from the board of directors entirely to the finance committee, chaired by Morgan's partner, George W. Perkins, and Schwab resigned in late 1903. He was followed in the presidency by another Carnegie steelmaker, William E. Corey, who lost his job in 1909 for siding with the presidents of subsidiaries against Gary; many of the presidents were ignoring central directives and continued to do so for many years.

The efficiency of the new merger was exhibited by the financial crisis that gripped the corporation during its first years. Henry C. Frick, anticipating that the overcapitalization and the new managers might ruin U.S. Steel, quietly began unloading nearly $50 million of his shares in the company. His suspicion was justified. U.S. Steel common shares, which sold at a high of $55 in 1901, reached a low of $9 in 1904. The market value of the firm's stocks and bonds fell $270 million below par value during its first year. In 1902 the company decided it needed $50 million cash to further integrate its component companies and failed to raise one-quarter of that amount. Even more alarming, however, was the precipitate drop in the profits of the corporation at the end of 1903, when a general slump affected the steel industry. In the fourth quarter of 1903 the common dividend of U.S. Steel was cut in half, and it was dropped altogether for the next two years. In 1904 U.S. Steel earned 7.6 per cent on its investments, as compared to 15.9 per cent in 1902. Stabilization was clearly yet to be attained. Even more indicative was the fact that during 1901-1910 U.S. Steel ranked third among eight steel companies on their operating profits as a percentage of gross fixed assets. Profits, too, seemed disappointing in comparison to the promises.

"If the Steel Corporation is to be a permanent success it seems to me that it must at least accomplish two things," George W. Perkins wrote John D. Rockefeller in July, 1903. "1st. Regulate and steady prices, both in times of good and bad business conditions. 2nd. Be very far-sighted in its financial policy and management."[9] Price maintenance in periods of prosperity was an easy task, and save for a small decline in 1904, steel output increased steadily through 1907. The formation of U.S. Steel had not affected prices because of the company's desire not to attract new competitors, and during the boom of 1906-1907 the average price of steel was lower than it had been during the boom of 1901-1902. In late 1907, however, the market for steel began declining. In 1908, steel output was 40 per cent less than in 1907, and U.S. Steel faced its first real test of "bad business conditions."

On November 21, 1907, forty-nine steel industry leaders met at the Waldorf-Astoria in New York to participate in the first of what were soon dubbed the "Gary Dinners." Gary not only invited the steel men, however; he also notified the steel trade journals, the Department of Justice, the Department of Commerce, and the newspapers. Gary was anxious to avoid the impression that he was creating illegal price-fixing agreements or that there was anything secretive in his actions. At the meeting he stressed the need for industry cooperation and all the executives present attacked the demoralization of prices that had resulted from invasions of each other's markets. In the hope of attaining price stability, the group agreed not to reduce prices without mutual consultation, and a committee of five, including Gary, was elected to give advice and conciliate differences. Gary insisted that the meeting was not an effort to fix prices but was instead an effort to maintain them by "gentlemen's agreements."

In late January, 1908, a larger number of steel executives, representing over 90 per cent of the industry, met again at the Waldorf. According to Gary "every manufacturer present gave the opinion that no necessity or reason exists for the reduction of prices at the present time. . . ." This viewpoint was based not on a formal agreement, but on a consensus. The industry wanted competition, but not "bitter warfare." Gary, at the same time, took steps to prevent government prosecution of his voluntary agreements. He wrote Attorney General Charles Bonaparte in February, 1908, that the understanding had been made at the initiative of large steel customers with expensive inventories who wanted the steel industry to maintain prices. Still insisting no formal agreements had been made, Gary wrote that "We are perfectly satisfied to limit the amount of our business to our proportion of capacity and to do everything possible we can to promote the interests of our competitors; and by frequent meetings and the interchange of opinions we have thus far been able to accomplish this result without making any agreements of any kind."[10] The meetings continued.

By May, 1908, however, breaks again began appearing in the united steel front. And Perkins complained to Morgan that U.S. Steel's independent barons, still oriented toward industrial production rather than financial control, were among the leading troublemakers. But rumors were circulating that price cuts were being made or were imminent, and in late May the steel men again gathered to reaffirm their loyalty to the Gary understandings. But it was of no use, and several weeks later they met again to reduce prices on a large number of major steel items to counter the secret price-cutters.

After June, 1908, the Gary agreement was nominal rather than real. Smaller steel companies began cutting prices and distressed U.S. Steel sales managers clamored for steps to meet the competition. Customers began hedging their buying in the hope that more price cuts would follow, and in February, 1909, the major steel companies met, admitted they had cut prices to meet competition, and formally terminated the Gary agreements without setting minimum prices. "So large a part of the current business has been going to those who were either willing or compelled to make lower prices that the situation finally became unendurable," concluded *The Iron Age*.[11]

The collapse of the Gary agreements is an important turning point in the history of steel, for it represents the final failure of the promised stability and profit that motivated the U.S. Steel merger. It represents, as well, the opening of a period of intense competition for steel markets, in which price competition was an important element, which lasted until World War I and the establishment of a working coordination over prices under the auspices of the American Iron and Steel Institute. In 1908 the prices of most important steel products fell sharply according to published data, and even more sharply if individual secret rates are taken into account. It was not until 1916 that the prices of the peak years of 1902 and 1907 were restored in most lines of steel, even though output in 1909 and subsequent years was as great, if not greater, than in 1907.

The formal termination of the Gary Dinners did not result "in as much demoralization" of steel prices as had been expected, Perkins wrote Morgan in March, 1909. But the demoralization had already gone as far as it could, and now steel makers expressed the fear that they were being forced to embark on expansion programs leading to overproduction and excess facilities. In October, 1910, Perkins jealously wrote Morgan that he admired the European steel industry's cartel structure and the fact that the members of the industry had resorted to cooperation "rather than cutting one another's throats. . . ."[12]

Even if the founders of United States Steel did not intend to extend control over the entire steel industry, it is at least certain that they were anxious not to lose their substantial original position. The new company pursued a fairly active policy of acquiring existing firms—Union Steel in 1902, Clairton Steel in 1904, and Tennessee Coal and Iron in 1907, as well as a few minor firms—but made no overtures toward the bulk of its competitors. Presumably the initial size and consequent industrial efficiency of the new giant would have left it with an open field in what was, in fact, a competitive steel market.

Despite its several significant mergers and a policy of keeping the price of iron ore high to exclude new competitors—it owned about three-quarters of the Minnesota ore fields—United States Steel during its first two decades held a continually shrinking share of the steel market. In 1901-1905 United States Steel accounted for 62.9 per cent of the nation's output of ingots and castings, as opposed to 52.5 per cent in 1911-1915 and 46.2 per cent in 1921-1925. U.S. Steel accounted for 43 per cent of the nation's pig iron production in 1901, 43 per cent in 1910; 50 per cent of finished rolled products in 1901, 48 per cent in 1910; 66 per cent of wire nails in 1901, 55 per cent in 1910. U.S. Steel's share of the entire steel output of the nation sharply fell from 61.6 per cent in 1901 to 39.9 per cent in 1920.

U.S. Steel's decline was in large part due to its technological conservatism and its lack of flexible leadership. The iron and steel industry as a whole was in a state of rapid growth and flux from 1900 on, and accounted for 6.9 per cent of the total capital of manufacturing in 1900 but 11.4 per cent in 1919. Technologically, open-hearth steel making replaced the Bessemer process; it accounted for

28 per cent of the steel ingot and castings tonnage in 1899, 79 per cent in 1919. U.S. Steel's basic investment in 1901 was essentially in the Bessemer process, and its expansion program was limited in the belief that its existing facilities were largely adequate. With the exception of the establishment of its Gary, Indiana works and its improvement of its Tennessee Coal and Iron property, U.S. Steel failed to alter the location of its facilities sufficiently or to improve its technology at a time when its competitors were rapidly moving ahead. Moreover, the market for steel goods began shifting radically to lighter steel products, a field which U.S. Steel was slow to enter. The introduction of alloy steels and the continuous rolling mill, and the increasing use of scrap rather than ore—U.S. Steel was heavily committed to ore—only aggravated the firm's decline. U.S. Steel, in short, was a technologically conservative, increasingly expensive operation that illustrates the inadequacy of the dominant theories on the positive relationship between size and efficiency current since the end of the nineteenth century.

U.S. Steel never had any particular technological advantage, as was often true of the largest firm in other industries. Charles M. Schwab admitted in 1901 that a monopoly could not be established without exclusive patents. With the exception of the Bessemer process, patents in the industry were traditionally used for collecting royalties rather than restricting entry. But patents were important to give a firm a lead in a field, as well as royalty income. When Henry Grey offered a new process for making structural steel to U.S. Steel, the corporation turned it down. Schwab, now president of Bethlehem Steel, bought it and established his firm's leadership in that area.

In 1909 there were eleven firms other than U.S. Steel with at least $25 million in assets engaged in some aspect of the steel industry. Since this is approximately the figure at which peak industrial efficiency was reached, each of these firms was capable of meeting U.S. Steel on most terms. Moreover, in 1909 there were still 208 companies with blast furnaces, a decline of only 7 per cent since 1899. The number of companies with steel works and rolling mills increased by one over the same period, to 446. The number of firms engaged in making tinplate and ternplate fell from fifty-seven to thirty-one over the period of ten years, but the number of wire mills using purchased rods increased from twenty-nine to fifty-six. U.S. Steel increased its total output 40 per cent during 1901-1912, thus having a growth rate far lower than any of its older competitors.

If nothing else, the steel industry was competitive before the World War, and the efforts by the House of Morgan to establish control and stability over the steel industry by voluntary, private economic means had failed. Having failed in the realm of economics, the efforts of the United States Steel group were to be shifted to politics.

The Oil Industry

The alleged triumph of Standard Oil over the oil industry was based in large part, as far as there was a triumph, on its ability to extract rebates from the railroads on its shipments. Rebates provided it with the capital and savings which were the key to its expansion, and Standard's defenders and critics alike acknowledge their importance to Standard's growth. Indeed, the secretive nature of the rebating made Standard among the most unpopular of trusts, and the fact that it continued receiving rebates long after the passage of the Interstate Commerce Act in 1887, and even after the passage of the Elkins Anti-Rebating Act of 1903, did little to enhance its popularity. Rebating left Standard naked before public attacks and accusations, and the company became the focus, standing almost alone, of a substantial part of the antimonopoly sentiment at the end of the nineteenth and beginning of the twentieth century. For many, not the least of whom was Theodore Roosevelt, Standard was not merely the reflection or example of the potential evils of trusts, but the evil itself.[18] The rebate, Attorney General William H. Moody concluded in 1906, was the key to Standard's monopoly.

However onerous the burden of rebates on the railroads—a burden which the railroads usually passed to the other shippers and eventually the consumer in the form of higher rates—it is nevertheless true that Standard treated the consumer with deference. Crude and refined oil prices for consumers declined during the period Standard exercised greatest control of the industry, 1875-1895, and rose thereafter along with prices for most consumer goods. Standard's ignominious reputation was based primarily on its relations to the independent oil producers: the company acted ruthlessly to keep prices low at the expense of small producers. Ironically, had the producers won, the consumers' price of oil would have been significantly higher. Indeed, the whole purpose of the Petroleum Producers' Union of Pennsylvania in the late 1870's and early 1880's was to raise prices by restricting output and controlling other producers unable to withstand the enticing and often enriching prospect of selling to Standard—"to make clear the way for a deliverance of the business from the condition in which it has been placed by the irrational course of producers, not less than by the unjust and unnatural restrictions placed upon it by those who seek to monopolize its control."[14] By controlling production, and creating their own monopoly, the producers hoped to become independent of the most powerful buyer, Standard Oil.

Standard never controlled a consequential share of the oil-producing industry, but restricted itself to refining and sales. As a producer of oil Standard accounted for 11 per cent of the output in 1906. Its somewhat ruthless relationship with the not altogether altruistic producers has often erroneously been projected onto its relations with competitive refiners. Standard attained its control of the refinery business primarily by mergers, not price wars, and most refinery owners were anxious to sell out to it. Some of these refinery owners later reopened new plants after selling to Standard.

In 1899 Standard refined 90 per cent of the nation's oil, and reached the peak of its control over the industry. During 1904-1907, however, Standard refined 84 per cent of the oil, and in 1911, the year of the dissolution, it refined 80 per cent. The dissolution decree left the component Standard companies in noncompetitive positions with one another, and the combined share of refining of this conglomeration declined to 50 per cent in 1921 and 45 per cent in 1926. It is clear that from 1899 on Standard entered a progressive decline in its control over the oil industry, a decline accelerated, but certainly not initiated, by the dissolution. And until 1920 it faced uncertainty and growing competition.

In 1899 there were sixty-seven petroleum refiners in the United States, only one of whom was of any consequence. Over the next decade the number increased steadily to 147 refiners. Until 1900 the only significant competitor to Standard was the Pure Oil Company, formed in 1895 by Pennsylvania producers with $10 million capital. It concentrated on the heavy lubricants field and grew despite Standard attacks, and after 1900 spread into other important phases of refining. By 1906 it was challenging Standard's control over pipe lines by constructing its own. And in 1901 Associated Oil of California was formed with $40 million capital stock, in 1902 the Texas Company was formed with $30 million capital, and in 1907 Gulf Oil was established with $60 million capital. In 1911 the total investment of the Texas Company, Gulf Oil, Tide Water-Associated Oil, Union Oil of California, and Pure Oil was $221 million. From 1911 to 1926 the investment of the Texas Company grew 572 per cent, Gulf Oil 1,022 per cent, Tide Water-Associated 205 per cent, Union Oil 159 per cent, and Pure Oil 1,534 per cent. In 1926 all of the Standard companies combined represented only 60 per cent of the industry's investment. This is not to say that the industry was competitive in the 1920's—important patent pools prevented that— but that the decline of Standard was substantial and continuous.

Standard's failure was primarily its own doing—the responsibility of its conservative management and lack of initiative. The American oil industry passed through a revolution from 1900 to 1920, and Standard failed to participate fully in it. The first factor in this revolution was the shift in the oil-producing areas from the East to the West in a few short years. Standard had developed its power over producers and railroads in the Appalachian and Lima-Indiana oil-producing fields, which in 1900 accounted for 95 per cent of America's crude output. But in 1905 this area was producing less than 40 per cent of the crude oil, and by 1912 the new California fields and the midcontinent fields were each producing more oil than the Appalachian, Lima-Indiana, and Illinois fields combined. Standard had important investments in both of these new areas, but its basic strength was in the East. Moreover, in the Gulf and Texas areas, as well as in the California and the midcontinent fields, large independent producers had made sufficiently large fortunes to move into refining. In the Texas and Gulf areas Standard was especially slow to compete, and by the time it entered the fight it was hopelessly handicapped.

The second major cause of Standard's decline was the radical transformation of the uses for oil as a result of the advent of the automobile and electricity. Standard made its early fortune primarily in illuminating oils and kerosene, which accounted for 63 per cent of the industry's production in 1899. By 1919, however, electricity had eliminated the demand, and this type of production accounted for a mere 15 per cent of the industry's output. Fuel oil spiralled from 15 per cent to 52 per cent of the output over the same period, and light oil products, including gasoline, increased from 14 per cent of the industry's output in 1899 to 27 per cent in 1919 and 48 per cent in 1929. Between 1910 and 1925 the number of auto registrations increased forty times, and gasoline and its distribution became the central core of the industry. In this area the independent oil companies led the field, pioneering in gas stations in the same way that they had surpassed Standard in developing improved tank cars and trucks as well as most of the major innovations in petroleum chemistry. In a spiralling market for oil such as existed from the turn of the century on, Standard, conservative and technologically uncreative, was no match for the aggressive new competitors. The dissolution decree of 1911 tended to knock Standard out of its lethargy, and its component companies began merging with many of the new independents to diversify and integrate in all regions. Without the managerial skills the managers of these independents brought with them to Standard, it is likely that the former near-monopoly would have been even weaker in the 1920's.

The oil industry, as well, had failed to establish stability and integration via voluntary economic means in the period before World War I.

The Automobile
Industry

The automobile industry is an excellent example of a fundamental technological innovation that led to a proliferation of wealth in new hands and the creation of new centers of power in the economy. And, in the Progressive Era, it was a source of additional intense competition.[15]

Entry into the auto industry was exceptionally easy prior to World War I. Technological innovation and managerial skill, not capital, were the key to success, though ample capital did not hinder progress and it saved at least one wild speculation. The extremes, while perhaps not fully representative, are interesting: Ford started with $28,000 capital and succeeded, the Electric Vehicle Company began with $20 million and failed. Many of the early auto manufacturers first started in the bicycle, carriage, or marine motor industry and diversified into automobiles. Most auto makers were really assemblers of parts produced by independent machine shops, and by requiring customer deposits on orders and cash on delivery they were able to shift the capital burden onto their parts suppliers. Only one of the successful major auto firms—General Motors—was able to attract significant investments from established investment centers before 1912. The other major promotions of organized finance, such as the United States Motor Company and the Electric Vehicle Company, failed. By 1926 seven of the eight major auto producers had managed to obtain virtually all of their invested capital out of their profits, and to thereby establish a new center of economic power in Detroit. The output of autos increased from 19,000 in 1904 to 122,-000 in 1909 and 1,557,000 in 1919, and in this type of market, with demand high and brand loyalties as yet weak, new companies might expect to survive, profit, and grow despite the furious competition.

Estimates on the number of companies entering the automobile field vary sharply, but even the conservative data indicate a high entry rate and competition. According to *Motor* in 1909, 502 companies entered the auto business during 1900-1908, 273 of these failed and 29 entered still other fields. In 1904 there were 104 auto builders, according to census data, and in 1909 there were 265. The most conservative figures, compiled by Ralph C. Epstein, indicate that in 1903-1924 there were 180 companies actually making and selling autos, as opposed to merely planning to do so. By 1926, 121 of this number died, leaving 59 in the field—still a rather substantial number. It is only after 1920 that new entries into the industry drop off sharply. The mortality rate was high even among the major firms. Of the ten leading producers in 1903 only one was in the top ten in 1924, and of the ten leading firms in 1912 only five were in the top ten in 1924. After 1912 the mortality rate declined and significant concentration began taking place within the industry. At the same time, the standardization of parts and integration within each company resulted in comparative stability for the major firms.

Given the incredible chaos in the industry, it is not at all surprising that steps were taken to bring it under control. The Electric Vehicle Company, among other things, acquired the Seldon patent on gas cars, hoping to collect a royalty on every gas car produced on the theory that they all infringed on its patent. The relatively powerful Packard Motor Company and Olds Motor Works were attracted to the patent as a means of destroying existing fly-by-night companies and preventing the creation of new ones. An Association of Licensed Automobile Manufacturers was formed in early 1903 to collect a royalty of 1¼ per cent of the retail price of each car made under the patent, with most of the revenues devoted to imposing the association's control over the industry. Ford was refused a license by the association, and in late 1903 it opened a suit against him. Ford, in the meantime, ignored the patent and in 1905 helped form a new competitive association. In 1909 Ford lost his patent suit, but an appeal brought him victory in January, 1911, and broke up the Seldon association.

The result of Ford's legal victory was to destroy partially the patent system within the auto industry. In 1915 the National Automobile Chamber of Commerce was formed by one hundred producers to freely cross-license routine patents among themselves. This policy lasted until 1935, and helped keep the industry competitive. After 1935 the possibility of patent exclusion and market growth became too great an attraction to resist, and the system largely collapsed.

General Motors is an excellent example of the interaction between major finance and the auto industry. G.M.'s involvement with organized finance at a time when all of the major auto firms were largely financing themselves was mainly due to the personality and grandiose ambitions of its first president, William C. Durant. Durant's philosophy was one of trying to absorb every promising company on the theory that in an industry in state of rapid flux any one of them might eventually emerge as the leading manufacturer. He started with Buick in 1904 and made sufficient profit to acquire twenty more firms, most of which were failures. Until 1910, despite earlier discussions with J. P. Morgan and Company, Durant largely financed his own expansion. In 1910 a banking syndicate under Kuhn and Loeb, Lee, Higginson and Co., and J. and W. Seligman and Co., took over General Motors for a five-year period, ostensibly to straighten out the financial chaos Durant had created. The syndicate loaned General Motors $15 million, taking for itself at least $2.5 million of it for floating the bond issues. "I consider it an excellent piece of business and the terms most liberal . . . ," Henry Seligman wrote in September, 1910.[16] By the time the syndicate had finished centralizing the company under the supervision of James J. Storrow of Lee, Higginson, General Motors' share of the American auto market had declined to 14 per cent in 1915 as compared to 21 per cent in 1908. Durant, in the meantime, continued his speculations, picked up Chevrolet and formed an alliance with Du Pont to buy back General Motors, which they took over in late 1915. In 1920 J. P. Morgan and Company moved into the alliance and Durant was pushed out, eventually dying in near poverty after losing at least $100 million. After Alfred Sloan, an engineer, took over as G.M.'s president in 1923, he reversed Durant's and the bankers' policy of equating efficiency with centralization by introducing a decentralization policy and eventually making G.M. the most profitable company in the industry. ". . . we would set up each of our various operations as an integral unit, complete as to itself," Sloan wrote about his new departure. "We realized that in an institution as big as General Motors was even then, to say nothing of what we hoped to make it, any plan that involved too great a concentration of problems upon a limited number of executives would limit initiative, would involve delay, would increase expense, and would reduce efficiency and development."[17]

The Agricultural Machinery Industry

The ostensible and probably actual reason behind the formation of the International Harvester Company in late 1902 was the intense competition in the agricultural machinery industry. But competition and overexpanded production and sales facilities within the industry had existed for many years, and repeated efforts by the McCormick Company and the Deering Manufacturing Company to merge led to repeated failures. It was only when the Deering organization began buying iron ore lands and building its own rolling mill in 1901, and the interests of Morgan and the new U.S. Steel merger were threatened, that progress was made. Gary directed the problem to the attention of George W. Perkins, and he, in turn, brought the full weight of the House of Morgan behind the existing merger sentiment.[18]

The amount of water in the $120 million preferred stock issued by the new corporation was slight, if there was any at all, mainly because of the strenuous insistence of the McCormick family that the stock be conservatively valued. But the new merger was singularly unprofitable during its first years, and the McCormicks and Deerings complained to the Bureau of Corporations in early 1907 that the 3 and 4 per cent dividends that the company paid "have been a disappointment to its organizers." More important, the Deerings and McCormicks soon began feuding with one another and nearly brought about a dissolution of the merger and a restoration of the separate companies. With dissension in the firm, inadequate profits, and many of the former brands still competing with each other in the industry at great cost of duplication, the company was forced to adopt radical organizational changes in late 1906 by eliminating the older managers inherited from the various firms. But the duplication of products continued until at least 1909. In 1910 the company finally began paying dividends on its common stock. Its rate of earnings on its capital stock increased from 4.7 per cent in 1902 to 9.9 per cent in 1911.

But the company's executives complained in 1907 that when International Harvester was formed the "selling agents went to sleep," and spent a good deal of time competing with the company's own brands.[19] Their lethargy, stimulated by poor organization and overconfidence, was most unfortunate for International Harvester. In 1903 the company sold 96 per cent of the binders in the United States; it sold 87 per cent in 1911. Its share of the mower market declined from 91 per cent to 75 per cent over the same period. And its share of the harvester market fell from 85 per cent in 1902 to 80 per cent in 1911 and 64 per cent in 1918. At the time that International Harvester was formed, Deere and Co., J. I. Case and Co., Oliver Farm Equipment Co., etc., were left out of the merger, and these firms quickly developed a full line of agricultural machinery. Although the number of manufacturers of agricultural implements declined slightly over the preceding decade, in 1909 there were still

640 in the United States. And after 1915, when Allis-Chalmers diversified into tractors, auto companies also began entering the industry.

The Telephone
Industry

From its foundation in 1877 until 1894, the Bell Telephone Company (A.T. & T.) had a virtual monopoly over the telephone industry.[20] Its position was based on its control of all crucial patents necessary for the industry, and its conservative Boston owners and managers restricted the extension of telephone service by financing most expansion out of profits. In 1894, with many of the key patents no longer in effect, vast areas of the United States were without service, and local capital was quite ready to finance independent companies. Bell immediately adopted a policy of harassing the host of aspiring competitors that sprang up in 1894 by starting suits against them—twenty-seven in 1894-1895 alone—for allegedly infringing Bell patents. It refused, in addition, to allow its subsidiary, Western Electric, to sell equipment to the new firms.

This policy failed largely because many of the new competitors had important patents of their own and were aggressive in research and development. At the same time, new firms, such as Kellogg Switchboard, Stromberg-Carlson, and Automatic Electric Company, sprang up to supply equipment to the new independents. The telephone market, especially in the West and in rural areas, was available to virtually anyone ready to take it.

But the telephone independents had no access to ample supplies of capital. The independents recognized that mutual cooperation was crucial if any were to survive, and in 1897 organized a national association designed to establish long distance service between their cities. In late 1899, however, it appeared as if the independents would finally receive major financial backing. The Telephone, Telegraph and Cable Company was formed in New Jersey, with $30 million capital, for the purpose of uniting the independent companies into a national network. Supporters of the company included John Jacob Astor, Peter A. B. Widener, Thomas Dolan, Frank Tilford, and other important public utility and oil industry figures—a formidable group indeed. Unfortunately for the new venture, J. P. Morgan became interested in the Bell System, though he did not control it at this time, and was in a position to help the Widener interests in an important gas utility war then going on in New York City. Widener, W. I. Elkins, and Dolan were induced to withdraw from the new telephone company, and it collapsed.

Despite massive capital support and the weaknesses of the independents, A.T. & T. faced intense competition and began losing control of the industry. In 1902 there were 9,100 independent telephone systems, and by 1907 there were 22,000. The number of phones in the independent system expanded so rapidly that in 1907, the year of peak relative strength for the independents, A.T. & T. had 3.1 million phones in service, the independents 3.0 million. The number of independent phones continued to grow in subsequent years, but by the 1920's A.T. & T. far outstripped them.

The pressure of competition increased A.T. & T.'s need for capital, and from early 1902 to early 1907 J. P. Morgan was an important minority faction within the board of directors; 1907 saw his victory over Boston control. Morgan's financial aid to the company, however, was singularly unsuccessful in 1906-1908. His major contribution was to reorient the company's policy from competing with the independents, where A.T. & T. had been most unsuccessful, to attempting to merge with them. Theodore N. Vail, the new president, asserted that the independents were all essentially promoters, that large size and "centralized general control" created economies, and that the public opposed competition in telephones. At the same time, however, A.T. & T. began selling equipment to the independents and trying to cut off their access to capital. The independents complained that A.T. & T. was treating them all as prospective mergers and was trying to obtain control over the independent telephone equipment companies.

By 1911 Vail was freely admitting that the policy of the company was to merge with independents. Reversing the earlier centralization of its organization, which Vail granted was largely based on accident, A.T. & T. broke up into eight to ten decentralized and semi-autonomous divisions. Thus able to compete more successfully with the independents, or to merge with them, A.T. & T.'s relative strength began growing. In early 1913 Attorney General Wickersham forced the company to dispose of Western Union, which it acquired in 1909, to agree to cease its merger policy, and to connect with the independents for toll service—an order that was effective only until 1919.

It is true that many of the independent telephone companies were poorly run, inadequately financed, and based largely on the power of local franchises. But the independents were primarily responsible for the rapid growth of the telephone system, and even the growth of the Bell System. During its period of total monopoly, 1885-1894, Bell's phones increased at a rate of 6.3 per cent a year; but during 1895-1906 they increased at an annual rate of 21.5 per cent. Moreover, by 1907 many of the independents were extremely well run and profitable firms. In 1907, a year of business decline, all but a few of the independents in Ohio, Indiana, and Illinois paid dividends of 4 to 12 per cent on their stock. A.T. & T. subsidiaries did no better, and many made smaller profits. Even more important, however, is the fact that independents forced telephone rates down and created a mass market for their services and for the industry. Comparative rate data is scarce, but every indication is that independent rates were substantially lower than A.T. & T.'s. In Philadelphia, for example, Keystone Telephone forced unlimited business service rates down from $160 to $90 a year in a few years' time. In 1895 Bell received an average of $88 revenue for each of its stations, but it received only $41 in 1914-1915. Vail admitted in 1911 that average A.T. & T. rates were higher than those of the independents, even where the independents had not fulfilled their initial promises of yet lower rates. In 1911 A.T. & T., despite its higher rates, paid dividends of only 6.3 per cent on its outstanding stock.

Even more significant is the fact that most of the important technological innovations in the industry were not produced by A.T. & T., and this often aided the competitive position of the independents. Until 1907 engineering and research was consciously relegated to a secondary role in A.T. & T. Loading coils, the mercury-arc repeater, and the three-element vacuum tube, for example, were all developed by independent inventors, and A.T. & T. was forced to buy them from the inventors.

The essential characteristic of the telephone industry in the first decade of this century was its competition and rapid change. And the industry, with its insecurity and unpredictability, serves as an additional example of the basic trend in the American economy at the beginning of this century away from centralization or monopoly.

The Copper
Industry

The history of the copper industry in this period is, in outline, one of attempted consolidations and pools, and a continuous unsuccessful effort to establish control over the industry.[21] The industry was viciously competitive, and the mood is best illustrated by Henry Seligman in 1885; upon hearing from his brother Albert in Montana that one Murphy, a competitor, had been lynched, Seligman said: ". . . as a rule I do not approve of taking the law into one's own hand, but in this instance I believe the result will prove very beneficial."[22]

In the first important copper producing area, upper Michigan, the Boston-owned Calumet & Hecla Company was able to control a peak of 65 per cent of the region's output in 1872. By 1883 it accounted for only 56 per cent of the region's production, and a number of efforts to establish price and output pools in the 1880's failed, in part because of the growing competition from Arizona copper. In 1887 a world copper pool organized by French interests involved many of the major American producers, but smaller American firms took advantage of the higher prices it created to increase their output, and the pool failed by 1889. Another effort was made in 1893, but it also failed.

Since voluntary means proved inadequate, in 1899-1900 six new combinations, stimulated by the doubling of the price of copper, were formed to exploit approximately two dozen older mines. Five of these combinations crashed. The most important copper consolidation of the period was the Amalgamated Copper Company, formed in 1899 by Thomas Lawson, Henry H. Rogers, William Rockefeller, and the Anaconda copper interests. The firm excluded the largest Michigan producer, Calumet & Hecla, and instead of extending its control over the American copper industry, by 1904 its share of U.S. output fell to about 40 per cent.

The efforts of private interests to control or consolidate the copper industry were singularly fruitless. Calumet & Hecla, with a conservative management, never seriously expanded into the Western mining areas, and the Michigan copper industry's decline eliminated it as a serious factor in the industry. It produced 23 per cent of the nation's copper in 1890, 13 per cent in 1900, seven per cent in 1910, and 11 per cent in 1920. The Anaconda-Amalgamated Copper interests accounted for 29 per cent of the nation's output in 1890, 39 per cent in 1900, 25 per cent in 1910, and 12 per cent in 1920. The nation's four largest producers of copper declined from 76 per cent of the output in 1890 to 66 per cent in 1900, 49 per cent in 1910, and 39 per cent in 1920.

The American copper industry is an excellent example of the rise of instability and competition during this period—instability due to the rapid shifts in the location of major deposits and the inability of any one group to control all the factors of production.

The Meat Packing
Industry

". . . here is something compared with which the Standard Oil Company is puerile," wrote Charles Edward Russell about the meat packing industry in 1905.[23] Russell's articles were a typical reflection of the dominant contemporary view of the industry and an excellent example of the general confusion on "the trust" that pervaded most discussions of corporate concentration at the beginning of this century. Among other things that Russell claimed for the trust was the power of absolute price-fixing and ownership of nearly all packing houses. The trust, if one looked beyond Russell's title, in reality consisted of the Big Six—something quite different than a totally unified Standard Oil.[24]

There is no question that the major meat packers cooperated with one another; the real issue is whether they were able to control the industry through their efforts. During the late 1880's the key Chicago packers—Armour, Swift, Allerton, Hammond, and Morris —attempted to fix prices and divide the market. In 1893 Cudahy and St. Louis Dressed Beef and Provision were brought into the agreement, and the pool met once a week to divide markets and adjust volume. From May, 1896, to January, 1898, the pool was unable to function because of competition from a major outsider, Schwarzschild & Sulzberger, but it resumed operation after bringing the intruder into the pool. In May, 1902, the pool disbanded under a Department of Justice injunction. For the most part, the pool was largely a way for the packers to maintain peace among themselves and to prevent imbalanced inventories of a perishable product in certain regions and during special times of the year. Since they had no way of regulating the output and supply of meat, which was the exclusive responsibility of thousands of stock raisers, it is doubtful the pool had any significant control over meat prices.

Armour, Swift, and Morris proceeded during 1902 to plan a merger of their own firms and other major packers, and collectively purchased thirteen packing companies. But lack of capital, the negative advice of Kuhn, Loeb and Co. as to the advisability of the merger, and public criticism destroyed the venture. The thirteen companies were then formed in 1903 into the National Packing Company, with Swift owning 47 per cent of the stock, Armour 40 per cent, and Morris 13 per cent. Using National Packing as an umbrella, the three firms regulated their own affairs in much the same way as under the old pool. In 1912 the company was ordered dissolved, and the property was divided among the owners.

In 1900 most of the founders of the meat industry were dead and their children were in charge of their companies. The results were not altogether happy. Armour, Morris, and Schwarzschild all suffered in the hands of the second generation, and this tended to open the markets of the industry to additional competition. By 1906 competition within the industry was intense, and efforts to mitigate it by creating the American Meat Packers Association, failed to change the situation.

The price of meat rose consistently from 1890 to 1916, and this fact was often cited as proof of monopolistic control in the industry; but so did the prices of many other foods and the prices of all foods and farm products combined. It was easier for the large packers to obtain railroad rebates on large shipments than to try to have the consumer pay for allegedly greater than average profits. Profits were certainly substantial, but not because of higher than competitive prices. As Edward F. Swift explained in 1905, "Even if these large packers were acting in harmony [which they were!], they would not be able to control prices to any considerable extent, for the reason that there are a sufficient number of other individuals, companies, or corporations in the business, who would increase the volume of their business the minute abnormal profits appeared. Therefore they would gradually take away the business from the large packers, should the latter attempt to buy their cattle unreasonably low or sell their beef unreasonably high."[25] In smaller towns the packers frequently cut prices to meet local competition during certain times of the year when local beef was plentiful, but in most of these places the proportion of the total business done by the large packers was generally quite low.

Entry into the packing industry was, and still is, comparatively easy. The raw materials were freely available and could be produced virtually anywhere. The major difference in profits was the exploitation of the byproducts of meat. Local slaughterers had less expense per head for refrigeration and freight, and usually had lower administration, sales, and accounting expenses as well. For identical grades of meat, local meat often commanded higher prices than Western meat. Liabilities were many as well, ranging from the cost of slaughtering to economies of mass purchases of animals, but the assets were sufficiently important to create serious competition.

The Bureau of Corporations' study of the meat industry in 1905 concluded that the Big Six killed and sold about 45 to 50 per cent of the nation's beef. Packing firms other than the largest three companies accounted for 65 per cent of the meat output in 1905, and 78 per cent in 1909. The number of slaughtering and meat packing establishments increased sharply during our period—from 1,080 in 1899 to 1,641 in 1909. This increase in the number of packers by 52 per cent in one decade later had the greatest significance for the political role of the meat industry in the Progressive Period.

Numerous other examples of the trend toward competition and the failure of mergers can be found in other important fields. In industries where rapid technological innovation was the key to success, as in electrical manufacturing and chemicals, the major companies began losing their share of markets and new entrants swarmed in during the first decade of the century. Where the level of necessary investment was comparatively low, as in paper, textiles, and glass, the number of new companies entering the field grew consistently and often spectacularly. And even when entries were not great, the reallocation of market shares tended to deprive giant, well-capitalized mergers of their supremacy. In several industries, tobacco being the most notable, revolutionary changes in consumer tastes upset the dominance of key firms.[26]

Additional cases and examples abound, and there is no point in tiring the reader with them. The trend is altogether clear: the manufacturing sector of the economy after the period of numerous mergers in 1897-1901 was growing increasingly competitive. Private efforts to establish stability and control within the various manufacturing industries had largely failed.

The economic and industrial development of the United States from 1890 until World War I assured a fluidity of conditions that made economic rationalization and stability by voluntary means substantially impossible.[27] If the growth of big business was spurred by the expanding urban markets, the consolidation of the economy into a few hands was made impossible by the shifting locations of markets and resources—changes that meant few companies were sufficiently well managed to hold on to their share of the market and prevent new entries. America was too diverse, the economic resources and opportunities too decentralized, to prevent the creation of an American economic frontier. The idea that economic opportunities were closed to middle-level wealth is not in accord with the facts. There was sufficient product and service development—the distribution and service industries increase sharply in this period—to dispel that notion.

Rapid technological innovation in this period often meant, as Schumpeter suggested, innovation embodied in new firms. This was certainly true in totally new industries, such as the automobile and electrical manufacturing industries, where older wealth was loath to speculate, and generally true within established industries as well. New products, new methods of production, new markets, new sources of supply, and new business combinations always affected the existing distribution of power and shares in older industries. Established firms participated in this growth, but were rarely able to prevent intruders from grabbing their share as well. All grew, but the smaller entries generally grew more rapidly. Internal financing out of profits or rapidly decentralizing sources of cash made it possible for many of these new entries to prosper quite independently of the larger financiers whose major efforts went into the merger movement. It is, of course, true that the economic and industrial mobility described does not warrant a belief in the Horatio Alger myth which has been so thoroughly analyzed, and largely disproven, by William Miller and his associates. Occupational or educational mobility and income or power mobility are two separate questions, however, and the burden of Miller's work has been in critically examining the oversimplified notions of apologists of the status quo on the social origins of the business elite. Many of our new business leaders came from those wealthier educational and occupational backgrounds capable of providing the prerequisite for that genuine, decisive mobility which is significant in power and income terms. And the dynamics of economic growth were such in the period that those individuals with the educational criteria, social manners, and minimum capital could and often did obtain radically magnified positions of economic importance without necessarily altering their precise family educational status or formal occupational designations. What should not be ignored are the important distinctions within that broad category, "the upper class."

The failure of the merger movement to attain control over the economic conditions in the various industries was brought about by the inability of the consolidated firms to attain sufficient technological advantages or economies of size over their smaller competitors— contrary to common belief and the promises of promoters. The consolidations were formed not because of technological considerations but primarily to create profits for promoters and incidentally because of the desire to eliminate competition. The amalgamation of industrial facilities and resources on a massive scale often has the sort of "efficiency" in a capitalist economy which is guided less by purely technological considerations than by uniquely capitalist ones —economic warfare, private profit, market instabilities. But such considerations are insufficient to prevent the entry of competitors who often can operate successfully at levels of production well below those of the larger combinations, and can exploit new opportunities for profit more ably. In these circumstances the power of a giant corporation is based on transitory or variable factors, and the decentralization movement within many large corporations is a concession to the efficiency of the successful smaller competitors.

Voluntary agreements among corporations in the form of pools and agreements of every kind usually failed. Consolidations and mergers were the next logical step, and also failed. The proliferation of new competitors undermined the possibility of attaining economic rationalization, with profit, by voluntary economic means. But whether the passage of the control of an industry from one firm to ten or twenty is relevant to the social, as opposed to the political, role of business is quite another matter. To ignore the social function of business, and its relation to the remainder of society, by concentrating on internal organizational and structural changes within industries would be a great error. Whether there are a few or many companies does not change the basic control and decision-making power of the institution of business in relation to the other important classes of society, but only the detailed means by which that power is exercised and certain of the ends toward which it is directed.

CHAPTER THREE

THEODORE ROOSEVELT

AND THE

FOUNDATIONS OF

POLITICAL CAPITALISM,

1901-1904

ALL OF THE EFFORTS of Morgan and the corporate promoters to introduce economic stability and control over various industries, and to end the bane of destructive and unprofitable competition, were heading toward failure. Monopoly and business cooperation were raised to the pinnacle of desired goals at the very time that popular and academic advocates of conservative Social Darwinism were attempting to utilize the doctrines of Herbert Spencer and William Graham Sumner as a justification of the existing distribution of economic power and laissez faire. Laissez faire provided the businessman with an ideological rationale on an intellectual plane, but it also created instability and insecurity in the economy. The dominant fact of American political life at the beginning of this century was that big business led the struggle for the federal regulation of the economy.

If economic rationalization could not be attained by mergers and voluntary economic methods, a growing number of important businessmen reasoned, perhaps political means might succeed. At the same time, it was increasingly obvious that change was inevitable in a political democracy where Grangers, Populists, and trade unionists had significant and disturbing followings and might tap a socially dangerous grievance at some future time and threaten the entire fabric of the status quo, and that the best way to thwart change was to channelize it. If the direction of that change also solved the internal problems of the industrial and financial structure, or accommodated to the increasingly obvious fact that the creation of a national economy and market demanded political solutions that extended beyond the boundaries of states more responsive to the ordinary people, so much the better. Nor was it possible for many businessmen to ignore the fact that, in addition to sanctions the federal government might provide to ward off hostile criticisms, the national government was still an attractive potential source of windfall profits, subsidies, and resources.

Only if we mechanistically assume that government regulation of the economy is automatically progressive can we say that the federal regulation of the economy during 1900 to 1916 was progressive in the commonly understood sense of the term. In fact, of course, this assumption has dominated historical writing on the period, and historians have replaced the mythology of laissez faire with the mythology of the federal government as a neutral or progressive intermediary in the economy. This theory of the nature of political democracy and the distribution of power in America has shaped our understanding of the American political experience, our understanding of who directed it, and toward what ends. At the same time, I will maintain, this perspective has overlooked the informal realities, has failed to investigate the nature, motives and detailed character of each phase of the regulatory process, and has led to a facile misunderstanding not only of the full nature of the American political experience but also of the character of American economic development. If the criterion is not the presence or absence of government intervention but the degree to which motives and actions were designed to maintain or preserve a particular distribution or locus of power, the history of the United States from Theodore Roosevelt through Woodrow Wilson is consistently conservative. Nor is the extension of federal regulation over the economy a question of progressive intent thwarted by conservative administration and fulfilment. Important business elements could always be found in the forefront of agitation for such regulation, and the fact that well-intentioned reformers often worked with them—indeed, were often indispensable to them—does not change the reality that federal economic regulation was generally designed by the regulated interest to meet its own end, and not those of the public or the commonweal.

The course of business action in the federal political sphere was motivated by a number of crucial factors that too often have been ignored by historians. First in importance was the structural condition within the economy, described in Chapters One and Two, which imposed the need for rationalization on many American industries. The second is the fact that, in the long run, business has no vested interest in pure, irrational market conditions, and grew to hate the dangerous consequences inherent in such situations. Moreover, the history of the relationship between business and government until 1900 was one that could only inspire confidence in the minds of all too many businessmen. The first federal regulatory effort, the Interstate Commerce Commission, had been cooperative and fruitful; indeed, the railroads themselves had been the leading advocates of extended federal regulation after 1887. The ties between many political and business leaders were close, not merely because Mark Hanna ran the Republican Party or Grover Cleveland had been the partner of J. P. Morgan's lawyer, but for social and ideological reasons as well. As I shall show in the following pages, the business and political elites of the Progressive Era had largely identical social ties and origins. And, last of all, the federal government, rather than being a source of negative opposition, always represented a potential source of economic gain. The railroads, of course, had used the federal and local governments for subsidies and land grants. But various other industries appreciated the desirability of proper tariffs, direct subsidies in a few instances, governmentowned natural resources, or monopolistic privileges possible in certain federal charters or regulations. For all of these reasons the federal government was a natural ally.

Business reliance on the federal government may have been variable in its emphasis, but it was consistent in its use. It was perfectly logical that industrialists who had spent years attempting to solve their economic problems by centralization should have been willing to resort to political centralization as well. It is irrelevant whether one accepts, or dismisses, this phenomenon as a "conspiracy theory" of elites working out of public sight, or describes it as "open channels" between personnel with similar values or contacts. Labels are irrelevant, the phenomenon is not—and the facts still remain whether we like them or not, or even if we are unaware of them. It was never a question of regulation or no regulation among businessmen during the Progressive Era, or of federal control versus laissez faire; there was, rather, the question of what type of legislation at what time. On the fundamental proposition that the government was to be utilized freely, if not for someone else's problems then at least for one's own, there was never any disagreement in practice, and frequently little in theory as well. If American business did not always obtain its legislative ends in the precise form it wanted them, its goals and means were clear. And the dominant trend in the political decisions that were made, with few exceptions, preserved the type of distribution of power and decision-making that also insured the power of regulated industries.

It is possible, of course, to find division in the ranks of "business" if the opinion of a Morgan lawyer is balanced off by a resolution of the Alabama Board of Trade. Such a procedure assumes that there are no operational power centers and that one opinion is as influential as another—a proposition almost disproven by stating it in a manner which allows one to realize what it really alleges. What is crucial is the opinion of key power groups, first of all, and the majority of all interests within a specific industry in which state or federal regulation is an issue. And, as so often happens, even if groups in different industries disagree on the broader theoretical propositions implicit in the general regulation of the economy by the federal government, it is the opinion of key power groups with interests in many fields that is the dominant concern to anyone studying general trends. It is possible to state that many businessmen—the drugstore operator being equated with the steel company president—opposed government regulation most of the time, even though most businessmen supported it at least when it was to their interest to do so. The group that supported it consistently, the men in the top echelons of finance and industry attempting to attain economic centralization and stability, and with important political connections, are the men who will primarily concern us here.

Outside of the realm of legislative and political activity there remained the larger intellectual issue of accepted social values. The view that government and business were equally valued in the Progressive Era, or that government was given higher value, is incorrect. For business held the ultimate reins of accepted ideology and defined the outer limits of potential reforms; all major parties paid tribute to the basic institutional rights and interests of business, and to the mythology of social values which allowed it to survive all onslaughts. More important, the net effect of federal legislation, and usually the intent, was to implement the economic-political goals of some group within an industry. The pervasive reality of the period is big business' control of politics set in the context of the political regulation of the economy.

The Antitrust
Legacy

The antitrust legacy handed to Theodore Roosevelt was little more than an amorphous social sanction—vague and subject to broad interpretation, or to inactivity. Ignoring the pro-laissez faire predisposition of the majority of intellectuals and academicians, the belief in competition as an abstract proposition was shared by the average middle-class businessman. But this commitment, with all its fuzziness, never was defined in any intellectually or politically meaningful way, and its obscurity was reflected in the Sherman Act and the role of the "trust issue" in the political history of the 1890's.

The Sherman Antitrust Act, written by Senators Sherman, Edmunds, Turpie, George, and others, was the only politically concrete heritage of the antitrust movement bestowed on Roosevelt. It is difficult enough to give a legal definition of monopoly power, short of 100 per cent control, acceptable to any large group of economists. The Sherman Act merely referred to a definition—the common law—which was as vague and multidimensional as the last lawyer's interpretation. Senator John Sherman made it clear in March, 1890, that

the object of this bill, as shown by the title is "to declare unlawful trusts and combinations in restraint of trade and production." . . . It does not announce a new principle of law, but applies old and well-recognized principles of the common law to the complicated jurisdiction of our State and Federal Government . . . . This bill does not seek to cripple combinations of capital and labor, the formation of partnerships or of corporations, but only to prevent and control combinations made with a view to prevent competition, or for the restraint of trade, or to increase the profits of the producer at the cost of the consumer. It is the unlawful combination, tested by the rules of common law and human experience, that is aimed at by this bill, and not the lawful and useful combination.[1]

The result, if not the intent, was clearly to establish a rule of reason with a variable, if not ambiguous, definition of the "restraint of trade."

Despite Sherman's disclaimer that the law would not be applied to trade unions or farmer organizations, many of his colleagues in the Senate predicted that "It would be a weapon in the hands of the rich against the poor," and they anticipated the law's subsequent use against unions.[2] But the law, with its loose emphasis on "intent" rather than specific actions, and its curiously abstruse lack of precision, was clearly ready-made for free interpretation by some administrative agency. If the Attorney General, Richard Olney, happened to be a former State Street lawyer for the Boston & Maine Railroad, a member of "good clubs," and a director of railroads, the results justified the anxieties of the skeptical Senators when Olney ordered federal troops to intervene in the Pullman strike of 1894. And if the Supreme Court, deeply committed to laissez faire and a literalist interpretation of the law, saw the Sherman Act as a justification for thwarting big business desires for concentration and cooperation—as in the *Addyston Pipe* decision (1899) and the *Trans-Missouri* decision (1897)—the law could be as disturbing to business leaders as to labor unionists.

For the small merchant, beleaguered farmer, and unemployed worker "monopoly" was a political slogan, inherited in part from the earlier part of the nineteenth century when corporation charters were in fact equivalent to monopoly privileges. And, with the advent of economic concentration, vast aggregations of economic power, and a merger movement, it seemed indeed as if "monopoly" and "trust" referred to economic realities—or at least to the direction of things. In the political sphere, however, the trends were more definite. While it is not my purpose to give a history of the 1890's, the least that can be said of the political history of that "mauve decade," as Thomas Beer termed it, was aptly summarized in the exchange between Henry Clay Frick and his partner, Andrew Carnegie, on the election of 1892: "I am very sorry for President Harrison," Frick wrote, "but I cannot see that our interests are going to be affected one way or the other by the change in administration." "Cleveland! Landslide!" Carnegie replied. "Well we have nothing to fear and perhaps it is best. People will now think the Protected Manfrs. will be attended to and quit agitating. Cleveland is pretty good fellow. Off for Venice tomorrow."[3]

Cleveland was indeed a pretty good fellow. Upon leaving the Presidency in 1889 he entered a law partnership with Francis Lynde Stetson, J. P. Morgan's lawyer and a power in the Democratic Party. After Cleveland's re-election Stetson remained an important business pipeline to the President. Even more important was Richard Olney, who actively encouraged his Boston friends—the Forbes, Higginsons, Endicotts, Hallowells, and Jacksons—to send him their "observations and recommendations" on the business situation. This they did, as William Endicott, Jr. phrased it, in order "to get as near as possible to the source of power."[4] McKinley, no less than Cleveland, welcomed the aid of the Republican counterparts of the Olneys and Stetsons, especially during the expensive campaign of 1896, when Mark Hanna was responsible for raising the wherewithal to defeat William Jennings Bryan.

The Sherman Act was not, with rare exceptions, enforced throughout the 1890's. By the end of the century the issue could no longer be ignored, if only because it was becoming politically inexpedient to continue to do so in the face of mounting concern over the growth of big business. In June, 1898, Congress created the U.S. Industrial Commission to study the entire economic structure and to take testimony from those interested in the problem. Composed of House and Senate members, but primarily of representatives of a variety of economic organizations, the commission functioned for three years, and its nineteen volumes of testimony and reports are a goldmine of information on every aspect of the American economy at the beginning of the century.

The Industrial Commission accepted the necessity and inevitability of industrial combinations, urging that "Their power for evil should be destroyed and their means for good preserved." More significantly, the commission's hearings provided a forum for key businessmen on the question of federal regulation. The majority of the sentiment was for national regulation of some type in some specific area, and no interest was as strong in this demand as Standard Oil. John D. Rockefeller, John D. Archbold, and H. H. Rogers of Standard called for a national incorporation law and the federal regulation of accounts and financial publicity. Inconsistent state regulation, the Standard spokesmen claimed, was vexatious. There should be, Rockefeller suggested,

"First. Federal legislation under which corporations may be created and regulated, if that be possible. Second. In lieu thereof, State legislation *as nearly uniform as possible* encouraging combinations of persons and capital for the purpose of carrying on industries, but permitting State supervision. . . ."[5] They were joined by Elbert H. Gary, of Morgan's Federal Steel, who called for full publicity of financial data, and by John W. Gates and Max Pam of American Steel and Wire, who wanted strict federal incorporation laws and a national manufacturing commission to supervise incorporation, and by James B. Dill, the promotion lawyer, who also favored federal incorporation. There was, of course, significant opposition to federal incorporation from John R. Dos Passos, the promoter, and Francis Lynde Stetson, but it is clear that important, if not dominant, big business sentiment was very much in favor of federal regulation.

Standard Oil took its views seriously, and thought it crucial that the Industrial Commission's report not conflict with them. In early 1900 Senator Boies Penrose, the Republican political boss of Philadelphia, sent Archbold an advance copy of the proposed Industrial Commission report, and Archbold thought it "so fair that we will not undertake to suggest any changes." Having approved of the commission's preliminary report, Archbold tried to get Penrose appointed chairman of the commission when its original chairman died in mid-1901. Penrose did not want the job, however, for the commission never interested him, and Archbold switched his support to Albert Clarke, not a member of Congress, and rounded up the votes to elect him. We do not want, Archbold wrote Mark Hanna, a radical report making "political capital against the so-called trusts."[6] There was never, of course, a radical report.

By 1900 the politicians could no longer ignore the trust issue. Sentiment within the House for action was very great, and the 1900 Democratic platform pledged the party "to an unceasing warfare in nation, State and city against private monopoly in every form." Even the Republicans, after years of relative silence or indifference on the issue, managed to "condemn all conspiracies and combinations intended to restrict business, to create monopolies. . . . [We] favor such legislation as will effectively restrain and prevent all such abuses." Roosevelt, running for the Vice Presidency, was allowed to carry the burden of the trust issue in 1900, but McKinley, according to Roosevelt, "was uneasy about this so-called trust question and was reflecting in his mind what he should do in the matter."[7] McKinley resolved to press the issue with the Senate, after making changes in the reciprocity agreements, but in September, 1901, two bullets fired at the President by Leon Czolgosz left the matter to Theodore Roosevelt.

A New President

During the first year of his presidency, Roosevelt moved as cautiously on the trust issue as McKinley would have. He inherited McKinley's Attorney General, Philander Knox—formerly attorney for Andrew Carnegie—and the equivocal Republican trust plank written by Mark Hanna. Moreover, the Republican Party was still dominated by Hanna. But, most important of all, Roosevelt had no firm convictions on the question of antitrust policy. His Message to the New York Legislature on the question in January, 1900 was in large part a verbatim transcription of a letter that had been sent him by Elihu Root— the lawyer of Thomas Fortune Ryan and other major capitalists—in December, 1899. He had never written on the question, his understanding of economics was conventional if not orthodox, and his expressions on larger questions of social and economic policy were decidedly conservative. As Governor of New York he had cooperated handsomely with George Perkins and the New York Life Insurance Company in quashing a bill passed by the Legislature limiting the amount of insurance which could be carried by any state-chartered company. Perkins, in return, was very active at the Republican national convention in winning the vice-presidential nomination for Roosevelt, a conscious step, as John Morton Blum rightly suggests, in advancing the political career of Roosevelt. His relationship to Mark Hanna was proper, if not cordial, and Hanna's differences with Roosevelt were those of conflicting personal ambitions and not of principle. Hanna was as pro-union as one could be without giving up a commitment to the open shop. He, like McKinley, favored moderate action—or statements—on the trust issue, and he defended the economic advantages of corporate concentration in much the same terms as Roosevelt later did. The relationship between business and government was essentially a pragmatic one. More fundamental questions did not have to be discussed simply because neither Hanna nor Roosevelt conceived of a governmental policy which challenged in a fundamental manner the existing social and economic relationships. Both men took that relationship for granted. Both accepted the desirability of a conservative trade union movement, responsible business, industrial conciliation, and government action to stop the "menace of today . . . the spread of a spirit of socialism" among workers.[8] Both allied themselves with the pro-conservative union, pro-big business, welfare-oriented National Civic Federation.

Roosevelt's first Annual Message to Congress, on December 3, 1901, was carefully shaped to suit all tastes. Roosevelt discussed the matter with George Perkins, now a Morgan partner, at the beginning of October, and gave him a first draft for his comments and recommendations. Perkins regarded the draft as perfectly acceptable, and was particularly pleased by the section endorsing national rather than state regulation; but Roosevelt apparently mistook a few critical comments for opposition. He wrote to Douglas Robinson that he considered his older views on the topic to be "no longer sufficient." "I intend to be most conservative, but in the interests of the big corporations themselves and above all in the interest of the country I intend to pursue, cautiously but steadily, the course to which I have been publicly committed again and again. . . ." His old position in the New York Legislature, on one hand, was insufficient, but his insistence on carrying through "the course to which I have been publicly committed again and again" indicates Roosevelt was in reality most unsure of his course. To play it safe, however, he told Robinson he would "in strict secrecy let you show such parts of it as you think best to prominent men from whom we think we can get advantageous suggestions or who may state objections. . . ."[9]

By the time Perkins, Robert Bacon, another Morgan partner, and assorted "prominent men" got through with the draft, virtually nothing in Roosevelt's Message warranted anxieties on their part. His statement was a defense, if not a eulogy, of big business. "The process [of industrial development] has aroused much antagonism, a great part of which is wholly without warrant. It is not true that as the rich have grown richer the poor have grown poorer. . . . The captains of industry who have driven the railway systems across this continent, who have built up our commerce, who have developed our manufactures, have on the whole done great good to our people." Success was based on ability, and foolish attacks on corporations would hinder our position in the world market. "It cannot too often be pointed out that to strike with ignorant violence at the interests of one set of men almost inevitably endangers the interests of all." With the welfare of the nation thus dependent on the security and stability of big business, Roosevelt then attacked the "reckless agitator" and made it clear that "The mechanism of modern business is so delicate that extreme care must be taken not to interfere with it in a spirit of rashness or ignorance." Occasional evils that did arise, such as overcapitalization, could be taken care of by publicity, and "Publicity is the only sure remedy which we can now evoke."[10] And, as a final gesture of goodwill to business, Roosevelt advocated the supremacy of federal over state legislation as the solution to the anarchy of dozens of distinct state laws.

Such caution was indeed gratifying. But Roosevelt's next step was less pleasing, if not surprising. Philander Knox, certainly no radical before or after the Northern Securities Case, opened the case against the Northern Securities Company on behalf of the federal government. The details of the incident have been discussed in every standard history of the period. Suffice it to say here that the effort of the Harriman railroad interests to reach a formal accord with the Morgan–Hill interests to end internecine competition for the control of the Chicago, Burlington & Quincy Railroad via joint ownership resulted only in banning the formal device of the holding company. The actual ownership of the railroad by the two power blocs was not altered, nor did they have to give up their railroad holdings, which still faced competition for three-quarters of their traffic. Preparation of the case was begun secretly by Knox, and not even Elihu Root was consulted. Perhaps it is true that Roosevelt wanted to assert the power of the Presidency over Wall Street, or aggrandize his ego, but neither precedent nor the subsequent events justify such a view. The agitation for action against the company was intense in the Midwest, but this alone does not explain the event.

The Northern Securities Case was a politically popular act, and it has strongly colored subsequent historical interpretations of Roosevelt as a trustbuster. It did not change the railroad situation in the Northwest, the ownership of the railroads in that region, nor did it end cooperation among the Hill–Morgan and Harriman lines. Roosevelt never asked for a dissolution of the company, or a restoration of competition. Knox' motives can be evaluated quite explicitly, and Roosevelt's

intentions in the matter can be judged largely on the basis of his subsequent actions. Knox certainly never intended to restore competition
among the involved railroads, and his concept of alternatives never
reached a sufficiently articulate condition to allow either him or Roosevelt to shape the course of events toward some significant change.
"The final solution," Knox mused, "by which the good of combination
will be preserved for the community and the evils be excluded, may
combine a just measure of scope for the operation of both principles,—
competition, which is the healthful economic reminder of the law of
the 'survival of the fittest,' and combination which is the economic expression of the social force of cooperation; and both these forces may
therefore in this ultimate solution properly modify yet support each
other, rather than destroy and exclude." Regulated combinations, he
predicted, will "show even greater common benefits."[11] At about the
same time, Knox did not think there was anything incongruous in asking Henry Clay Frick, his former client and a major shareholder in
Morgan's United States Steel, to invest large sums of money for him
in Pittsburgh banks.

The Northern Securities Case caught Wall Street by surprise, less
because it actually damaged concrete interests than because it seemed
to threaten the autonomy of the business decision-making process.
This is not to say that business did not desire government regulation
in certain areas, but this was surely not one of them. The classic version of Morgan's response has it that J. P. Morgan, who allegedly regarded the President as little more than a businessman in politics,
visited Washington on March 10, 1902, to discuss the threatened
change in Washington–Wall Street relations with Roosevelt. The discussion, according to the initial source, included the following dialogue:

"If we have done anything wrong," said Mr. Morgan, "send your man
(meaning the Attorney General) to my man (naming one of his lawyers)
and they can fix it up." "That can't be done," said the President. "We
don't want to fix it up," added Mr. Knox, "we want to stop it." Then
Mr. Morgan asked: "Are you going to attack my other interests, the
Steel Trust and the others?" "Certainly not," replied the President, "unless
we find out that in any case they have done something that we regard as
wrong."[12]

Certain aspects of the version are incorrect on their face value.
Neither Roosevelt nor Knox ever intended "to stop it" if by that term
it is meant to dissolve the basic structure of ownership or control in

any industry. The significance of the discussion has never been fully appreciated. Morgan made an offer, and whether he consciously decided for it at the time or not, Roosevelt operationally accepted it. Indeed, the event was the most decisive in the subsequent history of Roosevelt's trust policy.

In June, 1902, Perkins approached Roosevelt, Knox, Root, and others about the government designating "some safe plan for us to adopt" in forming the International Mercantile Marine Company. Knox refused to comment on the scheme Perkins presented, but it is evident that the House of Morgan was quite serious about obtaining a government dispensation for its undertakings—especially since, in this case, a subsidy from Congress for the new shipping company was also desired. Their belief that such a détente might be arranged was undoubtedly stimulated by Roosevelt's speeches. "The line of demarcation we draw must always be on conduct, not on wealth; our objection to any given corporation must be, not that it is big, but that it behaves badly."[13] At the same time, Roosevelt turned to Perkins for aid in passing his first important legislation for federal regulation of industry.

Agitation for a Department of Commerce had been carried on by business organizations throughout the 1890's. The idea was not particularly controversial and was especially welcomed by advocates of expanded foreign trade; only lethargy and a desire to reduce expenditures prevented earlier action. Big business sentiment for comprehensive federal regulation eliminating troublesome state regulation also stimulated interest in a federal agency that might lead to this end. Federal incorporation seemed to hold out the possibility of solving these problems, and "Affording the protection of the national government against conflicting state legislation and local political enactments, and—what is equally important—enforcing well-considered regulations and wholesome restrictions incidental to national institutions. . . ."—as the important corporation lawyer, James B. Dill, phrased it.[14] Roosevelt's Second Message to Congress in December, 1902, couched in soothing, conservative terms, asked Congress to create a Department of Commerce. "A fundamental base of civilization is the inviolability of property." State regulation could not adequately prevent the misuse of corporate power that was possible. In calling for national regulation, Roosevelt insistently repeated that "Our aim is not to do away with corporations; on the contrary, these big aggregations are an inevitable development of modern industrialism, and the effort to destroy them would be futile unless accomplished in ways that would work the utmost mischief to the entire body politic." Making it clear where his loyalties lay, Roosevelt developed his commitment even further by suggesting, in a manner similar to France's comment on the rich man and poor man in a democracy having the equal right to sleep under the bridge at night, that he was not at all interested in a redistribution of wealth or power. "We are neither for the rich man as such nor for the poor man as such; we are for the upright man, rich or poor."[15] The problems incident to an industrial society, therefore, could be solved by a higher personal morality, and nothing was more conducive to personal morality than publicity.

To aid him in his efforts for regulation, Roosevelt turned to the conservative Republican and business elements. Bring pressure to bear on Speaker David B. Henderson to secure passage of the Department of Commerce Bill, he wrote Perkins in late December, 1902, and have Marshall Field see that Rep. James R. Mann, chairman of the Interstate and Foreign Commerce Committee, brings in "a thoroughly sensible report" on the topic.[16]

Perkins assured Roosevelt that he wanted the bill passed, and that the wheels were already moving. His legislative agent in Washington, William C. Beer, kept him fully informed of the progress of their joint efforts. At the same time, Perkins had Senator Joseph B. Foraker of Ohio ask Roosevelt about the possibility of additional trust prosecutions, and the Senator could confidently report that "nothing will be done *at present,* and I am confident nothing will be done hereafter."[17]

A bill to create a Department of Commerce and Labor passed the Senate in January, 1902. It made no progress getting through the House Committee on Interstate and Foreign Commerce until January, 1903, shortly after Perkins took up the task. Amended to the House Bill, however, was a provision for a Bureau of Corporations—the Administration's potential agency for publicity on corporate affairs. The Administration directed its efforts in January, 1903 toward the passage of the Nelson amendment and toward the defeat of the Littlefield resolution. The Nelson amendment—written by Knox at Roosevelt's request—would allow the President to withhold information gathered by the Bureau of Corporations, thereby using publicity as his major tool for policing corporations, and would give the bureau the right to obtain whatever testimony or documents it deemed necessary. Roosevelt, in effect, could decide at his own discretion which corporations to attack through publicity. The Littlefield resolution, which passed the House, would have required all corporations engaged in interstate commerce to file annual financial reports with the Interstate Commerce Commission. Its major provision barred from interstate commerce any corporation which used discriminatory rates or sought to destroy competition. Roosevelt and Knox made their opposition to the measure known in early January: they preferred publicity to destruction, and the Littlefield Bill was stopped in the Senate. Roosevelt gave all of his support to the passage of the Nelson amendment to the Department of Commerce Bill.

Passage of the bill was inevitable, but was given a sudden burst of support by a *faux pas* committed by John D. Rockefeller, Jr. On February 6 Rockefeller wired Senators Allison, Lodge, Hale, and Teller that Standard opposed the Bureau of Corporations Bill. Roosevelt seized upon the opportunity and called in the press, transforming Rockefeller, Jr. into Rockefeller, Sr., and exaggerating the number of Senators that had received the telegram—but his story was essentially correct. This gave the measure an aura of radicalism to alienated Congressmen irritated by Roosevelt's conservative opposition to the Littlefield resolution, and it undoubtedly made a few indifferent Congressmen vote for the bill. On February 10 the House passed the bill 252 to 10, and the next day the Senate casually approved the bill without debate or a roll call. Roosevelt signed his bill on February 14, and later sent one of the pens he used to George Perkins, telling him "Your interest in the legislation was strongly indicated at different times during the year or more of active discussion. . . ."[18]

The Bureau of Corporations Bill passed with conservative support and was motivated by conservative intentions. Perkins had actively campaigned for it, and the Department of Commerce aspect of the bill was welcomed by all businessmen. "You know that I have the highest hopes for the new Department, and sincerely believe that it will be of very great practical use to our Government and our vast business interests," Perkins wrote Roosevelt in July, 1903. Despite Standard Oil efforts to dissuade him, Senator Nelson Aldrich worked with Roosevelt in the passage of the bill, and Roosevelt relied on him at various times. Roosevelt, after all, had destroyed the radical Littlefield proposal, and nothing in his presidency justified serious apprehension as to what he might do with the new bureau. William Howard Taft, ironically, chided Roosevelt about his reliance on the conservatives in Congress, and the President's rationale for his cooperation with them was based not only on political opportunism but also on the inherent desirability of the alliance. "My experience for the last year and a half . . . has made me feel respect and regard for Aldrich as one of that group of Senators, including Allison, Hanna, Spooner, Platt . . . Lodge and one or two others, who, together with men like the next Speaker of the House, Joe Cannon, are the most powerful factors in Congress." He might differ with them on specific questions, but they were "not only essential to work with, but desirable to work with . . . and it was far more satisfactory to work with them than to try to work with the radical 'reformers,' like Littlefield."[19]

The Executive
and Business

Roosevelt's cooperation with Aldrich continued as a matter of course, and the President sought out the elder statesman's advice on crucial issues. "I would like to read over to you a couple of my speeches in which I shall touch on the trusts and the tariff. . . . I want to be sure to get what I say on these two subjects along lines upon which all of us can agree," he wrote to Aldrich in March, 1903. At the same time, George M. Cortelyou, the first Secretary of Commerce, assured George Perkins "We are making good progress in the organization of the Department [of Commerce] on careful, conservative lines."[20] The assurance was based on fact. In February, immediately after the passage of the law, Roosevelt asked James R. Garfield to assume the post of Commissioner of Corporations and direct the new bureau. Garfield's assets, so far as Roosevelt was concerned, were many, not the least of them being his tennis ability, which qualified him for Roosevelt's "tennis cabinet." Son of President Garfield, civil service reformer, active in Ohio Republican politics, Garfield also had powerful friends among businessmen. Francis Lynde Stetson, a fellow alumnus of Williams College who often saw Garfield at old school functions, was consulted and gave the approval of the House of Morgan. The Cabinet approved of the appointment, and although Hanna did not care for Garfield, a meeting between the two and a profession of conservative intent by Garfield won the political leader over.[21] Moreover, Garfield was friendly with important Standard Oil lawyers.

In August Roosevelt became concerned that the overcapitalization of many recent corporate promotions, especially by Morgan, was the cause of the recent stock market panic. But throughout the year Roosevelt retained the support of Republican conservatives, such as Platt, who advised his Wall Street friends to give direction to the essentially conservative Roosevelt and try to control him. Roosevelt's Third Annual Message to Congress on December 7, 1903, confirmed Platt's estimate of the President: Roosevelt stressed that the organization of the Department of Commerce and the Bureau of Corporations "proceeded on sane and conservative lines." Legitimate business and labor had nothing to fear from publicity, and the new organizations would not only lead to conciliation between capital and labor but to a better position in foreign trade as well. "We recognize that this is an era of federation and combination, in which great capitalistic corporations and labor unions have become factors of tremendous importance in all industrial centers."[22]

The Bureau of Corporations' major activity during its first year of existence was to define its own legal functions in corporate regulation and those of the national government as well. The issue of the federal regulation of insurance, and whether it could be considered a form of commerce, was, as we shall see, very popular among insurance men —and a number of studies on the problem were prepared by the bureau's legal staff. So far as federal incorporation was concerned, bureau experts concluded, Congress had the power to regulate corporations. Surely, it seemed, the Bureau of Corporations gave big business little to fear and at least something to hope for.[23]

Not a few businessmen remained unhappy with the President, however. Roosevelt retained the support of such conservative Republicans as Senator Joseph B. Foraker of Ohio, Aldrich, and Elihu Root, but the Supreme Court decision in 1904 confirming the Northern Securities prosecution, and the creation of a distinct appropriation— however minute—within the Justice Department for antitrust work, raised some apprehension. "I say to you that he has been . . . the greatest conservative force for the protection of property and our institutions in the city of Washington," Elihu Root warned his peers at the Union Club of New York in February, 1904. "Never forget that the men who labor cast the votes, set up and pull down governments. . . ."[24] The presence of men such as Root, Cortelyou, Paul Morton, Taft, Knox and many other former members of the business and social elite, as well as most of McKinley's major appointees, still testified to the conservative nature of the Administration. Moreover, Roosevelt filed only three antitrust suits in 1902, two in 1903, and one in 1904. There was perhaps a little bluster now and again, but virtually no bite, and big business knew it.

Business had many reasons for optimism as far as the Bureau of Corporations was concerned. And in December, 1902, Roosevelt invited Judge Elbert H. Gary to the White House. The President had never met the chairman of United States Steel, but the two men immediately took a liking to each other, and saw each other and communicated frequently over the next seven years. This mutual confidence was to be of vast importance.

In May, 1904, the Interstate Commerce Commission found the Morgan-controlled International Harvester Company guilty of obtaining rebates from an Illinois railroad which it owned. Earlier in the year Cyrus McCormick had told Commissioner Garfield that so far as the Bureau of Corporations' program was concerned, ". . . International Harvester was in entire sympathy with some program of this sort."[25] Instead of prosecuting it, Attorney General William H. Moody and Garfield agreed to an International Harvester proposal that if the company would in the future conform to the law after being told when and where it was violating it, the right of prosecution would be dropped; no formal means of fulfilling the agreement appears to have been arranged. That George Perkins had organized the company, and was the major Morgan representative in it, was probably of influence in the bureau's having so lenient an attitude. At about the same time, Garfield discussed his plans for the bureau with Virgil P. Kline, counsel for Standard Oil and a friend, and Kline relayed the information to H. H. Rogers. The bureau wanted information, and Garfield intimated it would not be used for purposes of prosecution. In June, 1904, according to Garfield, Kline told him "the Standard Oil Company would co-operate with the Bureau and would give me the information that I desire . . ." for a bureau study. They agreed that "we would confer with the representatives of the company" on all important matters related to the study and bureau plans.[26]

Garfield was rapidly formulating a course of action for the Bureau of Corporations that was to operationally determine the nature of

Roosevelt's trust policies. In March, 1904, in response to pressure from livestock growers, the House passed a resolution calling for a bureau investigation of beef prices and profits. Garfield did not want the job, but was forced to proceed nevertheless. In April and in subsequent months, working through Charles G. Dawes of the Central Trust Company of Chicago, Garfield met with the major Chicago packers and assured them any information he obtained would remain confidential and that he had no intention of harming their interests. Even before a formal policy on the function of the Bureau of Corporations had been formulated, Garfield had moved to make the organization a shield behind which business might seek protection. Informal détentes and understandings were regarded sympathetically, even if the law was circumvented, and nothing would be done to harm business interests.

The pending election did a great deal, of course, to mitigate any radical action Roosevelt might have contemplated. In September and October, 1904, Garfield and Roosevelt came to an understanding as to the nature and function of the bureau. Garfield decided that "The function of the Bureau of Corporations is not to enforce the anti-trust laws," or even to gather information indicating the need for their enforcement. Roosevelt was less clear as to whether its purpose was to gather information to enforce existing laws or to show what additional legislation might be necessary, but Garfield's position was to prevail. Information gathered by the bureau would be released only at the discretion of the President—as provided by the law—and even though the beef information gathered by the bureau was not given to the U.S. District Attorney of northern Illinois, then considering legal measures, the names of the bureau's informants were passed along. The bureau was charged with investigating for purposes of possible legislation, not enforcing existing laws, Garfield maintained, and its information could not be used by other departments for purposes of prosecution. ". . . the policy of obtaining hearty co-operation rather than arousing antagonism of business and industrial interests has been followed," he concluded.[27]

Garfield had, in fact, been most cooperative with business. And rather than recommending legislation, the bureau effectively served, with its time-consuming procedures, as a block to legislation. "The danger of remedial legislation," Garfield wrote, "is that in its efforts to strike down the abnormal, the unusual and the evil, it likewise strike[s] down the normal, the usual and the good, hence extreme remedial legislation results in disaster."[28] Garfield was giving the bureau a safe, conservative direction. Roosevelt was safe too, and so was the Republican platform he ran on in 1904. "Combinations of capital and of labor are the results of the economic movement of the age, but neither must be permitted to infringe upon the rights and interests of the people. Such combinations, when lawfully formed for lawful purposes, are alike entitled to the protection of the laws, but both are subject to the laws and neither can be permitted to break them." Thus having equated the power of the corporation with the power of a puny craft union movement, the Republicans resigned themselves to the movement of the age. Despite Roosevelt's insistence that the Party return a large donation from Standard Oil, the Roosevelt campaign received large sums of money from Perkins, E. H. Harriman, and businessmen convinced by Root—who was shaping many of Roosevelt's campaign speeches—and others in the Administration that the President was doing his best for business.[29]

It is possible, of course, that the commonly held conception of Roosevelt as the anticorporate radical biding his time until he was President by virtue of a ballot box, not an anarchist's bullets, is valid. But certainly nothing the President did or said in the months immediately following his victory in 1904 justifies such an interpretation. Quite the contrary, the remainder of Roosevelt's presidency was essentially a continuation of his first three years, adjusted for tangential personal qualities and idiosyncracies. Perhaps Roosevelt may have conceived of himself as an impartial, objective mediator between contending economic interests, seeking to mitigate class conflicts. "It would be a dreadful calamity," he wrote Philander Knox in November, "if we saw this country divided into two parties, one containing the bulk of the property owners and conservative people, the other the bulk of the wageworkers and the less prosperous people generally." Roosevelt persistently returned to this theme—reform to him was a means of preventing radical social change. And inevitably, as if by reflex, he identified himself with conservatism and a benevolent paternalism. "The friends of property, of order, of law, must never show weakness in the face of violence or wrong or injustice; but on the other hand . . . it is peculiarly incumbent upon the man with whom things have prospered to be in a certain sense the keeper of his brother with whom life has gone hard."[30] It never occurred to Roosevelt, who dwelt on this theme again in his Message to Congress on December 6, that the existing distribution of power was based on something more than talent and personal skill. "Great corporations are necessary, and only men of great and singular mental power can manage such corporations successfully, and such men must have great rewards." This did not justify unabashed exploitation, because Roosevelt nominally placed "good sense, courage, and kindliness" on a higher scale of priorities. But translated into specific terms, this always resulted in a defense of business interests, and a call for mutual charity between the unequal—"More important than any legislation is the gradual growth of a feeling of responsibility and forbearance among capitalists and wageworkers alike."[31]

Business was indeed gratified by the President's and Garfield's conservatism. The bureau's policy, Roosevelt announced in the only aspect of his 1904 Message bearing on industrial corporations, was "one of open inquiry into, and not attack upon, business, [and] the Bureau has been able to gain not only the confidence, but, better still, the co-operation of men engaged in legitimate business." Garfield's first report for the bureau, in December, 1904 was similarly reassuring.

In brief, the policy of the Bureau in the accomplishment of the purposes of its creation is to cooperate with, not antagonize, the business world; the immediate object of its inquiries is the suggestion of constructive legislation, not the institution of criminal prosecutions. It purposes, through exhaustive investigations of law and fact, to secure conservative action, and to avoid ill-considered attack upon corporations charged with unfair or dishonest practices. Legitimate business—law-respecting persons and corporations—have nothing to fear from the proposed exercise of this great governmental power of inquiry.[32]

Moreover, Garfield came out for federal licensing of corporations, and this was especially welcomed by many big businessmen. "After the first year," Garfield reported later, "the business interests of the country appreciated that the Bureau was not to be used as an instrument of improper inquisition. . . ."[33] With the exception of Francis Lynde Stetson, who did not like the idea of federal incorporation and represented only himself, spokesmen of business were delighted with Garfield's report and few were apprehensive about what Roosevelt might do next. Even Stetson was pleased with the other work of the bureau. Seth Low, chairman of the National Civic Federation and an important influence in Roosevelt's trust policies, approved heartily. Perkins called Garfield up and congratulated him, and Garfield responded by welcoming any suggestions he or his business friends might have. Business communications were overwhelmingly in favor of Garfield's report and proposal. John D. Rockefeller, Sr. praised Garfield's license plan, according to *Harper's Weekly,* because "the Federal government would scarcely issue its license to a corporation without at the same time guaranteeing to its beneficiaries an adequate degree of protection."[34]

The *Wall Street Journal* editorialized on December 28, 1904:

Nothing is more noteworthy than the fact that President Roosevelt's recommendation in favor of government regulation of railroad rates and Commissioner Garfield's recommendation in favor of federal control of interstate companies have met with so much favor among managers of railroad and industrial companies. It is not meant by this that much opposition has not developed, for it has, but it might have been expected that the financial interests in control of the railroads and the industrial corporations would be unanimous in antagonism to these measures, which would, if carried into effect, deprive them of so much of their present power.

The fact is that many of the railroad men and corporation managers are known to be in favor of these measures, and this is of vast significance. In the end it is probable that all of the corporations will find that a reasonable system of federal regulation is to their interest. It is not meant by this that the financial interests who are in favor of the administrative measures, approve of them exactly in the shape in which they have been presented by the President and Commissioner Garfield, but with the principle of the thing they are disposed to agree.

. . . Now as between governmental regulation by forty-five states and governmental regulation by the central authority of the federal government, there can be but one choice. . . . The choice must be that of a federal regulation, for that will be uniform over the whole country and of a higher and more equitable standard.

CHAPTER FOUR

ROOSEVELT

AS

REFORMER,

1904-1906

IN LATE 1904, while on one of his periodic visits to the White House, Judge Elbert H. Gary of United States Steel and Roosevelt entered into a debate on big business in America. At one point Gary promised Roosevelt that "If at any time you feel that the Steel Corporation should be investigated, you shall have an opportunity to examine the books and records of all our companies, and if you find anything in them that you think is wrong, we will convince you that we are right or we will correct the wrong." "Well, that seems to me to be about the fair thing," the President agreed.[1]

It is likely that Gary was aware of a similar arrangement that had been made with International Harvester, and perhaps even of the one with Standard Oil. In January, 1905, the House of Representatives ordered an investigation of U.S. Steel, and Gary had his opportunity. The matter was turned over to the Bureau of Corporations, and Garfield dallied on the matter for most of the year. Without anything more than the verbal understanding between Gary and Roosevelt, in September, 1905, the bureau began obtaining a large amount of data from U.S. Steel and interviewing Steel officials. Garfield made requests for information to Gary, and finally decided it would be best to formalize the understanding between the government and the Steel corporation. On November 2, 1905, Frick, Gary, Garfield, and the President met at the White House. Gary freely declared his company "desires to co-operate with the Government in every possible way that is consistent with the proper protection of the interests of its stockholders in their rights and property. . . ." He was apprehensive, however, about the possible misuse of detailed information the corporation was to supply. Garfield reassured him Roosevelt only wanted information "upon which recommendations for legislation might be made." Gary requested that the bureau use only publicity to punish the company in the event it found something amiss. In return, Gary agreed formally to give Garfield full access to the Steel books, and any disagreement on the use of the material would be submitted to Secretary of Commerce Victor Metcalf or, ultimately, the President himself. Garfield drew up a memo on the understanding, and Gary and Roosevelt agreed with its contents.[2] This cordial understanding was supplemented the following week by mutual reassurances between Gary and Garfield. "I think I should say there has been no disposition on my part to endeavor to bind the Government to any promise or undertaking for the protection of our corporation," Gary wrote. "On the other hand, the public utterances of the President, and your statements to me from time to time, have been such as to show conclusively to my mind that there was no intention of doing or saying anything that would injure our Corporation or disturb business conditions." The government would not act to damage U.S. Steel's interests, Garfield responded, "unless it was shown to be the Government's clear duty to take it."[3]

Roosevelt, in formalizing his understanding with United States Steel, acted out of solicitude and not because it was the only way he could obtain desired information. The bureau was legally able to compel the production of evidence and witnesses, and the creation of a détente with Steel, in effect, altered the character of the Bureau of Corporations. More important, it allowed the bureau to become a shield behind which certain select corporations might hide from state and Congressional inquiries. To Garfield, the agreement was "a long step ahead in fixing the work of the Bureau on the lines I wish."⁴ Roosevelt had, in effect, institutionalized the policy of formalizing détentes with select companies. Morgan's offer to send his man to consult with the President's man, International Harvester's proposal that it would be happy to obtain government advice if they could avoid prosecution, and Standard's offer of a détente were now well on their way to at least partial embodiment in official policy.

The Bureau of Corporations' delay in investigating U.S. Steel during 1905 was in part caused by other concerns. Garfield was still committed to the investigation of beef prices and profits the House had forced upon the bureau. Garfield wished to keep the information he was gathering from the Department of Justice. Chicago packers grew increasingly apprehensive of his ability to maintain his promises that the data would be kept confidential, and became more reluctant to supply information in light of the fact that Roosevelt was less certain about the desirability of withholding information. In January, 1905, much to Garfield's embarrassment, Roosevelt ordered the bureau to hand its beef data over to the Justice Department for possible litigation. At the same time, the bureau rushed to complete its report on beef, and on March 3, 1905, released it to the public.

Garfield released the report with much trepidation. "Now will come the storm for its conclusions will not meet the popular demands —but it is the truth + I care not for popular clamor," he confided to his diary. The report certainly did not meet the popular demand, but it was largely accurate. It implicitly denied the widely-read charges of the muckraker Charles Edward Russell that "here is something compared with which the Standard Oil Company is puerile."⁵ The industry, the bureau announced, was substantially competitive, and the big packers were in no position to raise beef prices indiscriminately. Despite the strong supporting data for such conclusions, the public was irate at not being told what it wanted to hear, and the packers were angry at having their confidence betrayed. But the report was ultimately useful to the packers, and when the Justice Department initiated proceedings against the Big Four packers several months later, the bureau's *Report* turned out to be their best defense. Not only did it defend them from the accusation that they were a monopoly and gouging the public, but the packers had given the data to the bureau in return for a promise of immunity —even though such a promise was not necessary.

Roosevelt was displeased with the unfavorable press response to the beef report, and although he supported Garfield, he also requested a supplementary report. Garfield handed the matter over to Herbert Knox Smith, his chief aide and heir-apparent, who Garfield thought "has shown himself well qualified to take care of things."[6] Armour and Morris refused to provide Smith and his investigators with additional data, and he decided against a subpoena. An additional report to the President was never made.

The question of the beef industry went to the courts, and the bureau turned its attention to Standard Oil once again after allowing its understanding with Standard of June, 1904, to lie dormant for the time. In January and February, 1905, Garfield met with a group of Standard executives, including H. H. Rogers, John Archbold, and S. C. T. Dodd, and they decided to specifically investigate the numerous allegations of Standard rebating and monopoly in Kansas and the Midwest. Garfield was pleased. "Again I am in a position where I may be of great service to the public," he curiously concluded.[7] It was understood that information would be freely given the bureau in conformity with the June, 1904, agreement. Garfield told Roosevelt of the arrangement no later than January 21, 1905, and the President approved. Roosevelt's willingness to follow Garfield's lead was dictated by personal loyalties to his tennis partner, not by sympathy with Standard. The Standard Oil Company was Roosevelt's sole explicit criterion of a "bad" as opposed to a "good" trust, a definition that was later to assume great importance in the President's not too sophisticated thinking on the entire trust issue. Standard had opposed the formation of the bureau, and Roosevelt exaggerated this opposition into a general Standard dislike for regulation of any sort. In reality, Standard executives were early and leading advocates of federal incorporation, which they saw as a means of protection against burdensome state regulation. In August, 1904, Roosevelt favorably toyed with a suggestion by Nicholas Murray Butler, president of Columbia University, that it might be desirable to put the Standard tag on the Democratic Party. Despite the fact that virtually all of Roosevelt's critical comments on the "trust issue" were really attacks on Standard specifically and not on the larger economic order of which they were only a small part, during early 1905 he was willing to support Garfield's plan for an informal détente even with the oil corporation.

The bureau's investigation of Standard's Midwest and Western operations, especially in reference to railroad rebates, was begun in earnest immediately after the beef report was released. It was not initiated in a spirit of hostility, but Standard quickly reneged on its part of the agreement. During April, 1905, Garfield personally visited the Standard operations in the Midwest, and assigned investigators to tour other areas. In May, however, bureau representative Luther Conant, Jr. complained he was not receiving sufficient data from Standard's Pacific Coast subsidiary. Kline and Garfield met to discuss the matter, and according to Kline they agreed that the bureau would have access to all information save as it "in some manner touched the question of freight rates," but the company also insisted that "a needless disclosure of private rights and interests ought to be avoided."[8] Standard then tried to have the inquiry put off until the fall of 1905, but complaints by bureau field investigators that evidence was still being hidden and possible sources of testimony silenced alienated Garfield. The relationship between the bureau and Standard Oil for the remainder of 1905 became increasingly strained as the bureau's men closed in on Standard's obvious and well-known rebating practices. Garfield inevitably but reluctantly became highly critical of Standard. It appeared as if Standard was indeed the epitome of Roosevelt's "bad" trust.

Roosevelt As Reformer

1905 was not a year for victorious post-election antitrust action by a President presumably thought by most historians to have been chaffing for action; it was, instead, a year for more inactivity and détentes. Had Roosevelt been seriously interested in antitrust prosecutions he could have had more than five cases initiated by the Department of Justice in 1905. But the President was unable to break out of his traditional pattern of political alliances with big business conservatives. He did not continue his relations with them because of a consciously articulated desire to work with conservatives as such, but because he evaluated men and their motives on the basis of personal manners and character, and Ivy League men and moguls of industry seemed to have more polish and character than others he knew. Once convinced of the personal integrity and sincerity of such men, he was loyal to them even in the most embarrassing situations. And their word of honor, as in the case of Gary and Perkins, was often enough to vindicate their actions. On this basis, good trusts could be distinguished from bad ones, some corporations prosecuted and others encouraged. Perkins and Gary could speak of labor-management cooperation and mutual justice at the very same time that workers toiled twelve hours a day, seven days a week—at the very same time that unions were ruthlessly smashed. Roosevelt took their word at its face value and ignored the reality of a U.S. Steel labor policy no less exploitive than Standard Oil's.

1905 was a year of conservative consolidation within the Roosevelt Administration. Elihu Root, shortly after the 1904 election, had decided to retire as Secretary of War and return to private law practice. In a whirlwind period of less than one year, Root took substantial part in the reorganization of the Northern Securities Company, and in February, 1905, also at the behest of Morgan, he went to work on the reorganization of the Equitable Life Assurance Society shortly before Charles Evans Hughes descended upon it on behalf of the New York Legislature to seriously embarrass Morgan, Root, and Thomas Fortune Ryan, Morgan's ally. Deeply involved with Morgan, and with his reputation, conservative in any event, widely challenged, Root was nevertheless invited by Roosevelt in July, 1905, to become Secretary of State. Root accepted, and had Roosevelt appoint Robert Bacon, a Morgan partner, a Harvard man, and a friend of the President, Assistant Secretary of State. Big business was delighted, especially since Root began applying his energies to opening South America to United States commercial interests. Indeed, Roosevelt saw nothing ironic or incongruous in appointing Root to the Secretary of State's post just as he was deeply involved in directing Morgan's Chinese investments and the sale of the Canton-Hankow Railroad. Roosevelt, in brief, was personally devoted to Root. He considered Root as his leading and best qualified successor to the Presidency until 1906, when he finally realized that Taft would make a better candidate by virtue of the fact he was not widely regarded as a "Wall Street man." Moreover, Root rejected Roosevelt's urgings that he run.[9]

Roosevelt's personal loyalty to individuals, and his refusal to consider the possibility of a conflict of interest, began with his strong dependence on Philander Knox for the formulation and direction of his early trust program, and was to continue throughout his political career. To defend a friend and, incidentally, the reputation of his Administration, he was quite willing to brush political dirt under the carpet if he could. One example was his treatment of the Paul Morton affair in 1905. Morton was Secretary of the Navy and a former vice-president of the Atchison, Topeka, & Sante Fe Railroad. In February, 1905, the I.C.C. decided the Santa Fe was guilty of having accepted large rebates while Morton was an executive there. Morton, for his part, often represented the railroad cause while in the Cabinet, and was an important business pipeline to Roosevelt. Among other things, he had managed to convince Roosevelt of the desirability of railroad pools. When the affair broke in June, Morton naturally submitted his resignation to Roosevelt. Although he was forced to accept the resignation, Roosevelt insisted on publicly defending Morton: he proclaimed his selflessness and asserted that Morton alone among the railroad leaders had fought for the abolition of the rebate system —a proposition that conflicted with public knowledge. But Roosevelt realized he also had to order a further investigation of the truth of the allegations against the Sante Fe—Attorney General William H. Moody recommended he do so—and in ordering Moody to go ahead he stressed, without access to new facts, that Morton was innocent and that only the Sante Fe, and not its individual officers, be investigated. Moody, because of the case's importance, assigned former Attorney General Harmon to investigate the matter, and made no secret of the fact that he did not wish to prosecute the Sante Fe. Harmon, however, was contrary, and strongly advised prosecution of the Sante Fe on contempt charges. Moody was embarrassingly forced to hand the matter over to the courts for a decision, but since his own attorneys were in charge of the prosecution, no judgment was brought against the Sante Fe. Roosevelt's direction of the Morton affair indicates that personal loyalties, as well as his sense of public relations, were deep indeed.[10]

From the founding of the Bureau of Corporations until late 1906 Garfield was a major, if not the dominant influence in directing Roosevelt's trust policies. In late 1906 Roosevelt appointed Charles J. Bonaparte as his Attorney General. Bonaparte's assets were varied —he was a civil service reformer and a Baltimore attorney, and gave Roosevelt a Catholic in his Cabinet. His qualifications for handling antitrust activity, however, were more restricted. His public utterances on the issue revealed what was to follow. "I regard the tendency of combination as an inevitable feature of modern civilization," Bonaparte told the Civic Federation of Chicago's trust conference of September, 1899. "Emphatically no legislative action in regulation or restraint of combinations, whether by Congress or State legislature, is desirable. Our public men (with, I need not say, some honorable exceptions) are wholly unfit to deal with any such matters. The attempt will be highly demoralizing to all concerned, the practical results (except in the levy of blackmail) altogether nugatory."[11] Now, seven years later, Bonaparte was placed in charge of antitrust activity as an honorable exception.

Garfield, presumably another honorable exception, continued to maintain excellent relations with the business community throughout 1905, save with the big packers. United States Steel was happy with its détente as a means of protecting itself from Congressional attacks. Standard Oil, at least for the time being, appeared contented. In October, a group of visiting bankers saw Garfield and were cordial. Garfield was pleased and flattered: "Such conferences are valuable. I must try to have more of them," he confided in his diary. ". . . he left the impression that the majority of businessmen are bad," Garfield wrote commenting on an article by muckraker Ray Stannard Baker; "that I do not believe." His personal biases, needless to say, were reflected in the bureau's policies and, ultimately, in Roosevelt's as well. His annual bureau *Report* for 1905 strongly condemned penal remedies and enforcement of the antitrust laws as a means of regulating corporations. It was necessary to find the causes of industrial evils in order to remedy them, and Congress would be better advised to "provide a method by which reasonable combination may be permitted." A federal licensing law or federal incorporation would provide such a method, for it would assure proper publicity, and since "Existing business methods will be changed in accordance with public opinion," such publicity would give the public the facts.[12] Such a proposition pleased everyone and solved nothing.

The major concern of Roosevelt's Annual Message to Congress on December 5 was with railroad regulation, an area in which, as I have tried to show elsewhere, he was eminently conservative. ". . . these recommendations are not made in any spirit of hostility to the railroads," he insisted. As when discussing industrial corporations, Roosevelt identified the interests of "small investors, a multitude of railway employes, wage workers, and . . . the public" with those of the railroad tycoons. He never tired of reiterating that "In our industrial and social system the interests of all men are so closely intertwined that in the immense majority of cases a straight-dealing man who by his efficiency, by his ingenuity and industry, benefits himself must also benefit others. . . . The superficial fact that the sharing may be unequal must never blind us to the underlying fact that there is this sharing. . . ." There were, of course, "selfish and brutal men in all ranks of life." There were capitalists who acted in "disregard of every moral restraint," and laborers full "of laziness, of sullen envy of the more fortunate, and of willingness to perform deeds of murderous violence. Such conduct is just as reprehensible in one case as in the other." Such equations reveal much of Roosevelt's values. The man of power who helps control the shape and course of the economy is neutralized by powerless workers with "improper" attitudes and by hypothetical murderers—which to Roosevelt really meant militant unionists. Roosevelt was not willing to make a blanket defense of business either privately or publicly, but functionally he, along with all other members of the constituted establishment, paid homage to it. "Business success, whether for the individual or for the Nation, is a good thing only so far as it is accompanied by and develops a high standard of conduct—honor, integrity, civic courage." Business success is concrete, visible, and Roosevelt thought it a good thing. What is "honor, integrity, civic courage," tangibly? Roosevelt's ability to take such rhetoric seriously, to wax hot over platitudes, made him, for practical purposes, responsive to real business needs and desires.

So Roosevelt's 1905 Message, as far as it got down to real issues, was as pro-business as his earlier statements had been. "I am in no sense hostile to corporations. This is an age of combination, and any effort to prevent all combination will be not only useless, but in the end vicious, because of the contempt for law which the failure to enforce law inevitably produces. We should, moreover, recognize in cordial and ample fashion the immense good effected by corporate agencies in a country such as ours, and the wealth of intellect, energy, and fidelity devoted to their service, and therefore normally to the service of the public, by their officers and directors."[13] Specifically, Roosevelt again rejected state supervision of corporations as either possible or desirable. He thought the regulation of excessive over-capitalization might be desirable, but he asked for no concrete legislation. Instead, he restricted himself to the railroad regulation issue, and then turned to the problem of the regulation of insurance. Garfield, in his *Report* earlier in the month, had declared that the Bureau of Corporations had no constitutional or legal power to investigate insurance, which was not strictly a form of commerce, and had recommended a Congressional act regulating insurance to test the problem in the courts. Roosevelt attacked state supervision of insurance as inadequate and inconsistent. It led, he pointed out, to the creàtion of unscrupulous companies formed in one state and operating throughout the country. Roosevelt asked Congress to consider whether it had the power to regulate insurance. But he couched his request in such a manner as to leave no doubt that he desired federal regulation of insurance.

Ignoring railroad legislation, the creation of the Bureau of Corporations was the only significant step Roosevelt had taken on the trust issue during over four years as President. From late 1905, however, his demands for legislation, as well as his taking actual measures which have commonly been termed progressive, increased sharply. The bureau had proven abortive, and whatever progressive goals it might have achieved were frustrated by its genial Commissioner, working, of course, with the approval of the President. After the election of 1904, however, Roosevelt had few political obstacles or inhibitions. He had been given a mandate by the electorate, and he renounced the nomination for 1908. He now had the opportunity to move in new directions, presumably to try to redress the balance of economic power and to establish responsible public control over big business. The standard historical interpretation maintains Roosevelt did create a new frontier—perhaps not as radical as was once supposed, but nevertheless a system of regulation designed ultimately to bring big business under social control for public ends.

Insurance and
Regulation

The issue of the federal regulation of insurance during the Roosevelt presidency has been virtually ignored by historians. Had they been less delinquent, it is nevertheless likely that Roosevelt's demand for federal regulation would have been interpreted as another of his efforts to create progressive legislation, to bring big business under public control. The insurance industry, however provides an important example of how an industry sought to solve its internal economic problems by political means.

From the end of the Civil War and throughout this period the insurance business was characterized by cutthroat competition and warfare equaled in few, if any, other fields. In 1867 Henry B. Hyde of the Equitable Life Assurance Society introduced "tontine" insurance: if a policy holder died before the end of the term of his insurance he received its face value; if he lapsed in his payments he forfeited all; and if he reached the end of his term he received dividends plus a share of the forfeited reserves. The scheme was a form of gambling, and variations of it led to dividend wars, intensive commissions and raids on the sales forces of competitors, liberalized terms, rebates, and a gradual elimination of the number of life insurance companies until 1890. In the long run, the shrewd customer could benefit most from the anarchic conditions that existed, and given the enormous increase of insurance in force most conservative life insurance leaders regarded the entire situation as mutually damaging. At the same time, state regulation increased and was highly variable from state to state, as well as financially burdensome. Voluntary truces between Equitable and its chief competitor, Mutual Life, failed to solve the problems of aggressive outside firms and state laws, and invariably collapsed. The insurance in force more than doubled between 1876 and 1890, and then doubled again during the next decade. After 1885, there was a growing number of new firms. Indiana and Michigan discovered they could increase state revenues

by allowing irregularly managed firms to take out charters, and by
1900 over three hundred fraternal insurance companies were in existence. Between 1890 and 1905 the number of life insurance companies in operation more than doubled, although the numbers of new
entries and failures were even greater.[14]

State supervision was frequently ignorant, and often corrupt as
well. But the anarchy within the industry was so great, and the volume of new entries so high, that some large insurance firms preferred
state regulation to no regulation at all. During the 1870's, however,
a substantial and growing number of conservative insurance managers became convinced that only federal regulation could impose
order on the industry, protect them from dishonest companies, and
mitigate competition. As early as 1865 Congress had been petitioned
for a national incorporation act to save the insurance companies from
state regulation, and in 1868 a bill was presented to the Senate.
Additional efforts were made in the 1880's, but they failed. In 1889
an insurance journal devoted exclusively to agitating for federal regulation, *Views,* was founded in Washington. The great obstacle to
regulation, however, was not the reticence of Congress but the existence of the *Paul v. Virginia* decision of 1868, handed down by
Justice Stephen Field for the Supreme Court. Its thesis was simple:
insurance was a contract, a contract was not commerce, and the Constitution empowered Congress only with the right to regulate commerce. Despite the *Paul* decision, insurance men by 1892 were ready
to obtain federal legislation and hope for a more favorable Court
decision afterwards. In 1892, John M. Pattison, a member of the
House and also president of the Union Central Life Insurance Company of Cincinnati, submitted a bill providing for a Bureau of Insurance in the Treasury Department which could demand information
from insurance companies and had the power of subpoena. The
states were to continue issuing charters, but companies were to meet
federal standards thereafter. Companies were exempted from taxation save in the state in which they received their charter. Unhappily,
Congress was not moved by the plight of the insurance companies,
and although most insurance leaders supported the bill, they did not
work for its passage. By 1897, however, the deterioration within the
industry having accelerated, the *Ohio Underwriter* reported that "Officials of life companies the country over are wishing that the dream
of national supervision be realized." Their dream came one step

closer to realization when Senator Orville Platt of Connecticut introduced a bill at the request of some of his important insurance con-
stituents. The bill was identical to the earlier Pattison Bill, save that
it required Congress and not the insurance firms to pay the cost of
regulation, and allowed state taxation in areas where a company held
property as well as its charter. ". . . it is the duty of Congress to so
legislate from time to time, as to keep the laws of the country abreast
with modern ideas," the influential insurance journal, the *Spectator,*
announced.[15] The best way to test the constitutionality of the bill,
it concluded, was to pass it. Unfortunately for the industry, Platt's
Bill, like its predecessor, died in committee.

If the federal government would not get into insurance, many
insurance men reasoned, it would be necessary for them to get into
state politics to protect themselves. George Perkins, who as vice-
president of the New York Life Insurance Company had initiated
branch offices in the industry in the late 1880's and helped his company become the largest insurance company by 1900, was familiar
with the importance of politics. He realized that competition was
costly, and his efforts at voluntary cooperation among the giant companies had failed. New York Life's legislative agent, Andrew Hamilton, had spent about one million dollars in Albany over a ten-year
period, at least $235,000 of which even the company admitted went
for political payoffs. Perkins was deeply involved in these political
machinations, and through them became close to Theodore Roosevelt. William C. Beer, New York Life's national political expert, was
involved in Republican politics in its cruder aspects, and went with
Perkins to the House of Morgan. Indeed, it was Beer who later
worked with Perkins on the passage of the Department of Commerce
Bill. In early 1900, however, Perkins' special problem was a bill in
the New York Legislature limiting the amount of insurance any New
York chartered company could hold in force to $1.5 billion. It was
his work with Roosevelt, then Governor, in successfully opposing the
bill that attracted Perkins to the Rough Rider, and it marked the
beginning of their friendship. In June, 1900, Perkins threw his substantial weight at the Republican convention behind Roosevelt for
the vice-presidential candidacy.

The addition of Perkins as a Morgan partner in 1901 acknowledged the fact that insurance was now an important aspect of Wall
Street, and the interlocking of insurance and finance in a massive

way begins about this time. The need for regulation increased along
with the growth of the big insurance companies. The proliferation of
new insurance companies continued, and after 1905 accelerated even
more rapidly. State regulation, in addition to failing to prevent the
spawning of new companies, was increasingly costly. Direct fees collected from insurance companies by thirteen states alone in 1902
amounted to $3.6 million, while the expenses of supervision were a
mere one-ninth of that sum. Indirectly, moreover, the costs were
probably much greater, or at least insurance companies thought so.
Valued policy insurance laws, existing in many states, forced companies to pay the entire face value of a policy in the event of fire
or loss, rather than the actual value of the loss. Many insurance men
were convinced that such policies increased fires, and that they were
forced to raise their rates to cover losses.[16]

While the Department of Commerce Bill was being discussed in
1902, insurance interests unsuccessfully maneuvered to include a
Bureau of Insurance in the new department. Insurance men became
increasingly desperate over the growth of new and often dishonest
competitors, as well as the deluge of state legislation. In late 1903
the Committee of Insurance Commissioners prepared a bill to deny
the mails to insurance companies not authorized by the insurance
department of the state in which they were operating. The bill embodying this rather oblique approach was introduced in the Senate
by John F. Dryden of New Jersey, who also happened to be president
of the Prudential Insurance Company and the leading spokesman for
federal regulation of insurance. Dryden's bill was immediately opposed by major clients for insurance, who feared it might sharply
reduce the amount of insurance that could be obtained by large risks.
It, like all its predecessors, died a quiet death.

The Bureau of Corporations, however, offered hope to the har-
ried insurance industry. One of its first tasks was to investigate the
problems of the industry and to evaluate the legal issues involved in
federal regulation of insurance. In June, 1904, after completing a
number of legal briefs, the bureau sent one of its investigators,
Charles S. Moore, to interview leading Eastern insurance executives
and obtain their views on federal regulation. Arriving in Philadelphia,
Moore concluded that insurance opinion was unanimously in favor
of federal regulation, especially to counter the costs of valued policy
laws and, as Clarence E. Porter of Spring Garden Insurance phrased

it, federal regulation would "remove the harassing conditions and onerous expenses of the various States and would reduce the supervision of the insurance companies to that of one Government Department at Washington." Moore found insurance sentiment in New York, where he talked to the leaders of about eight companies, enthusiastically in favor of federal regulation.[17]

The realization that there was some hope for sympathetic action by the federal government galvanized insurance industry support for federal regulation. During the last two months of 1904 the industry mounted a campaign to obtain legislation. "I earnestly hope that the time is not far distant when, as a permanent relief from the needless and increasing burdens of over-supervision, over-legislation, and over-taxation . . . we shall have an act of Congress regulating insurance between the States," Senator Dryden announced.[18] At the same time, Dryden sent Prudential's statistician to see Garfield to obtain data to support federal legislation. A few weeks later, in line with a recommendation from Garfield, Roosevelt appealed to Congress in his 1904 Annual Message to consider whether it had the power to regulate insurance. The *Spectator,* the most influential of the insurance journals and close to New York Life Insurance, was encouraged. It had supported federal regulation for thirty years, and now had hopes for seeing its goal attained. "It is not the public that requires further supervision by the national government, but it is the insurance companies, with their millions of dollars of capital, that need protection from the inharmonious, exacting and often conflicting laws of fifty different States." To prove its point, the journal ran a symposium on the question for insurance men, and concluded that nearly all wanted strong national legislation.[19] The enthusiasm of the other insurance journals for federal legislation ranged from mild endorsement to, in most cases, very strong backing. John McCall and other major insurance presidents wrote letters of vigorous support for regulation to the journals.

The insurance men would have preferred an even stronger public stand for regulation from Garfield and Roosevelt, and an outright declaration that insurance was in fact commerce and therefore open to federal regulation. Despite Garfield's hedging in public, behind the scenes he worked closely with the strong pro-regulation group. After consulting with Dryden's statistician in November, 1904, in January, 1905, he met with James M. Beck, lawyer for the giant Mutual Life

Insurance of New York, who was preparing a comprehensive federal regulation bill to include a Bureau of Insurance in the Department of Commerce. Beck, who was in contact with Senator Dryden
on the matter, accepted a number of Garfield's proposals on the legislation, and handed the draft to Dryden, who then introduced it in the
Senate. The new Dryden Bill was strong. Insurance companies were
compelled to file annual reports with the new bureau, and its books
and records could be demanded and inspected at company expense.
Each company had to file its charter and by-laws and post a $100,-
000 bond as a guaranty of faithful performance of duty. States could
supervise companies they chartered, but not those of other states,
and state laws for the purpose of raising revenues or harassing interstate commerce were sharply restricted. Unsafe companies could have
their charters revoked by the bureau. Neither Beck nor Dryden
seriously expected the bill to pass at the time, but by submitting it
and raising the general principle they hoped to prepare the ground
for its eventual passage.

In surveying the opinions of the big Eastern insurance men on
federal regulation, or the insurance journals, the Bureau of Corporations initially overlooked the Hartford insurance companies. Herbert Knox Smith visited Hartford in early 1905, and discovered that
most presidents of the major companies favored federal regulation.
But the opposition, led by Senator Morgan Bulkeley, president of
Aetna Life Insurance, strongly feared that their New York competitors would dominate a federal bureau by weight of money and influence, and exploit the advantage. Their fear was especially shared by
the fire insurance companies. Most important, this opposition was
articulate and organized.[20]

Had it not been for the Equitable Life Assurance scandal, the
issue of federal regulation would have met an early death. Competing factions struggling for the control of the Equitable in early
1905, and the effort of Morgan to take over the most cutthroat giant
in the industry, led to the investigation of the New York insurance
industry by a New York Legislative Committee under William W.
Armstrong. The Armstrong Investigation, which began in July, was
directed by a brilliant lawyer, Charles Evans Hughes, who was to
create a milestone in the history of the Progressive Era. In the process of the investigation, which has been frequently discussed elsewhere, the many years of cutthroat competition and shaky finances

in the industry were exposed. What was not appreciated at the time, however, was that most important insurance men loathed a condition that had often been imposed on them quite as much as the righteous legislators disliked it. The public pressure for federal action was never greater than during the Armstrong revelations, and it played into the hands of the big Eastern insurance companies. In August, 1905, Roosevelt met with key government officials to discuss the Dryden Bill and the legal status of federal regulation. But the President refused to take a public position at the time. In late August, however, the cause of regulation received an additional boost from the Committee on Insurance Law of the American Bar Association, which concluded that federal regulation was constitutional and desirable if it could eliminate state valued policy and retaliatory laws. Even the National Convention of Insurance Commissioners supported the constitutionality of federal regulation, and regarded it as inevitable.

Despite the growing pressures for action and the insurance scandals, Roosevelt was confused as to what should be done. Senator Bulkeley opposed regulation, Senator Dryden favored it, and although Roosevelt knew Dryden spoke for the mass of the big companies, he used their disagreement as an excuse for avoiding action. In November, however, Francis Lynde Stetson approached Garfield about the matter. Stetson favored federal regulation but felt a constitutional amendment would be required to give Congress jurisdiction. He recommended Garfield investigate the views of a friend of his, Carman F. Randolph, who had been consulted by several insurance companies for a legal opinion on the matter and essentially supported Stetson's view. Randolph's brief was published in the *Columbia Law Review* in November, and Garfield considered it. Randolph sympathized with the desires of the large companies for federal regulation in order to escape state regulations, but he felt the Supreme Court's 1868 opinion that an insurance contract was not commerce was correct. Short of a Constitutional amendment, the only alternative for the federal government was to create a model insurance law in the District of Columbia and the territories and hope that the states would voluntarily duplicate it. Despite his Message to Congress the following month calling on Congress to consider the legal issues involved and stressing the desirability of uniformity through national legislation, Roosevelt had been converted to the

Stetson-Randolph position. He had asked Root, Moody, and Knox for their legal opinions on the matter, and only Root, who had recently completed a stint reorganizing the Equitable, thought comprehensive federal regulation was legal. A model law, Roosevelt reluctantly concluded, was the only practical alternative.[21]

The small Midwest and Western insurance companies regarded the movement for federal regulation as a menace, and organized to fight back. In October, and again in December, 1905, a conference of small Western companies met in Chicago to discuss technical standards and, more important, to oppose federal regulation that was "to be sprung by the large Eastern companies at any time they are ready to attempt to crush the life out of the Western companies."[22] Favoring state regulation, the small insurance companies realized that standards would nevertheless have to be raised if they were to avoid ultimate federal supervision. At the same time, the revelations of the Armstrong investigation and the desire to retain at least some control over the profitable insurance industry convinced the state governments that a housecleaning was in order. In February, 1906, at the initiative of Governor John A. Johnson of Minnesota and with the endorsement of Roosevelt, about one hundred governors, attorneys general, and commissioners of insurance met at Chicago to attempt to make state legislation uniform throughout the country. The convention endorsed the idea of a model insurance code in the District of Columbia, and appointed a committee of fifteen to prepare a bill for Congress.

Roosevelt had no real commitment on the issue of insurance, and freely admitted he had no knowledge of the field. The Armstrong revelations, although they created political pressures for action, did not terminate or complicate his friendly relationship with Elihu Root and George Perkins, both of whom were seriously attacked by the New York Committee. The issue of federal insurance regulation had been forced to his attention by the large insurance interests. Although he undoubtedly sympathized with the assumption that federal regulation was superior to state control, the constitutional obstacles, and his lack of serious interest in the issue, caused him to take the path of least resistance. By endorsing the model law movement, Roosevelt undercut the Dryden Bill and backed Stetson's alternative to comprehensive federal control or state anarchy.

In late March, 1906, the House Committee on the Judiciary decided that Congress did not have the power to control or regulate insurance, thereby killing any chance of extensive federal control. A few days later Roosevelt elected to support the model bill proposal drafted by the committee of fifteen chosen at the Chicago insurance convention in February. On April 17 he sent a special message to Congress endorsing the proposal, also admitting "I have no expert familiarity with the business."[23] The Senate supported the House interpretation of the constitutionality of federal regulation, and finally killed the Dryden Bill. But both branches of Congress were unresponsive to Roosevelt's disinterested plea for a model law in the District of Columbia, and the bill implementing it was never reported out of committee.

Having fought to a deadlock, the advocates of state versus federal regulation re-formed their ranks. But the pressure for action disappeared as Roosevelt and the public turned to other issues. Moreover, in 1907 about one dozen states enacted the model law for insurance despite the failure of the federal government. In September, 1906, the American Life Convention was formed by thirty-four small Western and Southern companies, representing a mere 4 per cent of the legal life reserves, to fight federal regulation and work for uniform standards and procedures. The issue was never joined. Eastern life insurance remained strongly in favor of federal regulation of insurance, but Roosevelt and Taft dropped the issue altogether. The problems that in the past had stimulated the demand for federal regulation only grew greater. Between 1905 and 1915 the number of life insurance companies alone more than doubled, and state taxes, licenses, and fees in 1907 amounted to $11 million—or 2.1 per cent of premium income. During the Wilson Administration the issue was consciously allowed to lie dormant, despite a campaign by Darwin P. Kingsley, president of New York Life, to unite the hundreds of presidents favoring federal regulation behind him. In 1914, when Kingsley managed to get a joint resolution before Congress providing for a Constitutional amendment, his effort had no public support. What was necessary was another public scandal similar to the Equitable revelation that would allow a President to take decisive "progressive" action to satisfy the public—and the large insurance companies. The scandal never occurred, and the issue of the federal regulation of insurance died.[24]

Meat Inspection:
Theory and Reality

In October, 1904, a young man named Upton Sinclair arrived in Chicago with a $500 stake from Fred S. Warren, editor of *The Appeal to Reason*. After seven weeks of interviews and observation in the stock yard area, Sinclair sent back stories to Warren on the working conditions, filth, and gore of the packing industry, and his novel *The Jungle* electrified the nation, spreading Sinclair's name far and wide and, finally, bringing the Beef Trust to its knees. The nation responded, Roosevelt and Congress acted by passing a meat inspection law, and the Beef Trust was vanquished. Or so reads the standard interpretation of the meat inspection scandal of 1906.

Unfortunately, the actual story is much more involved. But the meat inspection law of 1906 was perhaps the crowning example of the reform spirit and movement during the Roosevelt presidency, and the full story reveals much of the true nature of progressivism.

Alas, the movement for federal meat inspection did not begin with the visit of Sinclair to Chicago in 1904, but at least twenty years earlier, and it was initiated as much by the large meat packers themselves as by anyone. The most important catalyst in creating a demand for reform or innovation of meat inspection laws was the European export market and not, as has usually been supposed, the moralistic urgings of reformers. And since the European export market was more vital to the major American meat packers than anyone else, it was the large meat packers who were at the forefront of reform efforts.

Government meat inspection was, along with banking regulation and the crude state railroad regulatory apparatus, the oldest of the regulatory systems. In principle, at least, it was widely accepted. The major stimulus, as always, was the desire to satisfy the European export market. As early as December, 1865, Congress passed an act to prevent the importation of diseased cattle and pigs, and from 1877 on, agents of the Commissioner of Agriculture were stationed in various states to report on diseases.

In 1879 Italy restricted the importation of American pigs because of diseases, and in 1881 France followed suit. Throughout the 1880's the major European nations banned American meat, and the cost to the large American packers was enormous. These packers learned very early in the history of the industry that it was not to their profit to poison their customers, especially in a competitive market in which the consumer could go elsewhere. For the European nation this meant turning to Argentine meat, to the American consumer to another brand or company. The American meat industry, as indicated in Chapter Two, was competitive throughout this period, mainly because the level of investment required to enter packing was very small and because there were no decisive economies in large size. In 1879 there were 872 slaughtering and meat packing establishments, but there were 1,367 in 1889. Chicago in the late 1870's had established a municipal system of inspection, but it left much to be desired and was weakened over time. In 1880, after England banned the importation of cattle with pleuropneumonia, the livestock growers initiated a campaign for legislation designed to prevent the spread of the disease. The Grange and many state legislatures joined the movement, and in 1880 Rep. Andrew R. Kiefer of Minnesota introduced a bill to prohibit the transportation of diseased livestock from infected to clean areas. Similar bills designed to halt the spread of pleuropneumonia followed, but failed to gather sufficient support. In late 1882, however, exposés in the Chicago papers of diseased meat led to reforms in municipal inspection, and the major packers cooperated with the city health department to set up more examining stations to root out disease. Other cities also created inspection systems at this time, although they varied in quality.

Despite the failure of Congress to legislate on the matter, in 1881 the Secretary of the Treasury created an inspection organization to certify that cattle for export were free of pleuropneumonia. Such limited efforts and haphazard municipal inspection, despite packer support, were inadequate to meet exacting European standards. In March, 1883, Germany banned the importation of American pork, cutting off another major export market. Congress was forced to meet the threat to the American packers, and in May, 1884, established the Bureau of Animal Industry within the Department of Agriculture "to prevent the exportation of diseased cattle and to provide means for the suppression and extirpation of pleuropneumonia and other contagious diseases among domestic animals." Despite the research and regulatory activities of the bureau, which by 1888 cost one-half million dollars per year, the Department of Agriculture from

1885 on began appealing for additional federal regulation to help improve exports to Europe. Its major impetus was to fight European restrictions, not to aid the American consumer, and in doing so it effectively represented the interests of the major American packers who had the most to gain from the Department's success.[25]

Rather than improving, the situation further deteriorated with a hog cholera epidemic in 1889 worsening the American export position. Congress acted to meet the challenge, and in August, 1890, responding to the pressure of the major packers, passed a law providing for the inspection of all meat intended for export. But since provision was not made for inspection of the live animal at the time of slaughter, the foreign bans remained in effect. Desperate, in March, 1891, Congress passed the first major meat inspection law in American history. Indeed, the 1891 Act was the most significant in this field, and the conclusion of the long series of efforts to protect the export interests of the major American packers. The Act provided that all live animals be inspected, and covered the larger part of the animals passing through interstate trade. Every establishment in any way involved in export was compelled to have a Department of Agriculture inspector, and violations of the law could be penalized by fines of $1,000, one year in prison, or both. Hogs were required to have microscopic examinations as well as the usual pre- and post-mortem inspections. The law, in brief, was a rigid one, and had the desired effect. During 1891 and 1892, prohibitions on importing American pork were removed by Germany, Denmark, France, Spain, Italy, and Austria.

The Act of 1891 satisfied the health standards of European doctors, but greatly distressed the European packing industry. Slowly but surely the European nations began imposing new medical standards in order to protect their own meat industries. Major American packers failed to appreciate the retaliatory tactics of their foreign competitors, and protested to the Department of Agriculture, which pressured the Department of State into helping it defend the vital interests of the American meat industry. The government's meat inspection organization, in the meantime, gradually extended control over the greater part of the interstate meat commerce, and in 1895 was aided by another act providing for even stronger enforcement. In 1892 the Bureau of Animal Industry gave 3.8 million animals ante- and post-mortem examinations; it examined 26.5 million animals in 1897. It maintained 28 abattoirs in 12 cities in 1892, 102 abattoirs in 26 cities in 1896. The inspection extended to packaged goods as well, despite the rumors that American soldiers during the Spanish-American War were being served "embalmed meat" that damaged their digestive systems—rumors strongly denied by Harvey W. Wiley, the leading American advocate of pure food legislation. By 1904, 84 per cent of the beef slaughtered by the Big Four packers in Chicago, and 100 per cent of the beef slaughtered in Ft. Worth, was being inspected by the government; 73 per cent of the packers' entire U.S. kill was inspected. It was the smaller packers that the government inspection system failed to reach, and the major packers resented this competitive disadvantage. The way to solve this liability, most of them reasoned, was to enforce and extend the law, and to exploit it for their own advantage. They were particularly concerned about the shipment of condemned live stock to smaller, non-inspected houses, and applied pressure on the bureau to stop the traffic. When the Association of Official Agricultural Chemists created a committee in 1902 to determine food standards for meat products, the major meat companies cooperated with the effort and agreed with the final standards that were created.[26]

When Sinclair arrived in Chicago in late 1904 to do a story for *The Appeal to Reason* he was primarily interested in writing a series on the life of Chicago's working class. His contact with the local socialists led him to Adolph Smith, a medically qualified writer for the English medical journal, *The Lancet,* and one of the founders of the Marxist Social Democratic Federation of England. Smith proved to be of great aid to Sinclair, supplying him with much information. In January, 1904, Smith published a series of articles in *The Lancet* attacking sanitary and especially working conditions in the American packing houses. Smith's series was hardly noticed in the United States—certainly it provoked no public outcry. In April, 1905, *Success Magazine* published an attack on diseased meat and packer use of condemned animals. This article also failed to arouse the public, which was much more concerned with alleged monopoly within the meat industry than with sanitary conditions.

The inability of these exposés to capture the attention of the public was especially ironic in light of the unpopularity of the packers. Charles Edward Russell had just completed his series in *Everybody's*

Magazine on "The Greatest Trust in the World," an exaggerated account that nevertheless did not raise the question of health conditions. The Bureau of Corporations' report on beef displeased the public, and made the Roosevelt Administration especially defensive about the packers. The Bureau of Animal Industry, at the same time, feared that attacks on the quality of inspection would reflect on the integrity of the bureau and damage the American export market—and advised against the publication of the *Success Magazine* article.[27]

Roosevelt had been sent a copy of *The Jungle* before its publication, but took no action after it was released. The controversy over it was carried on for several months by J. Ogden Armour, Sinclair, and the press, and Roosevelt was dragged into the matter only after Senator Albert J. Beveridge presented a new inspection bill in May, 1906. In February, shortly before *The Jungle* received wide attention, the Department of Agriculture ordered the packers to clean up their toilet and sanitary conditions for workers, even though it had no legal power to do so. J. Ogden Armour, in early March, took to the *Saturday Evening Post* to defend government meat inspection. He pointed out that the Chicago packing houses had always been open to the public, and that the stockyards, for the past six years, had been in the process of total reconstruction. The large packers, Armour insisted, strongly favored inspection.

Attempt to evade it would be, from the purely commercial viewpoint, suicidal. *No packer can do an interstate or export business without Government inspection.* Self-interest forces him to make use of it. Self-interest likewise demands that he shall not receive meats or by-products from any small packer, either for export or other use, unless that small packer's plant is also "official"—that is, under United States Government inspection.

This government inspection thus becomes an important adjunct of the packer's business from two viewpoints. It puts the stamp of legitimacy and honesty upon the packer's product and so is to him a necessity. To the public it is *insurance* against the sale of diseased meats.[28]

Armour's reference to the small packers reflected his genuine concern with the increasing growth of competitors, the number of companies in the field increasing by 52 per cent from 1899 to 1909. And since the six largest packers slaughtered and sold less than 50 per cent of the cattle, and could not regulate the health conditions of the industry, government inspection was their only means of breaking down European barriers to the growth of American exports.

In March, at least, Roosevelt was not thinking of legislative reform in beef. Although he favored "radical" action, he told Sinclair in a discussion over socialism, "I am more than ever convinced that the real factor in the elevation of any man or any mass of men must be the development within his or their hearts and heads of the qualities which alone can make either the individual, the class or the nation permanently useful to themselves and to others."[29] Roosevelt was ready to allow the triumph of personal conversion rather than legislation in March, but in April his alienation with the packers went somewhat further. In March, 1906, a District Court dismissed the Justice Department's case against the Big Four packers on the grounds that their voluntary production of evidence to the Bureau of Corporations in 1904, on which evidence the suit was heavily based, gave them immunity under the Fifth Amendment. On April 18, Roosevelt sent Congress a message denying the packers' contention that Garfield had promised them immunity—which he had—and calling for legislation denying immunity to voluntary witnesses or evidence. By May, when Beveridge brought in his proposed meat legislation, the unpopular and grossly misunderstood major packers were ready to welcome the retaliatory legislation against them.

Historians, unfortunately, have ignored Upton Sinclair's important contemporary appraisal of the entire crisis. Sinclair was primarily moved by the plight of the workers, not the condition of the meat. "I aimed at the public's heart," he wrote, "and by accident I hit it in the stomach." Although he favored a more rigid law, Sinclair pointed out that "the Federal inspection of meat was, historically, established at the packers' request; . . . it is maintained and paid for by the people of the United States for the benefit of the packers; . . . men wearing the blue uniforms and brass buttons of the United States service are employed for the purpose of certifying to the nations of the civilized world that all the diseased and tainted meat which happens to come into existence in the United States of America is carefully sifted out and consumed by the American people."[30] Sinclair was correct in appreciating the role of the big packers in the origins of regulation, and the place of the export trade. What he ignored was the extent to which the big packers were already being regulated, and their desire to extend regulation to their smaller competitors.

In March, 1906, sensing the possibility of a major public attack on its efficiency, the Department of Agriculture authorized an investigation of the Chicago office of the Bureau of Animal Industry.

Although the report of the inquiry admitted that the inspection laws were not being fully applied because of a lack of funds, it largely absolved its bureau. Soon after, realizing that the Department of Agriculture report was too defensive, Roosevelt sent Charles P. Neill, the Commissioner of Labor, and James B. Reynolds to Chicago to make a special report. Neill, an economist with no technical knowledge of the packing industry, and Reynolds, a civil service lawyer, had never been exposed to the mass slaughtering of a packing house, and like Sinclair were sensitive, middle-class individuals. Roosevelt regarded the Department of Agriculture report as critical, but he hoped the Neill-Reynolds report would vindicate the worst.

Senator Albert J. Beveridge, in the meantime, began drafting a meat inspection bill at the beginning of May. Drafts passed back and forth between Beveridge and Secretary of Agriculture James Wilson, and Reynolds was frequently consulted as well. Wilson wished to have poultry excluded from the law, and diseased but edible animals passed. By the end of May, when a final bill had been agreed upon, Wilson strongly defended the Beveridge proposal. The measure was submitted as an amendment to the Agriculture Appropriation Bill, and the big packers indicated at once that they favored the bill save in two particulars. They wanted the government to pay for the entire cost of inspection, as in the past, and they did not want canning dates placed on meat products for fear of discouraging the sales of perfectly edible but dated products. Save for these contingencies, the Beveridge Amendment received the support of the American Meat Packers' Association and many major firms.[31] The packers' objections were embodied in the amendments to the Beveridge proposal made in the House by James W. Wadsworth, chairman of the Committee on Agriculture.

Roosevelt immediately opposed the Wadsworth amendments, and threatened to release the Neill-Reynolds report if the House failed to support his position. The House supported Wadsworth, and Roosevelt sent the report along with a special message to Congress on June 4. He must have had qualms as to what it would prove, for he hedged its findings by asserting that "this report is preliminary," and that it did not discuss the entire issue of the chemical treatment of meats. The report, the packers immediately claimed, reluctantly but definitely absolved them, but also "put weapons into the hands of foreign competitors."[32]

The Beveridge Amendment passed the Senate on May 25 without opposition. To strengthen his position, Wadsworth called hearings of the Committee of Agriculture for June 6 through June 11. Two significant facts emerge from the testimony, both of which Wadsworth intended making. Charles P. Neill's testimony revealed that the sight of blood and offal, and the odors of systematic death, had deeply shocked the two investigators, and that they had often confused the inevitable horrors of slaughtering with sanitary conditions. Roosevelt had erred in sending to the slaughterhouses two inexperienced Washington bureaucrats who freely admitted they knew nothing of canning. The major result of the hearings was to reveal that the big Chicago packers wanted more meat inspection, both to bring the small packers under control and to aid their position in the export trade. Formally representing the large Chicago packers, Thomas E. Wilson publicly announced "We are now and have always been in favor of the extension of the inspection, also to the adoption of the sanitary regulations that will insure the very best possible conditions," including nearly all the recommendations of the Neill-Reynolds report. "We have always felt that Government inspection, under proper regulations, was an advantage to the live stock and agricultural interests and to the consumer," but the packers strongly opposed paying for the costs of their advantage.[33] The packers opposed dating canned food because of its effects on sales, but had no objection to reinspection of older cans or the banning of any chemical preservatives save saltpeter.

Although segments of the press immediately assumed that the packing industry opposed regulation that presumably damaged their interests—and historians have accepted their version—most contemporaries, including Beveridge, knew better. Upton Sinclair was critical of the bill from the start, and called for municipal slaughter houses. On June 29, as the packers and livestock growers were urging passage of the Beveridge amendment with the government footing the expenses, Beveridge announced that "an industry which is infinitely benefited by the Government inspection ought to pay for that inspection instead of the people paying for it." The value of meat inspection for the export trade, Senator Henry C. Hansbrough of North Dakota declared, is obvious. What was wrong with the entire measure, Senator Knute Nelson pointed out, was that "the American consumers and the ordinary American farmer have been left out of the question. Three objects have been sought to be accomplished—

first, to placate the packers; next, to placate the men who raise the range cattle, and, third, to get a good market for the packers abroad."[34]

The battle that followed was not on the basic principle of a meat inspection law, but on the issue of who should pay for the cost of administering it and on the problem of placing dates on processed meat. During the committee hearings, Wadsworth asked Samuel H. Cowan, the lawyer of the National Live Stock Association, to prepare a bill with the modifications acceptable to the big packers. This he did, and it was rumored in the press that Roosevelt had given Cowan's efforts his tacit approval. If an agreement between Roosevelt and Wadsworth was, in fact, reached, it was surely secret, although the two men had at least two private discussions between June 1 and 15. On June 15 the President dashed off an attack on Wadsworth's bill that was intended for the press. Wadsworth, Roosevelt claimed, was working for the packers. "I told you on Wednesday night," Wadsworth answered, referring to their private conversation, "when I submitted the bill to you, that the packers insisted before our committee on having a rigid inspection law passed. Their life depends on it, and the committee will bear me out in the statement that they placed no obstacle whatever in our way. . . ."[35]

The House stood firm on its bill, and there was a stalemate for a week. Since an efficient inspection bill was to the interests of the packers, the New York *Journal of Commerce* announced on June 18, they should be willing to pay its costs. But the House conferees could not be made to budge on the issues of the government assuming the cost of inspection and the dating of cans and processed meats. Beveridge abdicated, and on June 30 the bill was signed by the President. The bill, George Perkins wrote J. P. Morgan, "will certainly be of very great advantage when the thing once gets into operation and they are able to use it all over the world, as it will practically give them a government certificate for their goods. . . ."[36]

The most significant aspect of the new law was the size of the appropriation—$3 million as compared to the previous peak of $800,-000—for implementing it. The law provided for the post-mortem inspection of all meat passing through interstate commerce. In this respect, the law was a systematic and uniform application of the basic 1891 Act, but it still excluded intrastate meat. Indeed, even in 1944 only 68 per cent of the meat output was covered by federal laws. The new law was unique insofar as it extended inspection to meat products and preservatives, and determined standards for sanitation within the plants. The basic purpose of Sinclair's exposé, to improve the conditions of the working class in the packing houses, could have been achieved either through better wages or socialism. Although they now had cleaner uniforms at work, their homes and living conditions were no better than before, and if they became diseased they were now thrown out of the packing houses to fend for themselves. "I am supposed to have helped clean up the yards and improve the country's meat supply—though this is mostly delusion," Sinclair later wrote. "But nobody even pretends to believe that I improved the condition of the stockyard workers."[37]

Yet historians have always suggested that Sinclair brought the packers to their knees, or that The Greatest Trust in the World collapsed before the publication of the Neill-Reynolds report. Given the near unanimity with which the measure passed Congress, and the common agreement on basic principles shared by all at the time, there is an inconsistency in the writing of historians on this problem. If the packers were really all-powerful, or actually opposed the bill, it is difficult to explain the magnitude of the vote for it. The reality of the matter, of course, is that the big packers were warm friends of regulation, especially when it primarily affected their innumerable small competitors.

In late August the packers met with officials of the Department of Agriculture to discuss the problem of complying with the law. ". . . the great asset that you gentlemen are going to have," Secretary Wilson told them, "when we get this thing to going will be the most rigid and severe inspection on the face of the earth." According to the minutes of the meeting, the packers responded to this proposition with "loud applause" and not with a shudder. The purpose of the law "is to assure the public that only sound and wholesome meat and meat food products may be offered for sale," Swift & Co. and other giant packers told the public in large ads. "It is a wise law. Its enforcement must be universal and uniform."[38]

Meat inspection ceased to be a significant issue during the remainder of the Progressive Era. Beveridge, for several years after the passage of the 1906 Act, tried to restore his defeated amendments, but he had no support from either Roosevelt or other important politicians. Secretary of Agriculture Wilson, among others, opposed Beveridge's efforts to have the packers pay for the expenses of inspection. The packers naturally resisted all attempts to saddle them with the costs, but strongly defended the institution of meat inspection and "the integrity and efficiency of the Bureau's meat inspection service."[39] Despite the urging of the American Meat Packers' Association, which wanted action to eradicate tuberculosis and other diseases in livestock, the issue of meat inspection died.

On the same day that Roosevelt signed the Meat Inspection Act he also signed the Pure Food and Drug Act, and these two measures have been commonly regarded as companion bills representing the triumph of progressivism, health, and decency. The pure food story, however, vividly illustrates the confused understanding by many historians of what factors actually motivated legislation in the Progressive Era.

The history of the pure food movement is the history of Harvey W. Wiley. Before Wiley's rise to importance in the movement, the campaign for unadulterated, honestly marked food was carried on by the National Board of Trade with the aid of the Grange, various state legislatures, and special food interests whose markets were being damaged by cheap competition. One of the earliest campaigns was directed against the adulteration of sugar products with glucose. Wiley's advent on the scene came in 1883, when he went to work for the Department of Agriculture as an expert on sugar chemistry. His earlier work had been in developing acceptable glucose adulterants for cane and maple sugar, and he was regarded as a friend of the industry. Wiley's contacts with industry continued through his work as a private consultant, and in his agitation for pure food legislation he initially maintained the position that it was mislabeling, not the purity of the food, that was the primary problem. The poor, he felt, had to have cheap food, and "It is not for me to tell my neighbor what he shall eat. . . ."[40]

In early 1898 the advocates of pure food legislation called the First National Pure Food and Drug Congress in Washington. The body included a wide variety of official delegates appointed by governors, and representatives of professional drug associations and farmers' organizations, but it also obtained strong support from interests that would have been directly regulated under any reform law—the Creamery Butter Makers' Association, Brewers Association, Confectioners' Association, Wholesale Grocers' Association, Retail Grocers' Association, and so forth. From this time on the food reform movement was essentially supported by the food industry itself, directed by Wiley, and represented a desire of major food interests to set their own houses in order and protect themselves from more unscrupulous associates. At the same time as the First National Congress, a pure food bill was submitted to the House by Rep. Marriott Brosius, and pressure on Congress for legislation began building up.

The Brosius Bill was presented to subsequent sessions of Congress without success. Save for slight amendments, it had the endorsement of the National Pure Food and Drug Congress. Its main aim was to prevent poisonous adulteration and mislabeling, and to strengthen the ability of Wiley's Bureau of Chemistry in the Department of Agriculture to enforce the law. Pressure on Congress from wholesale and retail grocers and candy makers to pass the bill continued. The food industry did not seriously disagree on the desirability of legislation, but segments of it wanted the law framed in such a manner as to give their product domination and approval. The oleo and butter industries immediately saw the possibility of interpreting a law against one another, and the alum and cream of tartar baking powder interests were similarly split.

In 1902 a bill drawn up by Wiley along the same basic lines as the Brosius Bill was presented to the House by Rep. William P. Hepburn and passed in December. By the end of that year the support for legislation was overwhelming. The National Association of Manufacturers, the American Baking Powder Association, and many individual food companies swung behind the movement. By 1903, however, the opposition to the measure organized, and was centered about the patent drug and whiskey industry and a few dissident grocers. Their line of attack was poorly conceived. The entire movement for legislation was designed, they claimed, to create a political lobby for Wiley and to aggrandize the power of the Bureau of Chemistry.[41] This opposition, however, was too weak and unrepresentative to alter the course of events.

Roosevelt showed little concern with the entire pure food and drug question. The movement grew in intensity, and was greatly aided by the related excitement over the conditions in meat packing. Wiley, who was a consistent Republican until 1912, maintained "it is not true that Mr. Roosevelt championed the law in its bitter fight for pas-

sage in Congress." Although Wiley was incorrect in his contention
that Congress opposed his bill strongly—it passed 63 to 4 in the Senate and 241 to 17 in the House—he was nevertheless right in maintaining that Roosevelt merely went along with the measure. Wiley,
despite his exaggeration of certain opposition, also admitted that the
"great majority" of the food manufacturers supported the bill once it
passed.[42] But the President and Wiley, the new head of the Board of
Food and Drug Inspection, soon ran afoul of one another, and Wiley
subsequently considered Roosevelt an enemy of pure food regulation.

The immediate issue between Wiley and the President was saccharin, which Wiley once casually indicated was dangerous and on the
road to being banned. Roosevelt, however, used the chemical in his
coffee, and strongly disagreed with Wiley. Moreover, there were loud
complaints from some food makers that Wiley was moving to ban
sulphur dioxide and benzoate of soda. In January, 1908, the President
cut Wiley down. He created a board, under Ira Remsen, the president
of Johns Hopkins and the discoverer of saccharin, to pass on all questions over which there were serious differences of opinion "among
eminent authorities." At the same time he began appointing less ardent devotees of the cause of food inspection to Wiley's organization.
Roosevelt, who was completely ignorant of such matters but a man of
strong prejudices, "tested him personally in reference to corn syrup,
the use of saccharine, and the importation of French vinegar."[43] Having failed the test, the President supported Wiley's less aggressive
associates during the remainder of the Presidency.

One other pillar supporting the image of Roosevelt as progressive
was the role of his Administration in the conservation movement.
Fortunately, Samuel P. Hays' brilliant *Conservation and the Gospel
of Efficiency* details the much more prosaic and less noble realities of
the conservation movement. "Conservation neither arose from a broad
popular outcry, nor centered its fire primarily upon the private corporation. Moreover, corporations often supported conservation policies,
while the 'people' just as frequently opposed them. In fact, it becomes
clear that one must discard completely the struggle against corporations as the setting in which to understand conservation history, and
permit an entirely new frame of reference to arise from the evidence
itself. . . . Conservation, above all, was a scientific movement. . . ."
The dominant motive behind conservation was a realization that

lumber resources were being permanently squandered by indiscriminate cutting, and that in the long run the fortunes of the lumber industry would decline as a result of such practices. Supported by the Northern Pacific Railroad, Weyerhaeuser Timber, King Lumber, and other giant corporations, Gifford Pinchot—the most famous of the conservationists—developed a program of sustained yield planting. Pinchot, who had the support of the American Forestry Association, regarded the forests as economic resources and strongly opposed using the forests as pure wilderness or game reserves. "The apostles of the gospel of efficiency subordinated the aesthetic to the utilitarian," Hays points out.[44] Roosevelt supported the Pinchot school against the "preservationists" opposing cutting of any sort. In this, as in most other matters, Roosevelt was fundamentally the conservative.

Roosevelt never ceased to maintain an incurable confidence that institutional reform could best be obtained by personal transformation of evildoers. He found, in the course of the many movements for legislative change, that the members of the press and the public wanted morality imposed on railroads, packers, and others. His response was pragmatic and contemptuous. He worked with reformers if it suited his purposes, but he virtually regarded them as the cause of evils by their consciousness of them. Roosevelt preferred to solve problems by ignoring them, and rarely took leadership during the earliest stages of discussion of industrial or political problems if it was led by those not in his class. Circumstances often forced him to intrude into affairs after intervention could no longer be avoided—he was, after all, conscious of votes and public pressures. But he never questioned the ultimate good intentions and social value of the vast majority of businessmen, nor did he ever attack an obvious abuse in business or take a stand on regulation without discreetly couching his terms with luxuriant praise for the basic economic status quo and the integrity of businessmen.

Nothing better illustrates Roosevelt's fundamental dislike of non-business reformers than his position on the "muckrakers." Exposé literature of the time was, admittedly, often careless and exaggerated, but it was also usually conservative in its motives, and for the most part avoided posing radical alternatives to existing evils. The invidious term "muckraker" was invented by Roosevelt in the midst of the agitation for food, meat, and railroad regulation, causes with which Roose-

velt presumably identified himself. On April 14, 1906, Roosevelt made
the headlines by attacking "the man with the muck-rake, the man who
could look no way but downward . . . who was offered a celestial
crown for his muck-rake, but would neither look up nor regard the
crown . . . but continued to rake to himself the filth of the floor."
Translated into concrete analogies, the celestial crown was apathy and
ignorance of the reality about him, a placid, optimistic complacency
toward the world as it stood. In the same speech Roosevelt hinted that
it might be theoretically desirable to someday have federal income
taxation, but in the context of his attack on reformers his innuendo
was not taken seriously, and Roosevelt never acted upon it.[45]

Roosevelt was quite sincere in his criticism of the exposé writers.
These journalists—Norman Hapgood, Osward Garrison Villard, and
especially David Graham Phillips—were the "friend of disorder." "Of
course," he confessed to William Allen White, "in any movement it is
impossible to avoid having some people go with you temporarily
whose reasons are different from yours and may be very bad indeed.
Thus in the beef packing business I found that Sinclair was of real use.
I have an utter contempt for him. He is hysterical, unbalanced, and
untruthful. Three-fourths of the things he said were absolute false-
hoods. For some of the remainder there was only a basis of truth."[46]
Roosevelt's thoroughly contemptuous attitude toward reformers indicates that their relevations were hardly enough to move him. Support
by important business elements was always the decisive factor.

La Follette, of all the contemporary reformers, especially aroused
Roosevelt's ire. He is "a shifty self-seeker," Roosevelt told William
Allen White in 1906; "an entirely worthless Senator," he concluded
several years later.[47] La Follette, for his part, condemned Roosevelt's
"equally drastic attack upon those who were seeking to reform abuses.
These were indiscriminately classed as demagogues and dangerous
persons. In this way he sought to win approval, both from the radicals
and conservatives. This cannonading, first in one direction and then in
another, filled the air with noise and smoke, which confused and ob-
scured the line of action, but, when the battle cloud drifted by and
quiet was restored, it was always a matter of surprise that so little had
really been accomplished."[48] La Follette was wrong, of course. A
great deal was accomplished, but for conservative ends.

CHAPTER FIVE

ROOSEVELT

AND

BIG BUSINESS,

1906-1908

The Good
Trusts

During mid-1906 Roosevelt signed his name to three major acts of legislation. Even though each of the industries involved—meat, food, and railroads—supported the specific measures regulating them, it appeared to subsequent historians as if the President had embarked on a decisive campaign for general regulation. Roosevelt had been cajoled into the meat and food campaigns, however, and top business circles were not apprehensive as to what the future held for them. "I believe that the powers that be feel that they have made splendid political capital out of what has been done in connection with the packers, the Standard Oil Company and minor matters," George Perkins reassured Morgan in June, 1906, "and are ready to rest on their laurels for some time." Especially comforting for the Morgan interests was the fact, as Perkins phrased it, that "the [U.S. Steel] Corporation is looked upon in Washington with more favor than perhaps any other one concern. . . ."[1]

Perkins' confidence was based on the understanding that had been reached between the Bureau of Corporations and U.S. Steel, as well as the excellent personal relations that he and Gary enjoyed with the President. The bureau investigation, U.S. Steel soon found, was a heavy drain on its time because the statistical data requested often took months to collect, but it at least kept the Administration happy. Indeed, the investigation dragged on interminably until 1911, and the relationship between U.S. Steel's leaders and President Roosevelt was to shift to other grounds.

The Tennessee Coal and Iron Company was the major steel producer in the South. Although its history until 1904 was not one of outstanding profit, from that year until 1907, when it earned gross profits of $2.8 million on sales of $13.3 million, it began to realize its tremendous potential. The promise of the company was based on its enormous reserves of iron ore, coal, dolomite, and lime located within a small region in northern Alabama and southern Tennessee. Its iron ore holdings were estimated at about 700 million tons, and its coal reserves were larger yet. Reliable estimates made by John W. Gates and Charles Schwab indicated that a ton of pig iron might be made by the firm at two to five dollars less than any competitor in the country, giving it a potential control over the entire Southern market. The company's inability to capitalize on its advantage was ended by a new management, and although the firm's raw materials had various imperfections, by 1907 it was actually charging more than the going average for its rails and getting vast orders from the Harriman lines. In 1907 alone Tennessee invested $6.6 million in new construction, and began a duplex steel process plant at Easley, Alabama that was technically outstanding and promised rich awards. Early in 1907 J. P. Morgan, considering the company's promise and resources, asked Gary and Frick about the desirability of buying it, but they advised against such a move. Although Gary later claimed that U.S. Steel was frequently offered Tennessee stock by individual stockholders in the company, John W. Gates testified before a Congressional hearing that his son was approached by U.S. Steel in late 1906 to sell his large holdings in Tennessee.

There can be no doubt that at least Morgan coveted the Southern steel company. In October, 1907, during the growing financial crisis on Wall Street, the investment firm of Moore & Schley came to U.S. Steel for a loan of $1.2 million to cover its commitments during the tight money market. A list of stock was offered the Morgan firm as sources of collateral to cover the loan, including large amounts of American Tobacco, Guggenheim Copper, and five others, including Tennessee Iron. U.S. Steel chose $2 million in Tennessee common shares. Its foot was in the Tennessee door.

Moore & Schley's problems, however, were not to end with the infusion of $1.2 million. Another $5 to $6 million was needed to help the firm meet its obligations, although Schley later denied that the issue involved was the ability of his company to avoid a crash. The company had about $25 million in shares to use as collateral, including large holdings of American Tobacco and Tennessee Coal and Iron. Again Moore & Schley approached Morgan, whose policy it was to help key firms during the crisis in order to prevent further declines and possible bankruptcies that might shake the very foundations of Wall Street. It was now up to the House of Morgan to decide whether it would take Tennessee stock as its collateral and move to control the entire company.[2]

On Saturday, November 2, Perkins, Morgan, and other key members of the concern met at Morgan's home to discuss the problem, "The idea being," in Perkins' words, "that possibly the Steel Corporation might be able to secure the property at an advantageous price." Later the same day, U.S. Steel's finance committee was called in for consultation. Frick opposed the purchase, alleging that production costs at Tennessee were too high, and Gary feared what the federal government might think of such a massive merger. "Mr. Morgan," according to Perkins, "felt as strongly the other way and urged that the coal and ore that this Tennessee Coal & Iron Company owned were, in themselves, worth the company's capitalization."[3] The next day, Sunday, the president of Tennessee was called in and discussed the progress the company was making in lowering costs and expanding production. The objections met, U.S. Steel's financial committee agreed to buy. An earlier rejected bid to Moore & Schley to buy the stock at less than par was raised to par, and Moore & Schley were offered $12 million for their shares. As for the federal government, it was agreed that Frick and Gary would immediately seek the approval of the President to consummate the deal.

That same night Gary and Frick boarded a train for Washington and arrived at the White House the following morning while the President was at breakfast. Garfield, perhaps coincidentally, arrived on the scene at the very same time, and obtained an immediate audience with Roosevelt for the steel men. Since Attorney General Bonaparte was out of town, Elihu Root was called in for an opinion on the matter. Gary and Frick did not identify Moore & Schley specifically, but explicitly indicated to the President that unless U.S. Steel acquired its stock in Tennessee, an important firm would definitely collapse and possibly cause a major crisis on Wall Street. U.S. Steel, they claimed, did not particularly care to acquire Tennessee Coal and Iron, because it was unprofitable, but they regarded it as a public duty. Roosevelt was not told that Moore & Schley had considerable alternate collateral, and he apparently was not aware that it needed a mere $6 million loan rather than the $45 million the total stock of the firm was to cost U.S. Steel. The cost of the stock, Gary indicated, was 35 per cent more than its real value.

Roosevelt took the statements of Gary and Frick at their face value, since the word of gentlemen could not be questioned. Roosevelt later insisted until the bitter end that he had not been deceived as to their truthfulness or the nobility of their motives. On the basis of their explanation, Roosevelt promised he would not prosecute U.S. Steel. Root and Gary then cooperatively drafted a formal statement on the understanding, consisting of a letter from Gary to Root on November 7, which was confirmed by the President and filed with the Department of Justice as a guide to policy. The final November 7 letter did not actually reveal everything that went on at the meeting in the White House; it was discreetly edited so it could not embarrass the Administration in the future. The following is Gary's November 7 letter, the bracketed sections having been cut from the final version.

At the recent interview at the White House between the President, yourself, Mr. Frick and myself, I stated, in substance, that our Corporation had the opportunity of acquiring more than one-half of the capital stock of the Tennessee Coal, Iron & Railroad Company at a price somewhat in excess of what we believed to be its real value; and that it had been represented [to us by leading bankers in New York] that if the purchase should be made it would be of great benefit to financial conditions, and would probably save from failure an important business concern; that under the circumstances Mr. Frick and I had decided to favor the proposed purchase of stock unless the President objected to the same. I further stated that the total productive capacity of our Companies would not be materially increased by the ownership of the properties of the Tennessee Company, and, after the purchase, would probably not amount to more than sixty per cent of the total steel production in this country, which was about the percentage our Companies controlled at the time of the organization of the U.S. Steel Corporation; that our policy was opposed to securing [that our policy was not to secure] a monopoly in our lines or even a material increase of our relative capacity [not to materially increase our relative capacity].

I understood the President to say that while he would not and could not legally make any binding promise or agreement he did not hesitate to say from the circumstances as presented he certainly would not advise against the proposed purchase.

[The President was also kind enough to state generally his favorable opinion of our Corporation and its management as ascertained by reports from the Department of Commerce and otherwise.]

If consistent will you kindly write me if the above statement is in accordance with your understanding and recollection.[4]

In consummating the agreement, U.S. Steel increased its ore reserves by 40 per cent and acquired a company worth, at the time, at least four times the purchase price.

Having secured Tennessee Coal and Iron at an "advantageous price" far in excess of the amount needed to save one of its stockholders, the House of Morgan and U.S. Steel proceeded to consolidate their position with Roosevelt in other areas as well. In late 1907, as has already been discussed in Chapter Two, the famous Gary Dinners were organized in an effort to fix and stabilize steel prices. Roosevelt and Bonaparte were fully informed of the activity from the beginning, and decided to allow the clearly illegal restraint of trade to continue without government interference. At the same time, the Bureau of Corporations' study of U.S. Steel continued at a leisurely pace.

In January, 1909, at the end of Roosevelt's tenure of office, several minor crises with U.S. Steel occurred. For over a year the bureau had patiently endeavored to obtain data from U.S. Steel on the capitalization of its original stock flotation as compared to the real value of the companies. It was widely known at the time that about one-half of the corporation's original stock represented water, and Gary and

Perkins were extremely defensive about the matter. Despite this breach by U.S. Steel in the agreement to supply the bureau with all data, the bureau and Roosevelt remained fast friends of Steel. This was especially true after Garfield was appointed Secretary of the Interior in March, 1907, and Herbert Knox Smith was made chief of the bureau. In January, 1909, the Senate decided that an investigation of U.S. Steel's absorption of Tennessee Coal and Iron was in order. Rumors were rife that the extraordinarily valuable company had been acquired at a bargain price during the panic of 1907 as a result of the President's promise of immunity from antitrust prosecution. Roosevelt and Bonaparte were seriously embarrassed, especially since they knew the rumors were true. They decided immediately to oppose the investigation. Roosevelt ordered Smith to send to the White House all confidential information gathered by the Bureau of Corporations relevant to the Tennessee merger, and he let it be known "that I could not be forced to give them . . . unless they were prepared to go to the length of trying to have me impeached."[5] On January 26, the Senate Committee on the Judiciary requested the bureau's data on U.S. Steel. On January 29, Secretary of Commerce Oscar Straus, with Roosevelt's permission, sent the Senate only what he termed nonconfidential material. U.S. Steel nervously watched the first real test of its détente with Roosevelt, and Gary anxiously reminded the bureau that "I hope our understanding will not be overlooked."[6] His confidence was not betrayed, for when the Senate Committee delivered its report in March it could not, for lack of information, pass judgment on the entire Tennessee Coal and Iron affair.

Roosevelt was incapable of doubting the honesty and good intentions of Gary and Perkins, and defended his actions and their statements on the Tennessee affair until his death. Given his sympathy, the Morgan group moved to use the President and the executive agencies in defending and protecting their other interests as well. From March, 1907 on, Roosevelt maintained an uneasy arrangement with Morgan's New Haven Railroad to allow it to absorb much of New England's railroad system. Despite vicissitudes in the arrangement, which I have discussed in detail in my study of railroads, Roosevelt permitted the effort, which was far more monopolistic than the Northern Securities Company, to be consummated. At the same time, Roosevelt never challenged the altruistic statements of U.S. Steel's leadership, and especially of Gary and Perkins, on labor-management cooperation. As leading figures of the National Civic Federation they publicly defended that organization's commitment to conciliation and arbitration between labor and management and its desire to see open shop unionism—at the time a seemingly radical position. Gary and Perkins were strong advocates of worker stock ownership, and introduced a stock participation plan at U.S. Steel. Roosevelt regarded them as model capitalists, and never once challenged the reality behind their statements.

The reality, of course, was very different. In 1901, during the strike by the Amalgamated Association of Iron, Steel and Tin Workers against U.S. Steel, the union movement in steel was virtually destroyed. Working conditions were notoriously bad, and they never substantially improved during this period; wages rose only very slightly. Like all other major corporations at the time, and despite the public relations image it tried to cultivate, U.S. Steel was autocratic and paternalistic, and it remained so for many years.[7]

In December, 1906, Congress passed a resolution ordering an investigation of Morgan's International Harvester by the Bureau of Corporations. The bureau and International Harvester, of course, already had an informal understanding, dating to May, 1904, that the company, if notified, would alter any illegal practice. In February, 1905, International's attorney met with Garfield and expressed his firm's desire to cooperate with any investigation or "in having new laws enacted for federal regulation."[8] The matter was allowed to lie dormant until Congress forced action. Perkins and Cyrus McCormick, referring to their earlier offer of cooperation, immediately renewed their pledge to aid an investigation in any way possible.

On January 18 and 19, 1907, Garfield, Herbert Knox Smith, Gary, Perkins, Cyrus McCormick, and Charles Deering met at the Waldorf-Astoria in New York to discuss the investigation. Gary, speaking for International Harvester, announced, in Smith's words, that the company "would take the same attitude toward the proposed investigation by this Bureau as has been taken by the United States Steel Corporation, and would ask the same treatment of the information furnished." U.S. Steel was fully satisfied with the treatment it was receiving, and Harvester expected to be also. It hoped that the information "would not be used for demagogic purposes," or in a manner that would help

its competitors. The bureau agreed to these requests. Gary informed
Garfield, again in Smith's words, that "he believed in the work of the
Bureau and the necessity of Governmental supervision of large corporations, and that he felt that the President and the Bureau, representing his policy, was a strong safeguard both to the removal of
abuses and to the prevention of violent attacks on private rights in
general that might otherwise come." Perkins and McCormick agreed
with Gary, and it was for this reason that Perkins had worked for the
establishment of the bureau. More specifically, they welcomed the
bureau's investigation because "the best thing that could happen to
the Harvester Company was a report by the Bureau showing the truth
of their claim that they were operating their American business at
a loss, for then they would have just ground for raising American
prices." Garfield was most obsequious about such business cooperation with the bureau. "It is most gratifying to find that the leaders
of business are thus recognizing the right of the Government to so
investigate."[9]

It did not occur to Garfield that Morgan's men were quite serious
when they stated they wished to use the bureau to raise prices, to prevent attacks from less friendly parties, and as a general shield. Garfield did not promise immunity from legal prosecution in the event of
violations of law, but he appeared to be friendly to the Morgan interests, and that was all that mattered. At the end of March, 1907, however, Harvester formally requested Attorney General Bonaparte to
defer any possible prosecution until a complete bureau report could
be finished. At about the same time, it urged the bureau to begin its
investigation in order that its objective analysis of the corporation
could be used to stem the tide of state prosecutions of International.
The bureau, the McCormicks asked, should point out any "irregular-
ities" in their company's practices, and they would immediately be
corrected. Smith, for his part, assured them "that it was not the desire
of the Bureau to harass the Harvester Company . . . and that our
Bureau was not a destructive agency. . . ."[10]

But the bureau still would not initiate its investigation on a serious
scale. In May, 1907, International's attorney visited the bureau, delivered information, and offered more. His hint did not change matters. During the interim, Attorney General Bonaparte took steps to
bring a suit against Harvester for certain of its overseas operations.
On August 22, Perkins took the matter in hand and visited Roosevelt

at his Oyster Bay home. Perkins complained about the lack of progress the bureau was making, and indicated his anxiety about the unnecessary antitrust action by the Department of Justice before the bureau's report revealed on the true facts about the company. Roosevelt wrote Bonaparte to defer a possible suit, at least until the matter could be straightened out, and Smith was notified of the meeting, thereby leaping to action. Perkins saw Smith several days later, and then discussed the matter with Bonaparte, who was feeling aggressive at the time. Bonaparte must have realized what was in store for him, and pleaded ignorance of the May, 1904, agreement between Attorney General Moody and International Harvester to work problems out privately. The matter was allowed to lie dormant until September 21, when Smith sent Roosevelt a long, impassioned defense of the system of mutual understandings and détentes with the House of Morgan that had been built by the bureau. Endorsing the policy of delaying any antitrust prosecutions until the bureau had time to complete its investigations, Smith also prejudged the inquiry by indicating "I have no knowledge of any moral grounds for attacks on the company." "The attitude of the Morgan interests generally, which control this company, has been one of active cooperation," and to initiate prosecution would be an abandonment of the policy of distinguishing between good and bad trusts. More important, Smith rejected the Sherman Act as a guide to corporate policy. "I believe that industrial combination is an economic necessity, that the Sherman law, as interpreted by the Supreme Court, is an economic absurdity and is impossible of general enforcement, and even if partially enforced, will, in most cases, work only evil. I believe the principle it represents must ultimately be abandoned." Business had supported, for the most part, the President's friendly policy of publicity as a means of regulation. More pointedly, Smith asked, "it is a very practical question whether it is well to throw away now the great influence of the so-called Morgan interests, which up to this time have supported the advanced policy of the administration, both in the general principles and in the application thereof to their specific interests, and to place them generally in opposition."[11] Straus endorsed Smith's position, and advised the President to do so as well. The threatened suit was called off.

The question of why and how the International Harvester suit was withdrawn later became a controversial issue in the 1912 campaign, when Taft accused Roosevelt of being subservient to the House of Morgan. The best Roosevelt could say of the accusation—Taft published many of the damning letters of August and September, 1907 —was that Taft failed to voice his protest at the Cabinet meeting that endorsed his decision. The point was irrelevant—ignoring Taft's denial that he was at the meeting—since the decision was ultimately Roosevelt's and Smith's alone. Taft also revealed that on September 26 Roosevelt ordered Bonaparte to stop the projected suit, and notified Perkins that a bureau investigation would precede any suit.

Roosevelt had the suit buried, but the bureau's investigation— which Smith had used as a bait for undercutting Bonaparte—continued to hang in limbo. His eyes fixed on state litigation, Cyrus McCormick, during October, 1907, felt compelled to write Smith to speed his inquiry. Smith continued to delay, and only in March, 1908, began the investigation in a serious manner. Perkins continued to badger Smith to move more quickly, and International sent in a considerable amount of data. In October, 1908, a temporary snag developed over International's reluctance to release appraisers' reports of the value of its 1902 pre-merger plants, but this obstacle was quickly removed. The study was not completed until March, 1913.[12]

The Evil
Trusts

The June, 1904, understanding between Garfield and the Standard Oil Company, by which information on oil would be gathered in a friendly, cordial manner, had led to difficulties by the end of 1905. As the bureau unavoidably closed in on the rebating practices of Standard and various railroads, the oil giant began throwing obstacles in the path of the inquiry. Kline insisted that Standard was giving the bureau all the information it had, but in this instance Garfield was unwilling to be put off. Kline, during March, 1906, seemed pleased with Garfield's work, but grew apprehensive as skeptical questions were put to Standard by bureau investigators. The press reported that on March 9, H. H. Rogers and John D. Archbold visited Roosevelt and offered the bureau all the information it desired in return for staving off a federal prosecution. If such an offer was indeed made, Roosevelt apparently turned it down, and although Kline tried to satisfy the bureau that no rebating was carried on, Garfield submitted a report to Roosevelt claiming extensive railroad rebating to Standard.

The report, as even historians friendly to Standard have admitted, was largely accurate. It came at an especially convenient time for Roosevelt, and since he still remembered Standard's opposition to the formation of the Bureau of Corporations, he did not hesitate to use it. The Hepburn Bill on railroads was being debated at that time in the Senate, and Roosevelt thought it would help the passage of the measure if he sent the bureau's report to Congress along with a Special Message. The bureau's report, sent to Congress on May 4, also convinced Attorney General Moody that Standard had violated at least the Elkins Anti-Rebating Act, and deserved to be prosecuted. Roosevelt was willing to allow Moody to go ahead, and in mid-November, 1906, the Department of Justice formally filed several cases against Standard and its affiliates. A decision on the major rebating case was not handed down until August 3, 1907, when Judge Kenesaw Mountain Landis fined Standard $29,240,000 for taking rebates on 1,462 counts. A bumptious, colorful figure, Landis immediately had to be brought into harness when he also threatened to open a case against the Chicago & Alton Railroad—which the government had promised immunity for supplying evidence.

Standard was unperturbed by Landis' fine, which it immediately appealed, but was far more disturbed by the Justice Department's suit in September, 1907, to dissolve the company. On September 8, Bonaparte was visited by a government attorney active on the Standard case who relayed the message that Standard was "very much dispirited and alarmed," and would open its books and correct all abuses if the government would not make individual indictments and would drop the case. Neither Bonaparte nor Roosevelt liked the proposition. To Roosevelt, Standard Oil and Harriman were "setting the pace in the race for wealth under illegal and improper conditions," and were the epitome of evil, as opposed to good, trusts.[13] Roosevelt, of course, was deeply involved at the time in a variety of friendly understandings with Morgan corporations, and there is little doubt that Standard was fully informed of all of the significant details. Standard also wished to establish a détente.

Bonaparte was not Standard's man, and the company next approached Garfield. On September 21, Fred Goff, one of Standard's Cleveland attorneys, visited Garfield and offered to reorganize the company in conformity with the law if the antitrust suit could be quashed. Garfield was obviously flattered. "Strange," he confided in his diary, "if such a change should come through my work + in my hands." Garfield favored the arrangement. He and Goff met again the following day, and they agreed to consult with their superiors. On September 27, Garfield discussed the matter with Roosevelt, who was skeptical but willing to send Garfield to Bonaparte for further discussions. The two Cabinet members decided that any future proposals would have to come from the responsible leaders of Standard themselves, and on September 29, with Archbold and J. D. Rockefeller's approval, Standard submitted its plan. Two commissioners —Garfield and Goff—could freely examine Standard's books at the corporation's expense, and would have the unanimous power to make Standard conform to their recommendations and the government to drop all suits. "A really astonishing proposal," Garfield concluded. "Goff has done well to induce them to make the offer."[14] Additional meetings followed, and during most of the month of October both Roosevelt and Bonaparte seriously considered the matter.

Then Standard made an error. Senator Jonathan Bourne, Jr. of Oregon visited Roosevelt and told him that if he agreed to the détente with Standard, the oil giant would help him win the nomination for the Presidency in 1908; it is likely that it was Archbold alone who sent Bourne. On October 25, the Cabinet met and decided to continue the prosecution.

There the matter rested until June, 1908, when Senator Bourne and Archbold tried to take the matter in hand with an even more bizarre proposition. During that month a reorganization plan for Standard was given to Bonaparte by the company, and Roosevelt left it to his Attorney General to decide whether it attained the object of the antitrust litigation. Linking the two proposals together, in late June Senator Bourne again visited Roosevelt about running for the Presidency with Standard support. Roosevelt dismissed the offer, and referred Bourne to Bonaparte. Still seeking some sort of grand alliance, Bourne asked Bonaparte to prepare an antitrust bill embodying the ideas of the Administration, which he would then try to have pushed through the Senate. Roosevelt and Bonaparte were evidently irritated by the Oregon Senator, and cut the matter rather short.[15]

On July 22, Circuit Court Judge Peter S. Grosscup decided to reverse the Landis fine on Standard. Roosevelt did not mind a reduction of the fine against Standard of Indiana, which he had always felt was excessive, but he reacted strongly against Grosscup's claim that the Landis trial was unfair and should be retried. Grosscup's decision, coincidentally, came at a time when Chicago papers were attacking his record for taking railroad passes during the late 1890's and Roosevelt was discussing his impeachment. Roosevelt's early opinion of Grosscup had been, first, that he was too radical and, after his past scandal, too conservative. In fact, however, Grosscup's position on the modern corporation—that it was inevitable and desirable—was similar to Roosevelt's, and in 1912 he supported Roosevelt in the Presidential election. The Grosscup decision, later sustained by the retrial, marked the end of negotiations for a détente between Standard and Roosevelt. Despite the victory of Standard in the rebating case—the antitrust case was still pending—a cordial relationship between top members of the Roosevelt Administration and Standard executives continued. Garfield saw Fred Goff from time to time. And in late July, 1908, shortly after Judge Grosscup had saved Standard $29 million, a party in his honor was given at Williamstown, Massachusetts by Rockefeller's son-in-law, T. Parmalee Prentice. Among the guests celebrating and feting the honorable judge from Chicago was Attorney General Bonaparte![16]

The tobacco industry was one of the few in which a single company had anything like monopoly control. Moreover, the American Tobacco Company followed an aggressive merger policy and was ruthless in fighting its competitors. Indeed, American Tobacco was strategically in a better position to maintain control over tobacco than Standard was to dominate the oil industry.

In 1904 American Tobacco absorbed Continental Tobacco, one of its few major competitors, and action by the government was inevitable. The nature of the government's approach, and the diverse interests that entered into the case, illustrate the relationship between the Roosevelt Administration and "bad" trusts with which détentes of the U.S. Steel variety were politically impossible.

Tobacco's man in the higher circles of government was Elihu Root. Root had worked for Thomas F. Ryan in 1905, and Ryan was interested in Tobacco. In late 1906 the Justice Department began taking steps leading to possible litigation against Tobacco. W. W. Fuller, Tobacco's counsel, persuaded Root to defend the Tobacco position within the Administration and, if possible, to prevent an antitrust suit. He sent Root considerable data to sustain Tobacco's case, and in February, 1907, when it became apparent that Taft and Bonaparte were pressing for an antitrust suit, Ryan suggested a possible compromise to Root. He had warned Tobacco executives to cooperate with the President, Ryan claimed, and he wished the company to distribute its direct stock holdings among the shareholders. In late February, however, the Justice Department subpoened various Tobacco executives. Although Root tried to reassure Ryan as to what the future held in store, Ryan decided to put his cards on the table. "I have just heard that the Harvester Company," he wrote in March, "has made an agreement with the Department of Justice (that is the President) to do what I want Am Tob company to do—I think you could try to find out if the President would like us to walk in that line[.] I feel sure he [would] . . . get much credit by our doing so."[17]

The key advocate of legal action against American Tobacco was James C. McReynolds, special assistant to Attorney General Bonaparte, who acted without interference from his superior. Root and Ryan decided to try to convince Roosevelt to accept Tobacco's stock distribution plan or else hand the entire matter over to the Bureau of Corporations for an investigation. During March, as McReynolds moved to convene a grand jury inquiry into Tobacco, the firm offered to dispose of its stock in British-American Tobacco, Reynolds Tobacco, and others. McReynolds, who was given complete jurisdiction over the matter by Bonaparte, refused to budge, and the grand jury inquiry went on.

An International Harvester-type détente was not consummated, but the bureau was brought into the matter nevertheless. The bureau had been toying with an investigation of Tobacco, and in early May an American Tobacco attorney visited Herbert Knox Smith to try to speed up its inquiry. The bureau's report, Fuller told Root, would be out by mid-summer. "But they already have come to their conclusions all along the line and they are very favorable to us—indeed Mr. Smith said that they were so favorable that he supposed the public would believe that his Department was stupid and deceived by us. . . . It may be that if the Presdt. wants a sort of advance idea of the discoveries of the Department of Commerce, he can get it by talking with Mr. Smith. It would show him how we have been slandered and misrepresented, and maybe change his feeling toward us."[18]

Neither Root nor the Bureau of Corporations was able to stop a suit against American Tobacco, but they were able to blunt some of McReynolds' more extreme proposals. McReynolds suggested that a receivership be created over American Tobacco, and that a general bill allowing this method of dissolution in other suits be recommended to Congress. The proposal was referred to Root and Bonaparte; both took a dim view of it and it died. Another suggestion, to take criminal action against James B. Duke, the founder and controller of American Tobacco, was also rejected. Root remained American Tobacco's main contact within the Administration, but he could not prevent the Southern District Court of New York from ordering the dissolution of the company in 1908. The entire question passed to the courts until 1911, when the Taft Administration was forced to make the final decision on American Tobacco's fate.

The Rule of
Reason

One can evaluate Roosevelt's relationship to big business both operationally and theoretically. Operationally there is the reality of détentes with the Morgan companies, and the President's refusal to take steps against them. At the same time there is the fact that the antitrust activity of Roosevelt's Administration was purely minimal, and substantially less, in terms of the number of cases initiated, than under Taft or Warren G. Harding.

Even without discounting Roosevelt's more exuberant political rhetoric, there was a remarkable correspondence between these operational realities and his theories. Although his views on the relationship of the corporation to society and politics developed somewhat through experience, the core of his ideas remained remarkably constant. He usually discussed the corporation in the context of an attack on "sinister demagogs and foolish visionaries" who "seek to excite a violent class hatred against all men of wealth." The corporation that created injustice, and the critic of injustice who did not accept the basic premises of the corporate economy, were invariably equated, and the injustices that Roosevelt attacked were not the structural evils inherent in an exploitive economy but those evils associated with a few exceptional corporations. "Under no circumstances would we countenance attacks upon law-abiding property," he declared in January, 1908, "or do ought but condemn those who hold up rich men as being evil men because of their riches. On the contrary, our whole effort is to insist upon conduct, and neither wealth nor property nor any other class distinction, as being the proper standard by which to judge the actions of men." Conduct, to Roosevelt, was a personal and not an institutional question, and in reality often was equated with the manners and class sensibilities upon which Roosevelt had been raised. "Sweeping attacks upon all property, upon all men of means, without regard to whether they do well or ill, would sound the death-knell of the Republic," he never tired of reiterating.

"In the modern industrial world combinations are absolutely necessary," Roosevelt concluded, and not merely among businessmen but among workers and farmers as well. Roosevelt resigned himself to the contemporary belief in the inevitability of trusts. "It is mischievous and unwholesome," he repeated again and again in different ways, "to keep upon the statute books unmodified, a law, like the anti-trust law, which, while in practice only partially effective against vicious combinations, has nevertheless in theory been construed so as sweepingly to prohibit every combination for the transaction of modern business." The law should not be repealed, he declared in December, 1907, but "it should be so amended as to forbid only the kind of combination which does harm to the general public." Combinations were "reasonable or unreasonable," and the way to determine which should be allowed was to grant supervisory power to the federal government. Antitrust suits as a means of enforcing the law, Roosevelt declared, were "irksome" and prolonged affairs. Instead, the government should have the right to approve "reasonable agreements" between corporations, provided they were submitted for approval to an "appropriate" body. National incorporation of combinations, with heavy emphasis of the regular publication of key data and publicity, would allow the government to regulate the corporate structure to protect both shareholders and the public. Barring this, federal licensing for the same ends might be tried. And only the national government was capable of effective regulation of this magnitude. Regulation, not repression, was the theme.[19]

Roosevelt's interpretation of the trust problem, his association of the evils of concentration with the personality of individuals, and his separation of "good" from "bad" combinations as a means of accepting the major premises of the corporate economy, were all part of the dominant thought of the day. His basic ideas, which were virtually identical to the attitude on the "trust problem" taken by the big business supporters of the National Civic Federation, were eminently acceptable to the corporate elite. The idea of federal incorporation or licensing was attractive as a shield against state regulation, and rather than frightening big business, as most historians believe they did, Roosevelt's statements encouraged them. Indeed, even his passing reference in his 1906 Message to Congress to the theoretical desirability of an income tax law was hardly radical. Andrew Carnegie was also attacking the unequal distribution of wealth as "one of the crying evils of our day," and the fact that Roosevelt took no concrete steps on the matter, and linked it with a Constitutional amendment, meant his rhetoric was not frightening even to reactionaries.

Early in 1908 George W. Perkins, the functional architect of the détente system and political capitalism during Roosevelt's presidency, attempted to articulate a systematic view on the relationship of the giant corporation to national government. The modern corporation, to Perkins, was the "working of natural causes of evolution." It must welcome federal supervision, administered by practical businessmen, that "should say to stockholders and the public from time to time that the management's reports and methods of business are correct." With federal regulation, which would free business from the many states, industrial cooperation could replace competition. In a defense of Roosevelt against unwarranted attacks from the business community—a community that was not obtaining the same benefits of business-government cooperation as Morgan firms—Perkins also suggested that Roosevelt shared his interpretation of the necessity of sympathetic regulation. "It is needless to say that I am in substantial agreement with most of the propositions that it contains," Roosevelt wrote his admirer upon receiving a copy of the speech.[20]

With the exception of Bonaparte, virtually all of Roosevelt's important advisers accepted his interpretation of the trust issue. Roosevelt ignored Bonaparte's objection that the terms "reasonable" and "unreasonable" were too indefinite for legal purposes and were subject to arbitrary interpretation. He did not feel that the antitrust law should be sweepingly applied, which it never was, but he suggested that Roosevelt's past distinctions between good and bad trusts had caused "those interested in certain trusts to claim immunity on the ground of their virtuous and benevolent purposes."[21] The détente system, Bonaparte sensed, was the logical conclusion of Roosevelt's philosophy. He was correct, but his influence was not sufficient to override it. Bonaparte, like his peers, was never concerned with the size of the corporate unit, but only with whether it violated the law. The difference was that the literal-minded Bonaparte thought an inflexible law was desirable, and Roosevelt did not.

Roosevelt sharply distinguished between good and bad corporations, and if the contemporary public was largely unaware of the subtle differences, at least Roosevelt and many big businessmen knew precisely what was happening. Roosevelt was consciously using government regulation to save the capitalist system, perhaps even from itself, for the greatest friend of socialism was the unscrupulous businessman who did not recognize that moderate regulation could save him from a more drastic fate in the hands of the masses. ". . . I think the worst thing that could be done," he wrote Henry Lee Higginson concerning the railroads, "would be an announcement that for two or three years the Federal Government would keep its hands off of them. It would result in a tidal wave of violent State action against them thruout three-fourths of this country." "The reactionary or ultraconservative apologists for the misuse of wealth assail the effort to secure such control as a step toward socialism. As a matter of fact it is these reactionaries and ultraconservatives who are themselves most potent in increasing socialistic feeling." ". . . we are acting in the defense of property," he reminded Lodge.[22]

Roosevelt was not alone in reiterating his conservative intent and function. Elihu Root as Secretary of State and L. M. Shaw as Secretary of the Treasury were two of the bitterest opponents of popular government. Oscar S. Straus, his Secretary of Commerce from December, 1906 on, was formerly president of the New York Board of Trade and Transportation, and was close to the National Civic Federation; he allowed Herbert Knox Smith to run the Bureau of Corporations with a free hand. More interested in immigration problems than corporations, Straus was personally close to various New York banking interests.

Key businessmen knew that Roosevelt relied heavily on Nelson Aldrich, especially for banking and financial advice, and that major machine politicians, such as Boise Penrose, could publicly proclaim their alliance with Roosevelt without a denial from the President. But their most important connection remained the Bureau of Corporations and its commissioners, first Garfield and then Herbert Knox Smith. Garfield went to great extremes during the formation of the bureau to assure that "the business interests of the country appreciated that the Bureau was not to be used as an instrument of improper inquisition nor, as some of the extremists feared, blackmail." Upon leaving the bureau he wrote Straus that "the work of the Bureau has shown the absurdity of the antitrust act," and the need for federal supervision.[23] Smith took virtually the same position as Garfield and Roosevelt.

Important businessmen were fully aware and appreciative of the policies of Roosevelt and his chief aides, and hardly succumbed to the irritated clamor of the conservative press that criticized the President on the basis of deduction from its abstract theories rather than on an evaluation of his concrete actions. Roosevelt's special conflict with Harriman, which initially had nothing to do with the tycoon's conduct as a railroad operator, was caused by a conflicting interpretation of the basis on which Harriman had donated funds to the 1904 campaign. Until late 1905 their relationship was perfectly amiable, and even after the breach in their relationship Roosevelt never took antitrust action against any of the Harriman roads, despite the fact that Harriman and Standard Oil became the criteria for "bad" and "unreasonable" trusts. And big businessmen such as Perkins, Gary, and the leadership of the National Civic Federation, which included among its ranks Seth Low, August Belmont, Andrew Carnegie, and John Hays Hammond, knew better than most of their contemporaries that the Roosevelt Administration was eminently acceptable ideologically and politically.

The key to their appreciation of Roosevelt was his antitrust policies. During October, 1907, the National Civic Federation held a large trust conference in Chicago to develop its viewpoint on the inevitability and desirability of the large corporation. "There is, in my opinion, more danger to be feared from the ordinary tendencies of the various States than from the present National Administration or any future National Administration," Isaac N. Seligman told the gathering. Charles G. Dawes, Nicholas Murray Butler, Robert Mather, Herbert Knox Smith, and numerous lawyers, businessmen, and public figures rose to expound the basic principles of Roosevelt's economic philosophy. At the conclusion of the convention, and virtually unanimously, the gathering called for legislation to permit "Business and industrial agreements or combinations whose objects are in the public interest . . . ," the exclusion of unions and farmers' organizations from the jurisdiction of the Sherman Act, federal incorporation laws, and the expansion of the publicity functions of various federal agencies regulating business. They also called for a public commission to recommend comprehensive trust legislation.[24]

The Attempt at
Political Consolidation

The resolution of the National Civic Federation in 1907 represented an effort to unify a number of diverse currents inherent in the nascent political capitalism being created in the United States during the Roosevelt period. First, it appealed to the federal incorporation movement and the widespread desire of many businessmen to free themselves from state regulation by hiding behind the shield of the federal government. Second, it reflected the desire of many businessmen to obtain an administrative agency ready to sanction anticompetitive action and provide security from possible state or federal trust prosecutions—to provide stability and predictability in a politically and economically fluid climate. And third, the position of the National Civic Federation on trusts reflected the hope of the Morgan companies to place their détentes on a firm, legal footing that might bind a political administration less sympathetic than Roosevelt's.

The subsequent history of the resolution provides a significant insight into the deep sentiment within the big business community for the consolidation of a political capitalism, Roosevelt's ambivalence, and the entire relationship between business and government in this period. The first important support for federal incorporation and licensing came from the Industrial Commission, and reflected the desires of Standard Oil more than any other single business interest. And although the Bureau of Corporations picked up the themes of federal licensing ard incorporation by late 1903, bills to introduce one or another form of regulation started being introduced in Congress. Six distinct bills were submitted before 1907, and the most important of these, submitted by Senator Francis G. Newlands in May, 1906, was largely drafted by Herbert Knox Smith with the approval of Garfield. Smith and Garfield's motives are clear; Newlands was a practical conservative Democrat who felt that national incorporation was the only way of heading off more drastic proposals for economic reform and nationalization. The Newlands Bill permitted mergers with proper capitalization and sharply restricted the scope of state taxation. Although many big business leaders wanted a federal incorporation or licensing law that would give the securities of their companies the federal government's stamp of approval, and protect them from the states, Congress made no concerted action to pass any bill.

Roosevelt's transition to a supporter of federal incorporation or licensing was inevitable, given his position that the federal regulatory process should be supreme. In his 1905 Message to Congress he reiterated his belief in the supremacy of national government, in his 1906 Message he endorsed regulation "by a national license law or in other fashion," and in his 1907 Message he finally came out for a federal incorporation law with a national commission to enforce it. During October, 1907, just before his Message to Congress, Roosevelt was apparently considering the entire issue seriously for the first time. At the end of the month, upon receiving the resolution of the National Civic Federation, Roosevelt wrote Seth Low, chairman of the organization, that a federal incorporation law should be accompanied by "a modification of the Sherman law permitting combinations when the combination is not hostile to the interests of the people."[25] When Roosevelt publicly endorsed federal incorporation in December, the stage was set for action.

The idea of a revision of the Sherman Act and advance government approval of mergers or big business actions greatly attracted many businessmen. At the same time, not a few capitalists, especially those supporting the National Civic Federation, were willing to pay deference to conservative labor unionism in theory if not in practice, especially if they could obtain labor's political support for revisions of the Sherman Act that might provide big business with stability and political security.

As soon as the National Civic Federation's position on trust regulation was formulated, and Roosevelt's statement on federal incorporation strengthened, Francis Lynde Stetson and Victor Morawetz, a major railroad attorney with Morgan connections, began drafting a bill. Gary was frequently consulted about general principles, and from time to time Herbert Knox Smith was asked for advice. Perkins also became involved in the political and legislative aspects of the measure, and on February 27, 1908, met with Samuel Gompers and other labor leaders and won their support. The bill, in brief, was virtually the total creation of the House of Morgan.

Perkins was unsure of Roosevelt's attitude toward the bill Rep. William P. Hepburn was introducing for the National Civic Federation, but he was confidently willing to experiment. The bill was presented as an amendment to the Sherman Act, and was fairly simple. Any corporation could voluntarily register its financial status, contracts, and vital data with the Bureau of Corporations. Once registered, a corporation could file any proposed contract or merger with the Commissioner, and if the Commissioner did not declare the proposal illegal within thirty days the government effectively removed its right to prosecute the company under the Sherman Act. Railroads as well as industrial corporations could register under the law, and individuals were granted the power to sue corporations for alleged injuries in U.S. Circuit Courts. And, most controversial of all, unions and strikes were explicitly removed from the jurisdiction of the Sherman Act.

The Hepburn Bill was introduced in March, 1908, and an immediate attempt was made to pin Roosevelt's approval to the measure. During early March Seth Low visited Roosevelt twice, and although he seemed to give his approval the first visit, the second time Roosevelt asked for a few small revisions. On March 11, Roosevelt discussed the entire matter with Stetson, Low, Gary, Gompers, and Herbert Knox Smith, and after they accepted his suggestion that railroads be excluded from the bill, Stetson felt Roosevelt had "substantially agreed upon a bill. . . ." Despite Stetson's confidence, the fact remained that Roosevelt was undecided about the entire Hepburn Bill. On the one hand Herbert Knox Smith advocated a "nationalization of the legal conditions of corporations," and helped formulate the bill. Although Roosevelt had long advocated an identical position, Attorney General Bonaparte strongly opposed the measure and Roosevelt's philosophy of "good" and "bad" trusts embodied in it. His major line of attack was the difficulty of courts' defining "reasonableness," and the mass of paper work such a law would create.[26]

Roosevelt was frankly sympathetic to the assumptions motivating the Hepburn Bill, but the major liability of the bill, as he privately saw it, was its provision excluding labor from coverage under the Sherman Act. The proponents of the bill continued their campaign to convince the President. Perkins went to Washington to obtain Root's and Aldrich's support, and had International Harvester and Charles G. Dawes, the powerful Chicago banker, join the fray on his side.

During late March and April the House Committee on the Judiciary held hearings on the Hepburn Bill, and Seth Low appeared as the major spokesman for it. Low freely admitted that Stetson and Morawetz were in charge of the primary drafting of the bill, but other important capitalists consulted and endorsing the measure included Gary, Samuel Mather, Henry Lee Higginson, Robert Mather, Isaac N. Seligman, James Speyer, W. A. Clark, August Belmont, and J. H. Ralston. The bill was frankly designed to avoid the legal disputes over federal-state powers that would result from a federal licensing or incorporation law, but it intended to achieve the same ends. Its philosophy was identical to Roosevelt's theory of the "reasonable" combination, and publicity was its primary tool for enforcement. And its major asset was to give business assurance that it would not be subjected to political attacks while trying to stabilize its own affairs.

Opposition to the bill centered almost exclusively on the labor clause. The National Association of Manufacturers strongly opposed the bill because of the clause, but was sympathetic to federal incorporation, which its special committee on the topic in 1908 declared would be "a national blessing . . . and protect one corporation from the oppression and rapacity of another." Andrew Carnegie endorsed the basic idea of the bill, but he wanted the administration of it handed over to a special commission—a proposal Low was ready to accept. The strongest opposition to the measure came from small business, merchants, and a few influential associations such as the Merchants' Association of New York and the New York Board of Trade and Transportation. Perhaps their emphasis on the question of excluding trade unions was purely opportunistic, but their frequent endorsement of federal regulation was certainly sincere in past instances.[27] It was clear, however, that in return for labor support the big business elements pushing the Hepburn Bill also won considerable small business and merchant opposition.

On March 25, Roosevelt sent a special message to Congress dealing primarily with the antitrust law. The message, on its face value, encouraged the advocates of the Hepburn Bill. "In the modern industrial world combinations are absolutely necessary," Roosevelt announced again. Such combinations had to be permitted not only in business, but among farmers and labor unions as well. The antitrust law needed modification, and, referring to the Hepburn Bill, Roosevelt said "Some such measure as this bill is needed in the interest of all engaged in the industries which are essential to the country's well-being."[28] Roosevelt suggested a few minor modifications of the bill, and by his absence of comment implicitly endorsed the entire bill in principle and the labor clause in particular.

It is not clear why Roosevelt sent his March 25 Message to Congress, but his heart was not in it—indeed, the message reeked of duplicity.

In late March, at virtually the same time, the Cabinet met and discussed the Hepburn Bill. Roosevelt indicated that he opposed the proposal because of its labor section. But to come out against a bill because of his fundamentally antilabor views was politically impossible, not only for himself but for the Republican Party. Roosevelt, in his own paternalistic way, was fond of calling himself a friend of labor, and now that he had a chance to prove it he failed abysmally. What followed was a series of crude rationalizations. On April 1, he wrote Seth Low that he might have to veto the bill because of its reliance on the courts for a definition of the term "reasonable," a matter that should be left to an executive agency in order to allow "proper control of the great corporations." On April 9 he again wrote Low that the "Stetson-Morawetz" bill "would be worse than passing nothing," and would be "ruinous politically." It would give the corporations "the chance to go into improper combinations without molestation."[29] Roosevelt was being dishonest with Low. The bill, in fact, left the determination of "reasonable" with the Bureau of Corporations, an executive agency, and the very concept of a reasonable trust was one that he had advocated for years. His real reason for opposition was the labor section of the bill, which he thought would lead "to the legalization of the blacklist and the boycott," and he freely admitted this to Herbert Knox Smith.[30]

During April the effort to force Roosevelt to actually endorse the Hepburn Bill continued. "The objection comes from the mercantile element, as distinguished from the corporation element," Seth Low tried to reassure him.[31] The bill embodies your view; why not endorse it? Low asked. Roosevelt apparently felt sheepish about his reticence, and passed the entire matter over to Smith, whom he asked to give the Administration position before the House hearings. Smith's presentation to the committee reflected Roosevelt's public ambivalence. While he refused to endorse the bill in its entirety, he proposed only minor amendments and effectively approved of those sections not referring to labor. Perkins tried to interpret Smith's position as an Administration endorsement of the bill, but Smith privately told Seth Low that the labor section was the major obstacle to Administration support.

By the end of April Roosevelt's obstinacy proved too much for the National Civic Federation, and some of its key leaders were prepared to temporarily give up the campaign to pass the bill. Although Perkins wished to continue the fight for the Hepburn Bill, perhaps because he feared Taft might be less responsive to Morgan needs than Roosevelt and he might lose the opportunity of legally consolidating the détente system, the bill was dropped. It is ironic that Roosevelt's consistently favorable attitude toward the desires of the House of Morgan should have been broken on the question of the trade union movement.

In July, as a part of Standard's effort to arrange a detente with the federal government, Senator Jonathan Bourne, Jr., wrote Roosevelt about enacting antitrust legislation with Standard's backing. Roosevelt's response was curious, given the fact that Standard's offer of support was rejected. He would make an effort during the next session of Congress to pass a federal incorporation bill drafted by one of his agencies or the National Civic Federation. In a defense of big business sponsorship of federal regulation—a defense that ignored motives—Roosevelt wrote "I have not the slightest patience with the foolish creatures who oppose a good measure because big corporations are wise enough to see that it is a good measure and to advocate it. . . ." Despite this generous position, Roosevelt continued to oppose the Hepburn Bill when a revised version was resurrected in November, and took no action on federal incorporation either. Bonaparte encouraged his opposition, although when John R. Dos Passos, the great promoter, presented an alternative measure Bonaparte was friendlier.[32] Roosevelt did not agree with Bonaparte's skepticism as to the distinction between reasonable and unreasonable trusts, but he preferred the informal détente system and was sufficiently antilabor not to want to lose a club over potential union radicalism. His corporate ideology remained constant, and he was unwilling to accept the position of a George Perkins who was prepared to take unions into a rationalized, predictable establishment as a junior partner. His rhetoric, despite his actions, did not vary throughout this period. Roosevelt's political capitalism had a stronger element of paternalism in it than even that of Perkins and the National Civic Federation.

CHAPTER SIX

THE

FAILURE OF

FINANCE

CAPITALISM,

1890-1908

HISTORIANS HAVE COMMONLY VIEWED the financial structure at the beginning of this century as highly centralized and tightly controlled. Certainly this was the preponderant contemporary view of the matter. "What is taking place is a concentration of banking that is not merely a normal growth but a concentration that comes from combination, consolidation, and other methods employed to secure monopolistic power," lamented the *Wall Street Journal* in describing the entry of banking into corporate finance. The Morgan of Brandeis' *Other People's Money* was an unrivaled, powerful mogul who commanded the entire financial structure almost arbitrarily—the Pujo Committee's Morgan. Morgan, suggested Lincoln Steffens, was a sovereign; he was the keystone of the financial structure, according to Lewis Corey.[1]

Morgan and Wall Street were, without a doubt, very powerful factors in the American economy. But had the complete centralization of capital been the dominant fact of the financial structure at the beginning of this century, the proliferation of new entries into most industries and the failure of the merger movement to establish industrial control would be inexplicable. For central finance would have withheld funds from undesirable competitors. Clearly, a much more complex situation existed, and the extent of this complexity has not been fully appreciated. The crucial fact of the financial structure at the beginning of this century was the relative decrease in New York's financial significance and the rise of many alternate sources of substantial financial power.

Throughout the 1870's and much of the 1880's, by far the largest number of banks were national banks, with their financial standards determined in Washington. By 1896, however, non-national state banks, savings banks, and private banks accounted for 61 per cent of the total number of banks, and by 1913, 71 per cent of the banks. The capital and resources of these non-national banks were small in the immediate post-Civil War period, but in 1896 constituted 54 per cent of total banking resources, and in 1913, 57 per cent.

The advantages of state banks were clear. The National Banking Act imposed relatively high capital requirements on national banks for issuing checks—$50,000 until 1900, $25,000 thereafter—and prevented their opening savings departments, prohibited the extension of real estate mortgage credit, and made domestic and foreign branch banking illegal. State banking laws, especially in the 1890's, became far more lenient in such crucial states as Michigan, California, and New York. Bank mergers were difficult for national banks, and large banks were forced to adopt the often unreliable method of interlocking directorates as a means of control. Moreover, national banks could not lend more than one-tenth of their capital to one borrower, and this meant that in 1912 there were only about sixty national banks that could lend more than $500,000 to one company. Larger national banks watched with considerable distress the growth of state banks. In California the young Bank of America was beginning to extend its power throughout the state by its aggressive policy of branch banking. The major New York banks also disliked having to compete, with interest on demand deposits and collections at par of out-of-town items, for the important deposits of state banks, most of which were loaned out as call-loans on the New York Stock Exchange. As one banker put it, "We love the country bankers, but they are the masters of the situation. We dance at their music and pay the piper."[2] And New York also found itself in the precarious situation, under such an arrangement, of being susceptible to heavy withdrawals of funds.

In 1903 the New York Clearing House tried to impose national reserve requirements on its rapidly growing state trust companies. Seventeen of them walked out and did not return until 1912. At the same time, some of the major national banks started accommodating to the new realities by organizing corporations for the purpose of buying state banks. And in 1903 the state-chartered Bankers Trust Company was organized with Morgan backing to compete with the independent state trust companies. J. P. Morgan and Co. were fully aware of the diffusion of banking power that was taking place through the state banks, and it disturbed them.

This diffusion and decentralization in the banking structure seriously undercut New York's financial supremacy. "There are some facts which seem to suggest the question whether our city may prove able to retain its past proportion of the vast settlements of this ever-growing continent," Henry Clews, the New York banker, said in 1888. ". . . and, although there is nothing to warrant very positive opinions about the future, it must be conceded as an unquestionable historic fact that in late years there have been symptoms of positive decadence in the status of our financial metropolis. . . . the natural development of national production of commerce is to build up independent financial centres of the interior, the effect of which can only be to check in some measure the growing ascendancy of New York."[3] Clews was correct in his estimate. Chicago's and St. Louis' growth were exceptionally rapid—the dollar value of the clearings of the Chicago Clearing House increased 410 per cent from 1866 to 1885, while New York's declined 12 per cent. In 1887 the National Banking Act was amended to allow cities with a population of over 200,000 to become central reserve cities, and hold the balances of smaller reserve cities of over 50,000 persons and country banks. Chicago and St. Louis immediately qualified, depriving New York of its exclusive status, and their bankers' balances and individual deposits, which had been only 16 per cent of the combined total of the three cities in 1880, increased to 33 per cent by 1910. The growth of smaller reserve cities was even more rapid. The dollar value of bank clearings of major cities outside New York was 24 per cent of the national total in 1882, 43 per cent in 1913. Henry P. Davison, Morgan's partner, declared in 1913 that New York's share of the nation's banking resources fell from 23 per cent in 1902 to 18 per cent in 1912.

Davison, Clews, and the New York banking community were well aware of their own relative decline and the growing diffusion of banking power and decision-making. Clews pondered about the problem in 1888 and came to the conclusion that New York's dominant role as a distribution point for imports and exports, and as a center of the nation's internal commerce, was being undermined. Even New York's position of supplying Midwestern and Western jobbers was being taken away from it by the giant manufacturers and distributors emerging in those areas.[4] There is ample evidence to suggest Clews was correct.

The power of J. P. Morgan and Co. was based initially on its ability to sell railroad stocks and bonds in the English and European markets. European investors placed $2.4 billion in the United States during 1880-1895, and owned a total of $4.5 billion in government and nongovernment bonds and shares in 1914. Morgan's activities in 1895-1896 in selling U.S. gold bonds in Europe were based on his alliance with the House of Rothschild; these activities added to Morgan's reputation as a rescuer of governments. That reputation was often the key to his power, and it lasted long after the power was greatly diluted. Morgan and a few large bankers saved the New York Clearing House in 1893, and, seemingly, the United States' financial standing only a few years later. Accomplishments of this magnitude enhance one's reputation indeed!

So long as large loans had to be placed in the European market, and so long as New York was the undisputed leader of American banking, Morgan's power was correspondingly great. Despite the fact that Morgan maintained the homily that character was the basis of commercial credit, and not money or property, it can be shown that Morgan's deficiency of sufficient amounts of all three seriously undermined his position after 1900. Morgan was swept into the industrial merger field, and the prestige of his firm allowed him to become the most important promoter. Since Morgan insisted on retaining substantial managerial control of his usually overcapitalized mergers, he must accept responsibility for their not altogether brilliant subsequent histories. We have already discussed the failure of International Mercantile Marine, the decline in the market shares of United States Steel and International Harvester, and the general fact that the financial record and stability for Morgan's promotions were no higher than par. Even Morgan could not overcome basic trends working against the success of the merger movement. Perhaps more significant was his inability to float American Telephone and Telegraph's 1907 bond issue, for it meant that Morgan, in a declining economy, was quite weak. The fact that he, unlike most others, retained control of management, forces one to conclude that in the process of trying to have his overcapitalization and organizational success as well, Morgan far overtaxed his financial powers and managerial abilities.

The ability to parlay key minor shareholdings into control of a powerful economic instrument also increased the dangers of competition. For better or worse, control of the majority of stock of a corporation was not the prerequisite for control of the corporation even in 1900, and ownership of a minority of stock coupled with active participation in management was often sufficient to exercise the total power of the corporation, both in relation to the general social order and in relation to actual or potential competitors. The railroads were generally controlled with less than 20 per cent of the stock. Even Morgan kept control of most of his properties with minority ownership. Harriman owned less than one per cent of the Union Pacific's shares in 1900, and 23 per cent in 1906. James J. Hill claimed he owned 2 per cent of the Great Northern's stock when he ran it.

Morgan in the 1890's could successfully maintain his independence in then significant flotations of $50–100 million. The sheer magnitude of many of the mergers, culminating in U.S. Steel, soon forced him to modify his stand, though at times he would have preferred total control. More important, by 1898 he could not ignore the massive power of new financial competitors and had to treat them with deference. Standard Oil, utilizing National City Bank for its investments, had fixed resources substantially larger than Morgan's, and by 1899 was ready to move into the general economy. Allied with Harriman and Kuhn, Loeb, this group was as powerful as the

Morgan-George F. Baker (First National Bank of New York)-Hill alliance. The test came, of course, in the Northern Securities battle, which was essentially an expensive draw. Morgan and Standard paid deference to each other thereafter, and mutual toleration among bankers increased sharply. Morgan, however, was always reluctant to accept Kuhn, Loeb as an equal, and in his 1906 flotation of A.T. & T.'s bonds he refused to allow Lee, Higginson to participate because of its alliance with Speyer and Company of New York. At the same time, the First National Bank of Chicago and the Illinois Trust and Savings Bank, among others, were largely independently directing substantial Midwestern capital into investment banking.

George F. Baker called Morgan the leader of Wall Street, and the designation is more correct than incorrect. George M. Reynolds, president of one of the largest banks in America, the Continental and Commercial National Bank of Chicago, realized that most of the antibanker sentiment was directed against Wall Street, and happily baited his erstwhile allies by telling the Pujo Committee in January, 1913, that "I am inclined to think that the concentration [of finance and credit], having gone to the extent it has, does constitute a menace."[5] Big bankers, then, were always very cautious of one another. But they needed each other for large security flotations, and competition could be costly. And by 1907 the old tycoons were growing old and were less ambitious—at least to the extent of being willing to pay greater deference to one another. A benign armed neutrality, rather than positive affection, is as much a reason as any for the high number of interlocks among the five major New York banking houses.

In 1907 a greater challenge to Wall Street overshadowed mutual rivalries and surreptitious aid to competitive industrial interests. The panics of 1879 and 1893 were weathered by the New York banks without decisive government intervention. The crisis of 1907, on the other hand, found the combined banking structure of New York inadequate to meet the challenge, and chastened any obstreperous financial powers who throught they might build their fortunes independently of the entire banking community. This crisis, discussed in detail later in this chapter, marks the conclusion of the New York banking community's consciousness of its own inadequacy. The nation had grown too large, banking had become too complex. Wall Street, humbled and almost alone, turned from its own resources to the national government.

The ability of industrial corporations to finance their own growth meant a corresponding decrease in the power of finance capital, which in turn allowed competition to arise and new firms to develop quite freely of finance capital. For mergers that did not have to bother with their promoters meddling in their managerial policies, it meant an ability to break free of their initial financial roots and follow an independent course. This, roughly, is what happened in many instances.

During 1899-1904, the intense merger period, a large part of corporate finance came from external sources. For the entire period of 1900-1910, however, 70.4 per cent of the new funds in manufacturing came from internal sources, and this led to a general independence from outside financial power. Indeed, since 1900 the formation of capital from external financing has not altered appreciably, and this has meant a corresponding decline in the power of finance capital institutions. In some industries nearly all the invested capital of successful firms came from profits; this was especially true for such new industries as automobiles, in which General Motors was the exception. And the banking community was fatally conservative in investing in new ventures. Standard Oil financed itself, and with its accumulated power then moved into the financial structure in a massive way. It was Du Pont, not Wall Street, that gave the first substantial support to any auto company and thereby acquired the dominant position in the industry. Such diversification from industry into finance or other industries—as in the case of autos and newspapers buying into or creating newsprint firms—meant a multiplication of significant financial groupings and a diminution of the power of the older investment and banking houses.

The very nature of the National Banking Act forced many companies to choose between the risks of self-financing and reliance on investment houses. Many chose the former and a sufficient number succeeded, radically affecting the distribution of financial power. Since a national bank could not lend more than one-tenth of its capital to one source, even as late as 1912 there were only twelve banks able to loan more than $1 million to one firm. This compelled most companies to rely on many banks rather than become dependent on any one, to try to finance their own expansion, or to turn to the investment houses. But the major New York houses were not available to many newer companies, much less aspiring competitors of mergers, and this led to the development of local investment houses more often than not dependent on specific industrial firms, and the creation of new dependent banks that were the adjuncts of industrial concerns in the smaller communities. At the same time, the merger movement provided substantial capital to the former owners of companies, and the very availability of funds to create the giant combinations also led to an availability of funds for the creation of new and often competing firms. The financial structure was too complex, too fluid. The Money Trust sitting in New York could not, despite Brandeis' allegations, control competition and entry through their direction of credit.[6] The economy by 1910 had moved well beyond the control of any city, any group of men, or any alliance then existing in the economy. The control of modern capitalism was to become a matter for the combined resources of the national state, a political rather than an economic matter.

Banking Reform Movements, 1893-1903

The conventional historical interpretation of financial reform in the 1890's has assumed that silver and Bryanism were the dominant movements of the time, and that the banking and business community took an essentially standpat position on reforms of any type. Silver, Bryan, and Populism were, without question, the only politically meaningful movements of financial reform in the 1890's, and the banking and business community opposed them all without any equivocation whatsoever, but most bankers in the 1890's and after were not standpatters. Quite the contrary, they favored financial reform—their kind of reform, for their own ends.

"From the time I came to Chicago in 1892 the necessity of new banking and currency legislation was appreciated by most bankers," James B. Forgan, the leader of Chicago banking recounted, "and the subject became a live one."[7] The major liability of the existing banking laws, in addition to aiding the diffusion of resources and the spread of small banks, was the inelasticity of the currency supply during certain times of the year and the inability of the banking system to move circulating media to areas with ample commercial credit but insufficient loan funds. Bankers tried to meet the problem with a wide variety of reform schemes. Bank notes secured by government bonds were safe, but did not provide sufficient elasticity, and various schemes to issue notes on bank capital were advanced. Some of these plans included cooperative reserve funds to pay off the notes of bankrupted banks.

The depression of 1893 increased the agitation for financial reform not merely among farmers but among bankers as well. At its 1894 convention, the American Bankers Association endorsed "the Baltimore Plan" for banking legislation. The heart of the plan was the issuance of new currency protected by a joint guaranty fund of all issuing banks. Despite the fact that it was formulated by a major New York banker, A. Barton Hepburn, it was met by indifference or hostility by the larger banks. Nevertheless, the topic of reform was raised at virtually every subsequent meeting of the A.B.A.

Banking reform became almost exclusively a banker's issue, and certain businessmen, such as Carnegie, feared banking reforms of any sort. But various banker schemes continued to pour into Congress. Some asked for clearing house currency and bills of issue on bonds and a variety of securities as means of overcoming the currency shortage. Not a few of these plans were carefully formulated, and some were actually presented to Congress as bills. George A. Butler, a New Haven bank president, campaigned for circulating notes issued by the Comptroller of Currency up to 75 per cent of paid up capital, and a common reserve fund. A bill submitted by Senator Daniel W. Vorhees of Ohio to the 53rd Congress would have allowed banks to issue circulating currency equal to the par value of U.S. bonds deposited as security; it received much banker support. Rep. Joseph H. Walker of Massachussets introduced a bill in 1896 to allow national banking associations run by the banks to issue new notes based on coin and legal tender and a large proportion of old greenbacks. And Rep. Charles Fowler of New Jersey, a friend of banking, submitted a plan to permit banks to issue notes equal to one-fifth of their unimpaired capital.[8]

Although the demand for reform was substantial among bankers conscious of economic problems, none of these plans obtained a significant following. During 1896 a group of merchants entered the scene and added momentum to the banking reform movement. In late 1896 the Indianapolis Board of Trade decided to channelize the sentiment for banking reform into a national convention to consider the entire problem. Aided by various boards of trade and supported by a number of large banks, the convention met in Indianapolis in January, 1897, to answer the threat of silver and bimetalism. The most important action of the convention was to call upon President McKinley to appoint a commission to formulate financial legislation or, if the President could not do so, to create an independent group. As guiding lines to the commission's work, the convention called for the gradual retirement of greenbacks, a continuation of the gold standard, and the creation of elastic credit facilities. McKinley was friendly to the Indianapolis Monetary Convention. In his Inaugural Address he had endorsed "some revision" of the financial system. On July 24, 1897, he sent a message to Congress calling for a special monetary commission, and a bill to implement it passed the House but failed in the Senate.

A private commission headed by Senator George F. Edmunds of Vermont, but really dependent on J. Laurence Laughlin of the University of Chicago for ideas and direction, was appointed by the executive of the Indianapolis convention. The commission began meeting in September, and H. Parker Willis, one of Laughlin's graduate students, was hired as an assistant to the commission. By December the commission completed its report, largely due to Laughlin's efforts, and in January, 1898, a bill implementing its recommendations was introduced in the House by Rep. Jesse Overstreet of Indiana. The measure proposed allowing national banking associations created and run by the banks to circulate notes on commercial assets issued by the Comptroller of Currency up to the amount of the unimpaired and paid-up capital. Among other powers, the associations could authorize the creation of branch banks. Despite a modest campaign for passage of the Indianapolis Bill, the proposal quickly died.[9]

The fact was that fundamental banking legislation was politically dangerous, and the Republican Party did not want to take risks by acting. Moreover, while the minority of the banking community concerned with the problem favored reform, the vast majority were too indifferent to apply political pressure. For a time the growth of clearing house associations in various cities throughout the 1890's appeared to some bankers to offer hope for controlling the financial practices of at least the major banks, and a bill to create elasticity based on the commercial assets of associated banks of clearing house associations was introduced in Congress at the behest of Theodore Gilman, New York banker. The only actual legislation came in 1900, when a few minor revisions of the national banking laws greatly increased the ease with which a small bank could obtain a national charter. In 1900 the Republican Party, although favoring greater elasticity, shied away from financial reform. The return of prosperity after 1897 and the virtual demise of silver agitation made the party anxious to avoid fanning the flames of Bryanism.

The need for banking reform could not disappear as long as the large bankers desired the flexibility which only greater centralization and federal control could bring. In 1900 Secretary of the Treasury Lyman Gage suggested the creation of regional central banks, and in his first Message to Congress in December, 1901, Roosevelt casually referred to the need for more elastic currency. But such fleeting references meant little so long as state banks maintained the dominant influence over most Congressmen and were able to thwart the desires of the reform-oriented big city bankers. And certainly there was no hope for legislation unless the President was willing to take a stronger position. Voluntary efforts to regulate local banking conditions, the *Bankers' Magazine* commented, would not solve the problem of developing an elastic bank currency. Government centralization was necessary, it granted, but as the ally of smaller banks it opposed any scheme that might allow large city banks to set up branches. Although it thought the natural process of consolidation might eventually create its own centralized banking system, in the meantime the *Bankers' Magazine* favored some type of central deposit bank that would issue notes in return for commercial paper.[10]

The bankers were split among themselves on the issue of additional federal regulation, the smaller bankers, especially in towns and rural areas, benefiting most from a perpetuation of the status quo. Despite the division which appeared in the meetings of the American Bankers Association, the pro-legislation elements were able to maintain the upper hand. A commission of the A.B.A., led by A. Barton Hepburn, chairman of the board of Chase National Bank, presented a draft of a bill to Rep. Charles N. Fowler of New Jersey, chairman of the amorphous Committee on Banking and Currency, and the basic ideas emerged in 1902 as the Fowler Bill. The proposal was conservative enough, allowing the issuance of bank notes against bond-secured assets, thereby providing an increased measure of elasticity. But it also authorized branch banking by the larger city banks, allowing them to compete with the state banks. This clause doomed the bill in advance, and various attempts to revive the Fowler measure over the next year failed. Many small bankers favored greater currency elasticity, especially based on commercial assets, but they were not going to allow their throats to be cut without a fight. Resolutions from Midwestern states and bankers convinced House members it would be politically judicious not to vote for a bill endorsed by big bankers.

Despite the failure of Congress and the President to act decisively for the legislation the major bankers desired, the federal government did take steps to try to stabilize the money market and banking system. Even before Roosevelt became President, Secretary of the Treasury Gage made a practice of depositing ever-increasing amounts of public funds in banks, and as government revenue increased due to taxes imposed during the Spanish-American War, the government became a more powerful factor in the money market. The big bankers were pleased when Leslie M. Shaw, who succeeded Gage in 1902, eased the type of collateral bonds and eliminated the cash reserves required for government deposits. Even these valiant efforts to make the Treasury a much greater factor in central banking were to little avail. The diffusion of American banking continued away from New York, and the rise of the merger movement and a market for industrial securities sharply increased the amount of speculative activity in finance. Indeed, as the money market became increasingly geared to the needs of stock speculation, Roosevelt and the federal government did virtually nothing to control the trend, and in fact had little power or authority upon which to act. More important, until 1907 there was no special concern with this problem.[11]

Roosevelt and Banking Reform

Financial problems confused Roosevelt. He admitted his ignorance of the topic and caused despair among those members of Congress interested in some type of reform. "I do not intend to speak, save generally, on the financial question because I am not clear what to say . . . ," Roosevelt wrote Grenville M. Dodge early in 1903. On financial matters he kept in contact with Nelson Aldrich, Orville Platt, Perkins, and other conservative spokesmen who, although often disagreeing with each other on details, were perfectly safe. Roosevelt exploited this disagreement as a convenient way to avoid confronting the issue seriously. He did not support the Fowler Bill or the Aldrich Bill of 1903, in large measure because "one great trouble has been the absolute inability to get anything like unity of judgment among the financiers."[12] Besides, "Uncle Joe" Cannon, speaker of the House, opposed any financial legislation—even minor changes. Cannon and a few others in Congress wished to put off acting on financial matters for fear of aggravating the speculators' panic of mid-1903.[13] So long as he could not get agreement among the leaders of both branches of Congress, Roosevelt was willing to let the matter slide.

The existence of financial instability only increased the desire for action among big banking and other conservative circles. Orville Platt, Aldrich, and various Morgan men continued to press Roosevelt, but to no avail. "When we were there," Platt reported to Aldrich concerning a visit to the White House, "he seemed to fall in with our opinions, but when Shaw, Carlisle and Cullom ventilate their ideas, he is just as apt to side with them. He will mix and muddle this thing all up I fear." To please Aldrich, Roosevelt proposed a few minor changes in the banking structure to "give confidence to the business community," but at least Platt felt no real action would be forthcoming. Roosevelt, for his part, tried to placate the pro-legislation bankers by at least talking with them and paying deference to their views. He invited Morgan, E. H. Harriman, Henry Lee Higginson, and H. C. Fahnestock to discuss the financial situation, and since they could not agree among themselves on what changes were desired, Roosevelt used their divisions as an excuse to justify his own indifference and ignorance of the matter.[14]

A sufficient number of bankers wished action, however, for Roosevelt to consent to the enlargement of the central banking functions of the Treasury from late 1903 on. Bankers, including a few small ones, were disappointed by the lack of legislative action, but Secretary of the Treasury Shaw offered them a temporary solution that did not need the approval of the legislative branch and which offended no one. From late 1903 Treasury monies, and not merely current revenue, were placed in depository banks as needed, allowing the Treasury over the next few years to regulate the flow of money and place reserves in strategic cities—providing a small measure of long sought-after elasticity. Still, after 1903 Roosevelt and Aldrich ignored the issue of financial reform, and prosperity removed the pressure for action and made the topic comparatively esoteric for several years.

Conservative financial leaders in New York and Chicago were nevertheless completely aware of the possibilities for financial instability inherent in the diffusion of the banking system and the rigidity in the supply of money. Henry Clews, always ready to comment on the matter, urged federal regulation to create an elastic currency based on commercial assets and a wider variety of bonds. And decisively new alternatives for reform were presented for discussion, especially by New York and Chicago financial interests. Earlier plans for reform had concentrated primarily on elasticity, and bank cooperation was restricted to proposals for essentially cooperative clearing house associations backed by the federal government. By 1906, however, much more extensive proposals for banking control were put forth. In January, 1906, Jacob H. Schiff warned the New York Chamber of Commerce that unless the currency system were reformed the country would face the most serious financial crisis of its history. The warning immediately led to the formation of a special committee within the Chamber to propose legislation. In March, the committee, composed of John Claflin, Frank A. Vanderlip, Isidor Straus, and similar big banking and investment leaders, recommended the creation of a far-reaching central bank "similar to the Bank of Germany," with the power to regulate currency supplies. Although the report was not supported by the New York Chamber as a whole, it is indicative of the extent to which big bankers were ready to revamp the entire banking structure in the hope of centralizing it. The American Bankers Association, during mid-1906, also organized a commission of big bankers representing the major cities of the nation, chaired by A. Barton Hepburn. Its report, released in November, 1906, declared "that changes in the existing bank note system are imperatively required."[15] Although not endorsing a central bank, the committee urged the creation of regional clearing houses through which bond-secured currency could be issued by banks in varying amounts and guaranteed by a common fund built up by taxes on such notes.

Such plans obviously differed, although their purported ends were identical, and Roosevelt used such distinctions as an excuse for avoiding serious action on financial reform. In his Annual Message to Congress in December, 1906, Roosevelt decided at least to acknowledge publicly the need for greater elasticity in the banking system. Although he carefully avoided endorsing any specific plan, he referred to Secretary Shaw's modest proposal for permitting national banks to issue temporary notes up to a certain proportion of their capital. The President remained unwilling to move decisively.

The Panic
of 1907

Insofar as there were bankers who thought about the problems of banking, by 1907 virtually all of them wanted federal reform legislation. 1906 had been a year of considerable stringency for financing and loans, and in late 1906 the currency commission of the A.B.A. and the special currency committee of the New York Chamber of Commerce merged their plans and had the combined plan introduced in the House by Rep. Fowler. But since neither Aldrich or Roosevelt approved of it, no action was taken on the bill, despite the A.B.A.'s strenuous support. Roosevelt informed Fowler that "it is useless to expect and a waste of time to ask for radical legislation at this session," and instead recommended the passage of a few minor measures, including a very conservative asset currency.[16] Such a measure to increase the central banking functions of the Treasury was, in fact, passed in 1907 as the Aldrich Bill, but without any asset currency provisions.

If J. P. Morgan had been, as many historians have assumed, the controller of the American financial structure, he would not have sat by during the obvious approach of the panic of 1907. Nor would he have turned to the federal government for salvation. In mid-March, 1907, after it became apparent that the financial stringency of 1906 would continue and the New York Stock Exchange experienced a sharp decline in prices, Morgan visited Roosevelt to ask about general government aid in the crisis. Roosevelt, according to the financial press, reassured Morgan that he would act responsibly not only in reference to financial matters but also in general industrial and railroad affairs upon which the ultimate health of the financial community was based. Shortly thereafter the Treasury began depositing large amounts of customs receipts in various banks and reducing its normal withdrawals of government funds. But despite this earnest gesture the shortage of money in New York continued, and Morgan sat by and watched inexorable fate move in for a reckoning with the speculators and weaker freebooters.

Not a few businessmen tried to blame financial conditions on the negligible antitrust activities of the President and their purported influence on financial "confidence." Historians have made much of this alleged breach of communication between Roosevelt and the financial community. Roosevelt tried to deny any responsibility for existing conditions, and it is difficult to believe that the major bankers did not accept his denials. After all, Morgan certainly knew of the convenient détentes with his interests, the railroads were pleased with the initial impact of the recent Hepburn Act, and the antitrust laws meant very little to the general business and financial community, save for Standard Oil. More important, Roosevelt's Treasury policy was designed to merely provide greater interest-free financial resources to the bankers without in any way defining or limiting the way in which they could be used. Insofar as Roosevelt did not take steps to inhibit the growing speculative activities of the bankers, he does share responsibility for the panic of October, 1907—but in this respect he aligned himself with the financial community.

Most bankers, in any event, were strangely indifferent to threats of impending crises, even as commercial loans in New York and Chicago became virtually unavailable at any price. Meeting at Atlantic City in September, all but 150 of the 2,000 members of the American Bankers Association present ignored the session on financial reform, preferring the beaches to discussions of means of saving themselves. Roosevelt's new Secretary of the Treasury, George Cortelyou, brought in to replace Shaw after certain of Shaw's private business dealings threatened a scandal that never materialized, took matters into his own hands. Indeed, after the Treasury began depositing five million dollars a week in national banks from early September on, it was obvious that the government would assume primary responsibility in meeting the crisis.[17]

During the early weeks of October the Hamburg and Amsterdam banks underwent a crisis and forced gold to be shipped from the United States. A crisis on the Montreal Stock Exchange followed, and Wall Street was shaken to its foundations. On October 16 the stock of the United Copper Company collapsed and threatened to take three important New York banks with it. The New York Clearing House

Association rushed to their aid, but a run on the Knickerbocker Trust Company forced it into bankruptcy on October 22. Then came the most trying and chastening experience in the history of the banking community.

The panic of 1907 was an indication of the extent to which the ability to control crises had moved out of the hands of the New York bankers. If it were merely a question of raising $50 million in a healthy European financial market, as in 1895, Morgan would have been able to handle the task. But the American economy, and the scale of its needs, had grown tremendously, and it was as much affected by conditions outside New York as in the city itself. By 1907, Morgan, Stillman, and other key leaders of finance were old men, and the strain of the situation was more than they could bear financially or psychologically. Moreover, Morgan and others were not being called upon so much to save themselves as they were to rescue the improvidently run trust companies that had mushroomed as a part of the banking diffusion that had taken place since the turn of the century.

On October 23 the Trust Company of America and the Lincoln Trust Company began tottering, and their threatened collapse promised general financial depression and bankruptcy. The day before, however, Cortelyou rushed to New York and met with Morgan, Stillman, George Baker, Perkins, and other leading bankers. He agreed to deposit $25 million with the major New York banks immediately "for the relief of the community generally." The banks could loan the money, which was interest-free, to whomever they pleased, including stock brokers and speculators; the substantial added interest on the loans remained with the bankers. Over the next eight days the government loaned an additional $10 million for the relief of trust companies, and plunged a total of $37,697,000 into New York. At the same time, Morgan and his associates, in a series of around-the-clock sessions that exhausted the men, decided they would all suffer the consequences unless a financial pool was formed to support the weaker trust companies and the stock market. But even substantial pledges of private funds were insufficient, especially since none were used, and within a few days the New York Clearing House was forced to suspend currency payments on behalf of clearing house certificates. On October 28, after shipping out nearly $30 million of their reserves to country banks in the South and West, the Chicago Clearing House also suspended cash payment on behalf of certificates. Currency scrip was issued throughout the nation and five states closed their banks and declared a moratorium on financial obligations.[18]

In the midst of the crisis, with the federal government doing everything the New York bankers could ask of it, Morgan coolly picked up Tennessee Coal and Iron. During November, by Presidential order, the Treasury issued $150,000,000 in assorted certificates and bonds at low interest rates, and allowed banks to issue currency on the bonds as collateral. The creation of emergency currency in Chicago also helped, and although the reverberations of the panic led to a substantial industrial depression throughout most of 1908, the immediate crisis was overcome. But the big bankers were thoroughly chastened, and serious financial reform could no longer be delayed.

Smaller merchants as well as the New York bankers now realized the urgent need for reform. During November and December, 1907, numerous generalized resolutions calling for a more flexible currency arrived in Congress from various merchants and business groups. Roosevelt, in his Annual Message to Congress in December, again in vague terms invited Congress to make the currency more elastic, but it was evident that he was loath to become involved in the complicated problems of banking, much less to provide leadership in the matter.

There was no shortage of proposals to suit every political and banking faction. In early January, 1908, two bills were introduced in Congress. The Fowler Bill, a departure from Fowler's earlier, banker-drafted bill of 1906, eschewed any type of central bank, although it provided for a joint guaranty fund and concentrated heavily on allowing banks to issue notes for loans on commercial paper so long as their reserves were primarily in gold. Senator Aldrich also submitted a bill designed to allow the creation of emergency currency backed by state, municipal, and railroad bonds. The currency commission of the American Bankers Association, however, met in mid-January and condemned both the Fowler and Aldrich Bills, and presented its own measure, written by J. Laurence Laughlin and similar to the earlier Fowler Bill. Further, merchant and banking interests immediately opposed the Aldrich Bill, which was regarded as a conservative effort to shore up the value of railroad bonds. Various clearing houses, the New York Board of Trade, the Merchants' Association of New York, and other important banking and merchant groups attacked the Aldrich Bill, while organizations such as the N.A.M. called for currency secured by commercial assets without endorsing any specific bill. The Wall Street bankers were divided on both the Fowler and Aldrich measures and neutralized one another, although George F. Baker and Perkins supported the Aldrich Bill. The two most important leaders of Chicago banking, James B. Forgan and George M. Reynolds (also president of the A.B.A.), led the fight against both bills, and Forgan convinced Roosevelt to oppose the guaranty of bank deposits.[19]

Roosevelt probably enjoyed the spectacle of the big bankers fighting one another, and although he opposed the Fowler Bill as inflationary, he admitted "This financial business is very puzzling." Banker divisions provided him with a convenient excuse for inactivity. "The trouble is that the minute I try to get action," Roosevelt wrote Henry Lee Higginson, an opponent of the Aldrich Bill, "all the financiers and businessmen differ so that nobody can advise me . . . and only Senator Aldrich has prepared a bill."[20] Still, Roosevelt was really partial to Aldrich's measure.

With the banking community so deeply divided over its specific objectives it is not surprising that a vague compromise had to be arranged. George Perkins saw Aldrich in March and convinced him to remove railroad bonds as collateral for emergency currency, since this feature of his bill patently favored the large Eastern banks and was a major source of opposition. Morgan had suggested a simpler bill that was capable of being passed, and he and Perkins were hardly surprised or displeased when the Aldrich Bill was later sharply watered down by Congress. In late March the Aldrich Bill passed the Senate.

Hearings on the Aldrich Bill were held by the House Committee on Banking and Currency, of which Rep. Fowler was chairman, during April. With the exception of representatives of the Standard Oil and Morgan banks of New York, virtually every major banking and commercial group testified or let its views be known. Former president of the A.B.A. John Hamilton was nearly correct when he stated "the sentiment is universally against the Aldrich bill."[21] Among others, the Chicago, Minneapolis, Philadelphia, and even the New York clearing houses testified against the Aldrich Bill. Despite this overwhelming opposition, everyone wanted regulation of some sort to prevent the recurrence of a terrifying panic similar to that of 1907. The Aldrich, Fowler, and A.B.A. forces had effectively neutralized one another, and the result was a compromise bill presented by Rep. Edward B. Vreeland for the Republican caucus in the House, which became law in May. The Act allowed government bonds and commercial paper to be used as collateral for an emergency currency issued by cooperative national banks of ten or more meeting certain capital and surplus requirements, but since the various conditions were so involved that the Act was never utilized until 1914, the most significant aspect of the measure was the authorization of a joint Congressional National Monetary Commission to study the entire financial and banking system and deliver a report. Roosevelt was relieved, and notified Taft that the entire problem of banking, on which "I am not sure of my ground," would now rest with the Commission.[22] The solution to the problem of the banking and financial structure, even the banking community agreed after its prolonged internecine dispute, would have to be left with the politicians. But the bankers had brought the problem to the politicians' attention, and in the process of doing so they made banking reform an issue to be ultimately defined and solved on bankers' terms.

CHAPTER SEVEN

THE

ORDEAL OF

WILLIAM HOWARD TAFT,

1909-1911

The Legacy
of Reform

William Howard Taft inherited an ambiguous legacy from the Administration of Theodore Roosevelt. And, given the deeper ambiguities in the very nature of progressivism, as well as in the new President's own values, his leadership was to be marred by innumerable contradictions and seeming inconsistencies. Had his wife been less ambitious, the new President would have preferred a quiet, predictable chief justiceship on the Supreme Court. But at the beginning of 1909 Taft was still the anointed successor to Roosevelt, elected with the support of big business during the furious campaign against William Jennings Bryan, and as yet untried in the uncharted seas of national politics.

Taft, of course, had campaigned on the record of Roosevelt, and endorsed the record as he understood it. Roosevelt's legacy is clear to the modern historian, but it was less so to the contemporary observer as well as to Taft. Roosevelt was known as the "trustbuster" despite the fact that he busted very few trusts. Many disliked his tone, and confused his critical verbiage in regard to the Harrimans and Rockefellers with a genuine enthusiasm for reform. Roosevelt had embarked on a campaign to save business both from its own folly and from the dangers the unthinking masses posed in a formal political democracy potentially capable of really operating as a democracy. Despite the rhetoric of serving as the President for the entire nation, Roosevelt felt naturally comfortable only in the company of Knox, Lodge, Aldrich, Root and other members of the Eastern social and business elite. He considered himself, quite appropriately, a conservative trying to avoid revolutionary chaos by bringing the industrial structure under reasonable control. He repeatedly accepted the inevitability of corporate concentration as the basis for any measure of control. By a series of détentes and administrative decisions, and by ignoring the vague Sherman Act, Roosevelt was able to create a rather arbitrary political capitalism dependent more on his personal whims than on any formally rationalized system. In virtually every area in which he acted, however, he responded to initiatives shown by others in formulating basic proposals. His major legislative measures reflected the desires and pressures of specific interests, and his détentes with corporations were invariably the result of their initiatives.

Reform journalism during the Roosevelt era—which the President rather cruelly dubbed "muckraking"—offered Taft little guidance to compensate for the quite arbitrary nature of Roosevelt's actions. It is significant that out of the entire muckraking literature, which was in effect a refutation of the existing theories on the character of the capitalist economy and state as well as a partial description of the operational nature of American institutions, no serious social or economic theory was formulated. In part this was due to the puerile character of many of the muckrakers, and their obscuring of many of the realities of the day by ascribing opposition to government control where there actually was none. More than anyone else, they should have been aware that there is no necessary incompatibility between capitalism and the government, since the burden of much of their writings was the control of government, at least on a local and state level, by business. But all too many of the prominent muckrakers were journalists rather than thinkers, with commonplace talents and middle-class values, incapable of serious or radical critiques. A few, at least, were opportunists. Ray Stannard Baker was celebrating U.S. Steel in 1901 for its "republican form of government, not unlike that of the United States. . . ." By 1903 he was writing about the dangers of the union closed shop. Ida Tarbell eventually took up the cause of Elbert H. Gary. Even the more consistent of the muckrakers, such as David Graham Phillips and Charles Edward Russell, regarded Roosevelt as an innocent in the entire process of political treason or regarded the simple elimination of rebating as a crucial step toward ending the "trust problem." The muckrakers, for the most part, thought capitalism could be reformed by replacing evil men with good citizens, and in this respect they very much agreed with Roosevelt.[1]

Roosevelt frequently referred to "mob rule" as a danger, and to the need for the federal government to protect the honest businessman from the wrath of the masses. In voicing anxieties over the potential power of the masses to uproot the rights of business, Roosevelt merely expressed a common denominator among most patrician "reformers" during this era. Indeed, many of the major reformers and "enlightened businessmen" at the turn of the century were primarily concerned with avoiding radical attacks. ". . . all popular forms of government . . . [will] be attended by the growth and development of communistic ideas," Marshall M. Kirkman, a railroad executive, had warned in 1885. By separating business from the masses through the creation of commissions, however, "the result has been in a measure to prevent misunderstanding and allay irritation on the part of the people."[2] During the 1890's the Interstate Commerce Commission served as precisely such a bulwark against the attacks of state legislatures on railroads, and the I.C.C. experience suggested that the federal government had a potentially important buffer role to play in a political democracy.

Big businessmen feared democracy, especially on the local and state levels where the masses might truly exercise their will, and they successfully turned to the federal government for protection. This fear was articulated, often quite frankly.

In 1901, the *Bankers' Magazine,* a perfectly conservative journal, speculated on the future and desirable political development of the nation.

The growth of corporations and of combinations tends to strengthen the forces which seek to control the machinery of the government and the laws in behalf of special interests. . . .

Theoretically, the ballot controls everything; but the spirit of political organization which has grown up outside of legislative enactment now goes far to control the ballot. Industrial and commercial organization, when it desires to control the government, either Federal or State, finds a political organization ready for its uses. The productive forces are the purse-bearers. They furnish the means by which alone governments can be made effective. They also furnish the means by which the political organization which produces the government is created and becomes effective. The business man, whether alone or in combination with other business men, seeks to shape politics and government in a way conducive to his own prosperity. . . . More and more the legislatures and the executive powers of the Government are compelled to listen to the demands of organized business interests. That they are not entirely controlled by these interests is due to the fact that business organization has not reached full perfection. The recent consolidation of the iron and steel industries is an indication of the concentration of power that is possible. . . .

Every professional man as well as all who pursue every other mode of livelihood will be affiliated by the strongest ties to one or the other of the consolidated industries. Every legislator and every executive officer will belong to the same head. Forms of government may not be changed, but they will be employed under the direction of the real rulers. Of course it is easy to see that individual independence, as now understood, is different from what it would be under such a novel state of things, but no doubt it would still be individual independence. Probably under a government directed by a great combination of industrial and productive powers, the degree of individual independence which each citizen sacrifices for the good of the whole would be no greater and perhaps not so great as the independence which each citizen now sacrifices in obedience to existing law and custom. The direction of the industrial and producing forces would enlarge independence in some directions while it might restrict it in others. Wisely conducted, every citizen might, according to his merit and ability, attain higher prizes in life than is possible at the present time.[3]

Nor did the values reflected in the *Bankers' Magazine* represent an isolated phenomenon, even if these values were never expressed quite as systematically. Roosevelt's view of the dangerous, potentially irresponsible character of the masses, and the need to channelize them along controllable lines, was expressed by many others as well. ". . . the day has gone by," Charles S. Mellen of the New Haven Railroad told the Hartford Board of Trade in 1904, "when a corporation can be handled successfully in defiance of the public will, even though that will be unreasonable and wrong. A public must be led, but not driven, and I prefer to go with it and shape or modify, in a measure, its opinion, rather than be swept from my bearings with loss to my self and the interests in my charge." Reiterating the theme of an irrevocable tension between the masses and "good government," William Dudley Foulke, a leading civil service reformer in this period, indicated that popular government and parties were the source of spoils, and that the aim of civil service reform, which Roosevelt so notably advanced, was to mitigate this evil of democracy.[4]

Increased state regulation of railroads, state suits against major corporations, and state efforts to implement economic and social welfare laws of every type, only illustrated the value of comprehensive federal regulation that was more responsive to big business than the majority of individual states might be. The Hamiltonian conception of the role of the national government as predominant, which was so central to the New Nationalism of Roosevelt, was motivated by the same fear of state and local initiatives that could express the genuine desires of the masses. When the détente between the Bureau of Corporations and International Harvester was created, Elbert H. Gary was explicit in suggesting that one of the advantages of the arrangement was to prevent violent state attacks on Harvester such as were then taking place in the Midwest. Gary consistently feared the masses, and for this reason hoped for a general institutionalization of the détente system into a formal political capitalism. "I think one of the great disturbers and objections to the conditions and proceedings of this country," he remarked to a Senate inquiry in late 1911, "is the frequent elections." A possible solution, he suggested, was the election of an "absolutely independent" President for a term of eight years.[5] Albert Stickney, a Harvard-trained New York attorney, suggested a few years earlier that periodic elections resulted in business instability and lost time. The solution was to merge both houses of Congress, abolish term limitations for Congressmen and the President, and have elections only at times of vacancies or upon removal of the President by a two-thirds vote of the Congress. "Mass rule is mob rule," he frankly stated. Representative government, according to Willard A. Smith, editor of the *Railway Review,* led to the victory of "the loudest mouthed."[6] It could be saved only if the businessmen took over.

The discontent of the masses, Francis Lynde Stetson remarked in

1917, "is to be allayed not by a policy of stern and unbending tory-ism," but by flexibility.[7] His advice had been followed by the big businessmen in the National Civil Federation, Brandeis, and other progressive capitalists, who acknowledged, along with Roosevelt, the right of trade unions to be organized in genuine open shops. However different their functional actions, which were antiunion, the Garys, Perkinses, Carnegies, and pro-regulation capitalists knew that labor would demand a place in the sun as well. The choice, they well real-ized, was between a lackadaisical A.F. of L. that accepted the ideo-logical premises of the status quo and a radical industrial union movement led by a Eugene Debs or a William Haywood.

Taft the
Trustbuster

Taft entered office in 1909 with the legacy of Roosevelt's progres-sivism: its informality, its conservatism, its loosely defined precedents. The Republican platform of 1908 ostensibly committed him to the amendment of a basically wholesome Sherman Act in such a way as to allow greater federal "supervision and control over" interstate cor-porations. And the new President was undoubtedly still sensitive to Bryan's allegation that the Republican Party had an alliance with big business. Taft also entered office with a number of political debts.

Taft's first debt was to Theodore Roosevelt, the man almost wholly responsible for his political fame and fortune. On Roosevelt's advice, the new President decided to work with House Speaker Cannon—as Roosevelt had always done—and the regular Republican Party lead-ers. Roosevelt was pleased with Taft's major appointees, and Taft was solicitous of his every wish during 1909. Largely on the basis of Roosevelt's record, the Taft campaign received $150,000 from the House of Morgan during the close campaign of 1908, and the dona-tion was given with the anticipation that the détente system would be perpetuated by the new Administration. Perhaps more significantly, Perkins, Gary, and other Morgan aides had arranged for the projected railroad rate advance during the summer of 1908 to be postponed, realizing any increase could cost Taft votes. Immediately after his nomination, Taft assured Nelson Aldrich, the party's leading conservative, that he would rely on him for advice. Business expected just as fair a hearing from Taft as they had received from his predecessor, perhaps even a better one, and this expectation seemed about to be realized. Commenting to Morgan on a confidential outline of Taft's inaugural address, Perkins thought it "in all respects conciliatory and harmonizing in its tone."[8]

But despite these auguries for a continuation of Roosevelt's basic policies, Taft was literal minded, molded by politics, and ultimately an enigma. So far as antitrust affairs were concerned, he never followed any policy consistently, despite the fact that he was eventually to destroy the détente system and initiate many more antitrust suits than had Roosevelt. Historians have regarded Taft as a President with an uneven record. He favored the income tax, but only if it were supported by an amendment to the Constitution. In 1909, however, George Perkins supported the principle of an income tax, and even Aldrich and Root endorsed a corporation tax as an alternative to the income tax. The differences between Taft and the Midwestern Insurgents in the Senate and House were quantitative rather than qualitative and there was a striking similarity on railroad matters. Taft was to rely on Aldrich rather than on the Insurgents in the Senate, but in doing so he merely followed Roosevelt's precedent, and in antitrust matters he acted quite independently of Congress.[9]

There can be no doubt that Taft was not a great conservationist—but neither were Roosevelt nor Gifford Pinchot for that matter. Taft was politically inept and, for better or worse, his Cabinet members were of some consequence in shaping Taft's more critical viewpoint toward the House of Morgan. The Attorney General, George W. Wickersham, while similar to Bonaparte in his general views on trust matters, was much more influential than Bonaparte had been with Roosevelt. Herbert Knox Smith, still head of the Bureau of Corporations, was committed to the détente system, but his new superior, Secretary of Commerce Charles Nagel, extended more control over the bureau than had his predecessors. There was no one similar to James R. Garfield close to Taft, and the President, with his long judicial experience, was used to thinking in terms of formal laws rather than informal understandings.

Publicly, at least, Taft's views on the regulation of big business were not substantially different from those publicly expressed by Roosevelt. By the end of 1909 Taft was unwilling to press seriously for a revision of the Sherman Act, or, for that matter, for any new laws pertaining to corporations. He wished to wait for the Supreme Court's decisions on the American Tobacco and Standard Oil cases; and, more important, he was unwilling to grant those concessions to trade unions which he knew would have to be a part of any new law. Still, politics has its own imperatives, and Taft knew that he must recommend trust legislation to Congress in his Special Message on January 7, 1910. That he was not seriously interested in obtaining it is quite another matter.

Taft's Message tried to make "as emphatic as possible" a distinction between giant corporations that had attained great economy in production and those trusts, irrespective of their efficiency, designed to stifle competition. But wholesale investigations and prosecutions of giant corporations would "tend to disturb the confidence of the business community," injuring "the innocent many for the faults of the guilty few." Since it was impossible to enact an amendment to the Sherman Act that would allow the courts to distinguish between "good" and "bad" trusts in a rational manner, Taft instead asked for a federal incorporation law that would allow the national government to pass on corporate practices, proposed mergers, and capitalization. Such a law would apply only to those corporations ready to come voluntarily under its jurisdiction, and would not "prevent reasonable concentration of capital. . . ."[10] Taft had taken a stand, not unlike Roosevelt's, which was certainly popular with big business insofar as it stressed federal incorporation, but it also allowed him full freedom to engage in antitrust prosecutions.

George Wickersham's position on antitrust matters was virtually identical to Taft's—that is, it was capable of very broad interpretation. There was an "economic necessity" to many large combinations, but unnecessary economic centralization was to be avoided when possible. Wickersham hoped, in early 1911, that the Supreme Court, in its forthcoming decisions on the Tobacco and Standard Oil cases, would clarify the Sherman Act for businessmen once and for all. But when it failed to do so, he essentially continued to maintain Taft's view of January, 1910, concentrating on federal incorporation as a solution. Herbert Knox Smith, with greater emphasis on the need for federal incorporation, continued to maintain the same view—and received much sympathetic encouragement from Gary and Cyrus H. McCormick, the two major beneficiaries of his détentes.[11]

The crucial distinction between Taft and Roosevelt, however, is not an ideological one. Taft, unlike Roosevelt, believed that the Sherman Act still existed and had some value, and he did not appreciate the possibilities for accommodation offered by private détentes. Beginning in 1910, Wickersham was to initiate a large number of cases under the Sherman Act—for a total of sixty-five during the four years of the Taft Administration as opposed to a total of forty-four under Roosevelt. More important, Taft was to bring to a conclusion the few major cases initiated during Roosevelt's Administration. Despite this seeming activity, as we shall see, Taft never had a consistent, coherent attitude toward the antitrust question.

In the Standard Oil antitrust suit initiated under the Roosevelt Administration, a Circuit Court decision ordering the industrial titan to divest itself of its subsidiaries was handed down in November, 1909. The case was immediately appealed to the Supreme Court, and in May, 1911, the Supreme Court handed down an order for Standard Oil of New Jersey to divest itself of its holdings in thirty-seven other companies, the distribution of ownership in each company to be according to the distribution of stock in Standard of New Jersey at the time of the dissolution. Included in the legal opinion of the Court was the altogether mercurial "rule of reason" specifying that only "unreasonable" combinations in restraint of trade were illegal under the Sherman Act, thereby greatly complicating the meaning of the law to big business.

There is no indication that Wickersham participated in the formulation of the Standard dissolution plan, but the scheme was eminently designed to fail. An immediate byproduct of the decision was the sharp increase in the value of Standard stock. Standard of New Jersey was left as the second largest corporation in the United States and retained 43 per cent of the net value of the pre-dissolution stock. The component companies remained near monopolies in their respective territories and did not compete with one another. The competition that eventually returned to the industry was due to factors, discussed in Chapter Two, that had nothing to do with the Court's decision. Over the next fifteen years the Standard empire was largely reintegrated.

Despite the eventual harmlessness of much of Taft's antitrust activities, he still managed to alienate considerable big business elements by his efforts. From the beginning of 1910, after Taft lost Insurgent support because of his alliance with the Eastern conservatives on the

Payne-Aldrich Tariff, the Mann-Elkins Bill, and similar measures, segments of big business began turning on Taft because of his rather literal dedication to antitrust activities. Herbert Knox Smith and his Bureau of Corporations were left hanging in limbo as Wickersham ignored him in his trust prosecutions. And since the House of Morgan had the most to lose from such changes, throughout 1910 the tension between the Morgan interests and Taft increased. In June, 1910, when Wickersham slapped an injunction on major railroad freight increases, George Perkins began fearing the worst from the once obliging Taft. After receiving a critical attack from his old friend, Francis Lynde Stetson, Wickersham rather plaintively wrote him that "Surely we may differ on economic questions without abating in any degree a friendship of many years. . . ." In July, 1910, after Wickersham ordered a grand jury inquiry into the National Packing Company—later dissolved in 1912—lawyers for the joint firm of Swift, Armour, and Morris desperately tried to arrange an out-of-court settlement with the adamant President and Attorney General.[12]

From mid-1910 on a key factor in shaping Taft's antitrust policy was Roosevelt's increasing hostility toward his protegé. Throughout 1910 the tension between the two men increased as Taft split the Republican Party apart on reform issues while playing the role of the erstwhile radical in the very area that Roosevelt believed in conservatism. In the early months of 1911 the political relations between the two men again became friendly, even cordial, notwithstanding the open opposition to Taft from Midwest Insurgents and a growing number of businessmen.[13]

The President was never able to establish that crucial rapport with all too many potential business friends. Some who had tolerated or rationalized his actions in 1910 were basically unhappy. Businessmen pleaded with Taft to restore business confidence by withholding further antitrust actions and having the Department of Justice pass on the legality of proposed business transactions; Wickersham and Taft merely tried their best to reassure businessmen that the Sherman Act was, in fact, explicit and that business really knew what the law was.

Taft and Wickersham, in mid-1911, took steps to halt the growing business disenchantment with the Administration. The American Tobacco antitrust suit had been in the courts since 1907, and in May, 1911, the Supreme Court ordered the Circuit Court, in conjunction with the Department of Justice, to work out a dissolution plan satisfactory to all concerned. The Circuit Court called in the attorneys for the Tobacco Company and for the government and asked them to submit a mutually acceptable plan. Wickersham failed to formulate a detailed proposal, and rejected out of hand a receivership scheme advanced by one of his key attorneys, James C. McReynolds. McReynolds, an ardent believer in laissez faire who was later to attain fame as a conservative member of Wilson's Cabinet and then in the Supreme Court, quit in a huff after Taft told Wickersham "I would not hesitate to run right over him."[14] American Tobacco's attorneys then proceeded to submit a plan very much like the one proposed by Thomas Fortune Ryan to Elihu Root in early 1907. The proposal was immediately challenged in public hearings by tobacco dealers, tobacco growers, and the attorneys general for a number of the Southern states. Perplexed, and aware of the fact that the Bureau of Corporations was preparing a study of the tobacco industry, Wickersham called in the bureau's leading expert, Dr. A. C. Muhse, for his opinion of the dissolution proposal. Muhse was very frank: the American Tobacco plan was merely a scheme to preserve monopolistic conditions in the industry. Three giant firms would remain, each with a monopoly in its type of product and two of them loaded with the old debt of American Tobacco, while the original company was to receive a very high return on its investment. "The proposed method of distribution . . . ," Muhse warned, "leaves very much to be desired if truly competitive conditions are to be reestablished."

Muhse's insights, however, merely confirmed the value of the Tobacco plan in the minds of Wickersham and Luther Conant, Jr. of the Bureau of Corporations, and Conant freely admitted that American Tobacco would soon control the industry once more. Amidst the protests of tobacco growers and dealers, Wickersham informed Taft he would "accept the principles and most of the details of the plan suggested by the tobacco company." The protests were dismissed by Wickersham with the assertion that he "relied on the report of Dr. Muhse as corroborating the statements made by the Tobacco Company."[15] Even if Wickersham was not deceiving the President, it is certain that he tried to deceive the public. The following month, after the plan was accepted by the Circuit Court, Wickersham announced that the Tobacco monopoly had been destroyed by breaking it up into fourteen competitive units. Muhse's predictions were immediately realized, as the three giants created by the dissolution increased their share of the cigarette market from 80 per cent as one firm in 1909 to 91 per cent in 1913.

U.S. Steel and
Roosevelt

While Wickersham was fishing in troubled water, damaging the reputation of the Taft Administration among trustbusters and trust-builders alike, the Democrats in the House initiated an investigation of U.S. Steel that was to mesh with other events to bring the nascent split between Taft and Roosevelt to a head. Taft was no more responsible for the inquiry that began in May, 1911, than was Roosevelt for an earlier Senate inquiry during the first months of 1909. But the new investigation by the Stanley Committee was to involve Roosevelt in one of his politically tender spots, the acquisition of Tennessee Coal and Iron by U.S. Steel.

Although there were vicissitudes in the relationship between Taft and Roosevelt during 1910 and the first nine months of 1911, it was apparent to many of Taft's allies that a conflict was inevitable. As early as September, 1910, Louis Howland, an Indianapolis newspaper man, had suggested that Roosevelt's reputation as an erstwhile reformer would be especially susceptible on the questions of Tennessee Coal and Iron and campaign donations, should Taft find it necessary to fight. Wickersham was relayed the message by Taft's secretary—it is not certain the President knew of it—but the Attorney General realized that such discussions would "be an open declaration of war" on Roosevelt.[16]

The House inquiry posed a simple bureaucratic problem and a larger question as to what was to remain of the détente with U.S. Steel. The Bureau of Corporations, after all, had been collecting data on United States Steel for years, and Smith was concerned about the problem of winning credit for any investigation of U.S. Steel for his bureau. Its first report, finally issued July 1, 1911, was a useful collection of fairly accessible data on the decline in the market position of the giant—a report hardly designed to offend U.S. Steel's officers. Irritated, the Stanley Committee entered the report in its records as an "exhibit" rather than as "evidence."

In July Herbert Knox Smith was brought in front of the Stanley Committee and asked to produce all the material on U.S. Steel in his possession—undoubtedly a deliberate Democratic effort to embarrass the President. Smith demurred on the grounds that the data had been given voluntarily and might aid U.S. Steel's competitors, and that only the President was able to release it. The tension between the Congressmen and Smith was poorly concealed. Smith's policy was simply to respect the confidence U.S. Steel had placed in him, and in this he had the support of Secretary of Commerce Nagel. One of his chief aides, William H. Baldwin, was unceremoniously fired by Smith when he complained that not enough data were being released. In August, it was agreed by Nagel, with Taft's apparent approval, that information received in confidence would not be given to the Stanley Committee. At the same time, Taft wrote Roosevelt that he should refuse to appear before the committee—advice he ignored.

By the end of August Wickersham thought it time to begin responding more aggressively to the political attacks of Roosevelt's friends in the Republican Party. After all, Roosevelt could have been thrown to the wolves so far as his progressive reputation was concerned, especially after defending his whole course of action in the Tennessee affair—and Taft was protecting him.

The temptation was too much, especially in light of the fact that U.S. Steel continued to drag its feet on the seemingly interminable bureau investigation. Since he was aware of the implications in October, 1910, there is little doubt that Wickersham knew he was declaring political war against Roosevelt when he initiated an antitrust suit against U.S. Steel one year later on October 26. That the Tennessee acquisition was a key point in the complaint made it certain that the suit was really against Roosevelt. Roosevelt, quite predictably, accepted the challenge and broke off relations with Taft. It marked the end of a long friendship. But Roosevelt's public defense, which followed several weeks later in *The Outlook,* was not merely a defense of the détente system with U.S. Steel, but of its acquisition of Tennessee Coal and Iron as well.[17] To the bitter end, despite the obvious political liabilities of his position, Roosevelt was unable to challenge the personal integrity or motives of his Morgan friends.

On October 27, Luther Conant of the Bureau of Corporations

was ushered into Judge Gary's office and told that U.S. Steel would furnish no more information to the bureau, save on advice of counsel. The bureau decided not to utilize its power of subpoena. During November, and with Taft's support, members of the Attorney General's office requested all information on U.S. Steel in the possession of the bureau. The Steel people hurried to Secretary Nagel and were able to prevent the release of the data until January, 1912, when a mutually satisfactory plan for the release of the data was agreed upon. A second bureau report on U.S. Steel was then rushed into print on January 22, 1912.

Smith was now left in an untenable position as head of the bureau, especially since the bureau's traditional functions were now unacceptable to his nominal superiors. In July, 1912, Smith resigned, ostensibly on the grounds of disagreement with the general Taft antitrust policy, and joined the Progressive Party. Taft, hoping to avoid unfavorable publicity, urged Nagel to allow the matter to pass quietly. By using data collected by the bureau, and exploiting the appeal that the company had acted "on the apparent approval of the Government and the public," U.S. Steel was, ironically, later deemed innocent under the antitrust law.[18]

Business and
Regulation

By 1912 the antitrust policy of the Taft Administration was in a shambles, in large part due to the desire of the Administration to defend itself against Roosevelt's partisans. Taft's position on the nature of the modern corporation, and even on remedial legislation, was decidedly Rooseveltian. But his wild and inconsistent antitrust cases had upset the corporate climate. Under Roosevelt it had been possible to attain a significant measure of stability, at least for the Morgan interests, without legislation. Taft, however, vividly illustrated the need for a more formal, predictable, and permanent basis for the relationship of the large corporation to the national government.

As it became evident that Taft would pursue antitrust activities far more seriously than was desired, businessmen turned to the discussion of legislative alternatives. Indeed, the President himself pointed to some of these alternatives. He had explicitly endorsed federal incorporation in early 1910, and Wickersham and Herbert Knox Smith had repeatedly referred to it as a solution to the "trust problem."

In addition to federal incorporation or licensing, however, more far-reaching proposals were to be made by important businessmen. The problem of the inequitable distribution of wealth, Andrew Carnegie announced in 1908, could be solved by the rich regarding their money "to be administered as a sacred trust for the good of others. . . ." So far as the price competition plaguing the steel industry was concerned, however, "it always comes back to me that Government control, and that alone, will properly solve the problem," ostensibly also solving the problem of "monopolistic industrial conditions." "There is nothing alarming in this; capital is perfectly safe in the gas company, although it is under court control. So will all capital be, although under Government control. . . . What is reasonable and proper will be for the court to determine." "There is nothing so absolutely impossible as uncertainty," George Perkins freely confessed in 1909 in reference to state regulation.[19]

Shortly after his January, 1910, speech endorsing federal incorporation, Taft asked Wickersham to prepare an implementing bill for Congress, where it was duly introduced in February as the Clark-Parker Bill. Seth Low and Perkins indicated their support for such a bill, but the matter was dropped by the Administration. The issue remained dormant until the end of 1910, when rumors began circulating around New York financial circles that Stetson had prepared a federal incorporation law at Morgan's request to be submitted to Taft—and that Taft was disinterested. Stetson denied the rumor, but Taft's simple renewal, in his second Message to Congress, of his earlier request for such a law certainly indicated that the President was not interested in obtaining it. "The Federal incorporation idea was generally approved by leading corporate and financial interests as a means of affording relief from oppressive State legislation and nullifying the obnoxious features of the Sherman anti-trust law," the New York *Financial America* announced.[20] Such supervision, Perkins told business audiences during late 1910 and early 1911, would tell stockholders and the public that business is honestly and fairly managed. "But federal regulation is feasible, and if we unite and work for it now we may be able to secure it; whereas, if we continue in our fight against it much longer, the incoming tide may sweep the question along to either government ownership or socialism." A "Business Court" in Washington, made up of businessmen and for the purpose of adjusting business problems, Perkins was suggesting in January, 1911, would give industry the freedom to act.[21]

Despite the growing businessmen's hatred of Taft's antitrust actions, on questions of policy they were largely in agreement. The President favored federal incorporation, as did Nagel and Wickersham, as a possible solution to the entire antitrust problem. The real block, so far as the attainment of legislation was concerned, was in the House. The House Democrats, especially, were entirely without alternatives to the business demand for federal incorporation or licensing. In June, 1911, appearing before the Stanley Committee, Judge Elbert H. Gary announced to the astonished members that "I believe we must come to enforced publicity and governmental control . . . even as to prices, and, so far as I am concerned . . . I would be very glad if we knew exactly where we stand, if we could be freed from danger, trouble, and criticism by the public, and if we had some place where we could go, to a responsible governmental authority, and say to them, 'Here are our facts and figures. . . . now you tell us what we have the right to do and what prices we have the right to charge.' " The reason Gary and Carnegie were offering the powers of price control to the federal government was not known to the Congressmen, who were quite unaware of the existing price anarchy in steel. The proposals of Gary and Carnegie, the Democratic majority on the committee reported, were really "semisocialistic," and hardly worth endorsing.[22]

Until late October, 1911, and the initiation of the suit against U.S. Steel, the outward unanimity between the Taft Administration and big business on federal regulation continued. Wickersham was still convinced of the "economic necessity" of big business, and despite growing business anxieties and insecurity over antitrust prosecution, letters of support for Taft's legislative proposals continued to arrive from important businessmen. Perkins, however, was already thinking beyond mere federal incorporation laws, as was the most consistent advocate of federal incorporation since 1905, Francis G. Newlands, Democratic Senator from Nevada. At the beginning of 1911 Perkins was proposing a federal business court or commission to pass on the legality of business action, proposed and actual. During the spring of 1911 Senator Newlands mulled over a similar idea, consulted with businessmen and Herbert Knox Smith about the matter, and obtained Perkins' support. In July a bill to create an Interstate Trade Commission was submitted to the Senate, and hearings that were to drag on until March, 1912, were begun in August. Newlands' bill was quite simple. The Bureau of Corporations was to be turned into a commission, and all interstate corporations with receipts in excess of five million dollars were to furnish organizational and financial data to the commission upon passage of the Act, and upon request thereafter. The bill was admittedly tentative, and Newlands indicated willingness to remove all serious penalty provisions from the bill. His major purpose, he frankly confessed, was to permit an official body to give its seal of approval to a corporation in order that public opinion might be placated and the market value of its shares maintained.[23] Although Herbert Knox Smith supported the basic publicity function of the proposal, the rather vague bill never became a serious political issue. Its real importance, other than significantly publicizing the commission concept as a solution to the antitrust issue for the first time, was in the forum it gave to businessmen in the course of its long hearings.

During the final two months of 1911, in conjunction with the Newlands hearings and the U.S. Steel suit, the big business-supported systematic legislative program emerged in coherent form. The first indication came from Roosevelt himself, who in his attack on the suit against U.S. Steel called for the formation of a national commission with "complete power over the organization and capitalization of all business concerns engaged in inter-State commerce," and possibly prices as well.[24] The proposal immediately won an enthusiastic response from Wall Street, and strongly raised Roosevelt's political stock. In late November Perkins visited Taft and presented him with a set of proposals, urging him to make the antitrust question his first order of business. The Sherman Act, Morgan's friend urged, should be revised to make guilt individual rather than corporate, with a greater stress on imprisonment than fines. A "court or commission" made up of businessmen, he further proposed, should be created under the Bureau of Corporations to gather voluntary information on corporate procedures and to approve certain corporate actions. Publicity and official endorsement of plans would be the keynote, with increasingly stringent rules being added with the passage of time.

And, Perkins stressed, until a Congressional investigation of the entire trust matter could be undertaken, prosecutions "of a nature disturbing to business" should be suspended.[25]

Several days after Perkins' audience with Taft, Gary appeared before the Newlands Committee with an even more elaborate plan. Big business, he reiterated, was inevitable and desirable.

The only regulation adequate in scope and power to deal with these aggregations of capital is regulation by the Federal Government, because the subject matter of the regulation is largely interstate commerce with which the states may not interfere, and the size and extent of the organizations involved is such as to require uniform and national regulation.

Every interstate corporation, he urged, should obtain a federal license if it met strict publicity, capitalization, and price requirements. A corporation commission similar to the Interstate Commerce Commission would be created to grant, suspend, and revoke licenses, subject to court appeal. It also could decide on the legality of matters submitted to it by businessmen and, in line with Carnegie's proposal, it could regulate prices. Such a system would prevent the evils of socialism, eliminate uncertainty, and give government "protection not only to the man who wishes to increase his business lines but to continue in business. . . ." Trade association agreements and prices, Gary suggested, should be enforced by a commission if the prices were fair.[26]

Seth Low, perhaps anticipating the legislative possibilities of Newlands' commission idea, early in November sent out a questionnaire to thirty thousand businessmen. He asked them, on the assumption that "the concentration of capital [is] essential to the full and efficient development of modern business," to comment on the desirability of a federal incorporation law, a federal licensing law, and a trade commission "with powers not unlike those now enjoyed by the Interstate Commerce Commission." Armed with the preliminary returns, Low appeared before the Newlands hearings at the end of November and announced that American business favored an incorporation law by a majority of nearly four to one, a licensing law by nearly two to one, and a commission by nearly three to one.[27] Thus strengthened, the president of the National Civic Federation took his predictable New Nationalist view of desirable government action, aligning himself with Gary, Perkins, and Carnegie.

In mid-December Perkins appeared before the committee and repeated the plan he had presented to Taft. He was followed by Henry B. Joy, the auto manufacturer, who favored a commission with price fixing powers. With the exception of Victor Morawetz, who favored a commission with powers to approve contracts and combinations but not to fix prices or grant charters or licenses, an impressive array of important business witnesses indicated that Low's statistics on business sentiment were very probably correct.

Ironically, Taft and Wickersham's position was not unlike that of Perkins. After all, Taft had told Wickersham that to injure those who own the capital of the nation, no matter how guilty they were of evil-doing, was to inflict an injury on the entire country as well. By November Wickersham was convinced of the necessity of a trade commission as an essential solution to the entire antitrust issue, although he was not explicit as to what its precise powers should be. Pressure on Taft to clarify his stand on the Sherman Act was exerted by business, and in his 1911 Annual Message to Congress he discussed the matter in greater detail than ever before. His basic premise was that the Sherman Act should be amended rather than repealed. And although he had paid little attention to the four federal incorporation bills presented in Congress during 1911-1912, Taft renewed his advocacy of such a voluntary measure. Taft recommended clarification of the law so that it would describe specific violations in detail, and he also proposed a federal corporation commission to which businessmen could submit proposed schemes and which might aid the courts with dissolution plans.[28] The differences between Taft and Wall Street were hardly discernible.

Although politics was to intrude into the discussion of the antitrust issue throughout 1912, the legislative desires of most important businessmen were constant irrespective of political conflicts. The Newlands Committee, after hearing the representatives of big business, heard representatives of the coal industry plead for revisions in the Sherman Act that would allow price and output agreements to end cutthroat competition, and drug store association representatives call for fair trade laws to defend themselves against the chains. The coal request was also tied to the creation of a commission to supervise such agreements. Carnegie, appearing before the Stanley Committee in January, 1912, reiterated his belief in a federal commission with the power to fix maximum prices, and throughout the previous month had vainly tried to swing Perkins to his view on prices. The publication of the National Civic Federation's complete survey in early 1912, with its sixteen thousand replies, certainly vindicated Low's earlier testimony before the Newlands hearings, although businessmen were reluctant to grant a trade commission price-fixing powers also. Pressure to revise the Sherman Act to eliminate the vague definitions introduced by the *Standard Oil* decision and the insecurity created by Taft's actions was universal among businessmen, whether they were eventually to side with Taft, Wilson, or Roosevelt in the political struggles of 1912. Perkins, in the meantime, kept encouraging the preparation of acceptable bills to implement his goals. Senator Albert B. Cummins, erstwhile Insurgent, submitted a preliminary trade commission bill to the Senate in February, 1912, and during March he and Perkins discussed the possibility of another bill.[29]

In proposing the federal regulation of business, advocates of the new Hamiltonianism were quite aware of the advantages such regulation would have in shielding them from a hostile public, as well as in introducing stability and control in economic affairs. "The leading companies should be, and I believe they are, prepared to accept the appointment of trade commissions both in the States and in the Federal Union," Francis Lynde Stetson announced in May, 1912. "No better buffer could be devised for absorption or avoidance of the shocks between the corporations and an impatient or critical public." There was "a world-wide movement of general dissatisfaction and of social unrest," Joseph T. Talbert, vice-president of the National City Bank of New York, told a group of his associates in the spring of 1912. "It would seem, therefore, to be the duty of all who influence public opinion, and have the power to lead and mould it, to seek not so much to check the movement as to direct its course in such manner that the blindly instinctive impulses of human nature may not destroy the economical organizations of capital. . . ." The trade commission idea appealed to Talbert, just as federal incorporation was thought by others interested in the preservation of capitalism to be the best solution to public hostility. A federal commission composed of businessmen of "broad experience," J. K. Gwynn of American Tobacco suggested, would not only protect business from a critical public, but it could bring some order to the industrial fabric to replace the "deceptive mirage" of unrestricted competition—unrestricted competition that was being rapidly displaced by "rational co-operation."[30]

Pressure to increase federal regulation came from many sources. Big business wished to have federal incorporation or a commission, or both, to escape from burdensome state regulation, to stabilize conditions within an industry, such as steel, where they had failed by voluntary means, to create a buffer against a hostile public and opportunistic politicians, and to secure those conditions of stability and predictability so vital to a rationalized capitalist economy. Small business, such as drug and other retailers, coal producers, and the like, sought the right to create and enforce price and output agreements— to end the burden of competition. Several efforts to create a politically stabilized capitalism deserve a more detailed consideration.

The telephone industry was highly competitive during the greater part of the Progressive Era, and highly unstable. The independents utilized, wherever possible, local political contacts as leverage in their fight against American Telephone and Telegraph. Seeing the struggle as primarily a political one, A.T. & T. responded with an intense public relations program and by relying on the federal government for whatever aid it could obtain. At the same time, it engaged in an active merger and expansion policy.

State telephone regulation existed in ten states by 1909, but seventeen more were added during 1909-1911, and another fifteen during 1912-1917. Moreover, many city regulations existed. During 1909, A.T. & T., seeing the trend, embarked on an active public relations program. Public hostility, E. K. Hall, vice-president of A.T. & T., declared in 1909, is

not only a serious danger to the property of the business but it is in my judgment the only serious danger confronting the company, because the natural tendency of such hostility, founded as it is on misunderstanding, prejudice, and distrust is, under slight incentive, to crystallize at any time into adverse legislation. . . .[31]

The I.C.C. experience showed that federal regulation could serve as an extremely valuable buffer between the public and industry, and A.T. & T. was pleased when the Mann-Elkins Act of 1910 placed telephones under I.C.C. jurisdiction. Rate wars were to become a thing of the past. On the other hand, the independent phone companies also favored the telephone provision of the Mann-Elkins Act.

Theodore N. Vail, president of A.T. & T., freely admitted in 1911 that the company had very little difficulty with state regulatory bodies and that any problems that did arise could be taken care of in the courts. One problem that was not easily worked out, however, was A.T. & T.'s acquisition of Western Union in 1909 and of many other companies as well. Wickersham, in January, 1913, made an arrangement with A.T. & T. for it to divest itself of Western Union, to give up its aggressive merger policy, and to connect with other independent companies for toll service. The company's merger policy, while moderately successful, nevertheless had failed to give A.T. & T. genuine control of the industry. Moreover, a number of cities expressed support for government ownership of telephones. In early 1913 at least twelve important city councils, including Cleveland, Los Angeles, Minneapolis, and San Francisco, endorsed the principle. A.T. & T. realized that its long-term objectives of political stability and economic rationality could be attained only by federal regulation, and its commitment to the cause was intensified. It preferred a commission with permanent members which would thus be free from the influence of politics, and it was explicit in admitting that, in a democracy, flexibility was necessary to prevent social upheavals. In 1914 Vail announced:

We believe in and were the first to advocate state or government control and regulation of public utilities. . . . that this control or regulation should be by permanent quasi-judicial bodies, acting after thorough investigation and governed by the equities of each case; and that this control or regulation beyond requiring the greatest efficiency and economy, should not interfere with management or operation. . . . in order that waste and duplication of effort may be avoided and uniformity of purpose and common control be enforced . . . there should be a centralized general administration in close communication with and having general authority over the whole on matters common to all or matters of general policy.[82]

Another important development that was ultimately to influence the fruition of a political capitalism was the growth and articulation of the trade association movement, centered primarily around Arthur J. Eddy, a Chicago lawyer who had worked for Standard Oil at various times. Eddy specialized in creating trade associations in competitive industries—associations that included the division of markets and price fixing. The technique was an old one, and probably illegal under the *Addyston* decision, but from 1911 on Eddy created associations among bridge builders, cotton fabric finishers, and others, stimulating a trend that in the 1920's resulted in many hundreds of such amalgams. In late 1911 Wickersham's office considered the problem, but failed to act on it.

As the Newlands hearings showed, even when opposed to big business or trusts the average small businessman wished to mitigate the effects of competition by what were essentially price, market, or output agreements—the basis of the trade association movement. He was, for all practical purposes, through with laissez faire, its costs, risks, and possible gains. Even such nominal devotees of the doctrine as Brandeis favored fair trade laws. For all practical purposes, both big and small business wanted modification of the Sherman Act in some substantial form.

Eddy realized that his trade association activities were of questionable legality, and in 1912 he published *The New Competition,* a book frankly committed to the proposition that competition was inhuman and war, and that war was hell. The Sherman Act encouraged competition, which inevitably led to consolidation and the destruction of small business. If trusts and unions were permitted, he argued in a terse, pointed style directed toward businessmen, so should price and output-fixing trade associations. His solution was explicit: repeal the Sherman Act and pass a federal licensing law. He urged creating a federal commission to adjust business controversies, demand complete accounting, and administer the newly legalized trade association movement. Trade associations would be given all bids and contracts, and it would be the responsibility of the federal commission to enforce price and market agreements. The commission would also have the power to fix prices. Eddy's program, vague as to precise size of the "small business" he was trying to save, nevertheless was to have an important impact on business and subsequent discussions of revisions of the antitrust law.[33]

The Banking
Reform Movement

The panic of 1907 exposed the basic weaknesses in the nation's banking structure, and no one was more aware of the fact than the bankers. But the bankers had shown themselves to be hopelessly divided on legislative matters and incapable of agreeing on any plan to stabilize interest rates and price levels and to reduce fluctuations —to introduce the much vaunted and poorly defined elasticity necessary for a national, profitable banking system.

Despite these divisions, the banking community—or at least that small portion of it that thought about such matters—was more seriously aware of the need for banking reform than ever before. Only through reform, Henry Clews declared, could the responsible, conservative bankers and businessmen be protected from the follies of the irresponsible few. But the alternatives were diverse, very diverse, and given the hostility of the House, the disunity among bankers tended to nullify their larger desire for banking reform. Although the majority of bankers favored some type of centralization of decision-making and greater elasticity of currency, their differences on the type of backing for a more elastic currency, or the form and control of the centralization, seemed insurmountable.[34] The Republican platform of 1908, reflecting the split in the banking community, merely endorsed banking reform in the broadest and vaguest terms. Taft, like Roosevelt, was bound to very little.

Nelson Aldrich still remained the key figure in politics concerned with banking reform. His close relationship with Taft on other issues was a crucial asset, but his reputation among Insurgents and Democrats was that of a blackguard conservative, and it seemed unlikely that Aldrich alone could have any measure passed. Moreover, Aldrich had strong feelings on banking reform that were not, according to such sympathetic associates as Paul Warburg, based on even a technically sound knowledge of banking principles. Aldrich's deficiencies were more than compensated for, however, by the many able and sophisticated individuals around him, and after he took his National Monetary Commission to Europe to study banking systems there, Aldrich quickly educated himself in the field. More important, Aldrich was soon to realize that his prominent association with the banking reform cause was a political liability, and he was anxious to play a somewhat less conspicuous role, at least so far as the public's view of the movement was concerned. Aldrich's associates, aware of the entire issue of public relations, also reiterated the need to avoid associating banking reform with Wall Street, even though Wall Street was the heart of the movement, if legislation was ever to be attained.

Aldrich's European tour convinced him of the virtues of central banking and the desirability of a broader-based asset currency utilizing sound commercial paper as well as gold, bonds, and other extremely restricted reserves. This change made it possible for Aldrich, whose 1907 and 1908 schemes had been roundly opposed by the American Bankers Association, to appeal to a much wider audience in the banking community. Indeed, Aldrich ceased being a sectarian on banking reform and was able from 1909 on, especially after a tour of Western banking centers that year, to count on greater sympathy for his views. For the better part of 1909 and 1910, however, the topic of banking reform was restricted primarily to a small segment of the banking community. Aldrich himself was increasingly occupied with other legislative matters, especially the tariff, and the return of prosperity after 1908 relaxed the pressure for change. Bankers, in the meantime, began searching for unifying plans that could solidify the banking community behind a single proposal. The compromise plans were not hard to predict, and by the end of 1909 they were all to emerge at about the same time. There were certain inevitable ingredients. Regional banking centers were implicit in the clearing house movement that the A.B.A. had endorsed in 1906. Central banking of the German and English type was widely appreciated, and every banking reformer realized that to be successful any central banking plan would have to avoid the appearance of being dominated by Wall Street, and they generally understood the need to use sound commercial notes to create an elastic currency.

Although Victor Morawetz, the Morgan lawyer and railroad executive, is generally credited as the author of regional banking schemes, the idea was already widely considered as an alternative when Morawetz delivered his famous speech on the topic in November, 1909. That very month, Maurice L. Muhleman, a New York attorney, had proposed a very detailed plan for regional banking centers in the *Banking Law Journal.* And a few weeks later, in a letter in the *New York Evening Post,* Theodore Gilman, a New York banker, outlined a system of regional clearing house associations, ultimately responsible to the Comptroller of Currency. Morawetz' plan assumed that a true central bank along English or German lines was impossible and inappropriate for the United States but that sectional banking districts under the ultimate direction of one central control board might be just as effective. Since political intervention in banking and currency had, in the final analysis, always been safe, it made little difference to Morawetz whether control of such a plan was entirely in the hands of the government or entirely private. That the bankers would support such a scheme was, quite coincidentally, verified when the *Banking Law Journal* in December, 1909, announced that its extensive poll among bankers showed that 59 per cent supported a central bank free from "Wall Street or any Monopolistic Interest." ". . . one cannot help feeling very confident," Paul Warburg wrote Nelson Aldrich.[35]

Taft was no more decisive than Roosevelt on the issue of banking reform during 1909 and 1910. Despite occasional pressure on him to act, he had no concrete proposals before him and personally understood very little about banking problems. Throughout most of 1910 the issue was a dormant one, even within the banking community, and only Paul Warburg persisted in presenting a comprehensive plan of reform. Rehashing his central bank-clearing house proposal of 1907 several times, in November, 1910, he announced his "United Reserve Bank Plan" to the Academy of Political Science in New York, with Aldrich present in the audience. The proposal would create twenty regional banking associations under a central bank board in Washington elected, save for one-fifth of the directors appointed by the government, by the regional banking associations and the shareholders of the central bank's $100 million capital. The central board would fix discount rates and define procedures for the regions, issuing circulating notes on commercial paper which it purchased from the regions.

Shortly after hearing his plan, Aldrich called upon Warburg to participate with Frank A. Vanderlip of National City Bank, Henry P. Davison of the House of Morgan, and Charles Norton of the First National Bank in a week-long secret conference on his estate on isolated Jekyl Island, Georgia. Aldrich was now ready to devote his major attention to banking reform, and the representatives of the most important Wall Street houses were to help him draft a bill. The confidential nature of the session was demanded if the bankers were to do their work without attaching obvious political liabilities to the final product. The plan which emerged from the conference was very much like Warburg's in principle, and Warburg claimed authorship for it even though Vanderlip actually drafted the final plan. A National Reserve Association would be created in Washington to preside over fifteen major regions. The regional banking centers, controlled by private banks, would elect the forty-five board members in Washington, but not more than four could come from any region—thereby eliminating the possibility of Wall Street control. The National Reserve Association could issue notes against bonds and commercial paper transferred to its vaults by member banks, and member banks could draw on the resources of the central bank by rediscounting commercial paper. The scheme seemed democratic enough, avoided Wall Street control, and was highly elastic. All that was necessary was to make it politically attractive.

Aldrich and his associates were fully conscious of their liabilities, not merely in the eyes of the public but with other bankers as well. President Taft, on the other hand, seemed to be most amenable to the new Aldrich Plan. Indeed, Taft had relied more on Aldrich for advice on banking and monetary affairs than on any other individual. But the President's seeming support for the Aldrich Plan was ultimately based on his opportunistic desire to utilize Aldrich for purposes other than banking reform. But on January 29, 1911, in any event, Taft wrote Aldrich: "I believe you have reached a most admirable plan and I want to assure you of my earnest desire to aid in every way you and your colleagues of the monetary commission in the movement to embody the plan in our statutes."[36] Yet Taft added, significantly, that he thought the plan would never pass a Democratic House, and that it might take several years to educate even the bankers to accept it. Taft continued to throw accolades at the plan, but was never willing to act on it, and by the end of 1911 he was trying to stop bankers from using bank funds to lobby for it.

Thinking the President was firmly with them, the architects of the Aldrich Plan turned their efforts to winning important banker and business support for it. A special monetary conference of all business organizations, convened by the National Board of Trade in January, 1911, passed a resolution, written by Warburg, endorsing the Aldrich Plan. At the beginning of February twenty-two key bankers from twelve cities met in Atlantic City to consider the Aldrich Plan. Sessions were closed, and all the conference publicly declared at the end of three days' discussion was that it endorsed the plan and would actively support it. In fact, the confidential minutes of the meeting—carefully edited by Aldrich to eliminate embarrassing passages showing his total control of the conference—reveal the innermost feelings of the nation's big bankers. James B. Forgan, the leading Chicago banker, made it explicit that everyone present accepted the Aldrich Plan in advance and that only "some little matters of detail" could be discussed. Indeed, the plan was endorsed at the outset. The real purpose of the conference was to discuss winning the banking community over to government control directed by the bankers for their own ends. It was made clear by the chairman of the meeting, Congressman E. B. Vreeland, that if legislation were not passed soon, the radicals would eventually try to do so. The participants were fully aware of the menace of the growing state banking movement, and referred to it many times. Although they agreed with Paul Warburg's statement that "it would be a blessing to get these small banks out of the way and have the branches" for national banks, it was realized that this would lead to terrific opposition from smaller banks.[37] It was generally appreciated that the plan would increase the power of the big national banks to compete with the rapidly growing state banks, help bring the state banks under control, and strengthen the position of the national banks in foreign banking activities. Concretely, the group discussed the problems of converting other businessmen and bankers to the plan, with special interest in the possibility of exploiting the recent Board of Trade conference on the Aldrich Plan.

The Aldrich Plan emerged as a broad approach rather than as a precise bill capable of immediate implementation. Indeed, it was understood that many details would have to be worked out or adjusted to bring as many diverse banking and business interests as possible behind the plan. In the meantime, it was generally conceded by the plan's architects that the important task was to create a powerful political backing for the plan—and then try to have it passed. It was especially crucial to remove the stigma of its having been originated by Wall Street interests and Nelson Aldrich. During the spring of 1911 the backers of the plan moved to create the National Citizens' League for the Promotion of a Sound Banking System to accomplish the task. Warburg and the other New York bankers behind the Aldrich Plan arranged to have the league centered in Chicago, presumably as an outgrowth of the National Board of Trade conference in January. New York was assigned the largest financial burden—$300,000—but George M. Reynolds and Forgan of Chicago were assigned primary organizational responsibility.

To administer the league the bankers turned to Professor J. Laurence Laughlin of the University of Chicago. Laughlin, nominally very orthodox in his commitment to laissez faire theory, was nevertheless a leading academic advocate of banking regulation. He had drafted the Indianapolis Plan of 1897, and was sensitive to the needs of banking as well as the realities of politics. Thoroughly conservative, Laughlin was no sycophant, no mere tool of the bankers behind the league. Created in April by the Chicago Association of Commerce, nominally acting on behalf of the National Board of Trade, the league's leadership and board was Chicago based, composed of businessmen, and was dependent on New York mainly for money. Its stated purpose was "to carry on an active campaign for monetary reform on the general principles of the Aldrich Plan without endorsing every detail of the National Reserve Association." Its principles included "Cooperation, with dominant centralization, of all banks by an evolution out of our clearing-house experience," financial liquidity based on commercial assets, uniform discounts to all banks, and, naturally, opposition to the domination of the banking system by any interest or area.[38]

So long as the Aldrich Plan remained a framework of discussion, as it did throughout 1911, most reform-minded bankers endorsed its rough outlines. Initially, at least, the proposal had seemingly unanimous support from the interested banking community. During May, 1911, the American Bankers Association approved its currency committee's strong amendments to the Aldrich Plan, sharply broadening the type of notes eligible to be rediscounted. Despite the initial unanimity of the major bankers, the united front of bankers began falling apart on many important particulars. An immediate problem was Theodore Roosevelt's passive opposition to the Aldrich Plan, which meant that all of the bankers' hopes depended on Taft. Even more serious was a nascent split within the National Citizens' League that grew wider by late summer, 1911. Laughlin was a political realist—as were many of the bankers interested in banking reform—and he was well aware that the association of a banking reform bill with the name of Aldrich would mean the kiss of death. He was entirely committed to the basic principles of the Aldrich Plan, but his commitment was to the principle and not the man. He had been warned by his former student and long-time aide, H. Parker Willis, that Aldrich was the worst possible leader of the movement, and Laughlin apparently agreed. Indeed, later Laughlin was even to suggest that the league never supported the Aldrich Plan at any time, but only "sound banking principles." (Warburg also made the same claim many years later, but the reality of his position during mid-1911 belies this claim.)

Warburg and the New York bankers had erred in allowing the Chicago reformer elements and Laughlin to run the league. The league printed vast quantities of literature for businessmen, especially in the South and West, where opposition was likely to be the strongest, but hesitated to tie itself entirely to the Aldrich Plan. Moreover, Laughlin's noncommitment to the plan had the support of the Chicago-based board of directors, and his conviction that this was the politically astute policy was strengthened by a personal survey of the political situation in the Democratic House in June, 1911. Before long there were two leagues in actual operation: the New York office under Irving T. Bush, pursuing its slavishly pro-Aldrich program, and Laughlin's. During July a critical exchange of letters between Warburg and Laughlin took place, and the latter freely admitted he felt Aldrich's name could kill a bill politically. Warburg stopped the flow of funds to Chicago, and the newspapers were soon reporting rumors of the division within the league. In New York on August 28 to try to patch up the now-public split, Laughlin was extremely conciliatory. He agreed that the league would not present its own bill, and that it would confer with the National Monetary Commission to make the bill the best possible. In the meantime, however, the league was to maintain its nonpartisan, educational role, thus increasing the impact of its endorsement of the final commission bill when it was formulated. In the same month Laughlin managed to convince Roosevelt not to take a stand on the banking issue, in which the former President had not the slightest interest. Despite these successes, and the very extensive educational work on businessmen and newspapers done by the league, the New York bankers ultimately failed to fulfill their financial obligations to the Chicago organization, and gave less than one-third of their quota. The league remained formally united, if not united on tactics, simply because Laughlin appreciated its usefulness in his work, which was to remain pragmatic and opportunistic, and to eventually reflect the sentiment of the large majority of bankers.[39]

The Aldrich Plan scored some successes in late 1911. In spite of the opposition of Edmund D. Hulbert, the important Chicago banker, and James J. Hill, the plan picked up significant banking and business support, in large part due to the effort of the league and to many speeches by the plan's supporters. In November the Aldrich Plan forces seemingly were able to obtain their biggest coup—the endorsement of the American Bankers Association—when Aldrich agreed to modify the plan to allow the board of the National Reserve Association, rather than the President of the United States, to remove the head of the Association. This triumph was the undoing of the entire Aldrich Plan movement.

On December 21, President Taft's Message to Congress included references to banking reform, which he endorsed in principle. Starting out by saying he was looking forward to the final bill of Aldrich's National Monetary Commission, and by praising the general outlines of the Aldrich Plan, he ended by throwing a damper on the core of the plan—private banker control. "But there must be some form of Government supervision and ultimate control, and I favor a reasonable representation of the Government in the management."[40] In effect, the President had rejected the basic premises of the Aldrich Plan. At the same time, Roosevelt was at best neutral toward it, and the Democrats were still an unknown quantity, though likely to be highly critical.

In January, 1912, the Aldrich Plan was submitted to Congress as the Aldrich Bill. It received very little publicity and never came to a vote. With Aldrich committed to retire, and a Democratic victory in November seemingly inevitable, banking reform appeared to be a dead issue.

CHAPTER EIGHT

THE

POLITICS

OF 1912

WILLIAM HOWARD TAFT had tried his best—and he had failed. He had blundered tactlessly into innumerable political traps, and he was grossly misunderstood by his contemporaries. He had inherited an ambiguous legacy from Roosevelt, but in the final analysis that legacy was reasonably conservative, and Taft was a conservative also. One cannot help admiring Taft's bumbling dedication to those noble conservative virtues, Reason and Moderation. Unfortunately for him, the period was one interested in action and change, however conservative in its ultimate intent, and Taft was simply out of step with his times.

The politics of 1912 were an outgrowth of the collapse of the détente system under Taft and the failure of his Administration to establish the political conditions necessary for economic stability. Taft's suit against U.S. Steel has already been discussed. Prior to the initiation of that suit in October, 1911, Taft had shown disturbing signs of disloyalty to the détente structure his predecessor had created. During June, 1911, Wickersham began considering antitrust action against

International Harvester, and in early July Perkins urged Smith to speed the Bureau of Corporations' inquiry into International Harvester, in the hope of forestalling action by Wickersham and vindicating the corporation. Several weeks later Perkins and Wickersham met, and the Attorney General claimed to be ignorant of the fact that the Bureau of Corporations already had an investigation under way. Prosecution was a possibility, he admitted, but he promised to look at the bureau's material. Perkins, for his part, offered to "meet [Wickersham] half way in an effort to do it by agreement rather than through a suit." The matter rested there until the outbreak of political war between Taft and Roosevelt. In November, 1911, Wickersham decided that progress with the Harvester people had been exceedingly small, and after fruitless negotiations with Harvester attorneys, in December Wickersham obtained a large amount of data on Harvester, with company approval, from the Bureau of Corporations.[1]

The International Harvester case was essentially politically motivated: it was directed against Roosevelt and his ties with the House of Morgan. After several conferences with Harvester's lawyers, on April 24, 1912, Wickersham filed a suit against the corporation. On the very same day, however, he sent a collection of documents on Roosevelt's détente with Harvester to the Senate, exposing to the public the entire collaboration between Roosevelt, the Bureau of Corporations, and the House of Morgan. Roosevelt was enraged, as were the International Harvester officials who for years had urged the Bureau of Corporations to release a report that would presumably spare them from such abuse. Roosevelt immediately charged Taft with having been at the Cabinet meeting at which the decision to postpone the prosecution of Harvester was made, and Taft promptly denied having been present. The charge became a major issue in the campaign of 1912, with Roosevelt suffering the worst damage in the fray. The Bureau of Corporations, however, later restored its confidential relationship with the Harvester people, promising not to release new information to the Department of Justice, and it even allowed Harvester to "offer corrections to possible inadvertent errors" before the publication of the bureau's report.[2] The bureau report, finally released on March 3, 1913, was actually quite critical of the price policies of International Harvester.

Taft's antitrust prosecutions, or intimation of them, motivated more by political considerations than by ideological commitments, were to cost the Republican Party dearly. By the end of 1911 Taft had not only managed to alienate the Midwestern Insurgents, but many of the party's key business supporters as well. The stage was set for decisive political change.

A Party
Is Formed

There is no question that Perkins would have preferred remaining with the Republican Party in 1912. In late 1910 he told Morgan that it seemed quite logical that Taft would be the party's choice in 1912, and at the time the prospect did not seem to disturb him. Although Taft's position on antitrust matters, and especially the détente system, was totally unacceptable to Perkins, he liked Taft's stated position in favor of banking reform, and endorsed Taft's stand against Gifford Pinchot's advocacy of government ownership of the hotly contested Alaska coal lands. During late 1910, when the La Follette forces in the Republican Party began organizing for the convention of 1912, Perkins was more concerned with the growth of the Socialist vote and the "rapidly approaching . . . crisis in this country ˙on the question of the relation between capital and labor and business and the State. . . ."[3] The National Progressive Republican League was formed in January, 1911, and Perkins had nothing to do with it.

The situation at the beginning of 1912 was entirely different. The rank and file of the Republican Party, a Chicago politician could report, were solidly for Roosevelt, who was not-too-coyly seeking the nomination as the reluctant candidate. More important, "I think that fully 90 per cent of the members of the [Chicago] Union League Club favor Roosevelt."[4] Roosevelt's article in *The Outlook* in November, 1911, sharply improved his standing in Wall Street, but despite his large and important backing, to win the nomination was a much more difficult proposition. As Roosevelt well knew from his own manipulation of the 1904 convention, the man who controls patronage can also control the delegates. But the vast rank and file sentiment for Roosevelt within the Republican Party was no myth, and the irritated, emotional outburst of La Follette in a speech to the nation's publishers in early February—Roosevelt supporters immediately described it as a nervous breakdown—eliminated the last major obstacle to a straight fight between Taft and Roosevelt for the Republican nomination.

The story of Roosevelt's political struggle for the nomination in 1912 has been reported in detail elsewhere—best of all by George E. Mowry in his *Theodore Roosevelt and the Progressive Movement*— and only a few key events need be reported here. What are more important, for our purposes, are the motives and ideology of the movement's key leaders. Although Roosevelt lost the support of Lodge and other regular Republicans by his endorsement of the recall of state judicial decisions in an otherwise strongly pro-big business speech in Columbus on February 21, powerful big business support came to Roosevelt's aid at the beginning of 1912. Perkins formally joined the Roosevelt cause in January, and was soon followed by Frank A. Munsey. Munsey was a rags-to-riches Maine farmboy who had invested a substantial part of his newspaper fortune in U.S. Steel, International Harvester, and other Morgan enterprises. He strongly admired Roosevelt as a personality, and having been alienated by Taft's antitrust policy, he wished to return to Roosevelt's policy on big business. He had not the slightest interest in reform for the masses, but was to be of great assistance in Roosevelt's campaign. Important aid also came from Dan Hanna, the son of Mark Hanna, and from Walter F. Brown of Ohio. Only the previous April, Brown and Hanna had been indicted by the government for taking rebates on ore shipments. Although the case was settled out of court, they were irate with Taft, and during January, 1912, Taft considered using the case to mete out justice for Hanna and Brown's treachery.[5] Supporters such as Hanna, Perkins, and Munsey made it possible for the Roosevelt forces to spend over $600,000 before the Republican convention in June. In addition, Roosevelt had the backing of many former aides as well as leading reformers. James R. Garfield, Medill McCormick, Gifford and Amos Pinchot, Albert Beveridge, William D. Foulke, and many others could be found with Roosevelt.

Although Roosevelt took the advice of Munsey and Lucius Littauer as well, Perkins soon became his most important adviser. In March, 1912, Perkins revealed his latest thoughts in the *Saturday Evening Post* on what was still his major preoccupation, "Business and Government." Attacking Taft's antitrust policies, Perkins praised the federal control of banks and railroads, and reiterated his belief in a federal commission of businessmen that could pass on business actions and plans. Perkins' ideas on the topic, in short, were the same as they had been over the prior two years. During March Perkins confidentially admitted he thought Roosevelt would not win the nomination because of Taft's control of the Republican political machinery. ". . . Mr. Roosevelt's candidacy I look upon as only an incident of a great development," and essentially as educational. And although Perkins managed to support other phases of Roosevelt's reform proposals, his primary, if not sole, concern was the issue of federal regulation.[6]

As Roosevelt began winning impressive victories in the fight for the various state delegations to the convention, especially in the West and North, Perkins realized it was quite possible that Roosevelt might win the nomination, and that it was likely that it could at least be kept from Taft. But Perkins, until the bitter end, was primarily committed to winning the public to his views, and not to the victory of any particular man. It was inevitable that the Taft forces exploit his connection with Morgan and try to link his support of Roosevelt to the antitrust prosecutions of U.S. Steel and International Harvester. The charge was made repeatedly, and rather than improve the cause of Roosevelt, Perkins refused either to resign or play a less conspicuous part in the Roosevelt movement. Perkins publicly tried to break the image of himself as a Morgan tool by suggesting that the nature of the Standard Oil and American Tobacco dissolutions had made Taft the most popular man on Wall Street, which "is laughing in its sleeve at what has been going on."[7] But these well publicized statements by Perkins, in addition to being incorrect, were beside the point—and the picture of Roosevelt the great reformer being sustained by Perkins was to cause incalculable damage to Roosevelt's cause.

When the Republican convention convened in Chicago during mid-June, Roosevelt had the support of many of the Republican machines, and a large majority of the votes cast in the direct primaries. The Republican National Committee had given virtually all of the contested delegates seats to Taft several weeks earlier, and the convention opened in a bitter atmosphere of mutual charges of deceit and bribery by the Taft and Roosevelt forces. When the convention voted to accept the National Committee's recommendation, thereby legitimizing itself, the Taft forces were firmly in control. Behind the scenes efforts to nominate a compromise candidate failed. On the night of June 20, crowded into a hotel suite, several dozen of Roosevelt's key advisers, including Perkins and Munsey, discussed the possibility of forming a new party. The decision was not merely a political one—it was primarily financial. Campaigns were expensive, and Roosevelt knew it. Munsey and Perkins were asked to consider whether they were willing to assure a Roosevelt campaign adequate financial support. While Munsey and Perkins immediately discussed the matter among themselves, Roosevelt and his political associates waited about the suite.

Perkins was not a man given to emotional or rash decisions. His initial strategy had been to utilize Roosevelt's candidacy for the Republican nomination as a means of creating pressure for the proper relationship between business and government. Even during his most sanguine moments Perkins thought merely that Taft could be stopped and someone more suitable—not necessarily Roosevelt—could win the nomination. Now that a proposal to split the party had been made, Perkins must have been even more pessimistic as to Roosevelt's chances—and his subsequent actions certainly indicate that Perkins was more devoted to creating conditions for the attainment of his legislative goals and principles than to the victory of Roosevelt. When, early in the morning of June 21, Perkins and Munsey walked over to Roosevelt and told him, "Colonel, we will see you through," the two capitalists were acting with utter realism. As Amos Pinchot, who watched the whole affair, put it: "Though we did not realize it, the Progressive party came into being, a house divided against itself and already heavily mortgaged. . . ."[8] The creation of the new party was announced, and its nominating convention called for early August, again in Chicago.

The Progressive Party meeting in Chicago in early August was less a convention than a revival. It was a foregone conclusion that Roosevelt was to be the party's candidate; the real issue was the principles upon which the party was to stand. The leaders of the new party, as Alfred D. Chandler, Jr., has shown, were not likely to be excessively radical, and all too many have confused their enthusiasm in early August with their politics. A good two-thirds were businessmen of consequence and lawyers, and hardly any farmers or workers could be found in important positions in the party. Professionals and editors composed the remainder, and the top echelons of the Progressives, on the whole, were urban, upper middle-class Anglo-Saxon Protestant refugees from the Republican Party. Some, such as the California Progressives, were bitterly antilabor.[9] The large bulk were psychologically committed to clean, efficient government compatible with their class interests. Their reform sentiments were flexible within the larger bounds of capitalism, and their feelings—and I stress the term "feelings"—lacked precision on any given topic save the personality of Roosevelt.

Given this plasticity, the ensuing events at the Progressive convention were quite logical. On August 5 Senator Albert J. Beveridge opened the convention with a speech that was unambiguous in its attack on "invisible government" in the two old parties. Beveridge had long taken a New Nationalist position on the inevitability of trusts and on the need to distinguish "good"' trusts from "evil" ones. "What we call big business is the child of the economic progress of mankind," he told the delegates. "So warfare to destroy big business is foolish because it cannot succeed and wicked because it ought not to succeed." Although he incidentally called for woman suffrage and child labor laws, as well as the revision of the tariff in some unspecified direction, the main burden of Beveridge's wildly received oration was the folly of Taft's antitrust policy. Referring to the fact that other nations encouraged their business, in soaring phrases Beveridge held out the golden image of the Progressive future:

And then we mean to send the message forth to hundreds of thousands of brilliant minds and brave hearts engaged in honest business, that they are not criminals but honorable men in their work to make good business in this Republic. Sure of victory, we even now say, "Go forward, American business men, and feed full the fires beneath American furnaces; and give employment to every American laborer who asks for work. Go forward, American business men, and capture the markets of the world for American trade; and know that on the wings of your commerce you carry liberty throughout the world and to every inhabitant thereof."[10]

Roosevelt was greeted by a thunderous crowd the following day, and in his "Confession of Faith" to the convention he opened by telling the fifteen thousand wildly cheering faithful: "Our fight is a fundamental fight against both of the old corrupt party machines, for both are under the dominion of the plunder league of the professional politicians who are controlled and sustained by the great beneficiaries of privilege and reaction." His tone was indeed radical, as he scorched his former political associates with his fiery invective, announcing "The first essential in the Progressive programme is the right of the people to rule." This should include direct Presidential primaries and direct election of Senators, as well as initiative, referendum, and recall, so long as it was not used "wantonly or frequently. . . . indiscriminately and promiscuously," which "would undoubtedly cause disaster." Such measures, he added, should be enacted where "government has in actual fact become non-representative." Roosevelt's welfare proposals were hardly more specific. He favored creating minimal occupational standards for workers, standards to be determined by independent experts—*a la* scientific management—rather than by the workers themselves. Minimum wage standards, he urged, should be determined by local commissions, but he hesitated to call for a minimum wage law for men. Workman's compensation laws that were "fair" were endorsed by Roosevelt, as well as a maximum hour law for women and a child labor law, but he failed to mention any age. Having established his Progressive credentials, however vague they were on specifics, Roosevelt then turned to the main and most extensive topic of his speech, "business and the control of the trusts."

The aim of Progressives, Roosevelt began, was to allow all decent men to prosper, "and we heartily approve the prosperity, no matter how great, of any man, if it comes as an incident to rendering service to the community. . . ." The wage worker and the consumer had a vital interest in business prosperity, which was the source of all welfare. Criticizing the Sherman Act and Taft's antitrust policies, he urged a revision of the law to recognize that "if we are to compete with other nations in the markets of the world as well as to develop our own material civilization at home, we must utilize those forms of industrial organization that are indispensable to the highest industrial productivity and efficiency." The Sherman Act, Roosevelt declared, ought to be revised to allow for a "national industrial commission" similar to the I.C.C. Such a commission could prevent overcapitalization, and would be able to tell businesses in advance what they could legally do if they voluntarily came under its jurisdiction. Again and again he reiterated the value of big business in foreign trade, and the need for honesty and fair profits.

Adding appropriately vague support for greater elasticity in the currency and for conservation, Roosevelt concluded by notifying the roaring audience that "We stand at Armageddon, and we battle for the Lord." "And while splendidly progressive it is," Munsey wrote to Roosevelt, "at the same time, amply conservative and sound."[11]

The next crucial event of the convention—the nomination was by this time merely an occasion for more enthusiasm—was the writing of the platform. The resolutions committee included Amos Pinchot, who was one of the few real radicals in the party, Charles McCarthy of Wisconsin, and others. As they completed their drafts on various issues, they sent them up to a room where Roosevelt, Munsey, Perkins, and a few others were gathered to edit them. When they reached the section on the Sherman Act, they drafted a statement beginning "We favor strengthening the Sherman law. . . ," and spelling out a few applicable areas. The statement was duly sent upstairs, and Perkins protested. Roosevelt concurred with him, and the plank was revised. The next day, however, as the chairman of the convention was reading the platform draft to a bored convention, the original Pinchot-McCarthy resolution was read. Perkins, who was seated next to Pinchot on the stage, immediately leaped to his feet and excitedly told Pinchot, "Lewis has made a mistake. That doesn't belong in the platform. We cut it out last night."[12] A conference with Roosevelt was immediately called, the statement was eliminated, and the press was duly notified. Perkins had won the day.

The basic problem for the Republican and Progressive parties was how to appear radical while really remaining conservative. The Republicans stood on Taft's record in matters of income and corporate taxation, postal savings, railroad reform, and other issues. The Republican platform called for banking reform without endorsing the Aldrich Bill, while the Progressives favored reform in vague terms, attacking the Aldrich Bill in the same manner that Taft had generally laid out in his 1911 Message. In a completely equivocal manner, the Progressive platform condemned the Payne-Aldrich Tariff and proposed an investigating commission instead, without the slightest indication whether the Progressives favored higher or lower tariffs. The Progressives favored ratification of the income tax amendment, as did Taft, but were unique in favoring woman suffrage. Direct primaries and direct election of Senators were endorsed by the Progressives, along with initiative, referendum, and recall—enacted by the states, not the federal government. The Progressives also endorsed a spate of very generally worded welfare reforms: prohibition of child labor, minimum safety and health standards for occupations, minimum wages for working women, the eight-hour day for women and youth, and one day's rest in seven for all workers.

But the longest section of the Progressive platform was devoted to "Business" and "Commercial Development," and it is here that the new party was to focus its attention. "We therefore demand," the platform declared, "a strong national regulation of interstate corporations. The corporation is an essential part of modern business. The concentration of modern business, in some degree, is both inevitable and necessary for national and international business efficiency." A federal commission similar to the I.C.C. was demanded to enforce active supervision and maintain complete publicity, to attack "unfair competition" and "false capitalization."

Thus the businessman will have certain knowledge of the law, and will be able to conduct his business easily in conformity therewith; the investor will find security for his capital; dividends will be rendered more certain. . . . Under such a system of constructive regulation, legitimate business, freed from confusion, uncertainty and fruitless litigation, will develop normally. . . .

Citing Germany as an ideal example for emulation, the Progressives suggested "that their policy of co-operation between Government and business has in comparatively few years made them a leading competitor for the commerce of the world. It should be remembered that they are doing this on a national scale and with large units of business. . . ." "The time has come when the federal government should co-operate with manufacturers and producers," the Progressives declared, ignoring Taft's economic imperialism, "in extending our foreign commerce."

The Republican plank on "monopoly and privilege" was virtually identical to the Progressive trust plank. They too endorsed an amendment to the Sherman Act to define offenses in greater detail, giving greater certainty to business. To help administer it, a "Federal trade commission" to "promote promptness" was also favored. Despite the substantial difference on welfare measures, the two parties were remarkably similar in their major proposals.

Indeed, Taft was well aware that the significant difference between the Republican and Progressive parties was not their platforms, and he shrewdly chose to emphasize the big business support for the Progressives. In this game, Perkins cooperated quite fully by concentrating on those issues which, in effect, vindicated Taft—but which were also the major reasons for Perkins' and Munsey's support for the new movement. Taft was sincerely convinced, at least from

the beginning of 1912 on, that Roosevelt had sold out to U.S. Steel
and the House of Morgan. ". . . letting the people rule when reduced
to its lowest terms, it seems, is letting the Steel Trust rule," Taft
commented on Roosevelt in April.[13] Taft also had important business
friends, but the House of Morgan was definitely *persona non grata* in
Washington in 1912. The Harvester suit, in all likelihood, was a consequence of this alienation.

Perkins' activities were not merely embarrassing for the House of
Morgan, but unsuccessful as well. Although Perkins had resigned as a
partner in the firm in December, 1910, he was still on the boards of
many of its major interests. In addition, J. P. Morgan, Jr., heir-
apparent to the firm, disliked Perkins and was jealous of his father's
dependence on him. Now, in retaliation for Perkins' political activities, the Morgan companies were being attacked by Taft. When
Perkins assumed the position of chairman of the executive committee of the new party, Morgan, Jr. moved to eliminate the thorn
in his side. On August 13 Morgan, Jr. suggested Perkins resign from
the board of U.S. Steel in order to give the corporation a nonpartisan
reputation. Several days later, after Perkins refused, Morgan, Jr.
bluntly wrote Perkins that the public associated his actions with Steel,
and that the company could not afford to get "identified with current
politics." Morgan again suggested that Perkins resign, and in this
request he claimed the support of Gary, Frick, and others. But
Morgan, Jr. apparently did not have the backing of his father—indeed, it is probable the elder Morgan knew nothing about the matter
—and it is unlikely that Gary was critical of Perkins' new role. Amos
Pinchot, who later regarded the Progressive Party as little more than
the tool of the Morgan interests, suggests that Gary secretly donated
to the party, and although he had only his intimate contact with
Perkins, Roosevelt and the party rather than concrete data as proof,
it is still unlikely that Gary would have been hostile to the new venture. Perkins' response to young Morgan's challenge was significant.

Were I, in this work, advocating anything that if put through would be
to the disadvantage of the Corporation, then I of course should leave
its board; but as much that I am advocating would be decidedly to every
corporation's advantage in a perfectly proper way, I can see no harm and
much possible good in what I am doing.[14]

Perkins stood his ground and remained with U.S. Steel, mainly because J. P. Morgan, Jr. had no real support for his position. The significant fact is not that an effort was made to fire Perkins for his politics, but that once having been tried it failed.

Having remained in both the Progressive Party and U.S. Steel to further policies to "every corporation's advantage," Perkins made the most of it. The trust issue, and Perkins himself, became the focus of the party's campaign. Western party leaders were irate, then indignant, when the only campaign literature they received explained the party's trust position, defended the Morgan companies, and explained away the growing attacks on Perkins as the political representative of Wall Street. Obtaining control of the New York office of the party, Perkins issued a weekly, *The Progressive Bulletin,* for national distribution, featuring the trust issue primarily. Amos Pinchot's much more radical and tediously long pamphlet on *What's the Matter With America* received comparatively small circulation. But as Pinchot was later to find out, it was really he who was out of tune with the Progressive song in 1912.

Munsey, in the meantime, controlled the new party's Washington office, which was located in the Munsey Building. Since Munsey's newspapers were among the very few supporting Roosevelt, he too shaped the party's functional program. Because the party lacked a paper in New York, Munsey purchased the *New York Press* for the occasion. Taft had betrayed the traditional economic policies of the GOP, Munsey announced in the *Press* in mid-September, and he freely admitted he supported Roosevelt "chiefly because I wanted to see the economic policies of the Republican party continued in force. . . ." "Of all the big progressives," Munsey announced in the introduction to a campaign pamphlet he distributed, "Roosevelt is to-day preeminently the biggest and sanest conservative—a progressive conservative."[15]

Taft failed to obtain any significant business support for his 1912 campaign, and so the obvious susceptibility of the Progressives because of Munsey and Perkins was doubly inviting. In April the Senate formed a new Subcommittee on Privileges and Elections under Republican Senator Moses E. Clapp, and in October the committee decided to investigate pre-convention campaign donations, those of Perkins and Munsey in particular. In order to assure maximum impact, Taft provided guidance and evidence behind the scenes, and he had advance knowledge of the major lines of questioning the committee would take. Of special interest to the President was the connection between International Harvester, Gary, Perkins, and the Progressive Party.

Taft unfortunately found Perkins and the Progressives less than obliging, for the issue of big business contributions in the 1904 and 1908 Republican campaigns was also interjected, much to the embarrassment of the President. The House of Morgan had given $150,000 to the Taft campaign in 1908, and if that was good enough for Taft in 1908, why was it wrong for Perkins and Munsey to donate to Roosevelt in 1912? Still, it was revealed that Dan Hanna had donated $177,000 toward Roosevelt's pre-convention expenses, Perkins had given $123,000, Munsey had contributed $118,000, and so forth. The Taft forces had accused International Harvester of having donated a major part of at least two million dollars contributed to the Roosevelt campaign, and Perkins demanded proof. The President overextended his case, and Perkins exploited the fact. Indeed, Perkins claimed, Cyrus McCormick favored Wilson, Harold McCormick opposed Roosevelt, and none of the McCormicks had donated to Roosevelt's pre-convention campaign. It is indeed true that the McCormicks did not donate to Roosevelt's pre-convention campaign, but Taft was correct in insisting that many of the family supported the new party; Perkins knew it, and kept the information confidential. The party's financial records for 1912 list C. K. McCormick, Mr. and Mrs. Medill McCormick, Mrs. Katherine McCormick, Mrs. A. A. McCormick, Fred S. Oliver, and James H. Pierce. The largest donations for the Progressives, however, came from Munsey, Perkins, the Willard Straights of the Morgan Company, Douglas Robinson, W. E. Roosevelt, and Thomas Plant.[16]

In fact, the Clapp inquiry embarrassed both Taft and Roosevelt. The voters gave Woodrow Wilson 45 per cent of their votes—and the Presidency of the United States.

Not a few Progressives felt cheated by the election, not only because of a fickle electorate but because of Perkins' militantly pro-big business activities. During the campaign ostensible unity was maintained, although there was substantial hostility toward Perkins, and at one point Senator Joseph Dixon, the party's chairman, nearly resigned because of him. In all of these conflicts Roosevelt ultimately supported Perkins. Now, the election lost, a number of Progressives demanded a reckoning.

Munsey deserted the party shortly after the election, although he donated a small sum in 1913. Roosevelt himself confided to Arthur H. Lee that "Whether the Progressive Party itself will disappear or not, I do not know." The story of the decline of the party has been told in detail elsewhere.[17] As the party lost votes in 1914, and as Roosevelt, Garfield, and others became more jingoist on the issue of the World War, the Progressives simply became a pawn in Roosevelt's and Perkins' efforts to shape the policies and candidates of the Republican Party. The strategy was to fail badly. But until 1916 the party lingered on, losing strength each year, and with Perkins as its head it stressed the trust issue more than any other. By October, 1914, Roosevelt confided to Perkins that he would never run again. At about the same time, much to the chagrin of Hiram Johnson and many Midwestern and Western Progressives, Perkins began suggesting the party be abandoned. During February, 1916, Perkins was referring to himself as essentially a true Republican, and he aided Roosevelt in a futile effort to have the Republicans nominate Lodge in 1916. The Progressive stalwarts, after the formal Roosevelt-Perkins switch to the Republicans in mid-1916, regarded their former leaders as traitors. The party, out of tune with dominant trends, simply disintegrated.[18]

Amos Pinchot felt he had been swindled. Hostile to the Perkins wing, and really a Jeffersonian Democrat at times on the verge of socialism, Pinchot wrote Roosevelt in December, 1912, about the domination of the party by Perkins and the Progressive stand for big business. Roosevelt strongly defended Perkins, as he did against all future assaults. During 1914 Pinchot was to lead the movement to depose Perkins, and Roosevelt publicly attacked him as the "lunatic fringe." Of all the disenchanted Progressives, only Pinchot tried to generalize his experience into a coherent view. From 1925 until 1933 he attempted to write a *magnum opus* entitled *Big Business in America*. He had, after all, personally known many of the principals in the history of the era, and he assiduously utilized the Stanley Committee hearings, Ida Tarbell's biography of Gary, and other public sources. The work was never patched together in any systematic form, but his rough thesis is clear: a plutocracy had taken over the United States as a result of the alliance of big business and government. Morgan and the U.S. Steel interests, in particular, had influenced Roosevelt and had had a decisive voice in every recent

presidential nomination. The steel company "needed political assistance" in attaining its initial goal of monopoly, since its efforts to
eliminate competition had failed. Gary's price-fixing proposals, he
suggested, were really an attempt to get the government to do something for U.S. Steel that it could not do for itself. Pinchot was fully
aware of the détente system between Morgan and the Roosevelt
Administration, and the Progressive Party was described as the result
of the failure of that system under Taft. Pinchot denied monopoly
was inevitable, and, in effect, he suggested a rough, unsophisticated
theory of political capitalism based on his own experiences and public
documents.[19]

Both Pinchot and Harold L. Ickes, another active Progressive,
believed that George Perkins had killed the Progressive Party, and in
a literal sense they were entirely correct. But the commitment of the
membership was primarily to a very fallible person, Roosevelt, rather
than to a program; and to the extent that program was considered, it
was substantially similar to that of Taft or Wilson. The Progressives
had no compelling, distinctive reason for existence. The party's
fortunes were based almost entirely on the desires of the Morgan
interests—most Insurgents stayed with the Republicans in 1912—
and when Woodrow Wilson was elected to the Presidency, it was to
Wilson that the larger business interests of the United States were to
turn for relief.

The Democratic
Victory

Woodrow Wilson's career before assuming the Presidency has
been exhaustively treated by Arthur S. Link, and only a few aspects
of it need to be recalled here. A Calvinist by faith, and trained at
Johns Hopkins in the classical liberalism of laissez faire and the political Whiggery of Burke, Wilson is probably incorrectly characterized
as a mere nineteenth-century liberal filled with certitude about his
opinions. Wilson was a conservative, and his early history was that
of the antilabor, paternalistic conservative who nevertheless believed
that child labor and factory laws were desirable if only to equalize
competitive conditions. But it would be wrong to make too much of

Wilson's early intellectual training and views, for although Wilson was formally an intellectual, the major part of his career prior to his active involvement in politics was spent as an administrator. Ideas were important to Wilson, but Wilson was not exclusively a man of ideas whose major preoccupation was with refining and defining them; and for this reason, when he was called upon to relate his ideas to his actions, there was always a natural amount of free play as to how they might be applied. This flexibility was not so much the result of opportunism as a lack of precision.

To suggest that Wilson was to later undergo a transformation as a political figure is to assume too much both for the intensity of Wilson's early conservatism and the extent of his later liberalism. There was a remarkable ideological consistency in Wilson's career, largely because his ideology was never so sharply defined that we may examine every change and intonation. Suffice it to say here, as Link and William Diamond have already shown, that Wilson's early career was that of a conservative, anti-Bryan Democrat who believed that reform was very largely a matter of good individuals replacing evil ones, and that only businessmen could ultimately understand business problems.

Wilson was in large measure the foil of Eastern conservative Democrats against the threat of William Jennings Bryan, and he was quite deliberately groomed for this role by George Harvey, a millionaire with important connections with Morgan, and then by Thomas Fortune Ryan, Adolph S. Ochs, and other major capitalists. Harvey, who started out as a newspaper man, made a fortune in electric traction and eventually acquired control of *Harper's Weekly,* from February, 1906, on openly advocated Wilson for President; he was the first to do so. Harvey had helped make the career of James Smith, Democratic boss of New Jersey, and it was Smith who imposed Wilson on the New Jersey party as its gubernatorial candidate in 1910. As Wilson entered the political arena, his views on public issues were sought after. In late 1907 he supported the Aldrich Bill on banking, and was full of praise for Morgan's role in American society. But progressivism, or the progressive tone, was the wave of the future, and Wilson responded to the pressure of the times. The individual had to be reintegrated into the community voluntarily, he told the American Bankers Association somewhat vaguely in September, 1908, while opposing Bryan, or the community would undertake the task. During the same period he opposed government regulation of corporations, trustbusting, and similar measures, although by 1910 he spoke highly of the trends in municipal reform. In emphasis, Wilson favored local rather than federal initiative, but he increasingly saw the advantages of federal legislation if it stressed individual rather than social guilt in, for example, corporate abuses. Perkins found this emphasis most compatible, and upon Wilson's election to the New Jersey governorship as a reformer, Perkins wrote him: "As to your views on the business questions of the hour, in my judgment they are absolutely sound."[20] By 1910 Wilson felt that giant business was axiomatic with efficiency. In an eminently conservative speech to the American Bar Association in 1910, he attacked trustbusting:

If you dissolve the offending corporation, you throw great undertakings out of gear . . . to the infinite loss of thousands of entirely innocent persons and to the great inconvenience of society as a whole. . . . I regard the corporation as indispensable to modern business enterprise. I am not jealous of its size or might, if you will but abandon at the right points the fatuous, antiquated, and quite unnecessary fiction which treats it as a legal person. . . .[21]

Wilson was to break his alliance with Boss Smith of New Jersey, thereby earning a reputation as a reformer, and in December, 1911, on the advice of Colonel Edward House, he finally broke with Harvey. Although Link is correct in characterizing many of Wilson's statements on public issues at this time as "vague, idealistic, and meaningless," some of these statements are important to understanding Wilson's feelings immediately prior to his nomination and his presentation of the New Freedom. As late as December, 1911, Wilson opposed the recall of judges, and he favored each state's deciding on initiative for itself, without specifying whether it would be desirable or not.

It was in the area of antitrust problems that Wilson showed the greatest conservatism, and his record in this field as Governor of New Jersey was later used against him by the Progressives. At the beginning of 1912 he was rather aggressively calling for the cultivation of foreign markets and the development of a powerful merchant marine. So far as competition was concerned:

. . . nobody can fail to see that modern business is going to be done by corporations. *The old time of individual competition is probably gone by.* It may come back; I don't know; it will not come back within our time,

I dare say. We will do business henceforth, when we do it, on a great and successful scale, by means of corporations.

I am not afraid of any corporation, no matter how big. I am afraid of any corporation, however small, that is bad, that is rotten at the core, whose practices and actions are in restraint of trade. So that the thing we are after is not reckoning size in measuring capacity for damage, but measuring and comprehending the exact damage done.[22]

To the obvious criticism that this sounded very much like Rooseveltian doctrine, Wilson frankly responded:

When I sit down and compare my views with those of a Progressive Republican I can't see what the difference is, except that he has a sort of pious feeling about the doctrine of protection, which I have never felt.[23]

Even after his nomination, Wilson retained a position on the trust issue remarkably similar to his earlier stand, despite the vague Democratic plank in favor of a strengthened antitrust law and a detailing of its standards of illegality, which committed Wilson to very little. Immediately after his nomination Wilson condemned the methods the trusts had used to establish monopolies, but then withdrew by declaring "that what we are seeking is not destruction of any kind nor the disruption of any sound or honest thing. . . ." "I am happy to say," he continued, "that a new spirit has begun to show itself in the last year or two among influential men of business . . . to return in some degree at any rate, to the practices of genuine competition." This conversion, miraculous as it seemed, promised "to show what the new age is to be and how the anxieties of statesmen are to be eased if the light that is dawning broadens into day."[24]

Historians have assumed that the meeting of Wilson and Brandeis on August 28, 1912, was to transform Wilson's emphasis on the antitrust question and to lead to the doctrine of the New Freedom. The problem of the coherence of the New Freedom, and the extent of its departure from Wilson's earlier views, can be examined later. The real question is: how radical was Brandeis' economic philosophy, and on what specifies did it add new dimensions to the great debates on economic issues during the Progressive Era?

Brandeis, unhappily, was antilabor in fact as well as in principle. He defended the right of labor to organize, but only in open shops, and he served as the attorney for the Boston printing employers during their antiunion struggles of 1904. If unions could be incorporated, he suggested, they might be sued—and therefore would act conservatively, setting up a wall against socialism. By 1910 Brandeis became enamoured of the "scientific management" doctrines of Frederick W. Taylor, and did more to popularize the theory in his attacks on the railroads in the Rate Case of 1910 before the I.C.C. than Taylor and his followers had been able to do in years of education. Brandeis was to defend the bonus system and proclaimed Taylor a genius, against intense union hostility. Although Brandeis was thoroughly hated by the Boston social elite for his attacks on the corruptly managed New Haven Railroad, his position on scientific management was to win him considerable business sympathy.

Scientific management was a thoroughly totalitarian philosophy, and merely a rationale for cutting costs. Taylor placed the movement in the same category as conservation, and if we understand that term to mean systematic exploitation he was correct. In the last analysis, its success depended on workers working harder and the elimination of loafers. Obedience, discipline, and imposed norms were required. "Scientific management makes collective bargaining and trade unionism unnecessary as means of protection to the workers," Taylor frankly stated.[25] In fact, although he incidentally promised higher wages, Taylor's reputation and fame were based on his promise of lower labor costs for businessmen.

Although Brandeis regarded such giants as U.S. Steel as artificial efforts to suppress competition, preserve inefficiency, and control a share of the market that could not be maintained without mergers, he primarily focused on the problem of efficiency rather than power concentration and the social relationships that resulted from it. Very much the same is true in his condemnation of the money trust—it was artificial and inefficient rather than a power concentration able to subvert the democratic process beyond the elimination of new entrepreneurs. It is primarily Brandeis' view of the contrived nature of much concentrated capital that is remembered, but several other paradoxes were intrinsic to his economic philosophy. He strongly favored price-fixing and fair trade laws because he regarded price cutting as the road to monopoly, but price-fixing was close to the hearts of Gary, Carnegie, and other big industrialists as well. Indeed, given lower costs, it was their best assurance of guaranteed high profits. Moreover, Brandeis was sanguine about the future of business as a whole, in large part because of the influence of scientific management on his thinking. Business was ceasing to be an exploitive enterprise, he stated in 1912, but rather "It is an occupation which is pursued largely for others and not merely for one's self. . . . It is an occupation in which the amount of financial return is not the accepted measure of success." As efficiency-minded business moved toward this goal, improving products and eliminating waste, "the great industrial and social problems expressed in the present social unrest will one by one find solution."[26]

Brandeis favored workmen's compensation, and was attracted to La Follette for a time, but he opposed direct government via the recall and initiative. He supported Roosevelt at the beginning of 1912, but felt uncomfortable about his trust position. When Brandeis wandered into the Wilson camp in August, 1912, he was hardly a crusading radical.

Nor was Wilson a great crusader either, and the New Freedom did not qualitatively alter his position on the problem of the government's relationship to big business. He turned to the topic not so much because he had anything obviously new to say on the problem, but because he was convinced by Brandeis that it was a good campaign issue. Wilson and his advisers were well aware of the importance of the business vote, let alone business donations, and that vote was very much sought after both by Wilson and Roosevelt. The New Freedom was general rather than specific in its assumptions and demands.

In terms of his analysis of the relationship of giant size to efficiency, Wilson took Brandeis' position. Trusts were not inevitable, but were artificially created and maintained by the control of credit, supplies, and raw materials. On the other hand, Wilson introduced a mitigating confusion. "I am for big business, and I am against the trust." This was safe enough, since the point at which big business became a trust was never defined, and the number of actual trusts— in the sense of having effective market control—was too small to fill big business as a whole with anxieties about Wilson's statements. "Big business is no doubt to a large extent necessary and natural. The development of business upon a great scale, upon a great scale of cooperation, is inevitable, and, let me add, is probably desirable." Some might argue that mere size, even without monopoly control, posed serious political and economic dangers, but not Wilson. "I admit that any large corporation built up by the legitimate processes of business, by economy, by efficiency, is natural; and I am not afraid of it, no matter how big it grows." If the law demanded "fair play" from all, small business could successfully compete with the giant corporations.

The focus of Wilson's New Freedom was not on the distribution and control of power, but on the freedom of entry to small business. ". . . we are rescuing the business of this country, we are not injuring it." Quite the contrary, Wilson was promising the freedom to exploit to all.

. . . not one single legitimate or honest arrangement is going to be disturbed; but every impediment to business is going to be removed, every illegitimate kind of control is going to be destroyed. Every man who wants an opportunity and has the energy to seize it, is going to be given a chance.[27]

How does one distinguish the New Freedom from Roosevelt's New Nationalism? Practically, one cannot; but, for obvious political reasons, Wilson was compelled to distinguish his view from that of Roosevelt's—ignoring his statement on their common beliefs in January, 1912. The Progressive Party, he declared, accepted monopoly and proposed making bad trusts good by utilizing an executive commission. Wilson, in fact, was not opposed to a commission, and since 1908 had favored one based on a "uniform process acting under precise terms of power in the enforcement of precise terms of regulation."[28] Roosevelt, he now claimed, wished to create a commission with arbitrary criteria of control, and he came remarkably close, at one brief point, to repudiating the commission idea. In a prescient statement he was later to forget, Wilson suggested, "If the government is to tell big businessmen how to run their business, then don't you see that big businessmen have to get closer to the government even than they are now?"[29] The very plan, he pointed out, was conceived by the men who were to be controlled.

Much of the New Freedom was defined by Brandeis, but the definition never went to the extent of binding the future President to anything concrete. Indeed, Wilson's speeches on the New Freedom must be regarded merely as campaign documents—to be used and forgotten. The New Freedom was against trusts and for big business. It was for big business and for little business as well. It promised equality of opportunity, but pledged no specific measures by which it might be guaranteed. Wilson assumed, in much the same way as Roosevelt, that businessmen were largely men of good will, and he saw no tension between the concentration of wealth and political democracy, save insofar as the power of wealth was used to exclude new members from the business class. There was justice in mobility, and the New Freedom was an imprecise interpretation of the economy rather than an effort to bring the economy under the control of a political democracy. Wilson implicitly rejected laissez faire, save insofar as he wanted to make its spirit relevant to the twentieth-century economy. But social change is rarely based on vagaries, and on specifics Wilson's New Freedom was to start out in a vacuum—a vacuum that was to be filled for him by men with more specific goals in mind, men who were able to play on the new President's weaknesses.

Wilson's reasonable, moderate stand on economic issues was to win him many important business supporters, although Henry Lee Higginson questioned whether Wilson really appreciated business problems.

It would do the Governor a deal of good to live in Wall Street for a year or two, and if Theodore Roosevelt could do the same, it would teach him many things that he never would learn otherwise. As for President Taft, I pity him so much that I wish him no experience except that of living quietly at home.

But Higginson felt Wilson had a "very keen" intelligence, and voted for him in 1912. Jacob H. Schiff, ordinarily a Republican, voted for Wilson also, and donated heavily to his campaign. Charles R. Crane, who had supported La Follette's presidential campaign and followed the Senator in his switch to Wilson, was the largest donor. Cleveland H. Dodge, Bernard M. Baruch, Henry Morgenthau, and other important financiers aided. Cyrus H. McCormick, Thomas D. Jones, and David B. Jones of International Harvester also gave heavily. George Harvey assisted with Wilson's publicity in the final days of the campaign, and Henry Seligman expressed what was probably the typical opinion of ordinarily big business Republicans when he wrote that ". . . I do not believe that [Wilson's] election can do much harm. . . ."[30]

In 1912, American society and politics were at a critical impasse.

Taft had shown how basically unstable the relationship between business and government could be, and how the idiosyncracies of a man
or the political needs of a party could undermine the desire and need
for a stable, rational, predictable business environment. Even more
important, by 1912 the competitive tendencies and the decentralizing
factors in industry and banking seemed ready to truly break out of
conventional bounds. New industries, new areas, new entrants—the
tendency appeared clear to all too many important businessmen. By
1912 big business was anxious for consolidation, a consolidation that
could not be obtained by another merger movement but only through
political means.

Wilson was attempting to generalize on the desirable relationship
of government to business, as was Roosevelt. These efforts were
superficial in their dep*h, and later capable of broad interpretation
by their originators. In the case of Wilson, the very vagueness and
lack of precision was, in itself, of the greatest consequence. For it
allowed others to add those crucial details that were to effectively
determine the operational nature of the New Freedom.

Others, besides Roosevelt and Wilson, tried to generalize on the
nature of the society they lived in, and the direction it should take.
To what extent were they more successful, both in their assumptions
and the clarity of their vision?

Robert M. La Follette critically evaluated the progressive movement, and Roosevelt in particular, and there can be little doubt that
the Senator from Wisconsin was the most consistent contemporary
critic of the political actions of his peers. Certainly only La Follette
has been spared the sort of comprehensive challenge to his reform
and liberal reputation that Roosevelt and Wilson have been exposed
to. It was La Follette who attacked Roosevelt for acting "upon the
maxim that half a loaf is better than no bread," suggesting that "a
halfway measure never fairly tests the principle and may utterly dis-
credit it." The Hepburn Act was such a measure, La Follette concluded, and equally damaging to the cause of reform were Roosevelt's
attacks on radicals and conservatives alike, and it was for this reason that the Roosevelt Administration left no permanent record of
importance.[31]

For all this, La Follette's vision of the good society was never
articulated, and the very vagueness of his alternative to the traditional

Republican view has allowed the La Follette reputation to stand by default. Yet it must be remembered that although La Follette fought Taft and Roosevelt, he was also a foe of the Socialists, and in Wisconsin the Socialists were a serious force to contend with. He was able to criticize Roosevelt's cooperation with the Morgan interests, and the more obvious injustices of the period, but La Follette never comprehended the direction or the mainstream of the relationship of business to politics in this period. Issues were distinct to him, good or evil, and not a part of a larger context of events. He took stands on many separate problems, but he never integrated them into a larger view of his times. Even at the end of 1911 he could praise the Bureau of Corporations, the central pillar of the alliance between big business and government, and he failed to probe very deeply into the operations of any single reform mechanism, save perhaps the I.C.C.

Yet La Follette spoke with indignation and passion for the cause of the small farmers and businessmen. And it was this sense of injustice, and his role as the great critic, that carried with it the impression of genuine radicalism. In fact, however, he alone among contemporary political leaders spoke for the small businessman and for true, unfettered competition. He felt, without proposing nationalization, that the rigorous destruction of big business' privileges would allow more small property owners to emerge and the threat of socialism could be destroyed. Later he was willing to work with the Socialists, if only because they also took an antiwar stand and were willing to meet his political terms in 1924. Related to his advocacy of the spread of small property was La Follette's belief that the application of efficiency principles to political administration would lead to political rationality. Perhaps to a greater degree than any contemporary political leader, it was La Follette who adopted the cult of expertise, science, and rationality. As Governor he exploited the combined talents of a great university, and let the political decision-making process increasingly fall into the hands of the presumably positivistic academics. By relying on the talents of the reform-minded professors at the University of Wisconsin, La Follette deferred confronting political and economic realities and theories for himself. Indeed, so long as he felt that difficult issues could be resolved by simple reference to experts, he was unable to call for little more than clean, impartial, and fair government run by a competent bureaucracy. He thus focused more and more on the formal political structure rather than on the political process in relation to the economy. The result was a brilliant career as a political critic, and a much more prosaic role as an economic reformer and advocate of specific economic changes.[32]

American intellectual currents during the Progressive Era have been exhaustively studied by others, and the sense of frustration and disillusionment on the part of the intellectuals, especially during and after the World War, is a thoroughly analyzed phenomenon. Yet this frustration was not due to a sense of discovery as to the true nature of the progressive ferment, save possibly for a few of those who followed Roosevelt's political wanderings, and it is this failure to delve into the roots of political frustration that resulted in the relatively sterile response to the whole process of disillusionment. This inadequate response was the result of a fundamental conservatism on the part of the large majority of contemporary intellectuals. With the exception of Thorstein Veblen, not one major social theorist emerged from the Progressive Era, if by "major" we mean one who profoundly understood and described the times he lived in.

The conservatism of the contemporary intellectuals, and the failure of their powers of insight during their period of disillusion, is quite explicable. The idealization of the state by Lester Ward, Richard T. Ely, or Simon N. Patten, was the understandable reaction to the Social Darwinism of Sumner and Fiske, for if the state could be said to be the highest form of cooperative human evolution, or a divine institution, then its actions could only be legitimized and declared good. But the idealization of the state was also the result of the peculiar training of many of the American academics of this period. At the end of the nineteenth century the primary influence in American academic social and economic theory was exerted by the German universities. The Bismarckian idealization of the state, with its centralized welfare functions designed to preserve capitalism and the status quo in its more fundamental aspects, was suitably revised by the thousands of key academics who studied in German universities in the 1880's and 1890's. A middle-class twist to the concept of state welfare made it quite acceptable to many essentially conservative professors by the beginning of this century. The menace of socialism could be met, Ely and John R. Commons felt, by recognizing and encouraging conservative unionism. Despite their unfortunate experiences with academic freedom during a period when it meant only the ability of students to choose their own electives, most of these theorists were dedicated to preserving the essential legal and economic prerogatives of the dominant economic classes.

Practically, the average liberal academic's view of the state was totalitarian as a consequence of his naïveté. He was very rarely concerned about formal, direct democratic control—this would have meant the end of private property as then understood—and only occasionally desired a balance of economic power that might have seriously limited business. Axiomatic and simplistic assumptions as to what might happen if some concrete legislation were enacted were generally the rule. Conservative in their ends, as were big business advocates of a far more extensive regulatory role for the federal government, the academics who proposed economic reforms failed to understand the process of political capitalism. Instead, the pressures and leverage created by their ideas helped make political capitalism possible.

The role of the intellectual as the reflection of the less formalized needs of powerful interests is perhaps best illustrated by Herbert Croly. Croly has become a favorite subject for American intellectual historians of this period, and there is no point in rehashing all of his ideas here. Suffice it to say that *The Promise of American Life* (1909) was not merely a theoretical systematization of the New Nationalism or Square Deal, although Croly took more of his programmatic ideas from Roosevelt than from anyone else, but a higher stage of its development. At the same time that he maintained there was an irreconcilable tension between the inevitable concentration of economic power and the existing decentralization of political institutions, and condemned the latter, he tried to make the "new meaning to the Hamiltonian system of political ideas" he was advocating attractive to labor as well.[33] In addition, however, to the recognition of unions as the representatives of labor, and the inheritance tax, was Croly's nationalist conception that traded social welfare for the regulation by the central government in commercial matters. Croly's book was fatally ambivalent on many of these matters, for, in the final analysis, he defended the desirability of economic inequality of a rather gross sort. And one is tempted to suspect that, given his eulogy of the social services of Morgan, Carnegie, Hill, and Harriman, when Croly advocated a new solidarity and attacked factions in society he was really talking about a utopia led by an alliance of Wall Street and Roosevelt.

Lest this analysis of Croly appear unfair, it should at least be observed that his next venture into social theory, a generous and sympathetic biography of Mark Hanna published in 1912, indicated an awareness of the functional political role of big business—a role he could only rationalize. Willard Straight, a Morgan executive who specialized in finding Morgan overseas outlets for investments, also shared the above analysis of Croly when he placed him in the editorship of his weekly, *The New Republic,* in 1914. In *Progressive Democracy* (1914) Croly exhibited a good deal more of his bureaucratic positivism and conservatism than he had in his earlier works. The Progressive Party alone stood for unequivocal change that recognized the necessity of "inequality and injustice" in the economic process as "the foundation of any really national and progressive economic policy."[34] Croly found the New Freedom's reliance on Jeffersonian doctrine—a reliance, as we shall see, that was more verbal than genuine—a retreat to the past.

Croly reflected the dominant political attitudes of Theodore Roosevelt, and this dependence made him incapable of viewing the operational realities of the society he lived in with sufficient perspective to truly understand it. When he finally broke with Roosevelt he passed through various phases of disillusion, having lost his source of ideas and inspiration, and ultimately ended his career writing editorials in praise of Mussolini's corporate state.

WOODROW WILSON

AND THE

TRIUMPH OF

POLITICAL CAPITALISM:

BANKING

BANKING REFORM at the beginning of 1912 seemed a dead issue, of interest only to a few bankers and the seriously divided National Citizens' League for Sound Banking. Despite the support of the American Bankers Association for the Aldrich Bill, the inclusion of the provision for total private control of the banking system managed to lose the bill the support of President Taft. And Aldrich's insistence that his name be attached to the measure guaranteed the opposition of the Democrats. The banking reform movement had neatly isolated itself.

Writing a
Reform Bill

The National Citizens' League was a substantial organization, its backers powerful and resourceful men. It was not at all evident to them that their cause was lost, although it was to become obvious that the politically flexible approach of Laughlin was increasingly relevant to the changed circumstances. The tension between Laughlin and the New York branch of the league, controlled by Paul M. Warburg, was to persist, but at the beginning of 1912 the National League unqualifiedly endorsed the Aldrich Bill. In the meantime, despite a few suggestions by bankers that the Aldrich Bill be regarded as less than sacred, the league continued to function as a large-scale education and propaganda organization for banking reform. Its periodical, *Banking Reform,* was in early 1912 supplemented by a volume by the same name. Edited by Laughlin, the book became the bible of the league, and a copy was sent to every member and distributed freely throughout the nation. Of the twenty-three chapters dealing with all phases of banking problems, eleven were written by Laughlin's former student, H. Parker Willis, who received $1,000 for his labors. Although avoiding Aldrich by name, the volume nevertheless endorsed the basic principles of his bill.

But the publication of a book rarely, if ever, led to the creation of a serious reform movement, and were it not for a set of fortuitous events, it is likely that the banking reform movement would have died an early death. The first, and perhaps most crucial accident, was the fact that H. Parker Willis, with whom Laughlin maintained continuous, intimate communication, taught economics at Washington and Lee University until 1905, as well as serving as the Washington correspondent of the New York *Journal of Commerce* and freelancing for Laughlin. In one of his classes he had taught the two sons of Carter Glass of Virginia, the ranking member of the Committee on Banking and Currency of the House of Representatives. Now, in early 1912, Glass was looking for an administrative assistant, and his sons recommended their old teacher to him.[1]

Carter Glass had virtually no technical knowledge of banking and needed an administrative assistant rather badly. As Glass himself put it:

He had no special qualification for the work beyond the information absorbed in these [ten] years of discussion and a reasonable amount of common sense acquired as a practical printer and successful newspaper publisher, supplemented by an observant service in Congress.[2]

Basically conservative, Glass had the confidence of Democratic House leader Oscar W. Underwood, who lined up behind Glass against the efforts of Arsène P. Pujo and his ambitious attorney, Samuel Untermyer, to assign the problem of banking reform to the Pujo Subcommittee on the "Money Trust." The House Committee on Banking was split into two subcommittees, and Glass was given the responsibility of considering banking reform. Totally unprepared, he hired Willis and first assigned him the tedious and harmless task of preparing a memo on the existing reform plans.

The Democratic Party had no special interest in banking reform, and although its 1912 platform specifically opposed the Aldrich Bill, it was extraordinarily vague as to its concrete alternatives. Certainly the seniority system of the House Committee on Banking, the personal ambition of Glass, and the learned summary by Willis were inadequate to fill the vacuum. Still, Willis' obtaining of his crucial role was a fortunate turn for the banking reform movement. Throughout the spring of 1912 Willis wrote Laughlin about his work for the Glass Committee, his relationship to his superior, and Washington gossip. The advice of the old professor was much revered. ". . . when you arrive," he wrote Laughlin concerning a memorandum he had written, "I should like to show it to you for such criticisms as occur to you."[3] The student-teacher relationship between the two men was still prominent.

This relationship between Willis and Laughlin is of great consequence to the subsequent history of banking reform, since it buttressed their virtually identical ideological and technical commitments. In June, 1912, Willis reported to Laughlin that "After a good deal of talk with Mr. Glass, I drew up a bill along the lines of which you and I spoke, and turned it into him."[4] But Glass had his reelection to worry about and thought nothing could be done that session, and instructed his expert to busy himself over the summer by working on a bill. At about the same time, both Willis and Laughlin concluded that the Aldrich Bill was politically impossible to pass, if only because the split in the Republican Party made a Democratic

victory appear inevitable. During May and June, 1912, Laughlin
traveled through the South, visiting conservative Democrats and
arousing their interest in banking reform. Of special importance was
Representative Oscar W. Underwood, House Democratic leader, who
responded to his suggestions enthusiastically but was to lose control
of the committee on resolutions at the Democratic convention to
the Bryan forces. Laughlin and the league, at the same time, found
it possible to praise the platform of both major parties as favoring
monetary reform, even though they could not help but point out that
the Democrats were more notable for what they opposed than for
what they supported.

If it had to depend on Willis, Glass, and Laughlin, banking reform as a cause would have died quickly enough. Fortunately for the
reformers, the Pujo Committee swung into high gear in its investigation of the Money Trust during the summer of 1912, and for eight
months frightened the nation with its awesome, if inconclusive,
statistics on the power of Wall Street over the nation's economy. The
Pujo investigation was to be a blessing in disguise. Five banking
firms, the elaborate tables of the committee showed, held 341 directorships in 112 corporations with an aggregate capitalization of over
$22 billion. The evidence seemed conclusive, and the nation was
suitably frightened into realizing that reform of the banking system
was urgent—presumably to bring Wall Street under control. The inquiry was directed by Samuel Untermyer, an opportunistic and
ambitious attorney who only the prior November was saying "The
fact is that the monopolies and substantial domination of industries
created in that form could be counted on the fingers of your hands,"
attacking "the political partisans who seek to make personal and
Party capital out of demagogic appeals to the unthinking. . . ."[5]

The ogre of Wall Street was resurrected by the newspapers, who
quite ignored the fact that the biggest advocates of banking reform
were the bankers themselves, bankers with a somewhat different view
of the problem of concentration in banking and in fear of the very
real trend toward instability and decentralization in finance. Yet it
was largely the Pujo hearings that made the topic of banking reform
a serious one. And, fortunately for the bankers, responsibility for
formulating reform measures was not under the jurisdiction of Pujo
but of Glass. And Willis, for all practical purposes, ran the Glass
Committee.

The Pujo inquiry opened up new dangers, and new promises as well. Laughlin, as early as May, 1912, had indicated his personal opposition to the control provisions of the Aldrich Bill. Now, in July, Willis wrote in the *Journal of Commerce* that if conservative banking reformers could not unite behind a reasonable substitute for the Aldrich Bill, which was now politically dead, the threat of legislation from the Bryan Democrats was real indeed. "In such a case it would be impossible to look for any conservatism."[6] Indeed, Pujo and Untermyer were to try again during the summer to win the legislative powers from the Glass Committee, and illustrated the truth of Willis' warning.

During July Willis continued to work on a draft of a bill, sending a copy to Laughlin for his comments. When the master failed to reply, the former student wrote he was "a little anxious" whether it arrived. At the same time, he tried to swing Laughlin to the compromise position Laughlin had shown signs of moving toward in May.

Yet I cannot help recognizing that an incomplete bill is all that can be had and that it is much better to take half a loaf rather than to be absolutely deprived of the chance of getting any bread whatever. . . . If the present condition of disunion and disagreement . . . continues, nothing will be done and the whole plan will fall flat. Indeed it may do worse than that for the so-called "progressive" element—such as Lindbergh and his supporter's—will be encouraged to enact dangerous legislation against Clearing Houses, etc.[7]

The league, Willis urged, should endorse any bill that carried reform further.

Laughlin clearly accepted Willis' argument, and needed no prodding. The New York league, barely able to contain itself, was infuriated when *Banking Reform* in September endorsed the principles of currency elasticity and centralization in any form, and by the journal's insistence on playing down the Aldrich Bill and maintaining that currency reform was a nonpartisan issue. As New York considered secession from the league, and tried to have Laughlin fired, Willis reassured him that "as a personal friend and loyal believer in your work," he would support him against his league opponents. To solidify his position, Laughlin had the state presidents of the league meet at the end of October to withdraw the league's exclusive support for the Aldrich Bill. Each of the three major platforms were inter-

preted so as to allow for adequate banking reform and the nonpartisan status of the league was reiterated. Only the prior month
the executive committee and the currency commission of the American Bankers Association had withdrawn its specific endorsement of
the Aldrich Bill in order to give itself freedom to push for the best
possible bill, working under the aegis of the league. Now, Laughlin
was free to formally take the same position and to end internecine
disputes within the league. "It is progress that the Aldrich plan came
and went," *Banking Reform* announced. "It is progress that the
people have been aroused and interested."[8]

Laughlin and the league were now free to "try to help in getting
a proper bill adopted by the Democrats," a bill that "In non-essentials
. . . could be made different from the old plan," and could be passed
if the league, the American Bankers Association, and the Chamber
of Commerce united behind it. The victory of Wilson made it possible to "hope that the changed administration will be more alive to
the commercial necessities of the country than the expiring one," as
A. Barton Hepburn put it. Fortunately, the new President admitted
"he knew nothing" about banking theory or practice.[9] Glass made
the same confession to Colonel House in November, and this vacuum
is of the utmost significance. The entire banking reform movement,
at all crucial stages, was centralized in the hands of a few men who
for years were linked, ideologically and personally, with one another.
The problem of the origin of the Federal Reserve Act, and the
authorship of specific drafts, was later hotly debated by H. Parker
Willis, Carter Glass, Paul M. Warburg, and J. Laurence Laughlin,
who greatly exaggerated their differences in order that they might
each claim responsibility for the guiding lines of the Federal Reserve
System. Yet all of these men were conservative by any criterion, and
although they may have differed on details, they agreed on major
policy lines and general theory. The confusion over the precise
authorship of the Federal Reserve Act should not obscure the fact
that the major function, inspiration, and direction of the measure was
to serve the banking community in general, and large bankers
specifically.

The exegetic problem of who wrote the Federal Reserve Bill still
remains, however. A final solution may not be possible, but certain
crucial facts can be isolated. Throughout November and December,
1912, Laughlin and Willis were in constant communication as the first

draft of a complete bill was finally written. Moreover, Laughlin, Colonel House, and Glass were to frequently consult with major bankers about reform, and provided an important and continuous bridge for their ideas while bills were being drafted.

On November 14 Laughlin and Glass met to discuss legislation, and Laughlin later claimed he was asked to prepare a bill. As Laughlin told Willis the following week:

Then it was agreed that as soon as I could complete the draft that we should have a private meeting somewhere unknown to the newspaper reporters, and go over the bill thoroughly from beginning to end. . . . Therefore, I shall go to work immediately to draft a bill embodying the general principles of the one I showed you, and try to adjust the machinery so that it might not be antagonized as a central bank. . . . I have little doubt that we shall have legislation in the spring session. What that measure will be depends largely upon what you and I can devise.[10]

The extent of centralization was to depend on President Wilson, but Laughlin was confident the problem could be taken care of adequately.

Willis responded in a friendly manner to Laughlin's efforts, although in early December he may have had second thoughts when he tried putting off a meeting with Laughlin for nearly a month. Laughlin, in any event, worked with the approval and advice of A. Barton Hepburn, James B. Forgan, and George Reynolds, who were kept informed of his efforts.

Laughlin prepared three drafts of a bill during the month of December, and sent each along to Willis. Plan A arrived at the beginning of December, and although Willis was courteous to his old professor, he sent it along to Glass with the comment, "It does not impress me very strongly." It was understood that an improved plan would follow the first one, and Willis hinted to Laughlin that whatever Glass "reports will be in fact the result of his own work and analysis," which was to say, Willis' work and analysis. The third draft —"Plan D"—arrived in Washington on December 22, and Willis thought it "decidedly better than the last and has much to commend it."[11] Several days later Glass was sent the draft.

The crux of Plan D was dominant public control of the central Treasury Board. Ten of its thirty-one members were to be chosen by banks, eight were to be appointed by the President, and the Secretary of the Treasury and the Comptroller were to automatically sit on the

board. The balanced board was to choose another ten from lists submitted by representatives of agriculture, labor, and commerce, and the
group of 30 was to choose a president. This board was to coordinate
the entire banking system belonging to the districts. Plan D provided
for an indeterminate number of district associations, whose capital
stock was to be owned by member banks, to be chartered by the
Secretary of the Treasury, the Comptroller of the Currency, and the
Attorney General, who could also fix the interest rates of the association. Laughlin never claimed that the details of Plan D were embodied in the final Federal Reserve Act, but he did claim that it
embodied the fundamentals.[12]

Various sections of Plan D consisted of extracts from the Aldrich
Plan, even though these were limited to the parts dealing with the
redeemability of Treasury Board notes by the districts in gold, the
foreign branch banking provisions, and the conditions for investments. On December 26 Wilson met with Glass and Willis to discuss
banking legislation and to consider Willis' draft outline. The distinction between the Willis and Laughlin proposals is on points of
emphasis rather than in the basic approach. The basic features of the
Glass draft were, in Glass' words:

(1) organization of a certain number of regional reserve banks of specified capital, with a view to decentralizing credits; (2) a compulsory
withdrawal of reserve balances as then impounded and their transfer to
these regional reserve banks; (3) compulsory stockholding membership
of national banks . . . ; (4) associate membership of state banks with
limited priviliges; (5) the rediscounting processes common to such plans;
(6) the issuance by the regional banks of federal reserve notes, based
on a gold and liquid paper cover; (7) the gradual retirement of national
bank bond-secured notes; (8) the joint liability of all the regional banks.[13]

The number of district associations was left indeterminate, and the
principle of a central board in Washington to replace the Comptroller
as supervisor was suggested by the President's urgings that such a "cap-
stone" be placed on the structure. By the end of December, as Colonel
House assured Paul Warburg, "the President-elect thought straight
concerning the issue."[14] But everyone else was thinking straight as
well.

Wilson's proposal to replace the supervisory power of the Comptroller with a central board made Glass speculate "that Mr. Wilson
has been written to and talked to by those who are seeking to mask

the Aldrich plan and give us dangerous centralization," but his immediate interpretation of the President-elect's orders, which he decided to accept, was much more to the liking of bankers than was required. Throughout the end of 1912, and during the first few months of 1913, Wilson and his intimates had ample opportunity to discuss banking reform with major bankers. E. D. Hulbert, the anti-Aldrich Chicago banker, and A. Barton Hepburn of the Chase National Bank, had direct links with the President and his advisers. Paul M. Warburg saw Secretary of the Treasury William G. McAdoo, Henry Morgenthau, and others during this period, and at Morgenthau's request he prepared a bill compatible with the Democratic platform. Laughlin, apparently unaware of the substance of Willis and Glass' December 26 meeting with Wilson, had more proposals to make—"Like Wilson he seems to want an additional centralizing mechanism of some kind but apparently is willing to reduce its scope a good deal," Willis reported to Glass. In early January Laughlin came to Washington, and Willis told Glass, "I think I had better go over his plan with him fairly carefully in order to see just what he has in mind in detail."[15]

Wilson's request, and the opinions of key bankers, meant that Glass and Willis had to be most flexible in working on their draft of a bill. Although they were careful to keep the contents of their work confidential, to aid the passage of any bill that might be agreed upon Glass deemed it desirable to hold public hearings on the topic and to make sure the course of these hearings was not left to chance. Willis visited Hepburn and Warburg and they were most cooperative, and Hepburn agreed to talk about banking ideas rather than plans. "This ought to mean that we can get a good deal out of him along lines that will be helpful in drafting our bill. Mr. Warburg takes the same view and I think wants to be as helpful as he can. . . ," Willis reported. The public assumption of the hearings was that no bills had been drafted, and Willis' draft was never mentioned, much less revealed. Laughlin also agreed to cooperate with this procedure. ". . . my appearance before the committee was largely *pro forma,*" Laughlin later wrote; "what I said at the hearings did not represent what I had already laid before them."[16]

The hearings of Glass' subcommittee in January and February, 1913, were nothing less than a love feast. A. Barton Hepburn started by assuring the Congressmen that the American Bankers Association would cooperate on "any good measure" that led to elasticity and cooperation in money reserve management. Regional banking would be far better than it was at present, he assured them, if it allowed for an elastic currency based on commercial paper and a bank association that "should be the dominant power in all commercial finance." He was followed by Warburg, who assured the subcommittee that the Aldrich Plan was one way, but not the only one, to solve the banking problem. ". . . you will find that you will come toward a centralized reserve system in some form," he predicted, even by following Morawetz' regional reserve plan. Indicating support for a centralized reserve system, as opposed to a central operating bank, only that month Warburg had submitted a confidential bill to Morgenthau that provided for four regional banks and a central issuing department and board of regents in Washington under ultimate government control.[17]

Festus J. Wade, St. Louis banker and member of the currency committee of the A.B.A., announced that "this association will cooperate with any and all people in devising a financial system for this country," even though he personally favored the Aldrich Bill. ". . . any bill you submit will be a vast improvement on our present system," and even if it were called "central supervisory control" rather than a "central bank," "It will be a central bank in its final analysis." George M. Reynolds joined the friendly chorus, confessing he had been opposed to a central bank for years, favoring only "some central overseeing or controlling board with common ownership of assets. By which I mean an organization with branches located in various section of the country, dealing only with banks and the Government." Any legislation in this direction, Reynolds declared, "will materially improve present conditions." ". . . you can count on at least good treatment and a reasonable measure of cooperation by the American Bankers' Association," he assured them.[18]

Many other bankers followed the leaders of the field, and most echoed their friendliness theme and offered a few conservative suggestions, but more tangible evidence of support was given behind closed doors. Festus Wade, Hepburn, and other major bankers met after testifying and decided to support a regional reserve plan—indeed, the Aldrich Bill was such a plan—and to improve it if necessary and possible, with special attention to the control mechanism. The currency commission of the American Bankers Association was also to be lined up, and the strong central bank advocates, such as

Forgan of Chicago, were to be brought under control in order to ease the modification of the A.B.A. position. Glass immediately saw the value of such assistance. "What I most earnestly desire to do," he wrote Wade, "is to aid in the construction of a measure of reform that will commend itself for soundness to the bankers of the country and, at the same time, secure the support of the business community for its fairness and sufficiency."[19] Wilson was given a copy of the draft bill on January 30, and it is likely that Laughlin was allowed to see a copy, or at least told of crucial details, not too long thereafter. Laughlin's contact with the subsequent drafts was purely minimal after the hearings, however, although he frequently communicated with Willis. The general plan, league members were publicly told at the beginning of February, would provide for regional banks with over-all central control.

The first draft of the Glass Bill given to Wilson on January 30 was very much like the one shown to him the prior December. It provided for a minimum of fifteen regional banks, the control of each being left largely in the hands of bankers representing various classes of banks. The important innovation was a Federal Reserve Commission in Washington to supervise the national system. Three of the commissioners were to be elected by the regional banks, and three were to be nominated by the President and confirmed by the Senate. The Secretary of the Treasury, the Secretary of Agriculture, and the Comptroller were also automatically members, giving the political appointees a majority.[20]

Glass tried to carry on his work quietly, but pressure for action was built up by various bankers and businessmen, and by attacks on the Money Trust by the Pujo Committee. The National Association of Credit Men sent sympathetic letters to Wilson throughout February and March, calling in general terms for currency legislation. Henry Lee Higginson, an old Wilson supporter, argued for regional banking centers with central control in his letters to the President. Colonel House, in addition, was talked to by Frick, Otto Kahn, and others in late February, and the following month also met Vanderlip, J. P. Morgan, Jr., and other bankers to discuss currency reform. The Morgan position was clear and public: what was necessary was comprehensive and thorough legislation on banking. Aiding this nearly universal sentiment among bankers was the Pujo hearings, for, as the *Wall Street Journal* admitted on March 7, "the fact that public interest is aroused will, it is believed here, lead to early action by congress by which legislation tending to perfect or reform our banking and currency system may be adopted."

To make sure the reform was more to the liking of bankers, a steady barrage of personal, unobstrusive communications with Glass, House, and Wilson was kept up throughout February and March.[21]

The Bankers and
the Glass Bill

Wilson's Inaugural Address included a passing reference to the inadequacy of the banking system, for which bankers were grateful. Despite the beginnings of slight signs of impatience on the part of Laughlin, the league was fulsome in its praise of Glass, and bankers felt greater and greater confidence as Colonel House began visiting Glass and showing interest in his currency measure. This sense of participation was undoubtedly aided by the fact that sometime in February or early March A. Barton Hepburn was called in by Glass to discuss, according to Willis, the banking community's concept of desirable reform. Although the true nature of the conversation can never be known, and Willis' account is inconsistent or implausible on its face value, there is no question that during early April the legislative committee of the A.B.A. met with Glass and Willis and "the main outlines of the bill, so far as then developed, were stated to them."[22] Shortly thereafter, sometime in mid-April, Colonel House passed a very detailed outline of the bill to Warburg, and before long it was circulating among the key bankers.

Strangely enough, on April 1 Laughlin stepped down from the leadership of the National Citizens' League, claiming that it had succeeded in its goal. He was thoroughly convinced that the Glass Bill would be based, in most of its important details, on his own "Plan D." The plan had been circulated among key league members, and on the assumption that Laughlin was correct, prominent officers of the organization were convinced "we ought to do all we can to have the Glass bill introduced at the special session. . . ." Paul M. Warburg, on the other hand, was less pleased, and on April 22 sent House a criticism of the outline of the Glass Bill that took point mainly with technical issues. Fifteen or twenty regional banks were not deemed too many over the long run, although Warburg preferred three to five. A number of specific details were questioned, but, according to his own claim, many of Warburg's objections were later met in subsequent revisions.[23]

Despite occasional complaints, which are too easily confused with serious opposition, the important bankers regarded the Glass plan favorably and looked forward to its passage. A perfect bill was not expected, George Reynolds told Glass, but something "in the right direction" would solve many problems. Regional banks controlled by a Treasury Board with note issuing functions would give elasticity in credit and note issues. ". . . I shall be only too glad to do what I can to assist in securing for you and your plans the cooperation of the bankers of the country as well as the American Bankers Association. . . ." Glass was soon to appreciate the importance of having the sympathy of the banking community. Colonel House was still very much interested in banking reform, as was Secretary of the Treasury McAdoo. In March, House was suggesting "that McAdoo and I whip the Glass measure into final shape . . ." in order to make the bill acceptable to the chairman of the Senate Committee on Banking, Robert L. Owen.[24] Samuel Untermyer, the ambitious attorney of the Pujo Committee, had been anxious to get jurisdiction over banking legislation for well over a year, and probably prodded by Untermyer, in mid-May McAdoo proposed a National Reserve Bank with far greater centralization than provided for in the Glass Bill; the proposal thoroughly frightened the bankers. By this time Glass had mobilized the major bankers behind him, and it was clear that only his plan would be acceptable to them. In mid-May, before McAdoo proposed his measure, Glass arranged a confidential meeting with major bankers to go over his bill. ". . . the bankers were swinging around into support of something like what we have been working on . . . ," Willis could report to his superior. At the same time, although Laughlin was not given precise details of revisions, Willis kept him informed of general progress.[25]

The crisis over the McAdoo Plan was to end in defeat for McAdoo on June 9 largely because the bankers stood behind Glass. Reynolds, Forgan, and Hepburn were especially important in coming to Glass' defense, and to their own as well. As they became more important as his allies, Glass sought their advice on technical aspects of his plan, and deepened the channels of communication that already existed. McAdoo, who was quite as conservative as Glass, and who perhaps was talked out of his plan by Reynolds and Forgan, only served to drive the bankers into Glass' arms. ". . . I am decidedly in favor of your plan," Reynolds assured Glass. Untermyer, who probably fathered the entire plot, irately suggested to Owen, Wilson, and McAdoo that the issue of banking reform be dropped entirely.[26]

In his next crisis, however, Glass was to be less successful than he had been with McAdoo. During most of his early work on a bill he had slighted Senator Owen. Not until June, 1913, was Glass elevated to the chairmanship of his committee—which he controlled rather completely—and Owen rankled at the relatively junior Congressman's brash ignoring of him. "The chief point of danger now seems to be the apparent intractability of our friend Senator Owen," Glass reported to Hepburn in early June. After Glass deigned to meet with Owen shortly thereafter, the Senator became more conciliatory and backed away from his probably vindictive support for the McAdoo plan. Owen was not prone to radicalism, for a decade as a bank president had made him amply conscious of the needs of the banking system.[27]

Nevertheless, Owen and Glass disagreed on two major points, and Wilson and his advisers were soon involved in the dispute. Owen insisted that the government choose all of the fifteen directors now proposed in the Glass Bill, and that control over the regional money supply be taken out of the hands of the regional banks. The first point was one of degree rather than of kind, since two-thirds of the board was to be "political" anyway. The second point called for increased centralization, but also for the removal of crucial power from the hands of non-political regional bankers. The Owen-Bryan wing of the Democratic Party wished the notes issued by the Reserve Board to be the obligation of the United States Government. Neither of these positions, in this writer's opinion, reflects any fundamental disagreements within the ranks of the Democratic Party, nor did they basically reduce the attraction of the Glass Bill to the majority of important bankers. Surely the regionalism of the Glass Bill was hardly more significant than that in the Aldrich Bill in establishing some decentralized control over the banking system, much less in breaking the power of the "Money Trust." Whether the bankers would be able to sit on the Federal Reserve Board did not change the larger functions of that board, and the functions were most emphatically approved of by the big bankers.

On June 17 Glass, McAdoo, and Owen were called to the White House and the Owen amendments to the Glass Bill were discussed. Glass strongly opposed the proposal, and argued for banker representation. The question was not decided that day, however, and the debate was allowed to rage while Wilson finally made up his mind. ". . . it would prove an almost irretrievable mistake to leave the banks without representation on the Central Board," Glass wrote Wilson on June 18. Perhaps, as McAdoo had suggested, the President might agree to pick the banker representation from lists submitted by bankers.

Glass did not give up on the right of the bankers to some board representation, and he was encouraged by Hepburn to keep up the struggle: "The cause is worthy of a good fight, and I have great hopes that you will measurably, if not wholly, succeed." In the meantime, Hepburn promised, the A.B.A.'s currency commission would be "contending for the currency principles upon which your measure is predicated." Wilson, during the same period, took tangible steps to make sure banking legislation would be seriously considered by Congress. Appearing before a joint session on June 23 "to urge action now," the President based his appeal on the need to increase business opportunity: "It is absolutely imperative that we should give the businessmen of this country a banking and currency system by means of which they can make use of the freedom of enterprise and of individual initiative which we are about to bestow upon them."[28] The speech hit a responsive chord among businessmen and bankers, and numerous letters and telegrams of congratulation were received in the White House.

The following day Wilson, Glass, Owen, and McAdoo met with Reynolds, Wade, Sol Wexler of New Orleans, and other representatives of the bankers to discuss the Glass Bill—which had been formally released to the public on June 20. Several important concessions were made to the bankers on the retirement of national bank notes and the control of regional discount rates. It is possible that additional compromises were made, since Reynolds later complained of government failures to comply with their agreement. But the major desire of the bankers was representation on the Federal Reserve Board. The conventional interpretation has it that Wilson parried this

demand by asking: "Will one of you gentlemen tell me in what civilized country of the earth there are important government boards of
control on which private interests are represented?" Unfortunately
for them, as Warburg later commented, the bankers failed to point to
England and Germany. Moreover, Carter Glass, the originator of the
story, also failed to point out that the subsequent sop given to the
bankers, a Federal Advisory Council of bankers and businessmen,
was suggested in essence by V. Sidney Rothschild, a New York
banker, on June 24. It was first proposed to Wilson, however, by
Brandeis on June 14.[29] Moreover, at least two of the five appointed
board members were required to have banking backgrounds.

The important bankers responded to this new situation with
mixed feelings, and it would be easy to confuse specific complaints
with general disagreement. After meeting with Wilson on June 24,
Sol Wexler and George Reynolds, speaking for the major bankers,
demanded several concessions on the bond refunding and bank reserve provisions of the bill. Also requested was a Federal Advisory
Council, such as had already been agreed upon by Wilson. Glass reacted favorably to these demands, as he had to their earlier pleas, but
was irked by the response of the bankers to the concessions after they
were made. Wexler and Reynolds, Glass claimed, had promised to
get the currency commission of the A.B.A. to endorse his bill "with
enthusiasm" in return for his concessions. Now having made them,
according to his view, he was distressed when Reynolds wrote him
on June 30 and told Glass that he would not oppose the bill but
would come out against "some of its provisions."[30] Glass was hurt,
and immediately wrote Festus J. Wade:

Having made many of the changes suggested by you and your associates,
I think the bill as it now stands is both "sound and wise" and should receive the support of men of your type.

It is difficult to know whether Reynolds and the big bankers were
trying to exact greater compromises from Glass or whether they were
correct in claiming he failed to conform to their verbal understanding
of June 25. Reynolds, on July 7, wrote Glass a letter indicating his
qualified support of the bill, support he had always given:

I am not hostile to and do not intend to be hostile to the whole bill; on
the other hand I hope that the bill may be passed, but I want to see it

modified to the extent the banks will have representation on the Federal Reserve Board, or that there will be an Advisory Committee, and I want to see a modification made in the reserve requirements along the lines our Committee recommended. . . .[31]

During the first part of July it became increasingly apparent that the larger part of the banking community would support the Glass Bill. *The Chicago Banker* reported on a survey of bankers in forty-two smaller Western and Southern cities, and found that bankers in twenty-two cities favored the bill in general while those in ten were opposed and ten were divided. The Northwest was favorable toward the bill on the whole, and the North, Central, and Midwestern states were largely unfavorable. Assuming the survey was fairly accurate, the important question was the nature of the opinion toward the bill among the big bankers and important journals.

"It can be easily criticized as to several of its provisions," the *Banking Law Journal* editorialized. "But in our opinion, if this bill be passed even in its present shape, when put in operation, it will bring about monetary conditions, far in advance of any that have existed in this country since the liquidation of the First Bank of the United States. . . . It is absolutely certain that the principle of central control, forming the basis of the Currency Bill is right. Many of its details may not be properly worked out. Experience alone can show what is superfluous and what is lacking. If Congress waits for a perfect bill which will meet every criticism and every cavil, it will never act effectually."[32]

The *Bankers Magazine,* which had been against the Aldrich Bill, granted the Glass Bill had some valuable assets, but strongly opposed it in August. A number of important expressions of support were received, however. Byron L. Smith, president of the Northern Trust Company of Chicago, told Glass his bill met with his "cordial approval," and was the sort of measure bankers had always clamored for. Josiah Quincy, former mayor of Boston and an insider in the city's elite, told Tumulty that Colonel William A. Gaston, an important Boston banker, had discussed the bill with many large bankers and that differences were friendly rather than irreconcilable. "Fundamentally I believe the proposed bill to be a good one," Samuel Ludlow, Jr. of the Union Trust Company of Jersey City, let Tumulty know, even though he wished banker representation on the Federal Reserve Board.[33]

The big bankers' policy of coyness in the hope of gaining concessions was disturbed by more ominous rumblings from Western radicals in Congress. Even more alarming, these Congressmen included
members of Glass' Committee on Banking. Led by Representatives
Robert L. Henry and Joe H. Eagle of Texas, these men attacked the
Glass Bill as being virtually identical to the Aldrich Bill in its basic
principles. The banks, Eagle claimed, were "to be guaranteed against
loss by the establishment of a paternalistic relationship or private
partnership with the government." The key objective of the dissident
faction was to include an amendment to the bill forbidding interlocking directorates among bankers. The eventual result could have
been predicted, given Wilson's readiness to back Glass to the hilt
with special conferences, political pressures, and the usual means
available to a determined President who also controls the party and
appointments. By promising the inclusion of such an amendment in
any future antitrust bill, and by having Bryan strongly endorse the
existing Glass Bill, Wilson was able to defeat the radicals while Bryan
was proclaiming the measure a people's victory. Although the Glass
Bill was to eventually pass the House on September 18 by a vote of
287 to 85, the possibility of much more radical alternatives to the
Glass Bill was broadcast to the banking and business community in
dramatic fashion.[34] During the midst of the controversy with the
Westerners, Glass wrote Festus Wade and other·key bankers to remind them of the option to his bill. ". . . unless the conservative
bankers of the country are willing to yield something and get behind
the bill . . . we shall get legislation very much less to be desired, or
have nothing done at all." Certainly if one takes on their face value
the histories of the bill subsequently written by Glass and Willis, the
position of the banking community appears as one of intractable
opposition. If one reads the contemporary financial and business
journals, accounts of bankers meetings, and the usual historical raw
materials, a much more complicated image of divisions, manuevering,
and subtleties emerges. Neither picture, in the final analysis, is a correct one, although the second one is obviously preferable. What cannot be measured is the large-scale indifference of the vast majority of
small bankers and businessmen and the extent to which the debate
within the banking community was concentrated among a relatively
few men. The president of the Massachusetts Bankers Association
sent three hundred bankers in his state an inquiry concerning their

opinion on the bill, and received fourteen replies. Henry P. Lason of DeFuniak Springs, Florida, was able to have more signatures sent to the Senate Committee on Banking and Currency in support of his funny-money plan than could either side of the Glass Bill for their positions.[35]

Still, the available records indicate that the banking community was virtually unanimous in its belief in the need for banking reform, however much it disagreed on specific means, and this fact was eventually to have the greatest significance. In the meantime, the bankers lined up on the issue of how to treat the Glass Bill. The large majority accepted the premises of the Glass Bill and sought to work within them, and it is here that the only significant division occurred. The large majority of the important bankers concerned about banking legislation refused to unqualifiedly endorse the bill, yet they strenuously condemned those who advocated opposing it. The goal was to obtain the best measure possible—but to get a measure.

Communications between Glass, Owen, and various bankers continued throughout July and August. But the resolution of the Wyoming Bankers Association favoring the Glass Bill with an amendment to allow for banker control, and the letter of the Richmond banker who suggested "we willingly waive all minor changes, rather than have no bill passed at this session," were relatively unimportant. Of much greater consequence were Vanderlip, Reynolds, Hepburn, Forgan, and bankers of their stature. On August 22 and 23 the leaders of the American Bankers Association met in Chicago to try to hammer out a common position on the Glass Bill. James B. Forgan led the fight for total opposition to the bill, and his stand was defeated by a large majority of the delegates. George M. Reynolds and A. Barton Hepburn, on the other hand, were able to convince the gathering to endorse specific amendments to the Glass Bill rather than oppose it. After all, as Hepburn put it:

The measure recognizes and adopts the principles of a central bank. Indeed, if it works out as the sponsors of the law hope, it will make all incorporated banks together joint owners of a central dominating power. Why, then, should not the principle, once recognized, be correctly applied?

To satisfy the Forgan faction, and perhaps to leave room for compromise, the amendments called for were sweeping in scope, making

national bank participation voluntary, limiting Federal Reserve
Board power in the regions, and in general decentralizing banking
rather than attaining the much desired centralization. The amendments were largely intended as a maneuver, and the details of the
position were sent along to Congress but not strictly adhered to in the
subsequent banker agitation.[36]

While the organized big bankers assumed a hostile position toward the Glass Bill, gestures of important conservative support from
other directions began coming in. Robert H. Treman, president of the
New York Bankers Association, assured Glass that "Personally I am
in sympathy with the Bill in general . . . ," and he wanted only a few
changes. Other indications of support from bankers also trickled in
during the end of August and the beginning of September, and Glass
was surely cognizant of the fact that only a handful of protests
against his bill arrived throughout 1913. The significant assistance,
however, was to come from businessmen's groups and, appropriately
enough, the National Citizens' League.

Laughlin had resigned from fulltime work with the league, but he
remained as chairman of the executive committee while James V.
Farwell, a Chicago businessman, ran the affairs of the organization.
The league took pride in its influence on the issue of banking legislation, and at the beginning of July publicly proclaimed the Glass Bill
as a good start only requiring several changes. Privately, the league's
key executives were much more pleased with the bill than it was
diplomatic to publicly acknowledge. On July 22 Farwell tried to
arrange an appointment with Wilson to discuss modifications of the
Glass Bill, since the league had spent much time educating on general
principles of sound banking, and "The present Glass-Owen bill, as
amended up to date, contains many of those principles." Wilson
would not see Farwell, but Glass, Owen, and McAdoo all discussed
the technical aspects of the bill with him, and Farwell could report
progress to Laughlin. Both Farwell and Laughlin felt that the league
had primary responsibility for the Glass Bill; despite suggested
amendments, at the beginning of September the league, and Laughlin
in particular, felt they had attained their major goals and that the
Glass Bill should be passed without delay.[37]

Businessmen, for the most part, were hardly concerned about
banking reform, but to the extent that they were they strengthened
the position of the Glass Bill. The National Association of Manu-

facturers' convention in May had left the door open to alternatives to the once desirable Aldrich Plan by not passing a specific resolution. Very few resolutions arrived in the Senate and House on the topic during the summer of 1913, but Harry A. Wheeler, president of the U.S. Chamber of Commerce and an active member of the National Citizens' League, in August wrote Glass of his impressions of business opinion on banking after returning from a national tour. There was "a strong desire on the part of the business interests of the country for the passage of a currency measure. There is a deeper interest on the part of the businessmen than I have been them heretofore exhibit in regard to any piece of national legislation." Wheeler favored the bill and suggested to Glass that he concentrate his efforts on winning the country bankers to his bill. Lest it be thought Wheeler was trying to swing Glass to his position, only the following week he wrote Laughlin "that the merchants of the country deeply desire the legislation. . . . The banks, on the other hand, are very much divided. . . . personally I have a large amount of confidence that it is likely to work out better than some of us now think."[38]

The attitude of the banking community toward the Glass Bill was deeply divided throughout September and October. As we shall see, much of the ostensible opposition was calculated to gain some concessions, but the basic principles, as had been the case in May and June, were heartily endorsed. The *Banking Law Journal* reversed its editorial stand and came out against the bill in September. The *Bankers Magazine* continued its traditional opposition to both the Aldrich and Glass Bills, recommending instead an expansion of the clearing house associations. But significant individuals were more reluctant to attack the bill in a wholesale manner. Senator Owen's Committee on Banking and Currency began its hearings in early September, and despite much criticism of the Glass Bill as it stood, much praise for many of its basic features was also heard. Reynolds and Wexler favored fewer than twelve banking regions, for example, but they thought twelve better than the status quo, and they admitted that the elasticity provisions of the bill were a sharp improvement over the situation existing in the banking system at the time. And even the strongest critics admitted that the banking system badly needed legislation.

The Senate hearings dragged on for nearly two months, and the delay encouraged numerous, once friendly, bankers to bargain for more concessions. Many bankers who supported the August 22-23 A.B.A. recommendations felt that the Senate was the proper ground for a fight. Even the critical bankers allowed themselves important loopholes for supporting the Glass Bill. "The administration's currency bill as it now stands in the Senate embodies many features that are fundamentally sound and consonant with the best traditions of banking theory and practice . . .," A. Barton Hepburn declared in mid-October. But what was necessary at this stage was "helpful criticism . . . rather than commendation." Despite the carping of some bankers, Irving T. Bush, the once diehard Aldrich Bill leader of the New York branch of the National Citizens' League, declared that the Glass Bill was a very good compromise which only needed a few revisions. Even Paul Warburg, who concentrated on the desirability of reducing the reserve regions to four, had favorable words for the larger conception behind the Glass Bill.[39]

From October 6 through 10 the American Bankers Association annual convention met in Boston to deal with the entire legislative picture. The currency commission, chaired by Hepburn, brought in a strong attack on the Glass Bill contradicting his statements immediately before and after the convention. There can be little doubt that the resolution was initially intended to serve as useful political leverage and a bluff to obtain concessions. The resolution, condemning the Glass Bill as a form of socialism, reached the floor and was immediately attacked by a number of bankers. Instead of trying to defeat the Hepburn report, friends of the Glass Bill attempted to get a resolution passed to the effect: "That we commend the President, the Secretary of the Treasury and Congress for their efforts to give this country an elastic as well as a safe currency, and pledge them our hearty support toward the enactment of proper legislation to that end."[40]

Hepburn, immediately seeing the obvious advantages such a statement would give him in supporting the Glass Bill and mitigating the harshness of his own report, seconded the measure himself. Although the currency commission report was to pass by a large majority, only the resolution commending Wilson was to pass unanimously. For all practical purposes, the A.B.A. gave its officers a free hand on legislative affairs.

"It is not true that the bankers are opposing legislation," one banker wired his Senator. "On the contrary, they, themselves, have brought about the demand for currency reform and there has been, and is now, a general apathy on the part of the public on this question." But at least a few bankers were willing to work for a wholesale defeat of the Glass Bill. Frank A. Vanderlip, president of the National City Bank had, since July, thought that it might be better to have no measure than one not fully acceptable to the bankers. The Senate Committee on Banking was obstructing the passage of the Glass-Owen Bill to the floor, as an alliance of Republican Insurgents and conservatives, including Democrats, blocked it in the interminable hearings. On October 23 Vanderlip presented the committee with the draft of a bill clearly unrepresentative of his true viewpoint, but ably designed to block the passage of any legislation. The scheme provided for a much more centralized national bank with total control over all branches, as well as smaller liabilities to banks that joined. For several weeks, until Wilson was able to break the impasse, the bankers were faced with the prospect of obtaining no legislation whatsoever.[41]

Earlier in October Glass had warned the bankers at a meeting of the Academy of Political Science:

the time for action on this great question is now, while the public interest is alive, and while we can act with that caution and deliberation which is impossible when the country is in the throes of a financial panic. . . . If legislation now is postponed until the public is goaded by another panic, you may rest assured that the resulting legislation will be more radical—yes, far more radical—than that contained in the present bill.

The logic of the argument was compelling and obvious, and major bankers immediately turned on the Vanderlip scheme. "I am unalterably opposed to obstructing any new banking and currency plan at this late date," Festus J. Wade wired Wilson. "I am confident the great masses of the American people are not willing to have a central bank inaugurated in this country." Jacob H. Schiff released an attack on the Vanderlip plan to the papers on October 27, and called for the speedy passage of the Glass Bill.[42]

A solid front between the Administration, Bryan, and the bankers was too much for the Vanderlip junto in Congress, and despite some exasperating moments for Wilson, the final outcome of the measure was never seriously in doubt. Some of Vanderlip's Senatorial supporters, after all, were damning the Glass Bill for having been written by Willis, who was identified as an agent of Wall Street. An alliance of this nature was not likely to last, and in late November the Glass-Owen Bill was sent along to the floor of the Senate for debate.

As the Congressional aspect of the controversy continued, the banking and business community debated the bill among themselves. Glass could count on the support of Bryan and, finally, Untermyer, and despite occasional opposition, the important bankers stopped playing coy and aimed directly at a victory for the Glass Bill. La Follette was insisting that the Glass Bill was "a big bankers bill," and he served to remind the bankers that there was a worse possible fate than the one being offered to them. Jacob H. Schiff was urging passage of the bill, and Festus J. Wade, along with his St. Louis colleagues, released a statement that the Administration's bill was the best one ever presented. When he heard rumors that he was allegedly against the Glass Bill, James Stillman notified his banks not to oppose the bill. Even Henry P. Davison gave up his hopes for the Aldrich Bill and joined the forces behind Glass' measure. Henry Lee Higginson, perhaps predictably, notified Richard Olney "I *very much* wish the bill success—I shall be glad for Wilson's glory if he succeeds."[43]

One incident illustrates the extent of the Glass Bill's true popularity in New York banking circles. Glass was invited to debate the issue of banking reform with Vanderlip before the Economic Club on November 13. Eleven hundred presumably hostile bankers and businessmen, according to Glass, gathered to see the battle. Only the prior month Vanderlip was attacking the "obnoxious" powers given to the Federal Reserve Board under the Glass Bill, nevertheless indicating that "as a matter of fact, I am extremely favorable to about eighty per cent of it." Now, Vanderlip was forced to justify a far greater political centralization. Glass was quite amazed at the massively favorable response to his speech and at the warm report on the proceedings in the pro-Roosevelt journal, *The Outlook*. Ignoring the fact that *The Outlook* had endorsed his bill several weeks earlier, and that the audience was not at all hostile to start with, the favorable response to Glass at this stage was perfectly consistent with everything else taking place within the banking and business community at the time. The most significant aspect of the entire affair, however, was the obvious extent to which Vanderlip felt uncomfortable in his new role. "Everyone concerned in this legislation is in pretty substantial agreement upon what result they are seeking," he admitted, "and within very broad lines upon the nature of the banking machine that must be set up to accomplish it." He made his criticisms, but he also praised Wilson for his stand for legislation, and reminded his audience, almost apologetically, that "For years bankers have been almost the sole advocates of just this sort of legislation that it is now hoped we will have, and it is unfair to accuse them of being in opposition to sound legislation."[44]

By the beginning of December, despite the strong attacks on certain phases of the bill by Elihu Root in the Senate—he still insisted he was for a strong reform measure—the direction of banker sentiment was overwhelmingly for the Glass-Owen Bill. In October the National Citizens' League's executive committee closed up shop on the grounds "that the work of the organization has been practically completed and success has been achieved." Although some bankers might oppose certain provisions of the Glass Bill, the league pointed out, neither the Aldrich nor the Glass Bill was perfect in all respects, "But either plan has obvious merits and forms a basis on which can be built up an operating success." ". . . . the Glass bill complies with approximate satisfaction to the principles of banking reform originally fixed by the League. . . ." This handsome endorsement, which was quite obviously sincere, was soon followed by many others. Midwestern bankers overwhelmingly favored the Glass-Owen Bill, Untermyer could report to Tumulty in mid-November. Hundreds of letters that poured into the White House from bankers, businessmen, and professionals confirmed this impression. When faced with the choice between the Glass Bill or none at all, nearly all banks opted for the Glass Bill. When faced with a choice between Glass' measure and Vanderlip's, they fought Vanderlip's. Glass had pleased the bankers in his debate in New York, and he wisely sought their advice on technical points during the following weeks. In mid-December the Vanderlip forces in the Senate, led by Senator Gilbert M. Hitchcock, seemed on the verge of defeating the Glass-Owen Bill. Glass notified Hepburn, Wexler, and Reynolds of the situation, and together with Wheeler of the U.S. Chamber of Commerce and J. H. Tregoe of the National Association of Credit Men they were able to mount a telegram campaign endorsing the *original* Glass Bill and attacking the Vanderlip Plan.[45] On December 19 the Senate passed the bill, with only one important modification (raising the gold reserve behind Reserve currency from 33⅓ per cent to 40 per cent), by a vote of 54 to 34. On December 22 the House passed the conference bill by a vote of 298 to 60, the Senate by a majority of 43 to 25.

The Authorship of the
Federal Reserve Act

A banking reform bill had been enacted and the bankers were pleased. Carter Glass immediately received congratulations from Hepburn, Wexler, Warburg, Forgan, James Speyer, and many other bankers. Businessmen such as John Wanamaker, James V. Farwell, Irving T. Bush, Charles R. Crane, and numerous others wrote him, full of praise for his work. Wilson also received hundreds of congratulations from bankers, businessmen, and business organizations. Important business organizations were also ready to endorse the new Act at their conventions during the subsequent months. The National Chamber of Commerce and the National Association of Credit Men were perhaps the quickest to respond. Among bankers, without doubt, the consensus was strongly favorable and perfectly consistent with their stand immediately before the final passage of the bill. Warburg was quite sincere when he wrote Glass on December 23, 1913, that "The fundamental thoughts, for the victory of which some of us have worked for so many years, have won out." The character of the board was of paramount importance to the future of the Act, he wrote Laughlin in February, 1914, but "the law on the whole is a great step in advance. . . ." Discussing the matter among themselves, bankers were equally friendly to the Act, and Laughlin was entirely correct when he stated, several months later, that "the sum and substance of the whole act is so remarkably good, that the combined support of both bankers and the public is certain to be given to it. . . ."[46]

Pride in the Federal Reserve Act was so great, in fact, that an intense controversy over its authorship was almost immediately to develop and simmer for well over a decade. The four major contestants for the authorship of the Federal Reserve Act were Willis, Glass, Warburg, and Laughlin, and one cannot understand the subsequent autobiographical accounts of the evolution and passage of the Act without also appreciating the fact that the desire to claim its paternity was uppermost in the minds of each of these men.

If one regards the Federal Reserve Act as part of the longer history of the banking reform movement, then certainly Laughlin's claim for the major responsibility for the Act is fairly well substantiated—despite numerous minor errors in his autobiography. But on all questions of important fact, none of the four major autobiographies is entirely accurate, and none can be accepted as the final version. No attention should be given to the numerous minor claimants, such as Owen and Untermyer. The bankers were the only significant group concerned with banking reform after 1897, and their problems and needs were the primary cause and motive behind the Act. For the Federal Reserve Act was the result of a movement led by bankers seeking rationalization, and hoping to offset the decentralization of banking toward small banks and state banks. The expansion and domination of banking by big city bankers was possible only with the aid of the federal government, and although the Act solved many of the problems of the small bankers, it held out the promise of reversing those larger tendencies within the banking system running against the big city bankers.

There was no disagreement among bankers in 1913 that legislation was desirable, but only over the precise form it should take. The best that might be said is that the Federal Reserve Act was the victory of Southern and Western banking, although even this view is inaccurate, but it certainly cannot be claimed that the Act was the victory of the people over the bankers. The significant support for reform came from the big bankers from 1909 on. Initially the major bankers favored, for the most part, the principles of the Aldrich Bill. They then supported the principles of the Glass Bill. The issue remains: to what extent did the big bankers obtain all or most of the principles of the Aldrich Bill in the Federal Reserve Act? And, far more important, to what extent did the Federal Reserve Act serve the interests of the big bankers irrespective of its differences from the Aldrich Bill?

Nelson Aldrich, for his part, was very strongly opposed to the Glass Bill as a whole throughout 1913, and although he felt it had "some features which were copied from the National Monetary Commission's plan . . .," it was "in the main . . . a very bad bill. . . ." Even when some of his old associates, such as Henry P. Davison,

tried to point out similarities on essentials, the dour ex-Senator refused to put his seal of approval on any major aspect of the Glass
Bill. He sourly pronounced to Taft that the bill was "revolutionary in
its character," and "will be the first and most important step toward
changing our form of government from a democracy to an autoc-
racy."[47]

Despite Aldrich's insistence that the Federal Reserve Act had
very little in common with his own proposal, he could not dissuade
many of his conservative friends from supporting the Glass Bill, or
from feeling that there was a direct continuity between the two plans.
Root was convinced, for his part, that "The Federal Reserve Act
was based directly upon the bill reported by the Monetary Commission. . . . It was the bill reported by that commission with some
modifications." Henry P. Davison, who helped formulate the Aldrich
Bill, also thought there was a direct continuity between it and the
Federal Reserve Act. Herbert L. Satterlee, Morgan's son-in-law and
official biographer, shared this judgment, and many years later an
Aldrich descendant, surveying the available evidence, came to the
same conclusion. Other contemporary commentators shared this view
also, and it has been passed along without any real resolution.[48]

From the vantage of crucial personnel and moving forces, the
theory of the direct continuity between the Aldrich and the Glass
Bills is certainly valid. The question remains, however, as to what
extent the specific provisions and functions of the two plans were
identical or significantly similar. Glass insisted that the two plans had
nothing in common "beyond a common use in some cases of indispensable banking technique and nomenclature," and that his bill
drew heavily on the clearing house experience of American banking.
Willis' interpretation of the matter was virtually identical.[49]

An analytical comparison of the text of the final Federal Reserve
Act and the Aldrich Bill reveals striking similarities, and in a number
of places the wording of the two plans is virtually identical or only
slightly modified. Warburg, seeking to vindicate his claim to the paternity of the Act, juxtaposed the texts of the two bills in parallel
columns, and by doing so greatly diminished the credibility of Glass
and Willis' claim that the Aldrich Bill was unimportant to the final
Act.

The Federal Reserve Act provided for eight to twelve districts
as opposed to fifteen in the Aldrich Bill. All national banks under the

Act were required to become part of the Federal Reserve System and to subscribe to capital stock in the Federal Bank equal to 6 per cent of their paid-up capital stock and surplus. State banks meeting certain requirements could voluntarily affiliate with the System. The Aldrich Bill made national bank affiliation optional, and fixed the capital subscription at 20 per cent of a bank's paid-in and unimpaired capital. The board of each Federal Reserve District, numbering nine, was to be divided into three classes of three members each. Class A directors were to be elected by the bankers, each bank having one vote. Class B directors were not to be bankers but were to represent those engaged in "commerce, agriculture or some other industrial pursuit." These men were nominated and elected, however, by the member banks of the district, and could be ex-bankers. Banks were to be divided into three groups, by size, and each could elect one director in classes A and B, or a total of six directors. Class C members were to be appointed by the Federal Reserve Board, and one was to be "a person of tested banking experience" designated as the chairman. The Aldrich Bill called for twelve directors, six chosen by banks irrespective of size, four by banks in proportion to their capital, and two who were to be representatives of nonbanking interests, elected by the ten previously chosen. The Aldrich Bill merely put control of the districts in the hands of the bankers, but the Federal Reserve Act made it possible for the bankers to take over each district, put nothing in the way of this happening, and gave them the means of controlling two-thirds of the directors.

The Federal Reserve Board was to consist of seven members, two of which were the ex officio Secretary of the Treasury and the Comptroller of the Currency. The five were appointed by the President with the approval of the Senate for staggered terms, and not more than one could be chosen from any district. At least two were to "be persons experienced in banking or finance," but none could be directors or stockholders of banks while in office. The board under the Aldrich Bill was entirely banker controlled, consisting of fifteen bankers and fifteen nonbankers, all elected by the branches, plus nine members elected by the nine largest branches and seven ex officio members, including the Secretaries of the Treasury, Agriculture, and Commerce, and the Comptroller. An executive committee of eight was to be chosen from this board, with not more than one from any branch. The Federal Reserve Board could fix the rates for rediscounted paper in the districts, suspend and adjust reserve requirements according to certain rules, issue and retire Reserve notes, and exercise very extensive controls over the various district banks. Since the Aldrich Bill allowed the branches to exercise the power to rediscount and discount within their area, and was far more decentralized in many other crucial respects, the Federal Reserve Act reflected a higher degree of centralization.

The various Federal Reserve Banks had primary responsibility for the actual discounting of less than ninety-day commercial notes, drafts, and bills as well as certain limited forms of agricultural credit for up to six months. The Aldrich Bill was virtually the same, except that it ignored agricultural credits. The open market provisions of both measures, allowing reserve banks to buy and sell bankers' acceptances, bills of exchange, gold, U.S. bonds and notes, were the same in most essential respects. The Aldrich Bill intended continuing existing reserve requirements, but the Federal Reserve Act fixed them at 12 per cent of total demand deposits for banks not in reserve or central reserve cities, 15 per cent for banks in reserve cities, and 18 per cent for banks in central reserve cities. Reserves in gold or lawful money against reserve notes in circulation were to be 40 per cent under the Reserve Act, as opposed to 50 per cent under the Aldrich plan. Federal Reserve notes under the Act were the obligation of the Treasury and were acceptable currency for all purposes, but under the Aldrich Bill notes were mainly for internal bank transactions. Both plans allowed clearing houses to be set up in the various districts and branches, and gave Washington the power to order their creation.

The Federal Reserve Act required the payment of 6 per cent dividends on the paid-up capital of its stockholders, as opposed to 4 per cent under the Aldrich Bill. Banks with a minimum capital and surplus of $1 million were permitted to obtain Federal Reserve Board approval to create foreign branches, as opposed to twice that amount in the Aldrich Bill.

Shortly after the passage of the Federal Reserve Act, and before the controversy over its authorship became intense, Willis wrote an outline of the new Act, admitting that "With regard to stock issues, kinds of paper eligible for rediscounts, and not a few other particulars, the Federal Reserve Act follows lines laid down in the measure which bore the name of Senator Aldrich."[50] Allegedly in order to reduce the opposition, in certain spots even the language of the two bills was identical. But despite this concession by Willis, the fact remains that the two plans differed in many particulars, and it is true that the identical language was not followed extensively in the most important parts of the new Act.

In major areas the differences between the two plans were of degree rather than kind, and, if anything, the new Act provided for substantially greater centralization. The crucial question is whether the intended functions of the two plans were identical, from the bankers' viewpoint. To what extent did the Federal Reserve Act serve the interests of the big bankers irrespective of its differences from the Aldrich Bill?

The Fruits
of Victory

The response of business and banking circles to the Act during its formative period, prior to its opening for actual operations in November, 1914, was overwhelmingly favorable. National banks had sixty days to join the system or give up their charters, and within one month after the passage of the Act three-quarters of the capital of the national banks was represented by the applications for admission to the system, including nearly all the large banks in the major cities. Four times as many state banks and trusts companies applied for national charters as during the same period of the prior year, and John S. Williams, Assistant Secretary of the Treasury, reported to Wilson that "The eagerness with which the banks have vied with each other in accepting the provisions of the new law is nothing less than extraordinary. . . ." Expressions of support for the new Act were to filter in throughout 1914.

The truly significant fact was not the overwhelmingly favorable attitude of the business community, but the realism of those bankers who were fully aware that the success or failure of the Federal Reserve System would depend not on abstract laws but on concrete administrators.[51] The selection of the personnel of the Federal Reserve Board was left very largely in the hands of Colonel House, although McAdoo also made several important recommendations.

Both men sought the advice of various members of banking circles, and the immediate rumors that Warburg or A. Piatt Andrews were being considered for board membership shocked Willis. "I fear from the types of names suggested for the Federal Reserve Board," he wrote Glass at the end of December, "that the old Aldrich central bank group is endeavoring to get into control or at least large management in the new system." If it succeeded, he feared, the law might be shaped along "central bank lines." On the other hand, such rumored appointments greatly encouraged former critics of the Glass Bill. Perhaps far more symbolic than the advice of George Perkins or Paul Warburg that it would be discreet to wait until Wilson made his appointments before criticizing the Act, was the private statement made by none other than Nelson Aldrich to John A. Sleicher of *Leslie's Weekly* on February 7:

Whether the bill will work all right or not depends entirely, as I stated, upon the character and wisdom of the men who will control the various organizations, especially the Federal Reserve Board. There is undoubtedly a general disposition to make the best of the legislation with the hope that it may turn out all right. . . .

The general effect of the act has unquestionably been helpful. While I have some doubts about the ultimate results, it seems to me no good purpose would be subserved by expressing publicly any doubts upon the subject.[52]

The first serious board candidate, eventually nominated and accepted, was W. P. G. Harding, the president of the largest bank in Alabama and apparently the proposal of House. House then recommended Richard Olney and suggested several businessmen for Wilson's consideration. Wilson, at the end of April, then offered posts to Warburg, Richard Olney, and Harry A. Wheeler, former chairman of the U.S. Chamber of Commerce, former National Citizens' League director, and president of the Union Trust Company of Chicago. Wheeler and Olney declined, but Warburg accepted the nomination.

Wilson had urged Olney to take the post because "the whole business world would be greatly heartened if you did." Businessmen were delighted by the Warburg appointment instead, but rumblings of a fight were immediately heard as Owen, Willis, and others protested. Warburg's friends, for their part, insisted that he had supplied most of the ideas for the Act and deserved the post. But the response to Warburg's appointment was nothing compared to the storm that broke out when Thomas D. Jones, a director of International Harvester and an old Princeton friend of Wilson's, was nominated. Wilson was deeply committed to Jones for personal reasons, and failed to get the Senate to approve his nomination despite his utilization of all the tools available to him. Warburg's confirmation, during July, was also delayed by reticent Senators curious as to how this Wall Street tycoon was to muzzle the Money Trust. Wilson could not understand the dislike for big capitalists among a number of Senators, and on July 8 he chose to remind the Senate, "It knows that the business of the country has been chiefly promoted in recent years by enterprises organized on a great scale and that the vast majority of the men connected with what we have come to call big business are honest, incorruptible and patriotic."[53]

Perhaps the Senate was chastened, but it had one victory and decided to spare Warburg if he would come for a "conference" rather than a hearing before the appropriate Senate committee. Besides, the President had fought hard and well, and his adamant posture dissuaded them from overriding him again. While the Warburg-Jones crisis raged, Wilson moved to fill his other board posts. Adolph C. Miller, formerly an economist teaching at the University of California, was offered a post and accepted. Several important Midwestern bankers were offered posts but declined. To take the place of one of these rejections, Frederic A. Delano, a railroad administrator and a former director of the National Citizens' League, was given the job.[54] Charles S. Hamlin, a Boston attorney, was given the fifth seat. In all, the banking community and those close to it were given three of the five board seats.

The Federal Reserve Board was chosen, and the banking community was satisfied. In the two most important Federal Reserve Districts the bankers moved to obtain the dominating positions of their regions, and throughout the nation they obtained many crucial posts. In Chicago, Reynolds was elected as a class A director representing the large banks, and Forgan was elected a class A director for the medium-size banks. Both men were nominated for the governorship of the district, but since both were unwilling to accept the decrease in pay they preferred having a government bank examiner in whom they had confidence appointed instead. More important, however, was the appointment of Benjamin Strong to the governorship of the New York Reserve Bank. Strong had been the president of the Bankers Trust Company and a director of many banks, as well as an early advocate of the Aldrich Bill. Many of Elihu Root's attacks on the Glass Bill in the Senate were drafted by Strong, but just prior to its passage he decided to give it critical support in the hope of "making the best of it." Now, due to the pleadings of Warburg and Henry P. Davison, Strong resigned from his many lucrative posts to take the leadership of the most important bank district in the nation.[55]

While the regional banks were working out their own organizational problems, the Federal Reserve Board in Washington moved to make specific the many general and flexible provisions of the Federal Reserve Act. Many points of disagreement were to arise, especially on the sensitive point of the relationship of the board to the Treasury Department. Warburg, Miller, and Delano feared that Secretary of the Treasury McAdoo sought to control the banking system—a contention McAdoo was quick to deny—and a conflict was inevitable. McAdoo was to win the battle but lose the war, since the board became a largely independent operation. The basic point of contention was the number of reserve districts. Warburg had never wanted twelve or even eight districts, and before his nomination was confirmed he frankly admitted to Colonel House, who passed the information to Wilson, that "it will become necessary to divide the country into four or five sections, each of which would be in particular charge of one member of the Federal Reserve Board. . . ."[56] Since each board member would be in charge of his home district, Warburg blandly announced, he was scheduled to take over New York, Philadelphia, Boston, and the entire upper Atlantic region. Wilson should have taken an unequivocal position on this suggestion, but he let it pass. It is no wonder, then, that Warburg was ready to contest the district structure handed to the board when it opened for business in late 1914.

The organization committee of the Federal Reserve System had created twelve districts before the board came into power. The Act itself allowed for as few as eight districts and permitted the board to readjust boundaries. By mid-1915, despite the protests of local banking interests, Warburg, Delano, Harding, and Miller moved to reduce the number of districts to eight. McAdoo, outnumbered on the board, managed to get the support of Wilson and Glass, and on

November 22, 1915, the Attorney General handed down a ruling forbidding the board to reduce the number of districts or change the location of existing reserve cities. In the last analysis, however, Wilson believed in an independent board free of political interference, and Warburg's faction won a number of successes, in large part because the outbreak of the war favored their arguments on the need for further centralization of the banking system. Reserve requirements were altered to meet the original standards of the Aldrich Bill, much to Willis' dismay. Such changes were relatively minor, however, and the Federal Reserve Act was not revised in any fundamental way in this period. Nor was such a revision advocated by the banking community, although the American Bankers Association was not inflexible on small changes. Had it been unhappy with the basic structure of the Act, or with the way it was being administered, it probably would have said so. Perhaps the machinery of the system was somewhat too complicated, the *Journal of the American Bankers Association* concluded late in 1915, but

It would be better to make no change at all than to have the act torn to pieces. It is certain that there has been created an agency capable of performing the work intended. There will be no further panics due to a bad currency system. Business will not be stifled by a defective banking scheme.[57]

The goal of nearly two decades of labor by banker-reformers had been attained!

". . . if all such prejudices, political and sectional, against New York and its bankers can be overcome by such measures as have been adopted in the Federal Reserve Act," Benjamin Strong suggested in June, 1915, "I should feel that the work now being done has been well repaid." The bankers, after all, managed their own regulation, and under the aegis of the federal government, Strong pointed out in 1919, the bankers of New York had ended anti-Wall Street sentiment and insulated themselves.[58] Strong was fully aware of the function of the Federal Reserve System in protecting the banking community, and he was conscious of his power within the New York District. Until the passage of the Federal Reserve Act the relative power of New York in national banking was declining, but from 1914 to 1935 it dominated American banking as it had only in the 1890's. And throughout this period Strong became at least as powerful as Morgan had been in his best years.

It was natural that New York became the dominant factor in the Federal Reserve System. The Federal Reserve Board was, for many years, either seriously divided or handicapped by directors who had no special leadership abilities—there was, in brief, a lack of firm, strong leadership with a definite policy. Warburg, the only real contender for such a role, left the board in 1918 at the end of his term, and refused renomination because of the strong anti-German sentiment in government. The Federal Reserve Act coordinated, if not centralized, the banking resources of the nation to an unparalleled degree. The continual and routine decisions of New York banking, because of this situation, affected the entire banking system in a much more important fashion than ever before. The presumably decentralized nature of the system allowed the most powerful of the interlocked districts to make innumerable operational decisions for the remainder.

Strong and a carefully selected staff of his former associates and aides ran the New York District, and the Federal Reserve Board found it easier to channelize its operations through New York. From 1916 on, the New York bank, with the approval of the Federal Reserve Board, began acting for the entire system on foreign operations, and the foreign trade of the nation was, to a large extent, financed through the New York money market. Moreover, the New York bank was appointed banker for the government in its foreign transactions. From 1915 on, New York served as agent for buying securities for all the Federal Reserve Districts, and it handled the traffic in acceptances, and from 1922 on the New York bank handled most of the open market functions of the system. Throughout the 1920's the increasing amount of call money sent to the New York Stock Exchange involved the Federal Reserve System in the stock market to an unprecedented extent. Perhaps most significant, New York discount rates became the leader for the entire system, and not only attracted reserve acceptances to New York, but in some respects introduced greater rigidity into the entire banking system.

The trend in the national banking system until 1913 was toward a reduction in the bankers' balances and individual deposits in New York, and in favor of the relatively more rapid growth in the Midwest and West. The most conservative estimate shows that New

York held 53.6 per cent of U.S. bankers' balances in 1915 and 52.7 per cent in 1928, and, thus, that it dominated the national banking system; some, such as Lawrence E. Clark, have argued that New York's relative share of reserves increased between the passage of the Federal Reserve Act and the Depression. The Federal Reserve System, for the most part, stabilized the financial power of New York within the economy, reversing the longer term trend toward decentralization by the utilization of political means of control over the central money market. Clark concluded:

So overwhelming has been the power of the New York Reserve Bank that the instrumentalities through which the Federal Reserve credit policy has been expressed may be brought into a grouping of three—the Federal Reserve Board, the Federal Reserve Bank of New York, and the other, or interior, Federal Reserve banks. At times the Federal Reserve Board has held the balance of power in the system and at other times the New York Reserve Bank. But the influence of the interior Reserve banks has always been weak. On the whole there is reason to believe that the Federal Reserve Bank of New York has been the dominant instrumentality which has controlled the credit policy of our central banking system.[59]

The question arises: To what extent was the evolution of the Federal Reserve System into a crucial aspect of political capitalism inherent in the very premises and specifics of the Act? As we have seen, the banking reform movement was initiated and sustained by big bankers seeking to offset, through political means, the diffusion and decentralization within banking. In 1895 the government went to Morgan for financial aid, but in 1907 Morgan came to the government. But in going to the government, banker-reformers brought concrete plans and specific personnel, and given the pro-capitalist frame of reference of all the major parties, it was the bankers who provided the legislative formulations of all significant bills.

It was no coincidence that the Glass-Underwood-Wilson Democrats created a measure very much to the liking of bankers and conservatives alike. During the war McAdoo found it useful to have the banking system centralized, as Willis put it, "by accepting the dominance of the Federal Reserve Bank of New York in the councils of the Reserve system and by employing the machinery of the Reserve Bank of New York for the purpose of directing and reorganizing the finances of the rest of the country." This centralization lasted after the war, but lest it be thought it was a necessity imposed by extraordinary circumstances, even Carter Glass, in a moment of frankness, admitted that it was hardly the destruction of the Money Trust that he sought in his bill. In April, 1916, well before the emergency reorganization of the American economy for war, Glass told a Washington audience that

The proponents of the Federal reserve act had no idea of impairing the rightful prestige of New York as the financial metropolis of this hemisphere. They rather expected to confirm its distinction, and even hoped to assist powerfully in wresting the scepter from London and eventually making New York the financial center of the world. Eminent Englishmen with the keenest perception have frankly expressed apprehension of such result. Indeed, momentarily this has come to pass. And we may point to the amazing contrast between New York under the old system in 1907, shaken to its very foundations because of two bank failures, and New York at the present time, under the new system, serenely secure in its domestic banking operations and confidently financing the great enterprises of European nations at war.[60]

CHAPTER TEN

THE TRIUMPH OF

POLITICAL CAPITALISM:

THE FEDERAL

TRADE COMMISSION

AND TRUST LEGISLATION

DURING MOST OF 1913 Woodrow Wilson and his aides were pre-occupied with banking reform and tariff legislation. But the pressure for more extensive federal regulation of corporations and business was great, and the New Freedom also obligated the Administration to take action in this area. To precisely what was Wilson committed? The New Freedom was, in the final analysis, intended to serve as a campaign document, and the doctrine was full of inconsistencies. "I am for big business, and I am against the trusts," Wilson declared, but he could not define the major differences between the two and he never gave the matter serious thought. He proclaimed that "The development of business upon a great scale . . . is inevitable," and also expressed satisfaction that businessmen were beginning to reform themselves.[1]

The guidelines utilized by Wilson were amorphous. What was certain, however, was the demand of leading businessmen for federal regulation designed to meet their problems. Since the failure of Perkins, Gary, and the National Civic Federation forces to enact the Hepburn Bill in 1908, important segments of big business had sought to overcome the condition of uncertainty that existed in innumerable industries. Federal incorporation had been prominently mentioned as a possible solution for well over a decade, but Congress was never willing to act on the principle. The idea of a trade commission similar to the I.C.C. was actively promoted by George W. Perkins and many others from early 1911 on, and both the Progressive and Republican Parties endorsed the proposal in 1912. Gary and Carnegie were even suggesting government price-fixing! Armed with the National Civic Federation's business opinion poll of late 1911, big businessmen stridently called for federal regulation of the economy.

It was obvious that without strong Executive support there could be significant legislative advances toward a political capitalism only as a result of irate public opinion manipulated to satisfy business ends. Save in railroad legislation, much of the real progress toward political capitalism from the beginning of the century until 1913 had been an incidental byproduct of scandals and amorphous reform enthusiasm among the wider public. In 1913 Wilson had little guidance save from fundamentally conservative individuals, of whom Colonel House was the foremost, who directed Wilson's unclear but moderate impulses toward conservative ends. Bryan, despite his emotional radicalism, was also a shrewd politician, and it was difficult to reduce his arsenal of phrases and clichés to specific proposals for concrete changes. Moreover, Wilson could barely tolerate Bryan's style and manners, and relied on him only when it was absolutely necessary. During 1913, despite a few dramatic antitrust cases by the fundamentally conservative but literal-minded Attorney General, James C. McReynolds, Wilson was responsive to the pressures and desires of big business. There was more progress in the fulfilment of big business interests through the Federal Reserve Act alone than there had been in well over five years.

Wilson's ideological conservatism has been appreciated by historians. The extent of that conservatism can only be fully under-stood, however, when we pass from Wilson as an intellectual to Wilson as an administrator. The New Freedom, after all, was not merely a doctrine—in any serious sense it was hardly that. The New Freedom was, more than anything else, government regulation of banking, industry, and railroads. Wilson during his eight years as a trustbuster initiated substantially fewer cases than Harding and Coolidge during their two terms. Wilson's other reforms were, for the most part, of no great significance to a wider public.

Wilson and
Business

Wilson did not enter office under any sort of cloud that might have made big business apprehensive. ". . . we shall get more experience with respect to economic and industrial policies," Senator Joseph B. Foraker predicted immediately after the election, and even Taft found it possible to approve Wilson's new Cabinet, an approbation that was eventually to blossom to admiration for Wilson in general. J. P. Morgan, on his deathbed, was full of optimism for the new Administration, and he offered his services to the President through George Harvey.[2]

Senator Francis G. Newlands, the old Democratic advocate of federal incorporation, by 1912 was ready to try instead to obtain a commission, and Wilson's victory made him chairman of the crucial Senate Committee on Interstate Commerce. Despite the increasing possibilities for action in 1913, very little was done. Pressure for action existed, of course, but it was mild in a prosperity year. Roosevelt kept up his demand for an interstate trade commission, but George Wickersham denied the need for any serious changes in the Sherman Act. Letters continued to pour into the Department of Justice, as they had in previous years, asking for opinions on the legality of various actions. And, as Arthur Eddy told a Department of Justice official, "I am interested in seeing passed broad and comprehensive legislation, legislation which will really reach the evils the industrial world suffers, at least as effectively as the Interstate Commerce Law reaches some of the evils in transportation."[3]

It was logical that the Department of Justice concern itself with the problem of the relationship of the government to business. It was even more logical, however, that the Bureau of Corporations try to reconsider the problem in light of the commitments of the New Freedom. Joseph E. Davies, the new head of the bureau, pondered about the matter and in July, 1913, sent Secretary of Commerce William C. Redfield a memo on the topic; Redfield approved it and immediately sent it along to Wilson. Perhaps the Davies memo was really a rationale for larger appropriations for the bureau—he asked for a tripling of its budget—but it is at least of significance as an example of an attempted definition of the role of the executive in the New Freedom. Big business had implications to the general political structure insofar as it had the power to create a state within a state, and it had the power to affect labor, Davies admitted. Both of these problems were beyond the interest of the bureau. What was of concern, Davies suggested, was the effect of big business on the costs of production and prices. In addition to its specific industry investigations, it was time for the bureau to discover "what principles or laws generally underlie industry and its relation to society and to the state. . . ." Questions to be explored were the relationship of size to efficiency and prices, and "whether the regulation of practically monopolistic units or the restoration of competitive units is the true and correct solution." This task, Davies modestly proposed, was to be completed in a five months period. As if this were not enough, state corporation laws and trade agreements would also be studied in great detail. If state laws could be made uniform it "would eliminate one of the principal arguments for centralization of power in the National Government for the regulation of corporations. . . ." Moreover, a really serious study of trade agreements could determine which ones ought to be exempted from the Sherman Act. The Davies memo indicated the doubt and confusion that existed among so many crucial leaders around Wilson, and left the door wide open to those who knew what they wanted. Davies' ambitious answers were never produced.

By October, 1913, however, it was increasingly obvious that Wilson's current legislative preoccupations were going to attain fulfilment and that "antitrust" legislation would be a serious issue in 1914. In late October, Ralph W. Easley, the director of the National Civic Federation, wrote McReynolds about antitrust legislation. Referring to the unhappy experience with the Hepburn Bill under Roosevelt,

Easley indicated that he had another draft bill available that had been produced by Seth Low, James R. Garfield, C. A. Severance, Samuel Untermyer, John B. Clark, and J. W. Jenks. An audience was requested and immediately granted. The federation's plan provided for a seven-man Interstate Trade Commission chosen by the President and with powers of investigation and subpoena, and the ability to refer its complaints to the courts and fine companies $5,000 for each violation. The commission could license corporations, and would require annual reports. Its jurisdiction would apply to companies with sales of $10 million and up. The proposal received an important circulation and a copy was sent to Wilson, while Davies also discussed the matter with Easley in detail.[4]

By the end of 1913 Wilson was feeling very mellow toward business. It had been most cooperative—indeed its aid had been crucial —in the campaign to obtain banking reform. On December 19 he wrote McReynolds that "I gain the impression more and more from week to week that the businessmen of the country are sincerely desirous of conforming with the law, and it is very gratifying indeed to be able to deal with them in complete frankness and to be able to show them that all that we desire is an opportunity to cooperate with them." During the same month, conscious of the long preceding effort to obtain a federal commission, the House Committee on the Judiciary, chaired by Henry D. Clayton of Alabama, opened hearings on the entire problem of trust legislation. And from late 1913 on the leaders of the business community began shifting their attention to the need for greater federal regulation of the industrial economy.

The President was fully aware of the fact that the business community resented the insecurity of the Sherman Act and wished to attain a measure of predictability and confidence that had been lacking under Taft. He was certainly familiar with the call for a "Federal Trade Commission" in the Republican platform of 1912, and the obsessive concern of the Progressive Party with the issue. Was it not Wilson, in the closing days of the campaign of 1912, who warned that "If the government is to tell big businessmen how to run their business, then don't you see that big businessmen have to get closer to the government even than they are now?" But the campaign was over, and by January, 1914, the pressure for a federal commission was very great indeed. Virtually everyone, from Rep. Dick T. Morgan of Oklahoma to members of top Wall Street circles, wanted some form of commission—for their own reasons. Only Senator William E. Borah and a few others condemned the movement toward commissions and boards, the movement which would take decisions "entirely away from the electorate," and expose these boards to "the influence and the power that affect other men. . . ."[5]

On January 20 Wilson appeared before a joint session of Congress and made it clear that future trust legislation would be just as responsible as banking legislation had been.

What we are purposing to do . . . is, happily, not to hamper or interfere with business as enlightened businessmen prefer to do it, or in any sense to put it under the ban. The antagonism between business and government is over. . . . The Government and businessmen are ready to meet each other half way in a common effort to square business methods with both public opinion and the law. The best informed men of the business world condemn the methods and processes and consequences of monopoly as we condemn them; and the instinctive judgment of the vast majority of businessmen everywhere goes with them.

There would have to be a prohibition of interlocking directorates, Wilson told Congress. But the main burden of his Message was to strike a most responsive chord.

The business of the country awaits also, has long awaited and has suffered because it could not obtain, further and more explicit legislative definition of the policy and meaning of the existing anti-trust law. Nothing hampers business like uncertainty. . . . And the businessmen of the country desire something more than that the menace of legal process in these matters be made explicit and intelligible. They desire the advice, the definite guidance, and information which can be supplied by an administrative body, an interstate trade commission.

Businessmen were delighted with the conservatism and reasonableness of the President's address, and messages of congratulation poured in from all over the country, from small and big businessmen alike. "It has had a very reassuring effect on the business community here in New York . . .," a member of Speyer & Co. wrote Wilson. "By your temperate, sober, earnest way in handling these important matters," a member of the Union League Club of New York assured Wilson, "you have in our opinion (the opinion of life-long Republicans) proved yourself a *safe* man to be at the head of the country!" Seth Low, however, wrote Wilson that he would have considerable difficulty defining a trust. The President, admitting he was aware of the problem, assured him "You may be sure we shall not attempt the impossible and will not even try to define a trust, but confine ourselves to very specific provisions."[6]

The Campaign for
Legislation

Although numerous bills for trust legislation and a federal commission had been introduced throughout 1913, the first politically serious bills were not introduced in Congress until January 22, 1914, when Rep. Clayton and Senator Newlands presented a rather timid bill, similiar to Newlands' earlier bills, providing for a five-man commission to supersede the Bureau of Corporations. The proposal allowed the commission to subpoena all necessary materials and to recommend action to the Attorney General, who had the power to arrange voluntary reorganization. The bill as it stood failed to appeal to the Attorney General's office, but it became the basis of discussion for subsequent legislation. To complicate the matter, Clayton also introduced four tentative bills amending the Sherman Act. The first forbade attempted efforts at monopolization via price discrimination, but contained so many clauses it became meaningless. The second extended "restraint of trade" to include agreements between companies, a position long maintained by the Supreme Court. The third bill forbade interlocking directors among banks, railroads, and competitive industries, and the fourth was intended to eliminate interlocking stockholdings.

In the meantime, the advocates of special proposals and concrete steps were given ample opportunity to exert pressures wherever possible, and to voice their criticisms of the tentative bills. The concept of a commission was never seriously opposed by any important segment interested in the topic, and Wilson was quite properly confident "that the businessmen themselves desire nothing so much as a trade commission."[7] At the hearings held by the House Committee on the Judiciary, and by the Senate Committee on Interstate Commerce during February-June, 1914, the three major business con-

cerns for future legislation were specifically with interlocking directorates, fair trade laws, and the status of trade unions under the
antitrust act.

Big business and bankers opposed a possible prohibition on interlocking directorships in industry and banking. There was, in fact,
little reason for their anxiety, since one or two interlocks on a board
are insufficient for control if the outside directors do not represent
some significant power, in which case the leverage the power provides exists even without interlocking directorships. In brief, short
of a total transformation of existing economic relations, the prohibition of interlocking directorships is not too important. Nevertheless,
many big businessmen found the suggestion obnoxious, and the
American Bankers Association, the Railway Executives' Advisory
Committee, and numerous individuals opposed any prohibitions.
Even Louis Brandeis suggested that a blanket ban on interlocks was
not desirable. At the same time that big business attacked the possibility of prohibiting interlocking directorates, representatives of small
business associations of merchants, druggists, and grocers, as well as
large manufacturers, called for the legalization and even the enforcement of fair trade price-fixing, a cause that Brandeis supported and
that was to be revived periodically.[8] Virtually all businessmen, big
or small, endorsed the general principle of a trade commission.

While the various tentative bills were under discussion, two business organizations were to become especially important among the
many petitioning their Congressmen and appearing before Congressional hearings, and were to shape the final legislation. The Chicago
Association of Commerce strongly desired a trade commission, and
under the leadership of Thomas Creigh, attorney for the Cudahy
Packing Company, it took a prominent part in the agitation for a
trade commission that could eliminate business uncertainty by giving business advice on the legality of proposed actions. This goal
became the heart of the Chicago Association's program, although it
also favored a commission with the power to issue desist orders
before handing a complaint over to the Attorney General. The National Chamber of Commerce also strongly endorsed the need for a
commission, but only a minority of the members of the Chamber,
led by Charles R. Van Hise, president of the University of Wisconsin,
accepted the Chicago position for a commission to advise business
on the legality of prospective actions. Although a few major city and

state groups, such as the Philadelphia Bourse and the New York State Chamber of Commerce, opposed the basic premises of the tentative bills, there is no doubt that the National Chamber of Commerce or the Chicago Association of Commerce reflected the overwhelming opinion of virtually all levels and types of business. And Congress knew business would support any action in this direction, since Senator Newlands had submitted three bills to businessmen in December, 1913, and favorable opinion in support of the basic principle flowed in.[9]

Until March 16, when the Trade Commission Bill was finally separated from the proposed amendments to the Sherman Act and unity imposed over the bevy of competing measures sponsored by the same men, no conclusive and final business position was possible. Moreover, the exact provisions of a future Administration bill were unknown. Various business organizations knew what they wanted, but they were not sure of what they had. La Follette regarded the existing bills as "flabby and without teeth," and Henry Lee Higginson opposed the assortment as they stood. The Interstate Trade Commission Bill of March 16 was so weak that there was little question that it would be amended. Introduced by Rep. James H. Covington of Maryland, the new bill provided for a five-man trade commission that could investigate a corporation to see if it was complying with the antitrust law, gather information, and advise the Attorney General concerning dissolutions and prosecutions. The bill, on the whole, was just as weak as it had been in its earlier confused form. And on April 14 Rep. Clayton merged the basic contents of his various tentative bills into one coherent draft, the Clayton Antitrust Bill.

The revision of the Sherman Act was entirely unsatisfactory to labor unions, who objected to the equivocal wording that "Nothing contained in the anti-trust laws shall be construed to forbid the existence and operation of labor organizations." Unionists wished an outright declaration that the antitrust laws did not apply to unions at all, and efforts by several members of the House Committee on the Judiciary to obtain such a clause failed. Changes in the wording of the Clayton Bill applying to unions were made, but as historians have commonly agreed, the Clayton Bill did not free unions from prosecution under the antitrust laws.[10] Despite intensive pressure by organized labor, Wilson regarded all efforts to have labor excluded from the law as class legislation, and the final bill, notwithstanding the embarrassed attempt of Gompers to find some concession in it to justify six years of support for the Democrats, was also hailed by antilabor elements.

The initial Trade Commission Bill was most unsatisfying to those business elements that had long been interested in such legislation. On the other hand, disunity among businessmen as to what type of legislation was desirable became increasingly apparent during the spring of 1914, although the sentiment for some form of legislation was nearly universal. Both the N.A.M. and the Chamber of Commerce split evenly on the desirability of a strong trade commission with the power to pass on proposed business actions. The N.A.M. convention, meeting in May, decided to take no stand whatsoever, and failed to approve a committee resolution condemning legislation. The Chamber of Commerce, on the other hand, began shifting its position, and it was apparent that Charles R. Van Hise, hitherto only a minority voice on the Chamber's committee on trust legislation, spoke for a significant proportion of the business community. In mid-April the Chamber sent a referendum to its members on the extent and form of trade commission legislation, asking them to vote on the trust committee's recommendations. On the creation of the commission and its power to investigate, the members endorsed their committee's positive recommendations by overwhelming majorities. The committee's refusal to endorse commission powers to pass on the legality of proposed actions, however, was reversed by a vote of 307 to 306. Even before the Chamber's committee received the results of the referendum, however, it moved to endorse the Clayton Bill in general, urging that legislation be "expressed in terms of principles only," but also favoring the prohibition of interlocking directors and stock ownership lessening competition. More significant was the committee's focus on the Stevens Bill, a hitherto obscure measure presented by Rep. Raymond B. Stevens of New Hampshire that assumed that it would be the function of a Federal Trade Commission to decide if a business' actions violated the more general provisions of the antitrust laws.[11]

The Stevens Bill was no coincidence. The Chamber's trust committee included among its members George Rublee, an attorney who had been in the Progressive Party and generally shared its trust orientation. The Chamber's committee held its first meetings in February, 1914, and Rublee was directly interested in the legislative history of the various bills from that point on. Rublee knew Stevens and the

Congressman agreed to allow him to draft a bill that was introduced on April 13. The Stevens Bill provided for a commission with powers to issue cease and desist orders, subject to court review, where unfair methods of competition were being utilized. The Stevens Bill, and the general concept of a strong trade commission, had few supporters in Congress, and its attraction was mainly to men like Rublee, Creigh, and Van Hise. On June 5, as an illustration of its unformulated casual attitude, the House passed the Covington Bill by a voice vote, defeating a motion to recommit by 151 to 19. No one was overly excited by the weakness of the measure, save those circles that had long advocated a trade commission as a means of giving business stability and predictability.

At the beginning of June, Rublee, Stevens, Brandeis, and Charles McCarthy went to see Wilson about the obscurity of the Clayton Bill, pointing to the need for a stronger trade commission to give it substance. The group's comments managed to swing Wilson from his not-too-firm position, and he indicated his willingness to see the heart of the Stevens Bill incorporated into the Federal Trade Commission Bill as Section 5.[12] Senator Newlands, always anxious to please and certainly no radical, responded to Wilson's new position by modifying his Senate equivalent of the Covington Bill to include the heart of the Stevens Bill. Despite some debate in the Senate on the meaning of unfair competition and the extent of judicial review, virtually everyone agreed the amended Newlands Bill was an important advance, and on August 5 it passed by 53 to 16.

The Clayton Bill, while the trade commission was being debated, passed the House on June 5 by a vote of 277 to 54, somewhat altered to allow the F.T.C. and I.C.C. to have greater responsibility for its enforcement and to eliminate imprisonment and fines for certain violations. It was obvious that legislation was almost universally desired, and the leaders of the small business organizations were especially pleased with the steps that had been taken by July, even though a reconciliation of the House and Senate Trade Commission Bills was still months off. Wilson, for his part, moved to reassure business, if assurance was needed, that the New Freedom could be trusted. He had, by mid-1914, attained considerable insight into the economy, and he was now able to evaluate the future needs of the nation in the light of recent progress. Speaking to the Virginia Editorial Association on June 25 "as a friend of business and a servant of the country," Wilson appraised the larger problem faced by a democratic society in an age of big business and industrialism. Perhaps it was once thought that America was ill and in need of progressive economic cures, but "as the diagnosis has progressed it has become more and more evident that no capital operation is necessary; that at the most a minor operation was necessary to remove admitted distempers and evils." The tariff and currency bills had been two minor operations, and the economy was now undergoing another operation in the form of trust legislation. But when this was completed "business can get and will get what it can get in no other way—rest, recuperation, and successful adjustment."[13]

Thomas Creigh of the Chicago Association of Commerce felt disappointed with the Trade Commission Bill and the even vaguer Clayton Bill, and in mid-July he and a group of his Chicago associates visited Wilson to discuss the entire legislative situation. They left Washington "feeling much encouraged," thinking the "objectionable parts" of the Clayton Bill would be dropped "and the Trade Commission Bills strengthened, especially, in Section 5, so that it would more fully embrace our ideas." The Chicago group, with its belief in a strong commission that could pass on the legality of business proposals, was doubly reassured when Davies privately indicated to it that many of its suggested changes would be made.

Davies' consolation was significant, for it was the head of the Bureau of Corporations, more than any other individual within the Administration, that helped formulate the Trade Commission Bill. Besides Wilson, he gave direction to the plastic Senator Newlands, the chief figure in the Senate. This was as it should have been, since the commission was to supersede the bureau. Davies, for his part, relied heavily on the advice of interested business lawyers such as Rublee, Creigh, and Gilbert H. Montague, the author of the Merchants' Association of New York's commission plan and a friend of the Chicago Association of Commerce's proposals. Montague, along with Creigh, sent Davies memoranda, letters, and proposals designed to strengthen the power of a commission, and even to protect any future commission from broad judicial review. Davies appreciated the assistance, and he used it in keeping Wilson behind a strong commission position while the debates on judicial review in Congress attracted attention during the summer. Business lawyers told him that they did not want long litigation, Davies assured Wilson, and that they preferred narrow judicial review. Although we cannot expect everything in the first bill, Davies assured

Creigh, the efforts of the Chicago Association of Commerce "have procured so much a better bill than I thought would be possible at this time. . . ."[14]

The Federal Trade Commission Bills of both the House and the Senate remained in conference until early September, when they were reconciled in favor of the Senate. The Senate passed the report 43 to 5, and the Act was signed by Wilson September 26. There was a moderate broadening of judicial review in the compromise bill, the debate over which historians have overexaggerated in importance; the final vote in the Senate is an accurate gauge of the seriousness of the disagreement. The Clayton Bill also passed through both branches with large majorities. The Senate approved it in early September by a vote of 46 to 16, over strong condemnation of its ineffectiveness by Western Senators. The conference report was passed by the House in early October by a vote of 244 to 54, and Wilson signed the law on October 16.

The End of the New Freedom

The Federal Trade Commission Act specified that a commission of five was to be appointed by the President with the approval of the Senate, with not more than three members from any party. "Unfair methods of competition" were declared "unlawful," and the commission was authorized to prevent them from being used. Upon calling a hearing, the commission could issue "cease and desist" orders which could be enforced by Circuit Courts. The commission might also compel the production of information and utilize the power of subpoena, with penalties for refusal to cooperate. The commission could gather and issue information of a more general sort, and advise the Attorney General on correcting illegal corporate actions. All in all, the Act was vague and unclear, failed to exclude businessmen from membership on the commission, and left a great area for free interpretation of the law.

By comparison to the Clayton Act, however, the Federal Trade Commission Act was a model of precision. It was the intention of Congress to allow the commission and courts to settle most of the vagueness in the Clayton Act, and no greater clarity in the antitrust law was established. Price discrimination was forbidden, but with ample "due allowances." The Act also condemned tieing contracts to prevent purchasers from buying from a company's competitors if they lessened competition. It forbade purchases of stock that reduced competition and prohibited interlocking directorates among banks with more than $5 million resources, between railroad directors or officers and construction or maintenance companies with which they did a substantial business, and directors of competitive industries. The new Act was most detailed in its specification of mechanical procedures for cease and desist orders and appeal procedures. On the whole, it reflected the deep ambivalence of Congress on the topic of business concentration. There were no means, needless to say, by which concentration could be reversed. Precedent was still the major criterion for action, and precedents were to be defined by judicial and administrative bodies dominated by men who, in the last analysis, had little more than their ideological commitments to guide them.

Although bankers disliked the interlock prohibitions, big business as a whole was very pleased, to put it mildly, with the new state of affairs. The provisions of the new laws attacking unfair competitors and price discrimination meant that the government would now make it possible for many trade associations to stabilize, for the first time, prices within their industries, and to make effective oligopoly a new phase of the economy. In part the new mood of confidence was a result of the President's repeated assurances that he favored a conservative approach to business—a public statement on the need for greater railroad profits on September 10 was only one of many examples—and a realization that a Federal Trade Commission was to serve as a stabilizing factor in the economy and a protector against public attacks. The unions were no better off, despite Gompers' effusive support of the Clayton Act, and the last stone in the foundation of a comprehensive political capitalism involving the banks, railroads, and industry had been laid.

The new measures were quickly endorsed by the long-time advocates of federal regulation, with the exception of George W. Perkins, now more deeply motivated by political considerations. ". . . these laws largely coincide with the principles we have urged," the president of the Chicago Association of Commerce telegraphed Wilson. "The Democratic National Administration deserves unmistakable approval," Francis Lynde Stetson announced in mid-October. Arthur J. Eddy, the architect of the trade association movement, also agreed that the new laws were progressive and constructive.[15]

What is truly significant about the passage of the two bills, however, is that it marked the conscious completion of the legislative objectives of the New Freedom just at the very time that the most important goals of business advocates of political capitalism were attained. In late 1914 Wilson drew the line on reform, and reiterated innumerable times his belief that federal regulation had gone far enough. In late October Wilson began explicitly formulating his retreat from legislative action. "The situation is just this," he wrote a friend: "the reconstructive legislation which for the last two decades the opinion of the country has demanded . . . has now been enacted. That program is practically completed." Further changes would have to await the end of the European war and the experience of using the "instrumentalities already created." By mid-November Wilson was ready to make a public statement of policy in a letter to McAdoo that was immediately sent to the press.

Ten or twelve years ago the country was torn and excited by an agitation which shook the very foundations of her political life, brought her business ideals into question, condemned her social standards, denied the honesty of her men of affairs, the integrity of her economic processes, the morality and good faith of many of the things which her law sustained.

Businessmen and politicians had been exposed to abuse, but any of the evils that may have existed were now corrected, and all of the older ideals and foundations were now being reasserted. "The spirit of co-operation which your letter breathes is an example to all of us," Frank Trumbull, head of the Railway Executives Association, immediately wrote Wilson. Stimulated by similar professions and the congratulations of Davies and urgings of Tumulty, Wilson bid his final farewell to the New Freedom in his Annual Message to Congress on December 8. Appearing before a joint session, Wilson's stand was unequivocal:

Our program of legislation with regard to the regulation of business is now virtually complete. It has been put forth, as we intended, as a whole, and leaves no conjecture as to what is to follow. The road at last lies clear and firm before business. It is a road which it can travel without fear or embarrassment.[16]

What the President ignored, of course, was that the road had never been charted by him, and that the New Freedom, in its concrete legislative aspects, was little more than the major demands of politically oriented big businessmen. They had defined the issues, and it was they who managed to provide the direction for change. If they did not always manage to shape every detail of each reform measure, it was only because, in a political democracy, legislative situations have their own unpredictable, uncontrollable qualities. But in its larger outlines it was they who gave progressivism its essential character. By the end of 1914 they had triumphed, and to the extent that the new laws were vague and subject to administrative definitions by boards and commissions, they were to totally dominate the extensive reign of political capitalism that had been created in the United States by 1915.

The Commission
Defines the Law

A Federal Trade Commission had finally been created; it was an unformed object guided only by vague legal prescriptions, to be shaped by the President and his advisers as they saw fit. Given Wilson's mood at the end of 1914 and the beginning of 1915, however, there was little question that the new organization would be amply conservative. The reassuring statements of the President continued into 1915 and were joined by those of Davies and others. "Nobody is henceforth going to be afraid of or suspicious of any business merely because it is big."[17] The practical reflection of the new stage in the New Freedom was the President's choice of the members of the F.T.C., the men with the responsibility of determining the functional meaning of the new law and setting the all-important precedents for the future.

It was only logical that Davies should be appointed the first chairman of the commission. Wilson appointed Edward N. Hurley of Chicago vice-chairman. Hurley had aided Wilson's political career in 1910 as an intermediary with the Democratic Party of New Jersey. Among other things he was a manufacturer and the president of the Illinois Manufacturers Association at the time of his appointment. William J. Harris, a Georgia businessman, was also appointed, as was Will H. Parry, former newspaperman and shipbuilder. It was only fitting that Wilson consider Rublee, and since the former Progressive received the endorsement of both Oswald Garrison Villard and the Chicago Association of Commerce, the President nominated him. But Rublee had once managed a campaign against Senator Jacob H. Gallinger in New Hampshire, and the Senator, not one to forget, blocked his confirmation in the Senate. Until the end of Congress, however, Rublee was appointed to the commission at the "pleasure of the President," and he served until September 8, 1916. Virtually the entire commission, therefore, was composed of individuals with business backgrounds or long pro-business records. The domination extended to even routine jobs in the bureaucracy, and applicants were asked to present "letters of endorsement from some good, sound businessmen."[18]

When the commission began defining its role in early 1915, therefore, it met in a general atmosphere of sympathy for business. Moreover, business was responding with enthusiasm. Hundreds of requests for information and advice poured in from businessmen, and calls for a maintenance of the era of good feelings came from all directions— Frank Vanderlip, Senator Albert B. Cummins, the Illinois Manufacturers Association. The commission had the law to guide it, but the law was vague. Commission members had their own views, and there was also the opinion of business. From April through June, 1915, the commission was to meet, debate, and consult outside advisers.

The mere existence of the commission served the obvious and valuable function as a buffer against public antagonism toward business, but most of the earliest advocates of a commission had also conceived of it as an agency that could give business legal advice and create predictability for their economic actions. The law quite explicitly avoided stating such advice could or could not be given, but it was clearly the intent of Congress not to include such a provision or to give the commission the power. Davies, more than any other individual on the commission, helped define future policy on this all-important question. He had always believed that a commission would be quasi-judicial and quasi-legislative as well as administrative in its functions. In addition to its explicit powers, he announced at the end of March, 1915, the new commission would provide some definition of what business could not do so that it might protect 99 per cent of business from the unfair competition of one per cent. Davies was fully aware that the law did not empower the F.T.C. to give advice, and he sought some means or rationale by which it might do so, and even drew up an amendment to the Act that was never submitted. Rublee, who was quite literal-minded in evaluating the law and could not find a convenient loophole, was very little assistance, and he and Parry concentrated on defining the F.T.C.'s functions in less complicated areas. The members of the commission could not solve the problem themselves; in late April they were forced to resolve the dilemma. The United Cigar Stores Company wrote the commission on April 20 about a proposed acquisition and asked "to ascertain the attitude of your Commission. . . ."[19] Perhaps only because it provided a convenient way to avoid giving up the powers it desired, the commission at this point decided to call on outside parties to help it attain its goal. Choice of the outside parties determined the final decision. Arthur J. Eddy, Victor Morawetz, Walker D. Hines, the railroad executive, Brandeis, and Van Hise, the most important outside consultants, were not prone to radicalism. Only Brandeis opposed the commission giving advice on the legality of proposed acts.

It was Eddy who managed to provide the rationale sufficient to get the commission to embark on a course without statutory warrant. Section 5, the advocate of trade associations pointed out, required the commission to "prevent" unfair methods of competition. If a company or association filed information on a proposed act, the commission could file a complaint if it thought the suggestion illegal. The principle, of course, had been suggested by Eddy only three years earlier, and Davies adopted the approach almost immediately. Rublee alone seemed to have some qualms about the legal basis of the decision, but the commission resolved to give rulings because, as Davies put it, "what men needed largely in the business world was not the menace of legal process, but some definite guidance and some information— some help."[20] At the end of June the commission adopted a plan of organization for its future work, and "conference rulings" were accepted as one of its key tasks. The structure of the commission was outlined along with its functions, not the least of which was to be the collection of statistics and information designed to help business. But it was the conference ruling decision that was of crucial value to business, and by the end of its first year the commission had issued forty-eight such rulings, and although they were not regarded as "conclusive," they could "be regarded as precedents in so far as they are applicable in proceedings before the Commission." At the same time the commission initiated a program of disposing of many of its incoming complaints through informal proceedings, "avoiding ill-founded prosecutions."[21]

This crucial interpretation of the function of the commission met with no opposition in Congress, and with only enthusiasm from business. Wilson accepted the shift entirely, and, along with the commission itself, misstated the original purpose of the law. ". . . the Federal Trade Commission was established," he declared in July, 1916, "so that men would have some place where they could take counsel as to what the law was and what the law permitted. . . ." The commission consistently regarded the new policy as inherent in the law. Its ruling and decisions, in addition to being designed "to promote business efficiency and . . . to co-operate with the business world in developing the best standards of commercial ethics," by 1919 were described as "furnishing that 'definite guidance and information' which the President and the Congress had in view in the establishment of the Federal Trade Commission, by the gradual working out of a code of business law."[22]

The response of business, quite predictably, was even more enthusiastic, and the cordial relationship between the commission and business became a virtual honeymoon of mutual praise. As Davies put it at the outset, "There is a great opportunity for this new agency in government to be of practical aid to the business of this country. That is, indeed, one of the purposes for which it was created. . . ." Of all the important business groups, only the N.A.M. stood off, neither attacking nor praising the F.T.C. But it stood alone. ". . . I found the members of the commission most cordial and not only willing but anxious to exercise their fullest powers to aid and assist business rather than to hinder and oppose it," one executive reported. The formation of a commission, the bulletin of the brokerage house Clark, Childs & Co. announced in May, "has taken some of the sharpest teeth out of the jaws of the Sherman Law. . . . The new Commission seems to be run with the main idea of helping business. . . ." It settled, for example, ninety-nine out of one hundred complaints with private, nonsensational conferences. "This is the most satisfactory development of the relation of the Administration to business that has developed in many years, and it will soon mean much to our stock market in freedom from fear of sensational attack."[23]

Business enthusiasm and support, of which the commission was fully aware and proud, centered increasingly on the dynamic activities of Hurley. Davies, nominally the head of the commission, shifted his focus from economic matters to foreign crises as Wilson became more concerned with foreign affairs, and vice-chairman Hurley shaped the larger program of the commission during late 1915 and 1916. Hurley wished to service business with information on standardized book-keeping, cost accounts, and credit systems. Such money-saving proposals especially struck the imagination of smaller businessmen, even though the commission's guides on the topic, which went through giant printings of 350,000 by the end of 1916, were also directed to manufacturers. This enthusiasm by business was maintained by Hurley's aggressive cultivation of the business community through a barrage of speeches and press releases.

The business response to Hurley was nothing short of overwhelming, and many hundreds of letters of praise arrived in the commission's office throughout 1915 and 1916. Their enthusiasm was due not merely to Hurley's fine sense of public relations, but to the remarkable content of his speeches. "Through a period of years the government has been gradually extending its machinery of helpfulness to different classes and groups upon whose prosperity depends in a large degree the prosperity of the country," Hurley told the Association of National Advertisers in December, 1915. The railroads and shippers had the I.C.C., the bankers the Reserve Board, the farmers the Agriculture Department. "To do for general business that which these other agencies do for the groups to which I have referred was the thought behind the creation of the trade commission." This total identification of the F.T.C. with business was, on Hurley's part, quite conscious. More important, he was able to obtain the complete support of Wilson for his position, and Wilson relied heavily on Hurley for guidance on his relations to business throughout 1916. Indeed, by May, 1916, Hurley was drafting some of Wilson's important statements on general economic affairs, including an endorsement of the work of the F.T.C. under Hurley.[24] In June, 1916, Davies resigned from the commission and Hurley, with strong business support, was chosen as chairman.

Was Wilson fully aware of the deep commitment of Hurley to business? All of the evidence indicates he was, and Hurley, too, claimed it. Speaking informally to the National Industrial Conference Board in July, 1916, the new chairman, in a remarkably frank address, freely revealed his own feelings and those, he claimed, of Wilson:

I am glad to meet with a body of businessmen like you gentlemen, and I will plead guilty on the start by saying that I do not know anything about the law, and that applies to the Clayton act and to the Federal Trade Commission act. In my position on the Federal Trade Commission I am there as a business man. I do not mind telling you that when I was offered the place I told the President that all I knew was business, that I knew nothing about the new laws nor the old ones, and that I would apply the force that I might have in the interest of business. I have been there since the sixteenth of March last year, and I think that the business men of the country will bear me out when I say that I try to work wholly in the interest of business.[25]

The enthusiasm within business circles for Hurley extended beyond the smaller business groups that benefited most from his cost and efficiency publications. Big business also responded positively to the commission, whose functions conformed to those outlined by its various spokesmen as early as 1907. The special attraction of the commission, and Wilson, to larger businessmen, however, was its position on trade associations in general and export trade associations in particular. The advantages of trade associations formed for domestic purposes were clear—the maintenance of prices and the elimination of internecine competition. Such associations were organized in abundance from 1912 on, but their legal status on issues of price controls and market divisions had never been thoroughly tested. The pressure to legalize them, on the other hand, was not great. Small retail business was more interested than big business in the legalization of fair trade pricing, and although businesses of every size generally favored such a law, no real movement for its passage ever was created.

Wilson and Hurley regarded trade associations with favor, and the trade associations respected the commission as a friend. The prevention of price cutting was commended by Brandeis and Davies, and Wilson, with Hurley's prodding, publicly stated in May, 1916, "that trade associations . . . and other similar organizations should be encouraged in every feasible way. . . ."[26] The real support of the Administration for the trade association movement came in the area of export associations. During the final days before the passage of the Trade Commission Act, both Davies and Secretary of Commerce William Redfield tried to have the bill amended to allow the commission to supervise export associations, but Wilson, although sympathetic, thought it better to make the change later. Wilson, ostensibly to help smaller businesses, took the position in early 1915 that "a method of cooperation which is not a method of combination" would be most advantageous "in taking advantage of the opportunities of foreign trade." The President was strident on this issue until American entry into the war, when all bounds on business were removed. Domestic markets were no longer sufficient for our economic development, he told a business convention in September, 1916, and the Federal Reserve Act, with its provisions for foreign branch banking, had truly prepared us for the world market. "Not only when this war is over, but now, America has her place in the . . . world of finance and commerce upon a scale that she never dreamed of before." "There is only one thing I have ever been ashamed of in America," Wilson, in a moment of satisfaction, declared, "and that was the timidity and fearfulness of Americans in the presence of foreign competitors."[27]

The commission's work on accounting and cost systems was equaled only by its concern for supporting the formation of export trade associations. By the end of its first year of operation the commission had ten specific investigations under way. The motives for investigating domestic industries were not at all hostile to the industries concerned. "We are making an inquiry into the coal industry today," Hurley announced, "with the hope that we can recommend to Congress some legislation that will allow them to combine and fix prices." Such impulses were hardly calculated to cause anxiety to an industry that for years had demanded just such rights. More significant is the fact that the first two inquiries completed dealt with export trade associations and the problems of South American trade. Ever since its formation, the commission favored a law to explicitly allow trade associations to be created. "The Commission does not believe that Congress intended by the antitrust laws to prevent Americans from cooperating in export trade for the purpose of competing effectively with foreigners, where such cooperation does not restrain trade within the United States. . . ." So long as such a law was not on the record, they claimed, potential exporters would be discouraged for fear of possible attack. The F.T.C., for these reasons, consistently supported the passage of the Webb Bill to allow export trade associations to operate and companies to acquire firms exclusively in the export business. Given Wilson's endorsement of the bill in December, 1916, industry pressure, and even occasional reminders by Perkins and others that Germany had become a great power because it was "taking care of her business interests" in seeking foreign trade, the passage of the Webb-Pomerene Act in April, 1918, was inevitable.[28]

The Democratic platform in 1916 was eminently conservative on the issue of "economic freedom." The reforms required to eliminate economic discrimination had been effected, and, for the future, the party pledged itself to "remove, as far as possible, every remaining element of unrest and uncertainty from the path of the businessmen of America, and secure for them a continued period of quiet, assured and confident prosperity." If there ever was a party plank intended to reflect the serious desires of the party, this was it.

So far as the larger issue of the relationship of business to government was concerned, the plank perfectly mirrored the new era of political capitalism and the New Freedom. Wilson was ready to accept the advice and direction of Hurley in handling the business community and the issues that had once figured so prominently in the campaign of 1912. Hurley reproduced Wilson's May 12, 1916, letter to him, which Hurley had really written, and reminded businessmen during September, 1916, that a President who endorsed the F.T.C. and the trade association movement was "a safe and sound man for the business interests of the country to champion." George Perkins, actively working for Charles Evans Hughes, might attack the commission as being vague, but businessmen knew better. The American Fair Trade League could condemn Perkins' verdict, and it was joined by other powerful business groups. The Federal Trade Commission, Wilson announced on September 25, "has transformed the Government of the United States from being an antagonist of business into being a friend of business."[29] Wilson was overly modest in his description of the situation.

Had Hurley remained with the F.T.C., his influence over Wilson would have continued, if not grown. In January, 1917, Hurley resigned "On account of certain large plant improvements requiring personal attention to my business affairs. . . ." Wilson regretfully accepted the resignation. The war was to keep the President occupied. The process of meeting the demands presented by that epic struggle made the traditional relationship of the federal government to business even more intimate. The F.T.C. was, very briefly, to waver from its safe, reliable path after the war, but its subsequent history and role did not disappoint the hopes and expectations of business.[30] Its success in this regard was due not so much to its structure and personnel as to the basic ideological assumptions and goals of the political machinery within which it existed. Its conservatism reflected the mandate from the President.

Bureaucracies have frequently determined conditions of political and economic development in a seemingly "nonpartisan" manner that has perpetuated a set of relationships and actions which were, in themselves, based on policy commitments with no formal affinity to those verbally accepted by the society around them. Such was not the problem, however, in the case of the Federal Trade Commission. The administrative outcome of the New Freedom was the logical conclusion of the premises of its initiators. The business community knew what it wanted from the commission, and what it wanted was almost precisely what the commission sought to do. No distinction between government and business was possible simply because the commission absorbed and reflected the predominant values of the business community. The platitudes and boosterism of Davies and Hurley were, in the final analysis, based on their deep commitment to the political capitalism that triumphed under the New Freedom. Wilson interacted with them, accepted their initiatives, and provided his own. The views and desires of Wilson and business were virtually identical.

CONCLUSION:

THE

LOST

DEMOCRACY

THE AMERICAN POLITICAL experience during the Progressive Era was conservative, and this conservatism profoundly influenced American society's response to the problems of industrialism. The nature of the economic process in the United States, and the peculiar cast within which industrialism was molded, can only be understood by examining the political structure. Progressive politics is complex when studied in all of its aspects, but its dominant tendency on the federal level was to functionally create, in a piecemeal and haphazard way that was later made more comprehensive, the synthesis of politics and economics I have labeled "political capitalism."

The varieties of rhetoric associated with progressivism were as diverse as its followers, and one form of this rhetoric involved attacks on businessmen—attacks that were often framed in a fashion that has been misunderstood by historians as being radical. But at no point did any major political tendency dealing with the problem of big business in modern society ever try to go beyond the level of high generalization and translate theory into concrete economic programs that would conflict in a fundamental way with business supremacy over the control of wealth. It was not a coincidence that the results of progressivism were precisely what many major business interests desired.

Ultimately businessmen defined the limits of political intervention, and specified its major form and thrust. They were able to do so not merely because they were among the major initiators of federal intervention in the economy, but primarily because no politically significant group during the Progressive Era really challenged their conception of political intervention. The basic fact of the Progressive Era was the large area of consensus and unity among key business leaders and most political factions on the role of the federal government in the economy. There were disagreements, of course, but not on fundamentals. The overwhelming majorities on votes for basic progressive legislation is testimony to the near unanimity in Congress on basic issues.

Indeed, an evaluation of the Progressive Era must concede a much larger importance to the role of Congress than has hitherto been granted by historians who have focused primarily on the more dramatic Presidents. Congress was the pivot of agitation for banking reform while Roosevelt tried to evade the issue, and it was considering trade commissions well before Wilson was elected. Meat and pure food agitation concentrated on Congress, and most of the various reform proposals originated there. More often than not, the various Presidents evaded a serious consideration of issues until Congressional initiatives forced them to articulate a position. And businessmen seeking reforms often found a sympathetic response among the members of the House and Senate long before Presidents would listen to them. This was particularly true of Roosevelt, who would have done much less than he did were it not for the prodding of Congress. Presidents are preoccupied with patronage to an extent unappreciated by anyone who has not read their letters.

The Presidents, considered—as they must be—as actors rather than ideologists, hardly threatened to undermine the existing controllers of economic power. With the possible exception of Taft's Wickersham, none of the major appointees to key executive posts dealing with economic affairs were men likely to frustrate business in its desire to use the federal government to strengthen its economic position. Garfield, Root, Knox, Straus—these men were important and sympathetic pipelines to the President, and gave additional security to businessmen who did not misread what Roosevelt was trying to say in his public utterances. Taft, of course, broke the continuity between the Roosevelt and Wilson Administrations because of political decisions that had nothing to do with his acceptance of the same economic theory that Roosevelt believed in. The elaborate relationship between business and the Executive created under Roosevelt was unintentionally destroyed because of Taft's desire to control the Republican Party. Wilson's appointees were quite as satisfactory as Roosevelt's, so far as big business was concerned, and in his concrete implementation of the fruits of their political agitation—the Federal Reserve Act and the Federal Trade Commission Act—Wilson proved himself to be perhaps the most responsive and desirable to business of the three Presidents. Certainly it must be concluded that historians have overemphasized the basic differences between the Presidents of the Progressive Era, and ignored their much more important similarities. In 1912 the specific utterances and programs of all three were identical on fundamentals, and party platforms reflected this common agreement.

This essential unanimity extended to the area of ideologies and values, where differences between the Presidents were largely of the sort contrived by politicians in search of votes, or seeking to create useful images. None of the Presidents had a distinct consciousness of any fundamental conflict between their political goals and those of business. Roosevelt and Wilson especially appreciated the significant support business gave to their reforms, but it was left to Wilson to culminate the decade or more of agitation by providing precise direction to the administration of political capitalism's most important consequences in the Progressive Era. Wilson had a small but articulate band of followers who seriously desired to reverse the process of industrial centralization—Bryan and the Midwestern agrarians reflected this tradition more than any other group. Yet ultimately he relegated such dissidents to a secondary position—indeed, Wilson himself represented the triumph of Eastern Democracy over Bryanism—and they were able to influence only a clause or amendment, here and there, in the basic legislative structure of political capitalism.

But even had they been more powerful, it is debatable how different Bryanism would have been. Bryan saw the incompatibility between giant corporate capitalism and political democracy, but he sought to save democracy by saving, or restoring, a sort of idealized competitive capitalist economy which was by this time incapable of realization or restoration, and was in any event not advocated by capitalists or political leaders with more power than the agrarians could marshal. Brandeis, for his part, was bound by enigmas in this period. Big business, to him, was something to be ultimately rejected or justified on the basis of efficiency rather than power accumulation. He tried to apply such technical criteria where none was really relevant, and he overlooked the fact that even where efficient or competitive, business could still pose irreconcilable challenges to the political and social fabric of a democratic community. Indeed, he failed to appreciate the extent to which it was competition that was leading to business agitation for federal regulation, and finally he was unable to do much more than sanction Wilson's actions as they were defined and directed by others.

There was no conspiracy during the Progressive Era. It is, of course, a fact that people and agencies acted out of public sight, and that official statements frequently had little to do with operational realities. But the imputation of a conspiracy would sidetrack a serious consideration of progressivism. There was a basic consensus among political and business leaders as to what was the public good, and no one had to be cajoled in a sinister manner. If détentes, private understandings, and the like were not publicly proclaimed it was merely because such agreements were exceptional and, generally known, could not have been denied to other business interests also desiring the security they provided. Such activities required a delicate sense of public relations, since there was always a public ready to oppose preferential treatment for special businesses, if not the basic assumptions behind such arrangements.

Certainly there was nothing surreptitious about the desire of certain businessmen for reforms, a desire that was frequently and publicly proclaimed, although the motives behind it were not appreciated by historians and although most contemporaries were unaware of how reforms were implemented after they were enacted. The fact that federal regulation of the economy was conservative in its effect in preserving existing power and economic relations in society should not obscure the fact that federal intervention in the economy was conservative in purpose as well. This ambition was publicly proclaimed by the interested business forces, and was hardly conspiratorial.

It is the intent of crucial business groups, and the structural circumstances within the economy that motivated them, that were the truly significant and unique aspects of the Progressive Era. The effects of the legislation were only the logical conclusion of the intentions behind it. The ideological consensus among key business and political leaders fed into a stream of common action, action that was sometimes stimulated by different specific goals but which nevertheless achieved the same results. Political leaders, such as Roosevelt, Wilson, and their key appointees, held that it was proper for an industry to have a decisive voice or veto over the regulatory process within its sphere of interest, and such assumptions filled many key businessmen with confidence in the essential reliability of the federal political mechanism, especially when it was contrasted to the unpredictability of state legislatures.

Business opposition to various federal legislative proposals and measures did exist, of course, especially if one focuses on opposition to particular clauses in specific bills. Such opposition, as in the case of the Federal Reserve Bill, was frequently designed to obtain special concessions. It should not be allowed to obscure the more important fact that the essential purpose and goal of any measure of importance in the Progressive Era was not merely endorsed by key representatives of businesses involved; rather such bills were first proposed by them.

One can always find some businessman, of course, who opposed federal regulation at any point, including within his own industry. Historians have relished in detailing such opposition, and, indeed, their larger analysis of the period has encouraged such revelations. But the finding of division in the ranks of business can be significant only if one makes the false assumption of a monolithic common interest among all capitalists, but, worse yet, assumes that there is no power center among capitalists, and that small-town bankers or hardware dealers can be equated with the leaders of the top industrial, financial, and railroad corporations. They can be equated, of course, if all one studies is the bulk of printed words. But in the political as well as in the economic competition between small and big business, the larger interests always managed to prevail in any specific contest. The rise of the National Association of Manufacturers in the Progressive Era is due to its antilabor position, and not to its opposition to federal regulation, which it voiced only after the First World War. In fact, crucial big business support could be found for every major federal regulatory movement, and frequent small business support could be found for any variety of proposals to their benefit, such as price-fixing and legalized trade associations. Progressivism was not the triumph of small business over the trusts, as has often been suggested, but the victory of big businesses in achiev·· ing the rationalization of the economy that only the federal government could provide.

Still, the rise of the N.A.M. among businessmen in both pro- and anti-regulation camps only reinforces the fact that the relationship of capitalists to the remainder of society was essentially unaltered by their divisions on federal intervention in the economy. In terms of the basic class structure, and the conditions of interclass relationships, big and small business alike were hostile to a labor movement interested in something more than paternalism and inequality. In this respect, and in their opposition or indifference to the very minimal social welfare reforms of the Progressive Era (nearly all of which were enacted in the states), American capitalism in the Progressive Era acted in the conservative fashion traditionally ascribed to it. The result was federal regulation in the context of a class society. Indeed, because the national political leadership of the Progressive Period shared this *noblesse oblige* and conservatism toward workers and farmers, it can be really said that there was federal regulation because there *was* a class society, and political leaders identified with the values and supremacy of business.

This identification of political and key business leaders with the same set of social values—ultimately class values—was hardly accidental, for had such a consensus not existed the creation of political capitalism would have been most unlikely. Political capitalism was based on the functional unity of major political and business leaders. The business and political elites knew each other, went to the same schools, belonged to the same clubs, married into the same families, shared the same values—in reality, formed that phenomenon which has lately been dubbed The Establishment. Garfield and Stetson met at Williams alumni functions, Rockefeller, Jr. married Aldrich's daughter, the Harvard clubmen always found the White House door open to them when Roosevelt was there, and so on. Indeed, no one who reads Jonathan Daniels' remarkable autobiography, *The End of Innocence,* can fail to realize the significance of an interlocking social, economic, and political elite in American history in this century.

The existence of an Establishment during the Progressive Era was convenient, even essential, to the functional attainment of political capitalism, but it certainly was not altogether new in American history, and certainly had antecedents in the 1890's. The basic causal factor behind national progressivism was the needs of business and financial elements. To some extent, however, the more benign character of many leading business leaders, especially those with safe fortunes, was due to the more secure, mellowed characteristics and paternalism frequently associated with the social elite. Any number of successful capitalists had long family traditions of social graces and refinement which they privately doubted were fully compatible with their role as capitalists. The desire for a stabilized, rationalized political capitalism was fed by this current in big business ideology, and gave many businessmen that air of responsibility and conservatism so admired by Roosevelt and Wilson. And, from a practical viewpoint, the cruder economic conditions could also lead to substantial losses. Men who were making fortunes with existing shares of the market preferred holding on to what they had rather than establishing control over an industry, or risking much of what they already possessed. Political stabilization seemed proper for this reason as well. It allowed men to relax, to hope that crises might be avoided, to enjoy the bountiful fortunes they had already made.

Not only were economic losses possible in an unregulated capitalism, but political destruction also appeared quite possible. There were disturbing gropings ever since the end of the Civil War: agrarian discontent, violence and strikes, a Populist movement, the rise of a Socialist Party that seemed, for a time, to have an unlimited growth potential. Above all, there was a labor movement seriously divided as to its proper course, and threatening to follow in the seemingly radical footsteps of European labor. The political capitalism of the Progressive Era was designed to meet these potential threats, as well as the immediate expressions of democratic discontent in the states. National progressivism was able to short-circuit state progressivism, to hold nascent radicalism in check by feeding the illusions of its leaders—leaders who could not tell the difference between federal regulation *of* business and federal regulation *for* business.

Political capitalism in America redirected the radical potential of mass grievances and aspirations—of genuine progressivism—and to a limited extent colored much of the intellectual ferment of the period, even though the amorphous nature of mass aspirations frequently made the goals of business and the rest of the public nearly synonymous. Many well-intentioned writers and academicians worked for the same legislative goals as businessmen, but their innocence did not alter the fact that such measures were frequently designed by businessmen to serve business ends, and that business ultimately reaped the harvest of positive results. Such innocence was possible because of a naive, axiomatic view that government economic regulation, per se, was desirable, and also because many ignored crucial business support for such measures by focusing on the less important business opposition that existed. The fetish of government regulation of the economy as a positive social good was one that sidetracked a substantial portion of European socialism as well, and was not unique to the American experience. Such axiomatic and simplistic assumptions of what federal regulation would bring did not take into account problems of democratic control and participation, and in effect assumed that the power of government was neutral and socially beneficent. Yet many of the leading muckrakers and academics of the period were more than naive but ultimately conservative in their intentions as well. They sought the paternalism and stability which they expected political capitalism to bring, since only in this way could the basic virtues of capitalism be maintained. The betrayal of liberalism that has preoccupied some intellectual historians did not result from irrelevant utopianism or philosophical pragmatism, but from the lack of a truly radical, articulated alternative economic and political program capable of synthesizing political democracy with industrial reality. Such a program was never formulated in this period either in America or Europe.

Historians have continually tried to explain the seemingly sudden collapse of progressivism after the First World War, and have offered reasons that varied from moral exhaustion to the repression of nonconformity. On the whole, all explanations suffer because they really fail to examine progressivism beyond the favorable conventional interpretation. Progressive goals, on the concrete, legislative level, were articulated by various business interests. These goals were, for the most part, achieved, and no one formulated others that big business was also interested in attaining. Yet a synthesis of business and politics on the federal level was created during the war, in various administrative and emergency agencies, that continued throughout the following decade. Indeed, the war period represents the triumph of business in the most emphatic manner possible. With the exception of a brief interlude in the history of the Federal Trade Commission, big business gained total support from the various regulatory agencies and the Executive. It was during the war that effective, working oligopoly and price and market agreements became operational in the dominant sectors of the American economy. The rapid diffusion of power in the economy and relatively easy entry virtually ceased. Despite the cessation of important new legislative enactments, the unity of business and the federal government continued throughout the 1920's and thereafter, using the foundations laid in the Progressive Era to stabilize and consolidate conditions within various industries. And, on the same progressive foundations and exploiting the experience with the war agencies, Herbert Hoover and Franklin Roosevelt later formulated programs for saving American capitalism. The principle of utilizing the federal government to stabilize the economy, established in the context of modern industrialism during the Progressive Era, became the basis of political capitalism in its many later ramifications.

In this sense progressivism did not die in the 1920's, but became a part of the basic fabric of American society. The different shapes political capitalism has taken since 1916 deserve a separate treatment, but suffice it to say that even Calvin Coolidge did not mind evoking the heritage of Theodore Roosevelt, and Hoover was, if anything, deeply devoted to the Wilsonian tradition in which Franklin Roosevelt gained his first political experience.

Marx and Weber:
Economics vs. Politics

What, then, can one say about the larger nature of the phenomenon of political capitalism in America? Certainly, if one looks at the formal traditions of economic and political theory there is little to be found that takes the American experience into account. For better or worse, the relationship of politics and the state to economic and social theory is a vast, uncharted region in the arena of going theories. This is not to say that theory has failed to develop a concept of politics and the state, but that none of them apply to the American situation. Classical economics, for example, offered little guidance. Adam Smith had a much more permissive concept of the state than is usually attributed to him, but his theory of accumulation was based on parsimony rather than state favors. The state was corrupt, to be conceded as little as possible, but necessary insofar as the maintenance of social order and property relations was concerned. *The Wealth of Nations* did not explain why the state was crucial to capitalism, and merely postulated a set of conditions Smith hoped could be implemented rather than describing or predicting a much more complicated historical reality. And insofar as Smith did believe the state was crucial to preserve social relations in their existing form, his utilitarian followers developed the same tradition in their advocacy of a centralized political administration capable of protecting the property of the rich against the poor. None of the subsequent major capitalist economic theorists ever tried to develop a comprehensive operational view of the integration of economics and politics. Descriptively, Keynesian analysis is based on the same separation of economic law and political reality which dominates classical theory, and Keynes never really examined the extent and form of state intervention into the economy. And the more technical specialized studies of imperfect competition and oligopoly have ignored the political consequences of this phenomenon on behalf of purely internal economic descriptions.

Yet there are several theoretical efforts dealing with politics, economics, or social relations that are worth considering here, if only because their deficiencies allow one to point more precisely to those areas where a theoretical synthesis of the American political and economic experience is necessary and possible. Despite their inadequacies, Marx, Max Weber, and Thorstein Veblen were concerned with genuine problems, and in this age of inconspicuous specialization in the social sciences the scope of their interests alone mark them as exceptional thinkers. Their errors can be cited, but there is, after all is said and done, something of significance worth criticizing.

Marx formulated an economic theory that was to have implications to social relations and politics, but he relied on purely economic categories of explanation. Indeed, although Marx the revolutionist was interested in economics only insofar as it had political implications, his economic theory is his only complete one and, for this reason, American development cannot be understood within the Marxist mold. This is not to say that Marxian economics is not useful for understanding specific situations, but the American experience extends well beyond Marx' economic categories, and his political theory is entirely inadequate. However much one can respect Marx' insights into the role of technology in economic history, or his intense commitment to a never clearly defined goal of social justice, the history of the past century does not readily allow one to share his mechanistic faith in tendencies in technology and economics that would develop those internal contradictions in capitalism that would lead to a better world for workers.

There is no point in an exposition of Marx's economics per se, given the excellent critical analysis that has been done by Paul Mattick and others.[1] Only several of his economic ideas need be mentioned. Although Marx believed moderate adjustments were possible, he strongly felt that society "can neither clear by bold leaps, nor remove by legal enactments, the obstacles offered by the successive phases of its normal development."[2] This position led to what must be considered the "original sin" of Marxism—the acceptance and justification of the boundaries imposed by capitalism on the industrialization process. It was not necessary for Marx to argue that technology as such made centralization and monopoly inevitable, but merely that there were certain tendencies within capitalist economics which, combined with technology, stimulated a movement in that direction. Worse yet, Marx made capitalism the prerequisite to industrialization, thereby becoming an unwilling apologist for the necessity of the system. Engels carried this argument the furthest in his attacks on utopian socialism.

Despite complications, Marx believed that the long-term tendency in capitalism was toward centralization and monopoly, a tendency stimulated by the utilization of new and better technology in the competitive economy. This centralization was crucial, and a part of a "progressive" development that was unavoidable and desirable, since "Modern Industry never looks upon and treats the existing form of a process as final."[3] It was the existence of such monopolies that would make capitalism ripe for expropriation. Marx did not anticipate any noneconomic intervention in the concentration process before it ended, and his analysis was based on the assumption that there were tendencies within the economy about which one could do nothing. Marx could condemn the injustice and misery which resulted from the industrialization through which he was living only because he was personally sensitive to suffering. His theory, as such, made such developments, in one form or another, necessary. Moreover, Marx made all of the facile assumptions as to size and efficiency that later became central in the writings of capitalist apologists. Marx saw total centralization as the conclusion of the capitalist economic process, and he had no intermediate theory of the nature of prices and competition in what is now referred to as an oligopolistic market in which the total economic victory of one large competitor over another is extraordinarily difficult. In this context, both Marxian and classical theories were thoroughly irrelevant as an explanation of the nature of the economic process. Neither could explain collusion based on solidarity among capitalists and a rationalized pursual of mutual interests and profits. In the American context, Marx was wrong in predicting that an ever smaller number of capitalists would share the market, for the rapid growth of the market and continuous technological innovations kept the economy sufficiently fluid to require the intervention of something more decisive than long-term impersonal natural economic processes.

Marx and Engels never formulated a comprehensive political theory. But such a system would not have made much difference to them in any event, since the entire theory of dynamics in Marxism is defined in purely economic terms. It was their failure to discuss the potential role of the state and politics in preserving capitalism that is the really fundamental reason why Marxism is not too useful in comprehending recent American history.

Marx and Engels applied inconsistent definitions of the state. They usually referred to it as the instrument of the ruling class, but the interpretation of the state as an independent, classless entity was used in certain crucial spots, and at times they mixed both definitions. The political element in Marxist economic theory, as opposed to commentaries on current events, is much more clearly defined. Marxian economics is a theory of circulation, accumulation, crises, and, ultimately, social relations. It is political only in the implicit sense that Marx believed economic developments would ultimately have social and political repercussions. But his theory of economic development, save in one particular, is primarily nonpolitical in its dynamic elements. Marx' political writings were intended for practical agitational purposes; his economic theory was self-sufficient and the state was not regarded as a means of preserving or enlarging economic power.

Historically, prior to the development of the modern economy in which capital was taken primarily from surplus value created by labor, Marx regarded the earliest capital accumulation—the stage of "primitive accumulation"—as dependent on political and essentially noneconomic factors of force and power. In the breakup of feudal society the land of the agricultural producer was expropriated, and this "is the basis of the whole process" of accumulation. Naked force was used first of all, but the Enclosure Acts in the eighteenth century were the political legitimization of robbery. The result was a free proletariat for nascent capitalists to exploit, and with which to initiate a process of accumulation based on surplus value. The political basis of primitive accumulation was also apparent in colonialism, as well as the public debt and mercantilist system. And although Marx cited numerous examples that should have caused him to modify this point—the English Banking Act of 1844, for example—he nevertheless maintained that "In Western Europe, the home of political economy, the process of primitive accumulation is more or less accomplished."[4]

Although Marxist theory relied on purely economic categories of explanation, Marx was confronted with any number of political incidents during his lifetime—the creation of maximum hour laws, child labor laws, and similar measures in England and France—that forced him to try to reconcile these events with his theory, and in the process of doing so he formulated several inconsistent theories of the state. When discussing the English Factory Acts "made by a state that is ruled by capitalist and landlord," Marx was hard pressed to understand why the hours of labor should be limited. Rather than show that the interests of various capitalist blocs could be very diverse, or that the state was independent of the capitalists, he tried to argue that these laws were to their self-interest insofar as they prevented the exhaustion of workers. Moreover, the possible loss to the capitalists was minimized by the increasing intensity of labor output per hour during the shorter work day. Later in *Capital,* however, Marx used another interpretation of the state and its motives, referring frequently to a nonclass "society" that stands above and beyond the interests of capitalists. ". . . capital is reckless of the health or length of life of the labourer, unless under compulsion from society." Not self-interest but charity was used as an explanation of state intervention. Child labor laws were "here and there . . . effected by the State to prevent the coining of children's blood into capital." When Louis Bonaparte tried to extend the legal work day in 1852, Marx wrote, "the French people cried out with one voice 'the law that limits the working day to twelve hours is the one good that has remained to us of the legislation of the Republic.' " The concept of "one voice" or "society" was a classless one, and a reflection on the nature of the state. Marx showed how courts were utilized to circumvent the proper application of the laws, or how factory owners pressured Parliament to obtain concessions, and he pointed to the various loopholes in the existing laws. But Marx greatly respected "The thoroughly conscientious investigations of the Children's Employment Commission . . .," and he exploited them to show the horrors capitalism was creating in the English manufacturing centers. Moreover, he extended this admiration to the Factory Act inspectors themselves, who applied the law ruthlessly and treated the objections of business "as a mere sham."[5]

The specific economic form . . . determines the relationship of rulers and ruled, as it grows directly out of production itself and, in turn, reacts upon it as a determining element. Upon this, however, is founded the entire formation of the economic community which grows up out of the production relations themselves, thereby simultaneously its specific political form. It is always the direct relationship of the owners of the conditions of production to the direct producers—a relation always naturally corresponding to a definite stage in the development of the methods of labour and thereby its social productivity—which reveals the innermost secret, the hidden basis of the entire social structure, and with it the political form of the relation of sovereignty and dependence, in short, the corresponding specific form of the state.[6]

But even though the state reflected the social and productive relations within society—the economy—it was not to be used to enlarge the power of the capitalists, to aid the process of accumulation, or to regulate relations among them. All of this was taken care of in the market place, which was precisely where the capitalist system was to be destroyed. The capitalists controlled the state, according to Marx' formal theory but they were not going to use it in the economic sphere. They might use it to club down workers, although Marx did not develop this realistic possibility in sufficient detail either. Where Marx actually saw the state operating, as in factory and labor laws, he gave it an implicitly nonclass character. Marx' dynamic economic theory was neatly isolated from the political sphere, and he naively assumed that the capitalist state would sit idly by while its material basis was destroyed by free economic laws.

Of all the writings of Marx and Engels on politics and the state, Engels' *Anti-Dühring* was by far the most systematic. Dühring's basic thesis was not entirely dissimilar to Marx' discussion of primitive accumulation. Early economic institutions were really "social-economic constitutional forms of a purely political nature," based on the force of the state. Even in modern civilization, Dühring argued, political conditions were the fundamental causes of the economic situation—direct political force was primary—proposing a theory quite the reverse of the Marxist concept. Engels, in a polemic that virtually threw out Marx' theory of primitive accumulation as well, took the opposite view. Force and politics could not alter inexorable economic developments, and politics either conformed to economics or was replaced by a political system capable of succumbing. ". . . the progressive evolution of production and exchange brings us of necessity to the present capitalist mode of production. . . . The whole process can be explained by purely economic causes; at no point whatever are robbery, force, the state or political interference of any kind necessary."[7] Indeed, in Engels' case the state and politics became so passive that he, much more than Marx, adopted an interpretation which made the state a classless, abstract entity—the state of bourgeois political theory. His discussion of the transition to socialism represents a hopelessly naive mix of both definitions of the state: the state as the tool of the capitalists and the state as the nonclass, independent agent.

Engels later went even further in advocating a theory of the neutral state. Bonapartism had been able to balance the proletariat and the bourgeoisie off against each other, and Bismarck was able to do the same, giving the state a character and interest separated from both classes, according to Engels. And, partly because it could be used through corruption, and also because the workers had yet to develop a politically dangerous class consciousness, the "democratic republic" was becoming the "inevitable necessity" of modern society, a condition with obvious implications to its class functions.[8] The fact that there were deep divisions between capitalists and emperors in a number of the modern states did not lead Engels to an analysis of internal divisions among power blocs, and the political expression that conflict might take. The power base of the emperors was also slighted, since it could not be subsumed within economic theory.

Marxist political theory was formulated mainly in response to specific political events, and on the basis of brief and inconsistent evaluations of the role of the state it is intended to be predictive. The predictions were based not on political understanding or theory that was especially serious, but on the anticipated outcome of economic developments. By effectively ignoring the role of the state in modern capitalism, Marxism lost sight of the possible resilience in capitalism, a resilience made possible by political rather than economic power. But if the state could determine the direction of the economy, an entirely new situation might be created, and in fact was.

Rosa Luxemburg excepted, European socialists tended to dissociate the economic activity and reforms of the state from the desire of capitalism to strengthen itself, and actually to endorse the state's activity. More important, they formulated alternate programs based essentially on the capitalist premises found in Marx: the assumption that concentrated industry was the price of technological efficiency, and that centralization and bureaucracy in decision-making were unavoidable. Luxemburg alone tried to think through an alternative theory, really breaking with the true Marxist tradition. She failed primarily because she did not go far enough in her consideration of the role of the state in internal economics, dealing with it rather merely as a sponsor of external imperialism; in the former respect her methodology was of more limited historical value. Marxist theorists, with a few uninfluential exceptions, have never seriously confronted the relationship of the modern state to the economy.

The term "political capitalism" was first coined by Max Weber, but the meaning I have given to it throughout this book has been one that Weber would have strongly opposed.[9] And quite rightly, for Weber's entire system cannot be reconciled with the American experience in any significant way. Although Weber, the titan of social theory in the twentieth century—a man who reflected and captured the intense disillusion with industrial capitalism that has shaped European social thought—frequently wrote about politics and economics on the basis of his German experience, he felt that no where in the world was his general theory more vindicated than in the United States. Ironically, it is in the United States that Weber is least applicable. Yet his concerns, if not his ideas, are precisely those of this study: the character of bureaucracy in the political sphere, the thrust toward rationalization in economic and political life, the nature of the state and its relationship to business. Weber was conscious, in a way that only a man who had lived through the First World War could be, of those complexities in modern society to which Marx was necessarily oblivious. But for all his insight, Weber, like Marx, abandoned himself to an impersonal future—to Historical Inevitability. Marx' future was optimistic, while Weber saw nothing ahead but the deadening triumph of a clinical, mechanistic industrialism. At the turn of this century neither alternative was inevitable, and the economic and industrial future was still capable of being molded—an opportunity we probably no longer have.

Although the America of the 1960's is, unfortunately, much closer to Weber's image than to Marx's, it did not become that way in the manner Weber predicted. Modern Western capitalism, according to Weber, had removed the state from the economy save in an external, impersonal sense. "Political capitalism" to Weber meant the accumulation of private capital and fortunes via booty connected with politics, the exploitation of opportunities provided by political bodies, colonialism, or tax farming. The basic argument of the entire Weberian system was to show how and why the Western economy had moved away from irregular forms of political capitalism—unpredictable to both the state and the economy—toward a political and economic rationalization of a sort very different from the one I have described in this volume. For Weber neatly separated the economic and political structure from one another in a way, so far as the American experience is concerned, that was historically meaningless. This bifurcation, I believe, was Weber's fatal error.

To Weber, rationalization in the political sphere attained its highest expression in the area of the law. The general trend in modern Western law was to make it classless in the sense that no group or faction was to have a favored position in the economic process once certain ground rules were defined. The basic thesis Weber tried to advance was that "To those who had interests in the commodity market, the rationalization and systematization of the law in general and, with certain reservations . . . the increasing calculability of the functioning of the legal process in particular, constituted one of the most important conditions for the existence of economic enterprise intended to function with stability and, especially, of capitalistic enterprise, which cannot do without legal security."[10] Once a rationally objective law was created the demands of concrete individuals or interests were ignored, a fact that would have been impossible in many nations under the favoritism prevalent during periods of political capitalism as Weber defined it. And while Weber acknowledged that the detached bureaucratic administration in charge of the implementation of the law was also protecting capitalism from the "irregular" demands of noncapitalists, which is to say the masses, he did not make much of the point. The significant fact to Weber was that capitalists were being protected from each other, and that modern Western law and states were taken out of the economic arena, leaving only certain minimal, universally applicable ground rules for economic activity. In the United States, of course, Weber's legal theory was nullified by Roosevelt's détente system and the application of the irregular "rule of reason" by both the executive and judicial branches of the national government.

Weber discussed the nature and origins of the modern Western state in detail, the basis of its legitimation, and especially the character of its administration. Politics and political parties interested him, but there is a disturbing impersonality about Weber's writings no matter how often one reads him. In part this is due to the sweeping numbered and lettered categories or ideal-typologies that Weber persistently used to catalogue all phenomena in virtually all places at all times. Such a method resists concrete historical application, save where Weber chose to make it. But the heart of the matter is that ultimately Weber did not really believe that the political institutions and structures of modern society had very deep or extensive consequences. His belief in a now impersonal legal structure, the impersonally administered state dominated by uncommitted bureaucrats, led him to outline a state and political structure that is somehow above or beyond the economic sphere, and is now virtually separated from it. Yet even within his own writings can be found ample random, untheoretical observations which disprove or raise serious doubts concerning his own systematic theory.

To Weber, whether he was discussing politics or economics, "Bureaucratization offers above all the optimum possibility for carrying through the principle of specialized administrative functions according to purely objective considerations."[11] The structure and operational rules of modern bureaucracies were essentially the same to Weber whether they functioned in industry or politics. Bureaucracies are crucial to the successful operation of large-scale organizations, and their efficiency is based ultimately on impersonal technical knowledge. Bureaucracy both reflected and accelerated the trend toward concentration and giantism in political and economic institutions. In politics, as in economics, according to Weber, no changes in the basic nature of the bureaucracy, or the dependence on it, could really be effected by a change in formal leadership. Both the state and the economy were based on organizational principles as well as formal economic relations. A change in a government or ownership might alter the specific leadership, but the essential organizational structure—the bureaucracy—would ultimately prevail. In effect, politics could not overcome the basic institutional legacy of the modern state and the systematized capitalist economy. It is for this reason that I consider Weber a determinist and a pessimist.

Yet politics remained. Weber was fully aware of the social and class character of modern parties and government, and that political battles would be fought over economic issues; but he failed to relate the consequences of those battles, once resolved, to the impersonality of law and bureaucracy—because he really did not believe politics could have serious consequences. Class and status were ultimately based on economic power, and party rule was class rule. And while the details of these facts were known to him, and he discussed the rich political amateurs or the American city bosses paid by financial magnates, the larger picture was overlooked by Weber. His discussion of political bureaucracies ignored *why* new bureaucracies were created. In the United States, for example, the technical knowledge of new administrative agencies that were created was not the source of their power. Power was created by decisions made in the political sphere by political agents, which is to say by class-oriented elements. It was the politically based bureaucracy that sought to rationalize the large-scale economic organization, to make economic decisions and profits predictable and secure through political means.

In large part due to his reliance on overschematized ideal-types that did not necessarily have concrete historical relevance, Weber ignored the specific value of his system. He categorized various types of modern political leaders, but ignored *why* they were there, other than legitimation provided by rational legal rules or charismatic hero worship. He overlooked *what* modern parties do when in power, but was concerned with only *how* they do it. Weber granted that elections disturbed modern economic life, but he failed to consider how capitalists responded to them.

If one looks at the detailed organizational structures of the administrative agencies created by the federal government from 1887 on, these agencies were seemingly neutral and Weber's argument may be vindicated. But if one regards their functions as a whole, and their genesis and original purposes, political bureaucracies are very much a part of the structure of political capitalism created in the United States during this period. Indeed, the formalization and independence from the legislative and executive branches imposed on many agencies was not due to a desire to find the technically best way of creating a bureaucracy, but to protect established economic interests from the buffeting theoretically possible in a political democracy with economic problems. Weber realized that monetary policy represented an important political intervention into the economy, but he ignored the implications of this fact to his conception of a modern capitalism that had "a horror" of political capitalism that relied on the government rather than "the harnessed rational energy of routine enterprise. . . ."[12] Capitalism, of course, was no longer able to fulfill its intense desire for rationalization, which Weber rightly ascribed to it, via private or personal methods. Even when discussing government regulation that patently contradicted his thesis he overlooked the purpose of such intervention—to attain stability, or profits, or even to preserve existing social relations.

Weber's discussion of economics, as opposed to the very distinct area of politics in modern society, was hardly more adequate. Weber did not really have an economic theory, although he discussed economics extensively. He dealt with the motives of capitalists and their personal qualities, and he discussed bureaucracy in a manner that frequently applied only to economic institutions. Yet he never came to grips with the crucial questions that preoccupied Marx: What were the laws of capitalist development, the working dynamics and *tendencies* of the economy? Weber's references to economics, like virtually his entire system, dealt in categories that were timeless and more pretentious than Marx'. For this reason Weber was incapable of identifying economic weaknesses that might require the intervention of the state. The bureaucracy of the modern business, with its efficiency and expertise, created the conditions of rationalization required by capitalism. So far as Weber was concerned, this self-regulation, along with intercorporate market agreements and monopolies, virtually exhausted the modern corporation's requirements. Market regulation by the state was largely assigned to past history, especially if it involved capital accumulation through political means. The state applied a limited set of laws uniformly, provided a suitable means of exchange by which rational economic accounting and calculation was possible, and left the rest to the capitalists themselves. Problems of crises, profit ratios, market insecurity, and those issues central to the general tradition of economic theory did not bother Weber very much, or at least he failed to relate them to his larger scheme. For this reason there is a certain lack of dynamics in Weber, an unnecessary, too convenient simplicity that goes beyond even that inherent in his incessant use of typologies.

Weber was correct in suggesting that "North America has offered the freest space for the development of high capitalism," but very little in his grand system is of aid in providing insights into that development.[13] He failed to take the role of ideas or interests in modern politics seriously enough. He separated the process of rationalization in economics and technology from the role of the positive state, and failed to see their dependence on one another despite the fact that he recognized the political and economic elites were frequently interlocked. The economic sphere had its own imperatives, the political sphere its neutral justification of bureaucracy as an end in itself. Weber rejected the possibility that victorious political parties, admittedly based on class interests, could determine the special form and direction economic, industrial, and political rationalization took. Instead, he imputed an internal, independent logic to developments in each of these areas that could ultimately be traced back to the theological origins of Western society. Weber ignored the genre of capitalists who, in addition to wanting a predictable political and industrial organization, also wanted one susceptible to aiding them in the process of profit-making via political means and favors, and to helping them attain industrial or financial rationalization. But such a group was crucial in shaping the American political experience and in defining political issues.

Despite his many shortcomings, only Thorstein Veblen, of all the American intellectuals of the Progressive Era, understood the main drift of American power relations in the period preceding the First World War. One can still read *Absentee Ownership,* published in 1923, with the utmost profit, for Veblen captured the indispensable reality of the domination of business over American politics, ethics, and the key institutions of society.

Veblen's concern with the material and industrial development of America focused on the vested legal and political institutions that were designed to preserve old social relations in new circumstances. He never ceased to reiterate the crucial fact that "the chief—virtually sole—concern of the constituted authorities in any democratic nation is a concern about the profitable business of the nation's substantial citizens."[14] Any administration had to represent the desires of big business, and Congress was little more than a "Soviet of Business Men's Delegates." Nowhere in the world did the big businessman influence the entire fabric of society and culture as in America.

Yet, for all his perception, Veblen failed to grasp the structural realities of the economy which the businessman ruled, and instead offered a rather oversimplified view of the source of the business-man's domination. It was his contention that the commanding heights of American business had expanded to such an extent that they were controlled by absentee financial and credit interests who assigned managerial responsibilities in the corporations to bureaucratic types. Investment banking, and Morgan was its major practitioner, had managed to take over the economy. In discussing this development, however, Veblen ascribed a natural power to finance capital which it did not have in fact, and he was unable to do more than explain away the origins of federal regulation of the economy, and especially the Federal Reserve Board. In its genesis, Veblen suggested, the Fed-eral Reserve Board was an event that was somehow brought under control, to the profit of finance. This legislation, like all others, was rechanneled because the personnel of politics was ultimately safe, a perfectly valid point that nevertheless failed to explain why legis-lation was enacted in the first place. Veblen, in short, ascribed an economic power to absentee ownership that it in reality did not have, and his approach to federal legislation was to try to explain it away.

Despite his correct understanding of the nature of political leadership as it stood, Veblen did not appreciate the tensions that were nascent in any formally democratic politics, and the extent to which action was necessary to direct this tension into harmless channels. More significantly, he was unaware of insecurity in the economic sphere and the extent to which government intervention was designed to overcome it. This oversight was due to the fact that finance capitalism had not developed to the degree he believed, and that the basic conditions in the economy were fluid to a larger extent than he appreciated. But for all this, Veblen was largely correct for the wrong reasons. The desire for security and predictability was real, and the efforts to attain it eventually produced the sort of centralization of decisions over the economy that Veblen ascribed to finance capital. The effects of federal regulation were conservative, even though Veblen slighted the intent. For all Veblen's deficiencies, his contribution toward a theoretical comprehension of American history in this century has never been equaled.

Theory and the American Reality

The American experience justifies different theoretical conclusions than those reached by Marx, Weber, or Veblen. Any reasonable generalization on the phenomenon of progressivism must necessarily take into account the economic realities and problems of the period, and the responses that were set in motion. Yet the crucial factor in the American experience was the nature of economic power which required political tools to rationalize the economic process, and that resulted in a synthesis of politics and economics. This integration is the dominant fact of American society in the twentieth century, although once political capitalism is created a dissection of causes and effects becomes extraordinarily difficult. The economy had its own problems, dictated by technological innovation, underconsumption, crises, and competition. But these difficulties were increasingly controlled by political means to the extent that the consideration of economic problems outside their political context is meaningless. The "laws of capitalist development" were not self-contained imperatives in the technological, economic, or political sphere, but an inseparable unification of all three elements.

The object of such a combination was not merely capital accumulation, although it was that as well, but a desire to defend and exercise power through new media more appropriate to the structural conditions of the new century: the destructive potential of growing competition and the dangerous possibilities of a formal political democracy that might lead to a radical alteration of the distribution of wealth or even its total expropriation. Politics and the state become the means of attaining order in the economic sphere and security in the political arena. And they were accessible tools because the major political parties and leaders of the period were also conservative in the sense that they believed in the basic value of capitalist social relations—of some variation of the status quo. The resilience of capitalism, under these circumstances, becomes something that cannot be evaluated in isolated economic terms. Behind the economy, resting on new foundations in which effective collusion and price stability is now the rule, stands the organized power of the national government. The stability and future of the economy is grounded, in the last analysis, on the power of the state to act to preserve it. Such support does not end crises, nor does it eliminate antagonisms inherent in the very nature of the economy, but it does assure the ability of the existing social order to overcome, or survive, the consequences of its own deficiencies. The theory of the national government as a neutral intermediary in its intervention into the economic process is a convenient ideological myth, but such a contention will not survive a serious inquiry into the origins and consequences of such intervention. The rhetoric of reform is invariably different than its structural results. Such mythology is based on the assumption that those who control the state will not use it for their own welfare.

It is important to stress that under conditions of political capitalism the form of the industrialization process, and of the political machinery of society, take on those characteristics necessary to fulfill the peculiar values, attributes, and goals of the ascendant class of that society. The rationalized, dominated, and essentially totalitarian decision-making process is not a consequence of forces inherent in industrialism, but in political capitalism in all its components. The organization of industry is based on the decisions of men whose motives have nothing whatsoever to do with inexorable destiny. Mergers, the scale of effective production, the nature of the production itself, and the direction given to the fruits of technology—all these were decisions made by men whose motives, interests, and weaknesses were peculiar to the basic capitalist assumptions upon which they operated. Their errors were many, as were the possibilities for their failure; but the national government stood behind them so that the consequences of their mistakes would not be calamitous. Perhaps industrialization would not have permitted democratic control and direct participation in the work process under any circumstances. All one can do is point to the large extent to which the concentration of industry in this period had nothing to do with considerations of efficient technology, and suggest that no effort whatsoever was ever made to democratize the work situation and industrial control, much less consider the desirability of reducing technological efficiency, if necessary, in such a way as to make decentralization or workers' control possible.

Nor is there any evidence to suggest that the bureaucratization of the political machinery of society, to the extent it took place, was as inevitable as the concentration of industry. It was perfectly logical for men who had spent years solving their economic problems or making their fortunes through political means to also welcome the intervention of a centralized state power to meet problems they could not solve themselves. Social forces, dynamic institutional factors, were the cause of bureaucratic developments in the form of new political agencies and the strengthening of many of the older ones. American capitalism was not merely interested in having law that operated like a piece of machinery, as Weber suggested, but in utilizing the state on terms and conditions which made bureaucratic functions class functions. Bureaucracy, in itself, needed a power base in order to operate in a roughly continuous, systematic fashion. Since it had no economic power itself, it had to support, and hence be supported by, powerful economic groups. This was especially true in a situation where the conditions of political activity were defined by political parties which in turn reflected economic interests, or where the idea of the bureaucracy originated with those operating in the very area in which the bureaucracy was to function.

The skeptical reader may ask whether political capitalism changed after 1916, or perhaps whether capitalism was made more socially responsible by virtue of the stability and rationalization it attained through political means. The question is a moot one, and would take at least one more volume to answer properly. All one can do is point to the continuity in the nature of the political parties and their key leaders, but, more important, to the perpetuation of the same distribution of wealth and the same social relations over the larger part of this century. The solution of economic problems has continued to take place in the political sphere, and the strength of the status quo is based ultimately on the synthesis of politics and economics. Crises have been overcome, or frozen, as much by the power of the state as by internal economic resources applied by business in isolation.

The question remains: Could the American political experience, and the nature of our economic institutions, have been radically different than they are today? It is possible to answer affirmatively, although only in a hypothetical, unreal manner, for there was nothing inevitable or predetermined in the peculiar character given to industrialism in America. And, abstractly regarding all of the extraneous and artificial measures that provided shape and direction to American political and economic life, and their ultimate class function, it would be possible to make a case for a positive reply to the question. Yet ultimately the answer must be a reluctant "No."

There can be no alternatives so long as none are seriously proposed, and to propose a relevant measure of fundamental opposition one must understand what is going on in society, and the relationship of present actions to desired goals. To have been successful, a movement of fundamental change would have had to develop a specific diagnosis of existing social dynamics and, in particular, the variable nature and consequences of political intervention in the economy. It would have, in short, required a set of operating premises radically different than any that were formulated in the Progressive Era or later. Populism rejected, on the whole, the values of business even as it was unable to articulate a viable alternative. Intellectually it left a vacuum, and, more important, the movement was dead by 1900. The Socialist Party suffered from the fetishistic belief in the necessity of centralization that has characterized all socialist groups that interpreted Marx too literally, and it had a totally inaccurate estimate of the nature of progressivism, eventually losing most of its followers to the Democrats. The two major political parties, as always, differed on politically unimportant and frequently contrived details, but both were firmly wedded to the status quo, and the workers were generally their captives or accomplices. No socially or politically significant group tried to articulate an alternative means of organizing industrial technology in a fashion that permitted democratic control over centralized power, or participation in routine, much less crucial, decisions in the industrial process. No party tried to develop a program that suggested democracy could be created only by continuous mass involvement in the decisions that affected their lives, if the concentration of actual power in the hands of an elite was to be avoided. In brief, the Progressive Era was characterized by a paucity of alternatives to the status quo, a vacuum that permitted political capitalism to direct the growth of industrialism in America, to shape its politics, to determine the ground rules for American civilization in the twentieth century, and to set the stage for what was to follow.

NOTES

The following code abbreviations are used in the notes:

NA Mss	Nelson Aldrich Papers, Library of Congress
AG Mss	Attorney Generals Files, Department of Justice Records, National Archives
CB Mss	Charles J. Bonaparte Papers, Library of Congress
BAI Mss	Bureau of Animal Industry Records, National Archives
BOC Mss	Bureau of Corporation Records, National Archives
FTC Mss	Federal Trade Commission General Records, 1914-1921, National Archives
FTCB Mss	Federal Trade Commission Files, F.T.C. Building, Washington
FDA Mss	Food and Drug Administration Records, National Archives
JG Mss	James R. Garfield Papers, Library of Congress
CG Mss	Carter Glass Papers, University of Virginia Library
HH Mss	Henry Lee Higginson Papers, Baker Library, Harvard Business School
HR	House of Representatives Records, National Archives
PK Mss	Philander Knox Papers, Library of Congress
JL Mss	J. Laurence Laughlin Papers, Library of Congress
WM Mss	William H. Moody Papers, Library of Congress
RO Mss	Richard Olney Papers, Library of Congress
GP Mss	George W. Perkins Papers, Columbia University Library
AP Mss	Amos Pinchot Papers, Library of Congress
HP Mss	Henry F. Pringle Notes on Taft, Theodore Roosevelt Collection, Harvard College Library
MP	*Messages and Papers of the Presidents* (New York, no dates). References are to the Bureau of National Literature editions for each President.
PP Mss	Progressive Party Records, Theodore Roosevelt Collection, Harvard College Library
LTR	Elting E. Morison and John M. Blum, eds., *The Letters of Theodore Roosevelt* (8 vols., Cambridge, 1951-1954)
TR Mss	Theodore Roosevelt Papers, Library of Congress
ER Mss	Elihu Root Papers, Library of Congress
HS Mss	Henry Seligman Papers, Baker Library, Harvard Business School
SEN	Senate Records, National Archives
FS Mss	Francis Lynde Stetson Papers, Williams College Library
WT Mss	William Howard Taft Papers, Library of Congress
WW Mss	Woodrow Wilson Papers, Library of Congress
PWW	Ray S. Baker and William E. Dodd, eds., *The Public Papers of Woodrow Wilson* (6 vols., New York, 1925-26)

All platform quotations are from Kirk H. Porter, ed., *National Party Platforms* (New York, 1924).

CHAPTER ONE—*Monopolies and Mergers: Predictions and Promises*

1. Dodd in James H. Bridge, ed., *The Trust: Its Book* (New York, 1902), 47; Hill and Logan in *North American Review*, CLXXII (1901), 647, 689.

2. *Bankers' Magazine*, LXII (1901), 657.

3. J. K. Gwinn in *The Annals of the American Academy of Political and Social Science*, XLII (1912), 126. Also see Schwab in *North American Review*, *op. cit.*, 655-59; U.S. Industrial Commission, *Preliminary Report on Trusts and Industrial Combinations;* 56:1 (Washington, 1900), I, 223.

4. Charles Francis Adams, Jr., *Speech Before the [Mass.] Joint Standing Legislative Committee on Railways* (Boston, 1873), 35; *The Federation of the Railroad System* (Boston, 1880), 19; *Railroads: Their Origin and Problems* (New York, 1878), 121.

5. Civic Federation of Chicago, *Chicago Conference on Trusts*, Sept. 13-16, 1899 (Chicago, 1900), 579.

6. John Moody, *The Truth About the Trusts* (New York, 1904), 494.

7. Frederick Engels, *Anti-Dühring* (Moscow, 1959), 226; National Campaign Committee, *The Socialist Campaign Book of 1900* (Chicago, 1900), 30; W. J. Ghent, *Our Benevolent Feudalism* (New York, 1902), 8 ff.; Caro Lloyd, *Henry Demarest Lloyd, 1847-1903* (New York, 1912), I, 287; Ira Kipnis, *The American Socialist Movement, 1897-1912* (New York, 1952), 112; Gaylord Wilshire, *Socialism Inevitable (Wilshire Editorials)* (New York, 1907), 140, 180; Sigmund Diamond, *The Reputation of the American Businessman* (Cambridge, 1955), 85.

8. See Gary in U.S. Senate, Comm. on Interstate Commerce, *Hearings on a Bill to Create an Interstate Trade Commission;* 62:2 (Washington, 1912), I, 693; data on merger movement from Ralph L. Nelson, *Merger Movements in American Industry, 1895-1956* (Princeton, 1959), *passim;* U.S. Industrial Commission, *Final Report;* 57:1 (Washington, 1902), XIX, 486-91; Thomas R. Navin and Marian V. Sears, "The Rise of a Market for Industrial Securities, 1887-1902," *Business History Review*, XXIX (1955), 105-38; Henry Clews, *Fifty Years in Wall Street* (New York, 1908), 768 and *passim;* Industrial Commission, *Preliminary Report*, I, 960-63; Burton J. Hendrick, *The Life of Andrew Carnegie* (Garden City, 1932), II, 84 ff.; Arthur S. Dewing, *Corporate Promotions and Reorganizations* (Cambridge, 1914), 523, 538.

9. Charles R. Flint, *Memories of an Active Life* (New York, 1923), 297-321; *North American Review, op. cit.*, 665-67. The return on capitalization at par was 7.4 per cent.

10. Francis Lynde Stetson, *Address Before the Economic Club of New York*, June 5, 1907 (no place, no date), 12. Also see Industrial Commission, *Final Report*, XIX, 616; *Bulletin of the Department of Labor*, V (1900), 670; Dewing, *Corporate Promotions*, 533; Industrial Commission, *Preliminary Report*, I, 249; Edward S. Meade, *Trust Finance* (New York, 1903), 181; U.S. Bureau of Corporations, *Report of the Commissioner of Corporations on the Steel Industry*, July 1, 1911 (Washington, 1911), pt. I, 37, 167-79, 251.

11. "Memorandum of Agreement," U.S. Rubber Papers, Baker Library, Harvard Business School, Jan. 21, 1892.

12. Sage in *North American Review, op. cit.*, 643; Clews, *Fifty Years*, 768. Also see Algernon A. Osborne, *Speculation on the New York Stock Exchange, September, 1904—March, 1907* (New York, 1913), 149-58; Thomas R. Navin and Marian V. Sears, "A Study in Merger: Formation of the International Mercantile Marine Company," *Business History Review*, XXVIII (1954), 291-328; N. R. Danielian, *A.T. & T.* (New York, 1939), 60-73.

13. *Iron Age*, LXVI (Nov. 22, 1900), 28 ff.

CHAPTER TWO—*Competition and Decentralization: The Failure to Rationalize Industry*

1. In 1909, however, 1.1 per cent of the total number of establishments accounted for 43.8 per cent of the value of all products. Many smaller firms were not full-line producers. U.S. Bureau of the Census, *Thirteenth Census of the United States: Manufactures—1909* (Washington, 1913), VIII, 32, 40, 181; *Historical Statistics of the United States, Colonial Times to 1957* (Washington, 1960), 570; *Dun's Review*, XXXIV (Jan. 9, 1926), 7-8.

2. Clews, *Fifty Years*, 767.

3. *Iron Age, op. cit.*, 28.

4. National Industrial Conference Board, *Mergers in Industry* (New York, 1929), 39; A. S. Dewing, "A Statistical Test of the Success of Consolidations," *Quarterly Journal of Economics*, XXXVI (1921), 84-101; Dewing, *Corporate Promotions*, 526, 547-58; Shaw Livermore, "The Success of Industrial Mergers," *Quarterly Journal of Economics*, L (1935), 75-89; Nelson, *Merger Movements*, 97-98, 161-62; George J. Stigler, "Monopoly and Oligopoly by Merger," *American Economic Review*, XL (1950), 29; Alfred L. Bernheim *et al.*, *How Profitable Is Big Business?* (New York, 1937), 107-14; A. D. H. Kaplan, *Big Enterprise in a Competitive System* (Washington, 1954), 145-46; Gabriel Kolko, *Wealth and Power in America* (New York, 1962), 60.

5. For decentralization, patents, and economies of size, see Alfred D. Chandler, "Management Decentralization: An Historical Analysis," *Business History Review*, XXX (1956), 111-74; John M. Blair, "Technology and Size," *American Economic Review*, XXXVIII (1948), 129 ff.; U.S. Temporary National Economic Committee, *Relative Efficiency of Large, Medium-Sized, and Small Business* (Washington, 1941), *passim;* and especially Joe S. Bain, *Barriers to New Competition* (Cambridge, 1956), *passim.* The number of patents issued to individuals increased over 50 per cent between 1901 and 1916, to 31,742. *Historical Statistics*, 607.

6. *New York Financier*, LXXV (1900), 1312.

7. For the general background of the steel industry, see Abraham Berglund, *The United States Steel Corporation* (New York, 1907); Bureau of Corporations, *Report . . . on the Steel Industry*; Hendrick, *Life of Andrew Carnegie*; U.S. House, Committee on Investigation of United States Steel Corporation, *Hearings*; 62:2 (8 vols., Washington, 1911-1912); George Harvey, *Henry Clay Frick—The Man* (New York, 1928); *Thirteenth Census*, X, 207-08, 228. For the early years of U.S. Steel, also see John A. Garraty, *Right-Hand Man: The Life of George W. Perkins* (New York, 1960), 96-119. The Gary Dinners are also covered in Senate Committee on Interstate Commerce, *Hearings on . . . an Interstate Trade Commission*, 704; BOC Mss, file 6518-8; *Iron Age*, LXXX (1907), 1549; LXXXI (1908), 1650-52, 1710-11, 1892; LXXXII (1908), 1757; LXXXIII (1909), 648, 1862-63. For decline of market shares also see Walter Adams, ed., *The Structure of American Industry* (New York, 1950), 157; Simon N. Whitney, *Antitrust Policies: American Experiences in Twenty Industries* (New York, 1958), I, 290-92; William Z. Ripley, ed., *Trusts, Pools and Corporations* (Boston, 1916), chap. V; Fritz Redlich, *History of American Business Leaders* (Ann Arbor, 1940), I, 132.

8. Charles Schwab to Perkins, July 3, 1901, GP Mss.

9. Perkins to John D. Rockefeller, July 8, 1903, GP Mss.

10. E. H. Gary to Bonaparte, Feb. 11, 1908, CB Mss; E. H. Gary, *Statement to the Public Press,* January 31, 1908 (no place), 1-2.

11. *Iron Age,* LXXXIII (1909), 648.

12. Perkins to J. P. Morgan, March 11, 1909, Oct. 15, 1910, GP Mss.

13. For the growth and general background of Standard, see U.S. Bureau of Corporations, *Report of the Commissioner of Corporations on the Petroleum Industry,* Part I, May 20, 1907 (Washington, 1907); Allan Nevins, *John D. Rockefeller: The Heroic Age of American Enterprise* (New York, 1940); George W. Stocking, *The Oil Industry and the Competitive System* (Boston, 1925); John S. McGee, "Predatory Price Cutting: The Standard Oil (N. J.) Case," *The Journal of Law and Economics,* I (1958), 137-69; Industrial Commission, *Reports,* I, 215, XIX, 597. For the growth of competition, see Melvin G. DeChazeau and Alfred E. Kahn, *Integration and Competition in the Petroleum Industry* (New Haven, 1959), 83 ff.; Warren C. Platt, "40 Years of Oil Competition," *National Petroleum News,* XXXXI (1949), 29-58; Raymond F. Bacon and William A. Hamor, *The American Petroleum Industry* (New York, 1916), I, 73, 262-70; U.S. Federal Trade Commission, *Petroleum Industry: Prices, Profits, and Competition* (Washington, 1928), 61 ff.; Whitney, *Antitrust Policies,* I, 107; Leonard M. Logan, Jr., *Stabilization of the Petroleum Industry* (Norman, 1930), 18-19.

14. Petroleum Producers' Union, *Address to Producers of Petroleum Issued by the General Council, July 13, 1878* (Titusville?, 1878), 3.

15. For the industry in general, see Allan Nevins, *Ford: The Times, the Man, the Company* (New York, 1954); Lawrence H. Seltzer, *A Financial History of the American Automobile Industry* (Boston, 1928); John B. Rae, "The Electric Vehicle Company," *Business History Review,* XXIX (1955), 302; John B. Rae, *American Automobile Manufacturers: The First Forty Years* (Philadelphia, 1959), chap. III; the studies by Ralph C. Epstein in *Harvard Business Review,* V (1927), 157-74, 281-92.

16. Henry Seligman to Isaac Seligman, Sept. 20, 1910, HS Mss.

17. Alfred Sloan, Jr., *Adventures of a White-Collar Man* (New York, 1941), 134-35.

18. See Garraty, *Life of Perkins,* 127-46; U.S. Bureau of Corporations, *The International Harvester Company,* March 3, 1913 (Washington, 1913); Cyrus McCormick, *International Harvester Company* (no place, May 20, 1907), 2-4; U.S. Temporary National Economic Committee, *The Structure of Industry* (Washington, 1941), monograph 37, 242; Whitney, *Antitrust Policies,* II, 230-31.

19. H. K. Smith, "Memorandum in Re Second Interview With International Harvester Company on January 19, 1907," BOC Mss.

20. For the industry in general, see U.S. Federal Communication Commission, *Proposed Report: Telephone Investigation* (Washington, 1938), chaps. I, II, IV, and *passim;* Danielian, *A.T. & T., passim;* Arthur Pier, *Forbes: Telephone Pioneer* (New York, 1953), 139-56; *Annual Reports, American Telephone and Telegraph Company, 1908* (Boston, 1909), 22; *1911* (New York, 1912), 27-32. For additional data on profits, rates, and innovation, see A. C. Lindemuth, *Telephone Mergers Illegal* (Chicago, 1908), 11-12; Edward M. Cooke, *The Case of the Keystone Telephone* (no place, ca. 1915), 4; U.S. Senate, *Investigation of Telephone Companies;* 61:2 (Washington, 1910), 136-44.

21. William B. Gates, Jr., *Michigan Copper and Boston Dollars: An Economic History of the Michigan Copper Mining Industry* (Cambridge, 1951), 44-89; Moody, *Truth About the Trusts,* 16; T.N.E.C., *The Structure of Industry,* 249.

22. Henry Seligman to Albert Seligman, Feb. 4, 1885, HS Mss.

23. Charles Edward Russell, *The Greatest Trust in the World* (New York, 1905), 5; also 2, 13, 145-47.

24. For the general background, see Whitney, *Antitrust Policies,* I, 31 ff.; U.S. Bureau of Corporations, *Report of the Commissioner of Corporations on the Beef Industry,* March 3, 1905 (Washington, 1905), *passim;* U.S. Federal Trade Commission, *Report on the Meat-Packing Industry,* Part I, June 24, 1919 (Washington, 1919), 46-48; Bertram B. Fowler, *Men, Meat and Miracles* (New York, 1952), 90-92, 134-36.

25. Bureau of Corporations, *Report . . . on the Beef Industry,* 59.

26. For the growth of competition in other industries, see Harold C. Passer, *The Electrical Manufacturers, 1875-1900* (Cambridge, 1953), *passim;* Richard B. Tennant, *The American Cigarette Industry: A Study in Economic Analysis and Public Policy* (New Haven, 1950), *passim;* Warren C. Scoville, *Revolution in Glassmaking: Entrepreneurship and Technological Change in the American Industry, 1880-1920* (Cambridge, 1948), 70-75; Paul L. Vogt, *The Sugar Refining Industry in the United States* (Philadelphia, 1908), *passim;* Melvin T. Copeland, *The Cotton Manufacturing Industry of the United States* (Cambridge, 1912), 143-45, 170; Whitney, *Antitrust Policies,* I, chap. IV, 353-57, II, 197-99, 258-60.

27. For data on the following discussion, see Harold Barger, *Distribution's Place in the American Economy Since 1869* (Princeton, 1955), 6, 13; Harold U. Faulkner, *The Decline of Laissez Faire, 1897-1917* (New York, 1951), *passim;* Simon Kuznets *et al., Population Redistribution and Economic Growth: United States, 1870-1950—Analyses of Economic Change* (Philadelphia, 1960). The output per firm during 1899-1914 in thirty-five industries increased 56 per cent, the total volume 76 per cent, and the number of companies 13 per cent. Frederick C. Mills, *Economic Tendencies in the United States* (New York, 1932), 36. For social mobility, see William Miller, ed., *Men in Business* (Cambridge, 1952).

CHAPTER THREE—*Theodore Roosevelt and the Foundations of Political Capitalism, 1901-1904*

1. U.S. Senate, *Bills and Debates in Congress Relating to Trusts;* 57:2 (Washington, 1903), I, 91, 94.

2. *Ibid.,* 156; also 23, 78, 121.

3. Harvey, *Henry Clay Frick,* 157.

4. William Endicott, Jr., to Olney, April 23, 1893, RO Mss. Also see Henry James, *Richard Olney and His Public Service* (Boston, 1923), 30; Henry Lee Higginson to Olney, April 19, 1893; Olney to Herbert L. Satterlee, April 15, 1914, RO Mss; H. C. Fahnestock to Stetson, June 27, 1893, FS Mss.

5. Industrial Commission, *Preliminary Report,* 5, 797; also 231-37.

6. U.S. Senate, Committee on Privileges and Elections, *Campaign Contributions;* 62:3 (Washington, 1913), 151, 154.

7. Roosevelt to Douglas Robinson, Oct. 4, 1901, LTR, III, 160.

8. Mark Hanna, *Mark Hanna—His Book* (Boston, 1904), 39 and *passim.* Also see Herbert Croly, *Marcus Alonzo Hanna: His Life and Work* (New York, 1912), 317; Philip C. Jessup, *Elihu Root* (New York, 1938), I, 210; Roosevelt to J. P. Morgan, March 27, 1901, LTR, III, 30; Perkins to John A. McCall, March 10, June 22, 1900, GP Mss.

9. Roosevelt to Douglas Robinson, Oct. 4, 1901, LTR, III, 159-60. Also see "First Draft, October 2, 1901. Corporations," and Roosevelt to Perkins, Oct. 17, 1901, GP Mss.

10. MP, 6645-48.

11. "Memorandum in Northern Securities Case: in re 'Overcapitalization' " (no date), PK Mss. Also see Knox to Henry C. Frick, June 28, Oct. 22, 1902, PK Mss; and Hans B. Thorelli, *The Federal Antitrust Policy: Origination of an American Tradition* (Stockholm, 1954), 420-25, for theories on the case.

12. Joseph B. Bishop, *Theodore Roosevelt and His Time* (New York, 1920), I, 184.

13. Speech of Sept. 20, 1902, in William W. Mills, ed., "The Trust Question: Statements by Theodore Roosevelt from December 3, 1901, to June 30, 1914," a manuscript in Roosevelt Collection, Harvard College Library.

14. James B. Dill, "National Incorporation Laws for Trusts," *Yale Law Journal,* April, 1902, 2 of reprint. For business agitation for a Commerce Dept., see petitions and letters in HR 51A-H6.5; SEN 54A-J18; HR 54A-F19.2; HR 54A-H14.5; HR 55A-F16.2; HR 55A-H9.3.

15. MP, 6716; also 6711.

16. Roosevelt to Perkins, Dec. 26, 1902; Perkins to Roosevelt, Dec. 27, 1902, GP Mss.

17. Joseph B. Foraker to Perkins, Jan. 3, 1903, GP Mss. Also William C. Beer to Perkins, Jan. 6, 7, 11, 15, 1903, GP Mss.

18. Roosevelt to Perkins, June 26, 1903, GP Mss. Also see Thorelli, *Federal Antitrust Policy,* 539-54; Arthur M. Johnson, "Theodore Roosevelt and the Bureau of Corporations," *Miss. Valley Historical Review,* XLV (1959), 571-77; Nevins, *John D. Rockefeller,* II, 516; Roosevelt to Knute Nelson, July 21, 1906, LTR, V, 334.

19. Perkins to Roosevelt, July 3, 1903, GP Mss; Roosevelt to William Howard Taft, March 19, 1903, LTR, III, 450. Also see George Cortelyou to Aldrich, Feb. 5, 1903, NA Mss.

20. Roosevelt to Aldrich, March 16, 1903, NA Mss; Cortelyou to Perkins, April 17, 1903, GP Mss. Also see Roosevelt to Aldrich, July 22, 1903, NA Mss.

21. For Garfield see Jack M. Thompson, *James R. Garfield: The Career of a Rooseveltian Progressive, 1895-1916* (Unpublished Ph.D. thesis, Univ. of South Carolina, 1958), 79-80.

22. MP, 6785-86. Also see Roosevelt to Henry Cabot Lodge, Aug. 6, 1903, LTR, III, 545; Louis A. Coolidge, *Orville H. Platt* (New York, 1910), 513-19; Roosevelt to Theodore Roosevelt, Jr., Oct. 4, 1903, LTR, III, 615.

23. A number of briefs are in FTCB Mss, and insurance studies are in BOC Mss.

24. Jessup, *Elihu Root,* I, 416. Also Everett Walters, *Joseph Benson Foraker: An Uncompromising Republican* (Columbus, 1948), chap. XIII.

25. William C. Beer to Herbert Knox Smith, Aug. 23, 1907, BOC Mss.

26. Garfield, "Conference With Virgil P. Kline of Cleveland, Counsel for the Standard Oil Co.," June 2, 1904, BOC Mss.

27. Garfield to Roosevelt, Oct. 1, 1904, BOC Mss; Roosevelt to Garfield, Sept. 30, 1904, BOC Mss. Also see Meyer H. Fishbein, *Bureau of Corporations: An Agency of the Progressive Era* (Unpublished M.A. thesis, American Univ., 1954), 72-73; Thompson, *James R. Garfield,* 105; Garfield to Charles G. Dawes, Aug. 17, 1904, BOC Mss.

28. "Hist. of Bur. of Corp. for Republican Campaign Book" [1904], in JG Mss. This draft was not used.

29. George Kennan, *E. H. Harriman* (Boston, 1922), II, 192 ff.; Jessup, *Elihu Root,* 429-30; Senate Committee on Privileges, *Campaign Contributions,* II, 1105; Roosevelt to George B. Cortelyou, Oct. 26, 1904, LTR, IV, 996.

30. Roosevelt to Knox, Nov. 10, 1904, LTR, IV, 1023.

31. MP, 6899.

32. MP, 6901; *Report of the Commissioner of Corporations, December, 1904* (Washington, 1904), 36.

33. Garfield to the Secretary of Commerce, March 4, 1907, BOC Mss.

34. *Harper's Weekly,* XLIX (Jan. 7, 1905), 8. Also see Garfield to Francis Lynde Stetson, Dec. 24, 1904, FS Mss; Stetson to Garfield, Dec. 27, 1904; Seth Low to Garfield, Dec. 23, 1904; Garfield to George Perkins, Dec. 24, 1904, FTCB Mss. The FTCB Mss contain about 50 letters of congratulations from businessmen.

CHAPTER FOUR—*Roosevelt As Reformer, 1904-1906*

1. Ida M. Tarbell, *The Life of Elbert H. Gary* (New York, 1925), 184.

2. "Conference at White House, Evening of November 2, 1905," Nov. 4, 1905, in BOC Mss. Also see Herbert K. Smith to Wm. J. Filbert, Sept. 22, 1905; James R. Garfield to Elbert H. Gary, Oct. 13, 1905; William H. Baldwin to Garfield, Oct. 17, 1905, BOC Mss.

3. Elbert H. Gary to Garfield, Nov. 10, 1905; Garfield to Gary, Nov. 13, 1905, BOC Mss.

4. Diary, Nov. 2, 1905, JG Mss.

5. Diary, March 3, 1905, JG Mss; Russell, *Greatest Trust in the World,* 5. Also Charles Dawes to Garfield, Sept. 13, 1904, BOC Mss; Diary, Sept. 15, 1904, JG Mss; Herbert K. Smith to Garfield, April 26, 1905, BOC Mss.

6. Diary, March 13, 1905, JG Mss.

7. Diary, Jan. 20, 1905, JG Mss.

8. Virgil P. Kline to Garfield, June 13, 1905, BOC Mss. Also Roosevelt to Lyman Abbott, Sept. 5, 1903, LTR, III, 591; Roosevelt to Nicholas Murray Butler, Aug. 6, 1904, LTR, IV, 883; Diary, Jan. 21, 1905, JG Mss; memos to Mortimer F. Elliott, June 8, 1905, and V. P. Kline, Nov. 1905; Garfield to Kline, Dec. 1, 1905, BOC Mss.

9. Jessup, *Elihu Root,* I, 431-41, 455, 489-90; Henry F. Pringle, *The Life and Times of William Howard Taft* (New York, 1939), I, 316.

10. E. H. Harriman to Roosevelt, Dec. 2, 1904, LTR, V, 450, is an example of railroad reliance on Morton. Also see *Railway and Engineering Review,* XLV (1905), 477; Roosevelt to William H. Moody, June 12, 17, 1905, LTR, IV, 1210, 1237.

11. Civic Federation of Chicago, *Conference on Trusts,* 620, 622.

12. Diary, Oct. 11, Nov. 28, 1905, JG Mss; *Reports of the Department of Commerce and Labor—1905* (Washington, 1906), 74-75.

13. MP, 6973-74, 6979-80, 6984-85.

14. J. Owen Stalson, *Marketing Life Insurance* (Cambridge, 1942), *passim;* R. Carlyle Buley, *The American Life Convention, 1906-1952: A Study in the History of Life Insurance* (New York, 1953), I, *passim.*

15. *Ohio Underwriter,* quoted in Buley, *American Life Convention,* I, 145; *Spectator,* LX (Jan. 13, 1898), 14. Also see Stalson, *Marketing Life Insurance,* 541; John F. Dryden, *Addresses and Papers on Life Insurance and Other Subjects* (Newark, 1909), 178 ff.; John M. Pattison to James R. Garfield, Dec. 29, 1904, FTCB Mss; C. A. Cook, "National Supervision of Insurance," Sept. 7, 1904, BOC Mss.

16. Garraty, *Life of George Perkins,* 180; Thomas Beer, *Hanna* (New York, 1929), 307-08; Perkins to John A. McCall, March 10, 1900, June 22, 1900, GP Mss; Charles S. Moore to James R. Garfield, June 15, 17, 1904, BOC Mss.

17. Clarence E. Porter to Garfield, June 10, 1904, BOC Mss. Also see W. W. Fuller to Aldrich, Dec. 9, 1903; John Wanamaker to Aldrich, Dec. 5, 1903, NA Mss; Charles S. Moore to Garfield, June 13, 15, 17, 1904, BOC Mss.

18. Dryden, *Addresses and Papers,* 196.

19. All found in files 0-6 to 160, BOC Mss.

20. James M. Beck to Garfield, Jan. 25, Feb. 7, 1905, FTCB Mss; H. K. Smith, "Memorandum of interviews with Presidents of Hartford Insurance Companies re Federal Supervision," 1905, BOC Mss.

21. See Burton J. Hendrick, *The Story of Life Insurance* (New York, 1907); Buley, *American Life Convention,* I, chap. IV; Roosevelt to Isaac W. Mac-Veagh, Oct. 8, 1905, LTR, V, 50; Francis L. Stetson to Garfield, Nov. 14, 1905, BOC Mss; Roosevelt to Thomas D. O'Brien, Nov. 24, 1905, LTR, V, 93.

22. Buley, *American Life Convention,* I, 251.

23. MP, 7290. Also *House Report No. 2491,* March 23, 1906, 59:1.

24. Buley, *American Life Convention,* I, 430-31; Dryden, *Addresses and Papers,* 163; *Historical Statistics,* 672; William C. Redfield to Joseph Davies, May 29, 1913; Davies to Redfield, July 14, 1913, BOC Mss; Darwin P. Kingsley, *Militant Life Insurance and Other Addresses* (New York, 1911), *passim.*

25. U.S. Dept. of Agriculture, Bureau of Animal Husbandry, *The Federal Meat-Inspection Service* (Washington, 1908), 8-10; "Report, 1888," BAI Mss; National Archives, *Preliminary Inventories,* No. 106 (Washington, 1958), 1-2; HR 46A-H2.2.

26. See "Letters to State Department, 1892-97," BAI Mss; "Reports, 1896, 1897," BAI Mss; Oscar E. Anderson, Jr., *The Health of a Nation: Harvey W. Wiley and the Fight for Pure Food* (Chicago, 1958), 128; Bureau of Corporations, *Report . . . on the Beef Industry,* 58; C. W. Baker to James Wilson, Dec. 27, 1900; Jacob Dold Packing Co., to B. P. Wende, Nov. 29, 1905, BAI Mss; Harper Leech and John C. Carroll, *Armour and His Times* (New York, 1938), 172-88; Records of Food Standards Comm. in FDA Mss.

27. D. C. Salmon to Orson S. Marden, April 10, 1905, BAI Mss.

28. J. Ogden Armour, "The Packers and the People," *Saturday Evening Post,* CLXXVIII (March 10, 1906), 6, italics in original. Also see Armour's *The Packers, the Private Car Lines, and the People* (Philadelphia, 1906), 342-55.

29. Roosevelt to Upton Sinclair, March 15, 1906, LTR, V, 179-80.

30. Upton Sinclair, *American Outpost: A Book of Reminiscences* (New York, 1932), 175; Sinclair, "The Condemned-Meat Industry: A Reply to Mr. J. Ogden Armour," *Everybody's Magazine,* XIV (1906), 612-13.

31. James Wilson to Albert Beveridge, May 14, 1906; A. D. Melvin to James W. Wadsworth, May 31, 1906, BAI Mss; Roosevelt to Beveridge, May 23, 1906, LTR, V, 282; Claude G. Bowers, *Beveridge and the Progressive Era* (Boston, 1932), 228-29; and resolutions in SEN 59A-J3.

32. MP, 7298; *Washington Post,* June 5, 1906.

33. U.S. House of Representatives, Committee on Agriculture, *Hearings on the . . . 'Beveridge Amendment' . . .;* 59:1 (Washington, 1906), 5, 55, and *passim.*

34. *Congressional Record,* XXXX, pt. 10, 59:1, 9657-58. Also *Washington Post,* May 31, 1906.

35. James Wadsworth to Roosevelt, June 15, 1906, in *Washington Post,* June 16, 1906. Also see the *Post,* June 11, 1906; Roosevelt to Wadsworth, June 15, 1906, LTR, V, 298.

36. Perkins to J. P. Morgan, June 25, 1906, GP Mss.

37. Sinclair, *American Outpost,* 175-76. Also Bureau of Animal Husbandry, *Federal Meat-Inspection Service,* 19-20.

38. "Packers' Convention on Pure Food and Meat Inspection," August 30-31, 1906, Washington, 46, in Bureau of Chemistry Records, National Archives; *Outlook,* LXXXV (Jan. 5, 1907), 52.

39. *National Provisioner,* XXXXI (Dec. 18, 1909), 19. Also see James Wilson to Redfield Proctor, Feb. 11, 1908, BAI Mss; George McCarthy to Taft, Nov. 18, 1910, WT Mss; Fowler, *Men, Meat and Miracles,* 113-15.

40. Anderson, *Harvey W. Wiley,* 127. Also see HR 45A-H12.1; HR 46A-H13.1; National Board of Trade, *Proceedings of the Eighteenth Annual Meeting, January 1888* (Boston, 1888), 19.

41. Petitions in SEN 55A-J51; HR 56A-H10.5; HR 57A-H11.9; also see *Pharmaceutical Era,* March 10, 1898, 365-66; Alex. J. Wedderburn to Chairman of House Committee on Interstate and Foreign Commerce, March 15, 1900, in HR 56A-F15.1; D. M. Parry to Harvey W. Wiley, Jan. 6, 1903; A. C. Morrison to Wiley, Dec. 19, 1902; Leonard M. Frailey to Wiley, Dec. 20, 1903, FDA Mss; Anderson, *Harvey W. Wiley,* 157-61; *The Interstate Grocer,* May 3, 1902, 1.

42. Harvey W. Wiley, *An Autobiography* (Indianapolis, 1930), 231-32. Also Oscar E. Anderson, "The Pure-Food Issue: A Republican Dilemma, 1906-1912," *American Historical Review,* LXI (1956), 550-73.

43. Roosevelt to Ira Remsen, Jan. 16, 1908; Roosevelt to Henry H. Rusby, Jan. 7, 1909, LTR, VI, 908-09, 1467-68. Also Wiley, *Autobiography,* 238 ff.

44. Samuel P. Hays, *Conservation and the Gospel of Efficiency: The Progressive Conservation Movement, 1890-1920* (Cambridge, 1959), 1-2, 127.

45. MP, 6685. Also see *New York Commercial,* April 16, 1906.

46. Roosevelt to Lyman Abbott, June 18, 1906; Roosevelt to William Allen White, July 31, 1906, LTR, V, 307, 340.

47. Roosevelt to William Allen White, July 31, 1906; Roosevelt to Kermit Roosevelt, May 30, 1908, LTR, V, 341, VI, 1044.

48. Robert M. La Follette, *La Follette's Autobiography* (Madison, 1913), 479.

CHAPTER FIVE—*Roosevelt and Big Business, 1906-1908*

1. Perkins to J. P. Morgan, June 25, 1906, GP Mss.

2. House Committee on Investigation of U.S. Steel Corp., *Hearings,* 8, 11, 126-27, 1073-96, 1133; Tarbell, *Gary,* 198-99; *Iron Age,* LXXXI (1908), 1583-99; Arthur Pound and Samuel T. Taylor, eds., *They Told Barron: The Notes of the Late Clarence W. Barron* (New York, 1930), 322-23; Perkins to J. P. Morgan, April 20, 1906, GP Mss.

3. Perkins, "The Financial Crisis of October 1907," 41-43, in GP Mss. Also see House Committee on Investigation of U.S. Steel Corp., *Hearings,* 1112.

4. This and subsequent letters are in ER Mss. Also see House Committee on Investigation of U.S. Steel Corp., *Hearings,* 7, 125, 135-40, 172-73, 198-201, 1127-34, 1375-79; Tarbell, *Gary,* 200-04; Roosevelt, "The Trusts, the People, and the Square Deal," *Outlook,* XCIX (1911), 649-50; Harvey, *Henry Clay Frick,* 302-06.

5. Roosevelt to Kermit Roosevelt, Jan. 23, 1909, LTR, VI, 1481. Also see Luther Conant, Jr., to Herbert Knox Smith, Dec. 25, 1908; William C. Baldwin to Elbert H. Gary, Jan. 7, 1909; George W. Perkins to Warren R. Choate, Jan. 18, 1909, BOC Mss; Charles J. Bonaparte memo of Jan. 9, 1909, CB Mss.

6. Gary to William Baldwin, Feb. 4, 1909, BOC Mss.

7. Charles A. Gulick, *Labor Policy of the United States Steel Corporation* (New York, 1924), *passim*; David Brody, *Steelworkers in America: The Non-union Era* (Cambridge, 1960), 149 ff., chap. VIII; U.S. Bureau of Labor Statistics, *Bulletin No. 218* (Washington, 1917), 15-16.

8. William C. Beer to H. K. Smith, Aug. 23, 1907; Smith to Cyrus McCormick, Aug. 8, 1907, BOC Mss.

9. H. K. Smith, "Memorandum of Interview in Re International Harvester Company, On January 18, 1907"; Smith, "Memorandum in Re Second Interview With International Harvester Company on January 19, 1907," BOC Mss; Garfield, Diary, Jan. 19, 1907, JG Mss. Also see George Perkins to Oscar Straus, Dec. 18, 1906; Cyrus McCormick to Garfield, Dec. 28, 1906, BOC Mss.

10. Smith, "Memorandum of Interview With Commissioner Smith on April 1, 1907, by Messrs. Harold F. McCormick and Cyrus H. McCormick . . .," BOC Mss. Also Paul D. Cravath to Charles J. Bonaparte, March 30, 1907, BOC Mss.

11. Smith to Roosevelt, Sept. 21, 1907, in *Senate Doc. No. 604*, 62:2, 4-8. Also see Roosevelt to Bonaparte, Aug. 22, 1907, LTR, V, 763; Bonaparte to Roosevelt, Aug. 26, 1907, CB Mss; William C. Beer to H. K. Smith, Aug. 23, 1907, BOC Mss; Oscar S. Straus to Roosevelt, Sept. 23, 1907; William Loeb, Jr., to Bonaparte, Sept. 24, 1907, *Senate Doc. No. 604*, 8-9.

12. Taft statement, April 28, 1912; B. D. Townsend to Charles D. Hilles, April 28, 1912, WT Mss.

13. Bonaparte to Roosevelt, Sept. 8, 1907; Roosevelt to Bonaparte, Sept. 10, 1907, CB Mss. Also see Virgil P. Kline to Garfield, Nov. 17, 1905; Garfield to Kline, Dec. 1, 1905; Kline to Garfield, March 21, 26, April 20, 1906; Garfield to Kline, April 13, 27, 1906; H. K. Smith to Kline, April 19, 1906, BOC Mss; *Washington Post*, March 10, 1906; Nevins, *John D. Rockefeller*, II, 559-78; *New York Tribune*, May 3, 1906; MP, 7293-96; William H. Moody, Memo on Standard Oil, June 21, 1906, WM Mss; Roosevelt to Moody, Sept. 13, 1906, LTR, V, 409; Roosevelt to Bonaparte, Aug. 17, 1907; Bonaparte to Roosevelt, Aug. 21, Sept. 20, 1907, CB Mss.

14. Diary, Sept. 21, 29, 1907, JG Mss. Also Standard Oil Co., to Bonaparte, Sept. 29, 1907, CB Mss.

15. Garfield Diary, Oct. 2, 25, 29, Nov. 5, 1907, JG Mss; Harvey, *Henry Clay Frick*, 308-09; Bonaparte to Roosevelt, June 26, July 2, 3, 6, 1908; Bonaparte to John D. Archbold, July 30, 1908; Roosevelt to Bonaparte, June 26, July 31, 1908, CB Mss.

16. Roosevelt to Bonaparte, June 6, 1908, LTR, VI, 1059; *Chicago Examiner*, June 1, 2, 1908; Peter S. Grosscup, "How to Save the Corporation," *McClure's Magazine*, XXIV (1905), 443-48; *Boston Journal*, July 27, 1908; Garfield Diary, Sept. 18, 1908, JG Mss.

17. Thomas Fortune Ryan to Root, [March, 1907], ER Mss. Also see W. W. Fuller to Root, Dec. 29, 1906; T. F. Ryan to Root, Jan. 15, Feb. 8, 1907; W. R. Harris to Fuller, Jan. 24, 1907; Fuller to Root, Jan. 30, 31, Feb. 23, 1907, ER Mss.

18. Fuller to Root, May 2, 1907, ER Mss. The first Bureau report was not released until February, 1909. Also see Fuller to Root, March 13, 20, 23, 27, 28, April 9, 1907; undated memo [March, 1907] by Fuller; T. F. Ryan to Root, [March, 1907], ER Mss.

19. MP, 7033, 7137, 7343, 7078-79; also see 7144, 7039, 7202-04.

20. Andrew Carnegie, *Problems of Today: Wealth-Labor-Socialism* (New York, 1908), 4; George W. Perkins, *The Modern Corporation, at Columbia University, February 7, 1908* (no place, 1908), 2, 13-17; Roosevelt to Perkins, Feb. 11, 1908, LTR, VI, 939. Also see MP, 7044.

21. Bonaparte to Roosevelt, Jan. 22, 1908, CB Mss. Also see Bonaparte to Roosevelt, Nov. 6, 1907; Bonaparte to Joseph Daniels, Oct. 2, 1908, AG Mss.

22. Roosevelt to Henry Lee Higginson, Feb. 11, 1907, LTR, V, 584; MP, 7039; Roosevelt to Henry Cabot Lodge, Aug. 14, 1907, LTR, V, 750.

23. Garfield to Oscar Straus, March 4, 1907, BOC Mss. Also see Elihu Root, *Addresses on Government and Citizenship* (Cambridge, 1916), 257-89; L. M. Shaw to Aldrich, Aug. 21, 1906, NA Mss; Oscar S. Straus, *Under Four Administrations: From Cleveland to Taft* (Boston, 1922), 195-214; William Loeb to Aldrich, Jan. 8, 10, Dec. 2, 1907, NA Mss; Roosevelt to Henry Lee Higginson, Feb. 19, 1908, LTR, VI, 948; *Washington Star*, June 9, 1906.

24. National Civic Federation, *Proceedings of the National Conference on Trusts and Combinations* (New York, 1908), 174, 453-55. Also see Kennan, *Harriman*, II, 192-208; Roosevelt to Thomas M. Patterson, April 8, 1907, LTR, V, 642.

25. Roosevelt to Seth Low, Oct. 30, 1907, LTR, V, 824-25; MP, 6977, 7039, 7079. Also see H. K. Smith to Francis G. Newlands, Dec. 2, 1905; Garfield to Newlands, Feb. 13, 1906; George B. Hanford to Garfield, May 23, 1906, FTCB Mss; Arthur B. Darling, ed., *The Public Papers of Francis G. Newlands* (Boston, 1932), I, 244-45; U.S. Senate, *Utility Corporations;* 70:1, Part 69-A (Washington, 1934), 32-36.

26. Francis Lynde Stetson to Perkins, March 13, 1908, GP Mss; H. K. Smith to John F. Crowell, March 2, 1908, FTCB Mss; Bonaparte to Roosevelt, March 12, 1908, CB Mss. Also see National Civic Federation, *Conference on Trusts, passim*; Gerald C. Henderson, *The Federal Trade Commission: A Study in Administrative Law and Procedure* (New Haven, 1924), 19-21; U.S. House, Committee on the Judiciary, *Hearings on House Bill 19745*; 60:1 (Washington, 1908), 10-11; Perkins to J. P. Morgan, Feb. 27, 1908; F. L. Stetson to Perkins, March 10, 1908, GP Mss.

27. N.A.M. report in Senate, *Utility Corporations*, 57. Also see Perkins to J. P. Morgan, March 16, 1908; Edgar Bancroft to Perkins, March 28, 1908, GP Mss; House, *Hearings on House Bill 19745*, 14 ff., 149, 153, 432-70, 665 ff.; U.S. House, Select Committee on Lobby Investigation, . . . *National Association of Manufacturers . . .*: 63:1 (Washington, 1913), I, 170 ff.; HR 60A-H19.18.

28. MP, 7344. Also see House, *Hearings on House Bill 19745*, 372 ff.; Perkins to H. K. Smith, April 18, 1908; Smith to Seth Low, April 13, 1908; Smith to Perkins, April 20, 1908, BOC Mss.

29. Roosevelt to Low, April 1, 9, 1908, LTR, VI, 987-88, 997. Also Oscar Straus, "Brief Personal Records as Secretary of Commerce and Labor . . .," 170, Oscar Straus Papers, Library of Congress.

30. Roosevelt to H. K. Smith, April 14, 1908, LTR, VI, 1007-08.

31. Seth Low to Roosevelt, April 11, 1908, BOC Mss.

32. Roosevelt to Jonathan Bourne, July 8, 1908, LTR, VI, 1115. Also Perkins to Seth Low, April 23, 1908; Perkins to J. P. Morgan, April 21, 1908, GP Mss; Roosevelt to Low, Nov. 21, 1908, LTR, VI, 1374; Bonaparte to Roosevelt, Dec. 2, 7, 1908, CB Mss.

CHAPTER SIX—*The Failure of Finance Capitalism, 1890-1908*

1. *Wall Street Journal* in U.S. House, Committee on the Judiciary, *Bills and Debates in Congress Relating to Trusts*; 63:2 (Washington, 1914), II, 2116. Also see *The Autobiography of Lincoln Steffens* (New York, 1931), 590-91; Lewis Corey, *The House of Morgan* (New York, 1930), 127.

2. Fritz Redlich, *The Molding of American Banking: Men and Ideas* (New York, 1951), II, 177; also chap. XVIII. Also see Bureau of the Census, *Historical Statistics of the United States, 1789-1945* (Washington, 1949), 266-67; Marquis James and Bessie R. James, *Biography of a Bank: The Story of Bank of America* (New York, 1954), chaps. IV, V; U.S. National Monetary Commission, *History of Crises Under the National Banking System* (Washington, 1910), 228.

3. Clews, *Fifty Years in Wall Street*, 577-79. Also see Redlich, *Molding of American Banking*, 179, 201-02; J. P. Morgan & Co., *Letter in Response to . . . the Committee on Banking and Currency of the House . . .* (New York, Feb. 25, 1913), 10; and esp. F. Cyril James, *The Growth of Chicago Banks* (New York, 1938), II, chaps. XVIII-XXI.

4. Clews, *Fifty Years in Wall Street*, 577-80; Margaret G. Myers, *The New York Money Market: Origins and Development* (New York, 1931), 240-41; *Historical Statistics, 1789-1945*, 640; U.S. House, Subcommittee of the Committee on Banking and Currency, *Money Trust Investigation: Investigation of Financial and Monetary Conditions in the United States*; 62:2 (Washington, 1913), III, 1959.

5. House Committee on Banking, *Money Trust Investigation*, III, 1655; also I, 611, III, 1993. Also see William Z. Ripley, *Railroads: Finance and Organization* (New York, 1915), 514; Anna R. Burr, *The Portrait of a Banker: James Stillman, 1850-1918* (New York, 1927), 108, 141; Corey, *House of Morgan*, 260; Redlich, *Molding of American Banking*, 379, 390-94; Danielian, *A.T. & T.*, 63.

6. Daniel Creamer *et al.*, *Capital in Manufacturing and Mining: Its Formation and Financing* (Princeton, 1960), 117, 121, 142; Redlich, *Molding of American Banking*, 175, 185, 380; Louis D. Brandeis, *Other People's Money— And How the Bankers Use It* (2d ed., New York, 1932), 48-49.

7. James B. Forgan, *Recollections of a Busy Life* (New York, 1924), 207.

8. George A. Butler, *A Practical Plan of Banking and Currency* (New York, 1893), *passim*; various plans filed in HR 53A-F4.1; Redlich, *Molding of American Banking*, 210; Henry P. Willis, *The Federal Reserve System* (New York, 1923), 7-8; Andrew Carnegie to Stetson, Feb. 12, 1895, FS Mss; George A. Butler, *Remarks to Committee on Banking and Currency, December 12, 1894* (New Haven, 1895), *passim*; SEN 53A-J4; U.S. House, Committee on Banking and Currency *Hearings and Arguments*; 54:1, 2 (Washington, 1897), 5-11, 107-08.

9. *The History of the . . . Monetary Convention at Indianapolis, January 12th and 13th, 1897* (no place, no date), 10 ff., 64-65; *Report of the Monetary Commission of the Indianapolis Convention* (Chicago, 1898), 11-20, 49-57; Willis, *Federal Reserve System*, 9-12; HR 55A-H2.1.

10. James, *Growth of Chicago Banks,* 740-41; MP, 6654; *Bankers' Magazine,* LXV (1902), 754; LXIV (1902), 171-72; LXII (1901), 10, 180, 657; LXIII (1901), 946.

11. U.S. House, Committee on Banking and Currency, *Banking and Currency Reform;* 62:3 (Washington, 1913), 9; HR 57A-H2.1; *Bankers' Magazine,* LXV (1902), 145; James, *Growth of Chicago Banks,* 736-37; Esther R. Taus, *Central Banking Functions of the United States Treasury, 1789-1941* (New York, 1943), 98-104; Osborne, *Speculation on the New York Stock Exchange,* 149-58.

12. Roosevelt to Grenville M. Dodge, April 22, 1903; Roosevelt to Lucius N. Littauer, July 22, 1903, LTR, III, 466, 525.

13. Roosevelt to Henry Lee Higginson, June 13, 1903; Roosevelt to Ebenezar J. Hill, July 21, 1903; Roosevelt to Joseph G. Cannon, Aug. 13, 24, 1903, LTR, III, 488, 522, 565, 570; William B. Allison to Roosevelt, Aug. 19, 1903; Mark A. Hanna to Aldrich, Aug. 20, 1903, NA Mss.

14. Orville Platt to Aldrich, Aug. 17, 1903, NA Mss; Roosevelt to Joseph G. Cannon, Aug. 24, 1903, LTR, III, 570-71. Also Roosevelt to J. P. Morgan, Oct. 8, 1903; Roosevelt to John Byrne, Dec. 29, 1903, LTR, III, 627, 684.

15. James, *Growth of Chicago Banks,* 742 ff.; American Bankers Association, *Report of the Currency Commission,* Nov. 15, 1906 (New York, 1906), 3. Also *Bankers' Magazine,* LXVII (1903), 155; Henry Clews, *Address Before the Minnesota Bankers' Association, June 21, 1905* (no place, 1905), 10-11; *New York Herald,* Jan. 5, 1906.

16. James, *Growth of Chicago Banks,* 746-47; Roosevelt to Charles N. Fowler, Jan. 20, 1907, LTR, V, 559.

17. *Commercial and Financial Chronicle,* LXXXIV (1907), 592; Corey, *House of Morgan,* 354; Perkins to J. P. Morgan, May 27, 1907, GP Mss; Roosevelt to Henry Lee Higginson, Aug. 12, 1907, LTR, V, 745-49; U.S. House, Committee on Banking and Currency, *Hearings and Arguments;* 60:1 (Washington, 1908), 88; Roosevelt to Charles Bonaparte, Jan. 22, 1915, TR Mss; James, *Growth of Chicago Banks,* 753.

18. House Committee on Banking, *Money Trust Investigation,* I, 434; also 430-51, 485. Also James, *Growth of Chicago Banks,* 756-66; "The Financial Crisis of October 1907," GP Mss; George F. Baker to Stephen B. Elkins, Jan. 16, 1908, Stephen B. Elkins Papers, Univ. of West Virginia Library.

19. SEN 60A-J38; HR 60A-H4.1; MP, 7082; Charles N. Fowler, *Address Before the Illinois Manufacturers Association,* Dec. 10, 1907 (no place, no date), *passim;* House Committee on Banking, *Hearings;* 60:1, 84-85, *passim;* James, *Growth of Chicago Banks,* 774-76; SEN 60A-K7; SEN 60A-K8; George F. Baker to Stephen B. Elkins, Jan. 16, 1908, Elkins Papers; Perkins to J. P. Morgan, March 16, 1908, GP Mss; Forgan, *Recollections of a Busy Life,* 189.

20. Roosevelt to Hermann H. Kohlsaat, Jan. 15, 1908; Roosevelt to Henry Lee Higginson, Feb. 19, 1908, LTR, VI, 908, 949.

21. U.S. House, Committee on Banking and Currency, *Hearings on the Aldrich Bill;* 60:1 (Washington, 1908), pt. VIII, 4. Also see House Committee on the Judiciary, *Bills and Debates . . . Relating to Trusts,* II, 2154; Perkins to J. P. Morgan, March 16, April 7, 21, May 22, 1908, GP Mss; *Annals of the American Academy of Political and Social Science,* XXXI (March, 1908), *passim.*

22. Roosevelt to William Howard Taft, Aug. 29, 1908, LTR, VI, 1203.

CHAPTER SEVEN—*The Ordeal of William Howard Taft, 1909-1911*

1. Ray Stannard Baker, "What the U.S. Steel Corporation Really Is, and How It Works," *McClure's Magazine,* XVIII (Nov. 1901), 7; David Chalmers, "Ray Stannard Baker's Search for Reform," *Journal of the History of Ideas,* XIX (1958), 422-34; David Graham Phillips, *The Treason of the Senate* (New York, 1953), 66, 70; Russell, *Greatest Trust in the World,* 232 ff.; C. C. Regier, · *The Era of the Muckrakers* (Chapel Hill, 1932), 197 and *passim.*

2. Marshall M. Kirkman, *The Relation of the Railroads of the United States to the People . . .* (Chicago, 1885), 30, 39-40.

3. *Bankers' Magazine,* LXII (1901), 497-99.

4. C. S. Mellen to Hartford Board of Trade, Jan. 21, 1904, ms in BOC Mss; William D. Foulke, *Fighting the Spoilsmen* (New York, 1919), 3, 257-58.

5. Senate Committee on Interstate Commerce, *Hearings on . . . an Interstate Trade Commission,* 103.

6. Albert Stickney, *Organized Democracy* (Boston, 1906), 222-24, 240, 267; Willard A. Smith, *Business Men and Public Service* (Chicago, 1915), 10-13.

7. *Remarks of Francis Lynde Stetson, Dinner to the Hon. Charles E. Hughes, New York, January 22, 1917* (no place, no date), 7. Also see Marguerite Green, *The National Civic Federation and the American Labor Movement, 1900-1925* (Washington, 1956), 314-22.

8. Perkins to J. P. Morgan, Feb. 25, 1909, GP Mss. Also see Pringle, *Taft,* I, 387-402; Senate Committee on Privileges, *Campaign Contributions,* I, 441, 445; Perkins to J. P. Morgan, July 21, 1908; Perkins to E. H. Gary, July 28, 1908; Gary to Perkins, Aug. 19, 1908, GP Mss; Taft to Aldrich, June 27, 1908, NA Mss.

9. Pringle, *Taft,* I, 433; Perkins to Taft, June 17, 1909, GP Mss; Taft to Guy W. Mallon, Jan. 17, 1910; Taft to Eugene Hale, June 22, 1910; Taft to Nelson Aldrich, Aug. 15, 1910, HP Mss.

10. MP, 7451, 7453-56. Also see H. K. Smith to E. A. Bancroft, July 26, 1910; E. H. Gary to Smith, Jan. 27, 1910; Smith to Filbert, Feb. 24, 1910, BOC Mss; Taft to J. B. Brannan, Dec. 1, 1909, HP Mss.

11. Wickersham, Memorandum to Charles Johnston, Feb. 23, 1911; Wickersham to Albert H. Walker, Feb. 28, 1911, AG Mss; George W. Wickersham, "The Enforcement of the Anti-Trust Law," *Century,* LXXXIII (1912), 618; *Reports of the Department of Commerce and Labor, 1910* (Washington, 1911), 396; E. H. Gary to Smith, Feb. 14, 1910; Cyrus H. McCormick to Smith, March 21, 1911, FTCB Mss.

12. Wickersham to Stetson, Sept. 5, 1910, FS Mss. Also see Perkins to J. P. Morgan, June 1, 3, 1910, GP Mss; Arthur Meeker to Charles Norton, July 14, 1910; Taft to Sec. of Treasury MacVeagh, July 12, 1910, WT Mss.

13. For the best account of political relations between the two men, see George E. Mowry, *Theodore Roosevelt and the Progressive Movement* (Madison, 1946), *passim.*

14. Taft to Wickersham, Sept. 1, 1911, HP Mss. Also see Henry Lee Higginson to Taft, Aug. 11, 1910, July 26, 1911; Charles G. Dawes to Charles Norton, March 23, 1911; Victor Morawetz to Norton, Oct. 11, 1910, WT Mss; Cyrus Adler, *Jacob H. Schiff: His Life and Letters* (Garden City, 1928), I, 290; Taft to Higginson, July 28, 1911, WT Mss; Wickersham to Albert H. Walker, Feb. 28, 1911, AG Mss. Throughout 1910-12 many businessmen wrote the Dept. of Justice asking about the legality of existing or proposed actions. The standard

response was that it was not policy to pass on the legality of contracts, thereby increasing business insecurity.

15. A. C. Muhse to H. K. Smith, Oct. 23, 1911, BOC Mss; Wickersham to Taft, Nov. 4, 7, 1911, WT Mss. Also see Thomas F. Ryan to Elihu Root, [March, 1907], ER Mss; Luther Conant, Jr., to H. K. Smith, Oct. 26, 1911, BOC Mss; *Annual Report of the Attorney General of the United States, 1911* (Washington, 1911), 4-6.

16. Wickersham to Norton, Oct. 8, 1910, WT Mss. Also Louis Howland to James P. Hornaday, Sept. 19, 1910, WT Mss.

17. Bureau of Corporations, *Report . . . on the Steel Industry*; Smith to Luther Conant, Jr., Aug. 29, 1911; Conant to Smith, Aug. 31, 1911, BOC Mss; House Committee on Investigation of U.S. Steel, *Hearings*, I, 474-75, 499-505, 521-22; II, 1370 ff.; William H. Baldwin to Charles Nagel, June 5, 1911; Nagel to Taft, Aug. 1, 1911, WT Mss; Wickersham to Taft, Aug. 30, 1911, HP Mss; Roosevelt, *Outlook*, XCIX (1911); Roosevelt to Everett P. Wheeler, Oct. 30, 1911, LTR, VII, 429.

18. *Summary of Argument for United States Steel Corporation . . . October 12, 1914* (no place, 1914), 12. Also see Luther Conant, Jr., to H. K. Smith, Nov. 3, 4, 1911; Charles Nagel to Charles D. Hilles, Jan. 17, 1912, BOC Mss; Nagel to Taft, Jan. 17, 19, July 17, 1912; Smith to Nagel, Jan. 18, 1912; Taft to Nagel, Jan. 20, July 17, 1912, WT Mss.

19. Andrew Carnegie, *Problems of Today*, 48; Carnegie in *New York Times*, Feb. 16, 1909; Perkins to E. A. Bradford, Nov. 27, 1909, GP Mss.

20. *New York Financial America*, Dec. 1, 1910. Also see B. J. Ramage, "Memorandum for Mr. Todd," Jan. 2, 1914, AG Mss; Senate, *Utility Corporations*, 32, 38-39; Seth Low to Taft, Feb. 19, 1910; Perkins to Carpenter, Feb. 8, 1910, WT Mss.

21. George W. Perkins, *The Business Problems of the Day, January 21, 1911* (no place, 1911), 12-13. Also see Perkins, *Address Before the Quill Club of New York, December 20, 1910* (no place, no date), 9.

22. House Committee on Investigation of U.S. Steel, *Hearings*, I, 79, VIII, 211. Also see Charles Nagel to Taft, June 27, 1911, WT Mss.

23. Henry Lee Higginson to Taft, July 31, 1911; William W. Laird to Taft, Aug. 11, 1911, WT Mss; *Papers of Newlands*, I, 420-22; Senate Committee on Interstate Commerce, *Hearings on . . . an Interstate Trade Commission*, I, 1-4, 7-14, 17-18, 23.

24. Roosevelt, *Outlook*, XCIX (1911), 649. Also see Mowry, *Roosevelt and the Progressive Movement*, 192.

25. Perkins to Charles D. Hilles, Nov. 28, 1911, WT Mss.

26. Senate Committee on Interstate Commerce, *Hearings on . . . an Interstate Trade Commission*, 694, 697; also 694 ff., 818, 843, 2407-12.

27. National Civic Federation, *The Trust Problem: Opinions of 16,000 Representative Americans* (New York, 1912), 5; Senate Committee on Interstate Commerce, *Hearings on . . . an Interstate Trade Commission*, 500.

28. Senate Committee on Interstate Commerce, *Hearings on . . . an Interstate Trade Commission*, 1089-1123, 1029-31, 1318-24, 1330-36, 1490, 1642-44, 1785; Taft to Wickersham, Sept. 1, 1911; Wickersham to Taft, Nov. 4, 1911, HP Mss; MP, 7652-55.

29. Senate Committee on Interstate Commerce, *Hearings on . . . an Interstate Trade Commission*, 2320 ff., 2354-81; *New York Times*, Jan. 13, 1912; Andrew Carnegie to Perkins, Nov. 29, Dec. 23, 1911, Andrew Carnegie Papers,

Library of Congress; Charles G. Washburn, *Address Before the Economic Club of Springfield, Mass., November 16, 1911* (no place, no date), 19-22; resolutions in SEN 62A-J49; Perkins to Albert B. Cummins, March 23, 1912; Cummins to Perkins, March 29, 1912, GP Mss.

30. Francis Lynde Stetson, *Address Before Williams College Good Government Club, May 8, 1912* (no place, 1912), 27; Joseph T. Talbert, "The Sherman Anti-Trust Law and the Business of the Country," *Annals of the American Academy of Political and Social Science*, XLII (July, 1912), 219; Gwynn, *Annals of American Academy*, XLII (1912), 126, 131. Also see Charles C. Batchelder, "The Character and Powers of Governmental Regulation Machinery," *Journal of Political Economy*, XX (1912), 397 ff.

31. Quoted in Norton E. Long, "Public Relations Policies of the Bell System," *Public Opinion Quarterly*, I (1937), 20-21. Also see resolutions in SEN 61A-J54.

32. Theodore N. Vail, *Mutual Relations and Interests of the Bell System and the Public* (New York, 1914), 6-7, 9. Also see *Annual Report, A.T. & T.*, 1911, 35; F.C.C., *Telephone Investigation*, 155-57; HR 63A-H12.10; Theodore N. Vail, *Views on Public Questions: A Collection of Papers and Addresses* (no place, 1917), 116 ff., 248-50, 263-65.

33. McKercher, "Memorandum For Mr. Fowler," Nov. 6, 1911, AG Mss; Milton N. Nelson, *Open Price Associations* (Urbana, 1922), *passim*; National Industrial Conference Board, *Trade Associations* (New York, 1925), *passim*; Arthur J. Eddy, *The New Competition* (New York, 1912), *passim*.

34. Clews, *Fifty Years in Wall Street*, 811; differences among bankers are illustrated in *Annals of American Academy*, XXXI (1908); J. Laurence Laughlin, *The Federal Reserve Act: Its Origins and Problems* (New York, 1933), 22; Paul M. Warburg, *The Federal Reserve System: Its Origins and Growth* (New York, 1930), 32 ff.; U.S. National Monetary Commission, *Hearings on Changes in the Administrative Features of the National Banking Laws*, Dec. 2, 3, 1908 (Washington, 1908), 113, 169.

35. *Banking Law Journal*, XXVI (1909), 942; Paul Warburg to Aldrich, Dec. 24, 1909, NA Mss. Also see Warburg, *Federal Reserve System*, 32-36; Andrew Frame to Aldrich, Oct. 22, 1909, NA Mss; Nathaniel W. Stephenson, *Nelson W. Aldrich: A Leader in American Politics* (New York, 1930), 363-66; Maurice L. Muhleman, "A Plan for a Central Bank," *Banking Law Journal*, XXVI (1909), 883; *New York Evening Post*, Dec. 10, 1909; Victor Morawetz, *The Banking and Currency Problem and the Central Bank Plan*, Nov. 24, 1909 (no place, 1909), *passim*.

36. Taft to Aldrich, Jan. 29, 1911, HP Mss. Also see Warburg, *Federal Reserve System*, 23, 50-53, 58-61; Laughlin, *Federal Reserve Act*, 15-16; Stephenson, *Aldrich*, 377-79; Taft to Aldrich, March 30, 1911, NA Mss; Taft to Franklin MacVeagh, Dec. 23, 1911, HP Mss.

37. *Proceedings of a Conference Upon the Suggested Plan for Monetary Legislation Submitted to the National Monetary Commission by the Hon. Nelson W. Aldrich, February 10-12, 1911*, typed ms in Aldrich Room, Baker Library, Harvard Business School, I, 4, II, 441; also see I, 16-17, 68-69, 92-93, II, 391 ff., 424, 437-40, 474-78, III, 766-69. Also Warburg, *Federal Reserve System*, 61-63; *Commercial and Financial Chronicle*, LXXXXII (1911), 430.

38. Warburg, *Federal Reserve System*, 71; Laughlin, *Federal Reserve Act*, 58. Also see James, *Growth of Chicago Banks*, 800-01. During its entire life the League received $340,000, $150,000 of which came from New York. J. Laurence Laughlin to Arthur H. Weed, April 4, 1914, JL Mss.

39. Andrew J. Frame, *Conservatism Our Watchword* (no place, 1911), *passim*; Roosevelt to Elisha E. Garrison, March 3, 1911, LTR, VII, 236; J. Parker Willis to Laughlin, Jan. 10, 1911, JL Mss; Laughlin, *Federal Reserve Act*, 43, 66, 68, 78-79; Warburg, *Federal Reserve System*, 76-77; Warburg to Laughlin, July 3, 6, 8, 26, 1911; Laughlin to Warburg, July 5, Sept. 15, 1911, JL Mss; *Chicago Daily Tribune*, Aug. 24, 1911.

40. MP, 7684. For opposition to the plan, see James, *Growth of Chicago Banks*, 806; *Railway World*, LV (1911), 871; for support, see James B. Forgan, *Address Before A.B.A. Executive Council, May 1, 1911* (no place, 1911); George M. Reynolds, *Address Before Texas Bankers' Association, May 16, 1911* (no place, 1911); Joseph T. Talbert, *Address Before New York State Bankers Association, June 22, 1911* (no place, 1911).

CHAPTER EIGHT—*The Politics of 1912*

1. Perkins, "Memorandum: July 13th, 1911," GP Mss. Also Perkins to H. K. Smith, July 3, 1911; Smith to Edgar Bancroft, Dec. 13, 1911; Bancroft to Smith, Dec. 16, 22, 1911, BOC Mss; Wickersham to Taft, Nov. 4, 1911, WT Mss.

2. Luther Conant, Jr., to Edgar Bancroft, Sept. 18, 1912, BOC Mss. Also see Taft to Wickersham, April 24, 1912, HP Mss; *Senate Doc. No. 604*, 62:2; Taft statement, April 28, 1912, WT Mss.

3. Perkins to Judson Harmon, Nov. 14, 1910, GP Mss. Also Perkins to J. P. Morgan, Oct. 11, 1910; Perkins to Roosevelt, Sept. 2, 1911, GP Mss.

4. Edwin W. Sims to James R. Mann, Jan. 6, 1912, James R. Mann Papers, Library of Congress.

5. John A. Garraty, *Henry Cabot Lodge* (New York, 1953), 286-87; George Britt, *Forty Years—Forty Millions: The Career of Frank A. Munsey* (New York, 1935), 144-50, 167-71, 182; Memo of Jan. 23, 1912 meeting in WT Mss.

6. Perkins to Alex. Hawes, March 21, 1912, GP Mss. Also Perkins to W. F. Wiley, March 29, 1912; Perkins memos to Roosevelt, March 11 [two], 12, 1912, GP Mss.

7. Perkins to William B. McKinley, April 29, 1912, WT Mss. Also Perkins to Alex. Hawes, April 22, 1912, GP Mss.

8. Amos Pinchot, *The History of the Progressive Party* (New York, 1958), 165-66. Also see Mowry, *Roosevelt and the Progressive Movement*, 248 ff.; Garraty, *Life of Perkins*, 262-63.

9. George E. Mowry, *The California Progressives* (Berkeley, 1951), chaps. II, IV; Alfred D. Chandler, Jr., "The Origins of Progressive Leadership," LTR, VIII, 1462-65.

10. Albert J. Beveridge, *Pass Prosperity Around* (no place, 1912), 8, 11.

11. *Theodore Roosevelt's Confession of Faith Before the Progressive National Convention, August 6, 1912* (New York, 1912), *passim*; Mowry, *Roosevelt and the Progressive Movement*, 266.

12. Pinchot, *History of the Progressive Party*, 173-77.

13. Taft to George B. Edwards, April 22, 1912, HP Mss.

14. J. P. Morgan, Jr., to Perkins, Aug. 19, 1912; Perkins to Morgan, Jr., Aug. 19, 1912, GP Mss.

15. Britt, *Career of Frank A. Munsey*, 167; Judson C. Welliver, *Catching Up With Roosevelt* [reprint from *Munsey's Magazine*, March, 1912]. Also see Pinchot, *History of the Progressive Party*, 178; Garraty, *Life of Perkins*, 273 ff.

16. Taft to Charles D. Hilles, Oct. 4, 1912, HP Mss; Senate Committee on Privileges, *Campaign Contributions*, II, 1124-29; "Party Contributions," PP Mss.

17. Roosevelt to Arthur H. Lee, Nov. 5, 1912, LTR, VII, 633. Also see Mowry, *Roosevelt and the Progressive Movement*, 284 ff.; Harold L. Ickes, "Who Killed the Progressive Party," *American Historical Review*, XLVI (1941), 306-37.

18. Donald R. Richberg, " 'Five Brothers' or 'Trust Triplets'," *Outlook*, CVI (1914), 638-48; George W. Perkins, *National Action and Industrial Growth, February 12, 1914* (no place, 1914); Hiram Johnson to Perkins, Nov. 17, 1914; Roosevelt to Charles Bonaparte, May 29, 1916; Roosevelt to Progressive Party National Conference, June 10, 1916, GP Mss; Perkins, mimeo circular, Feb. 18, 1916, CB Mss.

19. Pinchot, *History of the Progressive Party*, 76 ff., 184-200, 246-47; Mowry, *Roosevelt and the Progressive Movement*, 198; AP Mss, files 26, 69, 74, 138.

20. Perkins to Wilson, Nov. 10, 1910, GP Mss. Also see William Diamond, *The Economic Thought of Woodrow Wilson* (Baltimore, 1943), 17-19, 39-55; Arthur S. Link, *Wilson: The New Freedom* (Princeton, 1956), 62-63; George Harvey, *The Power of Tolerance* (New York, 1911), 174-78; Arthur S. Link, *Wilson: The Road to the White House* (Princeton, 1947), 97 ff., 113-20; Willis F. Johnson, *George Harvey—A Passionate Patriot* (Boston, 1929), 49-77, 105-41; PWW, II, 57-58.

21. PWW, II, 254-55.

22. PWW, II, 410-11. Also see II, 323-24, 358-59.

23. PWW, II, 420.

24. House Committee on the Judiciary, *Bills and Debates . . . Relating to Trusts*, III, 2953.

25. Robert F. Hoxie, *Scientific Management and Labor* (New York, 1915), 147. Also see Louis D. Brandeis, *Business—A Profession* (Boston, 1914), 13-27, 40-45; Oscar Kraines, "Brandeis' Philosophy of Scientific Management," *Western Political Quarterly*, XIII (1960), 191-201; Alpheus T. Mason, *Brandeis: A Free Man's Life* (New York, 1946), 142-49; Clarence B. Thompson, ed., *Scientific Management* (Cambridge, 1914), *passim*.

26. Brandeis, *Business—A Profession*, 2, 12; also 57 ff. Also see Mason, *Brandeis*, 368-78.

27. Woodrow Wilson, *The New Freedom* (New York, 1913), 164-66, 180, 190, 257.

28. PWW, II, 28.

29. Wilson, *New Freedom*, 201-02; also 205.

30. Henry Lee Higginson to Stetson, Aug. 22, 1912, FS Mss; Henry Seligman to Isaac Seligman, Oct. 1, 1912, HS Mss. Also see Link, *Road to the White House*, 485; Adler, *Jacob H. Schiff*, I, 302-12; Johnson, *George Harvey*, 216-18.

31. La Follette, *Autobiography*, 388. Also 479-81, 676.

32. For valuable insights into La Follette and his followers, see Frontis W. Johnston, *The Evolution of the American Concept of National Planning, 1865-1917* (Unpublished Ph.D. thesis, Yale Univ., 1938), chap. X; Charles McCarthy, *The Wisconsin Idea* (New York, 1912), 191 ff., 296 ff.

33. Herbert Croly, *The Promise of American Life* (New York, 1909), 154. Also see John R. Everett, *Religion in Economics: A Study of John Bates Clark, Richard T. Ely, Simon N. Patten* (New York, 1946), 140-44; Joseph Dorfman, "The Role of the German Historical School in American Economic Thought,"

American Economic Review, XLV (1955), 17-28; Charles F. Thwing, *The American and the German University* (New York, 1928), 41-45.

34. Herbert Croly, *Progressive Democracy* (New York, 1914), 113; also 16-18. Also see Croly, *Hanna, passim*; Croly, *Willard Straight* (New York, 1924), *passim.*

CHAPTER NINE—*Woodrow Wilson and the Triumph of Political Capitalism: Banking*

1. Paul Warburg to Laughlin, Jan. 8, 1912, JL Mss; *Banking Reform,* I (Jan. 29, 1912), 4, 12; H. Parker Willis to Laughlin, Feb. 15, 1912, JL Mss; J. Laurence Laughlin, ed., *Banking Reform* (Chicago, 1912); Laughlin, *Federal Reserve Act,* 90-91, 105.

2. Carter Glass, *An Adventure in Constructive Finance* (New York, 1927), 69. Also see Willis, *Federal Reserve System,* 109, 116, 136-38; Laughlin, *Federal Reserve Act,* 100-01.

3. Willis to Laughlin, May 2, 1912, JL Mss. Also Willis to Laughlin, March 23, 30, April 7, 1912, JL Mss.

4. Willis to Laughlin, June 17, 1912, JL Mss.

5. Samuel Untermyer, *Address Before the Economic Club of New York, November 22, 1911* (no place, no date), 25-26. Also see Laughlin, *Federal Reserve Act,* 81-84; *Banking Reform,* I (July 3, 1912), 1, 4.

6. *Journal of Commerce,* July 6, 1912; also Aug. 7, 1912. Also see House Committee on Banking, *Money Trust Investigation,* I, 101.

7. Willis to Laughlin, July 14, 18, 1912, JL Mss.

8. Willis to Laughlin, Aug. 26, 1912, JL Mss; *Banking Reform,* I (Nov. 1, 1912), 1. Also *Banking Reform,* I (Sept. 2, 1912), 1-5.

9. Laughlin to A. B. Hepburn, Nov. 4, 1912; Hepburn to Laughlin, Nov. 6, 1912, JL Mss. Also see Diamond, *Economic Thought of Wilson,* 101; Charles Seymour, ed., *The Intimate Papers of Colonel House* (Boston, 1926), I, 94.

10. Laughlin to Willis, Nov. 21, 1912, JL Mss. Also see Laughlin, *Federal Reserve Act,* 115-21.

11. Willis to Glass, Dec. 7, 1912, CG Mss; Willis to Laughlin, Dec. 18, 22, 1912, JL Mss. Also see Laughlin to A. B. Hepburn, Dec. 18, 1912, JL Mss; Laughlin, *Federal Reserve Act,* 121-22.

12. Laughlin, *Federal Reserve Act,* 121-24.

13. Glass, *Adventure in Constructive Finance,* 83-84.

14. Willis, *Federal Reserve System,* 141-43; Seymour, *Intimate Papers of House,* I, 161; Glass, *Adventure in Constructive Finance,* 83-84.

15. Glass to Willis, Dec. 29, 1912; Willis to Glass, Jan. 3, 1913, CG Mss. Also see Glass, *Adventure in Constructive Finance,* 91; Warburg, *Federal Reserve System,* I, 82.

16. Willis to Glass, Dec. 31, 1912, CG Mss; Laughlin, *Federal Reserve Act,* 131.

17. House Committee on Banking, *Banking and Currency Reform,* 4, 9, 69-75. Also Warburg, *Federal Reserve System,* 90-91.

18. House Committee on Banking, *Banking and Currency Reform,* 206, 233, 354-55, 377.

19. Glass to Festus Wade, Jan. 24, 1913, CG Mss. Also Willis to Glass, Jan. 18, 1913, CG Mss.

20. Laughlin to Glass, Jan. 21, 1913, CG Mss; Willis to Laughlin, Jan. 23, Feb. 6, 18, 22, 1913, JL Mss; Laughlin, *Federal Reserve Act,* 136; Laughlin to

Willis, Feb. 19, 1913, JL Mss; *Banking Reform,* II (Feb. 1, 1913), 6; Willis, *Federal Reserve System,* 1531-53.

21. Higginson to Wilson, Feb. 7, 27, 1913, HH Mss; Seymour, *Intimate Papers of House,* 161; letters in WW Mss, ser. VI, box 138; CG Mss, box 27; HR 62A-H2.1; HR 63A-H3.1.

22. Willis, *Federal Reserve System,* 391; also 169-93, 389-92. Also see Laughlin to Wilson, March 5, 1913, WW Mss; Laughlin to Glass, March 14, 1913, CG Mss; *Banking Reform,* II (March 5, 1913), 8; Seymour, *Intimate Papers of House,* 161-62; E. F. Swinney to Glass, March 31, 1913; Glass to Swinney, April 3, 1913, CG Mss; Warburg, *Federal Reserve System,* 91-92.

23. Charles A. Morss to Laughlin, March 18, 1913, JL Mss. Also see Laughlin, *Federal Reserve Act,* 136; Willis, *Federal Reserve System,* 177-91; Warburg, *Federal Reserve System,* 92-96.

24. George Reynolds to Glass, April 18, 1913, CG Mss; Seymour, *Intimate Papers of House,* 162.

25. Glass, *Adventure in Constructive Finance,* 95; also 96, 106-07. Also see Willis to Laughlin, April 16, May 13, 17, 22, 27, 1913; Laughlin to Willis, May 24, 31, 1913, JL Mss; Laughlin to Glass, May 2, 1913, CG Mss.

26. Reynolds to Glass, June 7, 1913, CG Mss. Also see Warburg, *Federal Reserve System,* 97; Glass, *Adventure in Constructive Finance,* 107-09; Link, *The New Freedom,* 210; George M. Reynolds to Glass, June 4, 9, 1913; Glass to Willis, June 9, 1913; Glass to A. Barton Hepburn, May 30, 1913; Hepburn to Glass, June 5, 1913, CG Mss; Samuel Untermyer to Robert Owen, June 13, 1913, WW Mss.

27. Glass to Hepburn, June 7, 1913, CG Mss. Also Glass to Willis, June 9, 1913, CG Mss.

28. Glass to Wilson, June 18, 1913; Hepburn to Glass, June 23, 1913, CG Mss; PWW, III, 37.

29. Glass, *Adventure in Constructive Finance,* 116. Also see V. Sidney Rothschild to Glass, June 24, 1913, CG Mss; Brandeis to Wilson, June 14, 1913, WW Mss.

30. George Reynolds to Glass, June 30, 1913, CG Mss. Also Glass, *Adventure in Constructive Finance,* 117-18.

31. Glass to Festus Wade, July 1, 1913; George Reynolds to Glass, July 7, 1913, CG Mss.

32. *Banking Law Journal,* XXX (1913), 554. Also see *Chicago Banker,* XXX (July 26, 1913), 1; *Bankers Magazine,* LXXXVII (1913), 131.

33. Samuel Ludlow, Jr., to Joseph Tumulty, July 28, 1913, WW Mss. Also see Byron Smith to Glass, July 3, 1913, CG Mss; Josiah Quincy to Tumulty, July 15, 1913, WW Mss.

34. "Congressman Eagle Analyses and Opposes the Glass Banking and Currency Bill," July 31, 1913, 10, in WW Mss. Also W. J. Bryan to Glass, Aug. 22, 1913, CG Mss; Link, *The New Freedom,* 218-23; Glass, *Adventure in Constructive Finance,* 127 ff.

35. Glass to Wade, July 23, 1913, CG Mss. Also see U.S. Senate, Committee on Banking and Currency, *Hearings on H.R. 7837;* 63:1 (Washington, 1913), II, 1183; SEN 63A-J4.

36. Vice-president of Bank of Commerce and Trusts, Richmond, July 29, 1913, in CG Mss; Senate Committee on Banking, *Hearings on H.R. 7837,* I, 30; also I, 5-21. Also see SEN 63A-J4; James, *Growth of Chicago Banks,* 810-12; Willis, *Federal Reserve System,* 397-98.

37. Robert H. Treman to Glass, Aug. 30, 1913, CG Mss; James V. Farwell to Wilson, July 22, 1913, WW Mss. Also see McLane Tilton, Jr., to Glass, Sept. 3, 1913, CG Mss; John S. Williams to Wilson, Aug. 23, 1913, WW Mss; HR 63A-H3.3; *Banking Reform,* II (July 1, 1913), 1 ff.; II (Sept. 1, 1913), 12 ff.; John V. Farwell to Laughlin, Aug. 12, 20, 1913, JL Mss; Laughlin to Glass, Sept. 3, 1913, CG Mss.

38. Willis, *Federal Reserve System,* 418; Harry A. Wheeler to Laughlin, Aug. 19, 1913, WW Mss. Also N.A.M., *Proceedings of the Eighteenth Annual Convention, May 19-21, 1913* (New York, 1913), 205-06.

39. A. Barton Hepburn, "Criticisms of the Proposed Federal Reserve Bank Plan," *Proceedings of the Academy of Political Science,* IV (Oct. 1913), 101. Also *Banking Law Journal,* XXX (1913), 703; *Bankers Magazine,* LXXXVII (1913), 369; Senate Committee on Banking, *Hearings on H.R. 7837,* 1, 27, 49, 223, 290, 546; III, 2131, 2170; HR 63A-H3.1; Irving T. Bush, "The Business Man and the Note-Issue Provisions of the Federal Reserve Act," *Proceedings of the Academy of Political Science,* IV (1913), 174-76; Paul M. Warburg, "The Owen-Glass Bill as Submitted to the Democratic Caucus," *North American Review,* CXCVIII (1913), 527-55.

40. American Bankers Association, *Proceedings of the Thirty-Ninth Annual Convention,* Oct. 7-10, 1913 (New York, 1913), 103; also 79, 87-88, 95 ff., 103, 113.

41. W. T. Fenton to L. Y. Sherman, Oct. 15, 1913, SEN 63A-J4. Also Samuel Ludlow, Jr., to Wilson, Oct. 7, 1913, WW Mss; Frank A. Vanderlip to Glass, July 24, 1913, CG Mss.

42. Carter Glass, "The Opposition to the Federal Reserve Bank Bill," *Proceedings of the Academy of Political Science,* IV (1913), 19; Festus Wade to Wilson, Oct. 25, 1913, WW Mss. Also W. G. McAdoo to Wilson, Oct. 28, 1913, WW Mss.

43. Belle C. La Follette and Fola La Follette, *Robert M. La Follette* (New York, 1953), I, 486; Henry Lee Higginson to Richard Olney, Nov. 1913, WW Mss. Also see Link, *The New Freedom,* 233-37; Adler, *Jacob H. Schiff,* I, 272-88; *St. Louis Republic,* Nov. 20, 1913; Burr, *James Stillman,* 280-81; Thomas W. Lamont, *Henry P. Davison* (New York, 1933), 103.

44. Frank A. Vanderlip, "The Rediscount Functions of the Regional Banks," *Proceedings of the Academy of Political Science,* IV (1913), 144; F. A. Vanderlip, *Address Before the Economics Club of New York, November 13, 1913* (New York, 1913), 6, 11 ff. Also see Glass, *Adventure in Constructive Finance,* 168-76; *Outlook,* CV (1913), 379.

45. *Banking Reform,* II (Oct. 1, 1913), 6-7. Also see Jessup, *Elihu Root,* II, 246; Samuel Untermyer to Tumulty, Nov. 16, 1913, WW Mss; Glass to Warburg, Dec. 3, 1913; Glass to J. H. Tregoe, Dec. 16, 1913; Glass telegrams to Hepburn, Reynolds, Wheeler, Wexler, Dec. 12, 1913, CG Mss.

46. Warburg to Glass, Dec. 23, 1913, CG Mss; Warburg to Laughlin, Feb. 2, 1914, JL Mss; Laughlin, "The Banking and Currency Act of 1913," *Journal of Political Economy,* XXII (1914), 435. Also see Glass, *Adventure in Constructive Finance,* 235; *Bulletin of the National Association of Credit Men,* XIV (Jan. 15, 1914), 15, 39; *Chicago Banker,* XXX (Dec. 27, 1913), 1, 21.

47. Aldrich to John A. Sleicher, July 16, 1913; Aldrich to Taft, Oct. 3, 1913, NA Mss. Also see H. P. Davison to Aldrich, July 18, 1913, NA Mss.

48. Jessup, *Elihu Root,* II, 247. Also see Lamont, *Henry P. Davison,* 103-04; Herbert L. Satterlee, *J. Pierpont Morgan: An Intimate Portrait* (New York,

1939), 550; Michael C. Rockefeller, *Nelson W. Aldrich and Banking Reform* (Unpublished honors thesis, Harvard College, 1960), 90 ff.

49. Glass, *Adventure in Constructive Finance*, 239 ff.; Willis, *Federal Reserve System*, 523-30.

50. Warburg, *Federal Reserve System*, I, 178-406, chap. IX; Elmer A. Lewis, ed., *Federal Reserve Act of 1913* (Washington, 1941), 1-27; H. Parker Willis, "The Federal Reserve Act," *American Economic Review*, IV (March, 1914), 1-24.

51. John S. Williams to Wilson, Jan. 24, 1914, WW Mss. Also California Bankers Association, *Proceedings of the Twentieth Annual Convention, May 27-29, 1914* (San Francisco, 1914), 87; Kansas Bankers Association, *Proceedings of the Twenty-seventh Annual Convention, May 21-22, 1914* (Topeka, 1914).

52. Willis to Glass, Dec. 25, 1913, CG Mss; Aldrich to John A. Sleicher, Feb. 7, 1914, NA Mss. Also see S. R. Bertron to Wilson, Feb. 14, 1914, WW Mss.

53. Wilson to Olney, April 30, 1914; Wilson Statement to the Press, July 8, 1914, WW Mss. Also see W. P. G. Harding, *The Formative Period of the Federal Reserve System* (Boston, 1925), 1-2; Wilson to House, March 30, 1914; House to Wilson, April 3, 1914; Wilson to Warburg, April 30, 1914; Warburg to Wilson, May 1, 1914; H. A. Wheeler to Wilson, May 15, 1914; Norbert R. Pendergast to Joseph Tumulty, May 5, 13, 1914, WW Mss; Willis to Charles F. Adams, Jr., May 14, 1914, Adams Papers, Mass. Historical Society; W. W. Flannagan to Glass, May 29, 1914, CG Mss; Link, *The New Freedom*, 452-56.

54. Wilson to E. C. Simmons, June 23, 1914; Edward W. Decker to Wilson, Aug. 3, 1914, WW Mss.

55. Lester V. Chandler, *Benjamin Strong: Central Banker* (Washington, 1958), 37 ff. Also see *Journal of the American Bankers Association*, VIII (1916), 872; James, *Growth of Chicago Banks*, 873-77; Jessup, *Elihu Root*, II, 248.

56. Warburg to House, May 12, 1914, WW Mss. Also see William G. McAdoo, *Crowded Years* (Boston, 1931), 285-86.

57. *Journal of the American Bankers Association*, VIII (1915), 467. Also see Opinion of T. W. Gregory, April 14, 1916, WW Mss; Glass, *Adventure in Constructive Finance*, 265-66; Harding, *Formative Period of Federal Reserve System*, 35-36; Warburg, *Federal Reserve System*, 157 ff., 439, 773; American Bankers Association, *Proceedings of the Forty-Second Annual Convention*, Sept. 25-30, 1916 (New York, 1916), 189.

58. Benjamin Strong, *Interpretations of Federal Reserve Policy* (New York, 1930), 8-9, 65.

59. Lawrence E. Clark, *Central Banking Under the Federal Reserve System* (New York, 1935), 397-98; also 161-63, 302-04, 353-58. Also see Chandler, *Benjamin Strong*, 41-47, 77-79, 93-103; H. Parker Willis, *The Theory and Practice of Central Banking* (New York, 1936), 90-102; William O. Weyforth, *The Federal Reserve Board* (Baltimore, 1933), 163-64; Benjamin H. Beckhart, *The New York Money Market: Use of Funds* (New York, 1932), 210; Benjamin H. Beckhart and James G. Smith, *The New York Money Market: Sources and Movements of Funds* (New York, 1932), 221, 260; Myers, *New York Money Market*, 428.

60. Willis, *Theory and Practice of Central Banking*, 95; *Congressional Record*, LIII, pt. 14, 64:1, 755.

CHAPTER TEN—*The Triumph of Political Capitalism: The Federal Trade Commission and Trust Legislation*

1. Wilson, *The New Freedom*, 180; House Committee on Judiciary, *Bills and Debates . . . Relating to Trusts*, III, 2953.

2. Joseph B. Foraker to J. G. Schurman, Nov. 19, 1912, Foraker Papers, Library of Congress; Pringle, *Taft*, II, 863-64; Johnson, *George Harvey*, 232-33.

3. Arthur Eddy to Clark McKercher, April 22, 1913, AG Mss. Also see Theodore Roosevelt, *The Progressive Party* (Washington, 1913), 25; *New York World*, March 3, 1913.

4. Joseph E. Davies, "Memorandum Re . . . Future Plan of Work of Bureau of Corporations," July 30, 1913, WW Mss. Also see Ralph W. Easley to McReynolds, Oct. 20, 1913; McReynolds to Easley, Oct. 21, 1913, AG Mss; N.C.F. proposal, Dec. 16, 1913; Easley to Joseph E. Davies, Jan. 15, 1914, FTCB Mss.

5. Wilson to McReynolds, Dec. 19, 1913, WW Mss; Robert E. Cushman, *The Independent Regulatory Commissions* (New York, 1941), 192-93.

6. MP, 7914, 7916; W. Speyer to Wilson, Jan. 22, 1914; Henry E. Smith to Wilson, Jan. 25, 1914; Wilson to Seth Low, Jan. 27, 1914, WW Mss. Also see Low to Wilson, Jan. 22, 1914, WW Mss.

7. Wilson to John S. Williams, Jan. 27, 1914, WW Mss. Also see Joseph Davies to Wilson, Feb. 10, 1914, WW Mss; U.S. House, Committee on the Judiciary, *Hearings on Trust Legislation*; 63:2 (Washington, 1914), 1567-83.

8. House Committee on Judiciary, *Hearings on Trust Legislation*, 133 ff., 167 ff., 191 ff., 335, 452 ff., 681, 767, 786, 1331, 1401 ff., 1682; Frank Trumbull to Wilson, Feb. 17, 1914; John P. Dwyer to Wilson, Jan. 29, 1914; Stuyvesant Fish to Wilson, Dec. 17, 1913; Edward L. Howe to Wilson, Feb. 10, 1914, WW Mss.

9. U.S. Senate, Committee on Interstate Commerce, *Hearings on Bills Relating to Trust Legislation. Interstate Trade*; 63:2 (Washington, 1914), 54 ff., 162-64, 662 ff., 688-94, 1009-1201; Chicago Association of Commerce, *Chicago Plan for Amendment to the Sherman Anti-Trust Law*, included with Thomas Creigh to Tumulty, Feb. 12, 1914, WW Mss; Chamber of Commerce of the State of New York, *Resolutions and Reports of Anti-Trust Legislation* (New York, 1914); SEN 63A-J37.

10. Belle and Fola La Follette, *La Follette*, I, 488. Also see Henry Lee Higginson to Elihu Root, Feb. 21, 1914, SEN 63A-J37; Marc Karson, *American Labor Unions and Politics, 1900-1918* (Carbondale, 1958), 77; Link, *The New Freedom*, 427-33; SEN 63A-J44; SEN 63A-J43.

11. Chamber of Commerce, *Referendum No. 8*, May 25, 1914 (Washington, 1914), 3, 6. Also see Senate Committee on Interstate Commerce, *Interstate Trade*, 688-89; National Association of Manufacturers, *Nineteenth Annual Convention*, May 19, 20, 1914 (New York, 1914), 125-27.

12. George Rublee, "The Original Plan and Early History of the Federal Trade Commission," *Proceedings of the Academy of Political Science*, XI (1926), 114-20; Franklin K. Lane to Wilson, July 10, 1914, WW Mss; Link, *The New Freedom*, 438.

13. PWW, III, 135-38. Also see J. R. Moorehead to Wilson, July 14, 1914; J. Leyden White to Wilson, June 18, 1914, WW Mss.

14. Thomas Creigh to Davies, July 23, 1914, FTCB Mss; Creigh to Wilson, June 15, 1914, WW Mss; Davies to Creigh, Aug. 12, 1914, FTCB Mss. Also see Davies to Creigh, Aug. 3, 1914; Davies to Wilson, Aug. 21, 1914; Gilbert H.

Montague to Davies, Feb. 24, 25, Aug. 19, 1914, FTCB Mss; Chicago Association of Commerce, *Notes on Federal Trade Commission Bill H.R. 15613* (Chicago, 1914); Merchants' Association of New York, *Report of Special Committee on Anti-Trust Bills* (New York, May 22, 1914).

15. Joseph H. Defrees to Wilson, Oct. 15, 1914, WW Mss; *Remarks of Francis Lynde Stetson on Taking the Chair Upon the Organization of the Martin H. Glynn Campaign . . .,* Oct. 13, 1914 (no place, 1914), no page. Also see Perkins in *New York Times,* Nov. 18, 1914; Arthur J. Eddy to Samuel J. Graham, Nov. 4, 1914, WW Mss.

16. Wilson to Powell Evans, Oct. 20, 1914, WW Mss; PWW, III, 211; Frank Trumbull to Wilson, Nov. 18, 1914, WW Mss; MP, 8015. Also see Davies to Tumulty, Nov. 23, 1914; Tumulty to Wilson, Dec. 4, 1914, WW Mss.

17. PWW, III, 258; also 267-79. Also see MP, 8033-34; Davies, "Government and Business," Dec. 17, 1914, in WW Mss.

18. F.T.C. to John M. Stanton, March 27, 1916; Secretary of F.T.C. to C. A. Dewberry, April 25, 1916, FTC Mss. Also Link, *Road to the White House,* 143; S. M. Hastings to Davies, April 13, 1915, FTC Mss; Pendleton Herring, "The Federal Trade Commissioners," *George Washington Law Review,* VIII (1940), 343; Herring, *Federal Commissioners: A Study of Their Careers and Qualifications* (Cambridge, 1936), 23; O. G. Villard to Tumulty, Dec. 12, 1914; Philip A. Crain to Brahany, Feb. 10, 1915, WW Mss; *Federal Trade Commission Decisions, March 16, 1915, To June 30, 1919* (Washington, 1920), 4.

19. United Cigar Stores Co., to F.T.C., April 20, 1915, FTC Mss. Also see AG Mss, box 3; FTC Mss, files 8501-05, for the F.T.C. effort to answer many requests and the requests themselves; Frank Vanderlip to Charles Ferguson, March 19, 1915; Albert B. Cummins to Davies, March 27, 1915; S. M. Hastings to Davies, April 13, 1915, FTC Mss; Davies to Wilson, Aug. 19, 1914, FTCB Mss; Davies, "Functions of Federal Trade Board," *Bulletin of Efficiency Society,* I (March 31, 1915), 1-5; Davies, "Memorandum in Re Suggested Powers of Trade Commission To Pass Upon Proposed Contracts, Agreements and Combinations," no date, FTC Mss; Rublee, "Outline of an Argument Against Making Final Orders of the Commission Under Section 5 of the Federal Trade Commission Act," no date, FTCB Mss; Rublee, Memo on powers and duties of FTC, handwritten, no date, FTC Mss.

20. Davies in stenographic report of hearings for Walker Hines, May 5, 1915, 28, FTC Mss. Also see Eddy, "Certain Powers of the Commission," no date; stenographic report of hearings with Louis Brandeis, April 30, 1915; Walker Hines to Rublee, May 4, 1915; Victor Morawetz to Rublee, May 11, 1915; Rush C. Butler to Davies, June 14, 1915; Cornelius Lynde to Davies, Aug. 23, 1915; Charles Van Hise to Davies, Aug. 23, 1915, FTC Mss.

21. *Annual Report of the Federal Trade Commission for the Fiscal Year Ended June 30, 1916* (Washington, 1916), 52, 8. 57 rulings were issued in the year ending June 30, 1917. In 1919 such rulings were extended to the proposed rules of industry groups and trade associations. Also see "Report of Commissioner Parry on a Tentative Plan of Organization for the Federal Trade Commission . . . Adopted June 29, 1915," FTCB Mss.

22. PWW, IV, 240; *Annual Report, 1916,* 26; *F.T.C. Decisions,* 3.

23. Davies to S. M. Hastings, April 21, 1915, FTC Mss; W. L. Petrikin in *Cleveland Plain Dealer,* April 20, 1915; Clark, Childs & Co. release, May 26, 1915, in WW Mss.

24. Edward Hurley statement, Dec. 1, 1915, in WW Mss. Also see the many examples of business enthusiasm for Hurley in FTC Mss, files 8140-2-2, 8140-4;

Hurley to Tumulty, April 26, 1916; Wilson to Hurley, May 12, 1916, WW Mss. This letter of May 12 was widely distributed, and drafted by Hurley.

25. Stenographic report in FTC Mss.

26. Wilson to Hurley, May 12, 1916, WW Mss. Also see Elbert H. Gary to Hurley, May 29, 1916; Charles Dawes to Hurley, June 14, 1916, FTC Mss; U.S. House, Committee on Interstate and Foreign Commerce, *Hearings on H.R. 13568*; 64:1 (Washington, 1916), 198 ff.; Bureau of Corporations, *Farm-Machinery Trade Associations* (Washington, 1915); Hurley speech of Dec. 1, 1915 in WW Mss.

27. MP, 8040; PWW, IV, 314, 322; also 234-44. Also see Davies to Wilson, Sept. 18, 1914; Wilson to Davies, Sept. 21, 1914, FTCB Mss; William Redfield to Wilson, Sept. 18, 1914, WW Mss.

28. Speech to N.I.C.B., July, 1916, FTC Mss; *Annual Report, 1916*, 35; Perkins to Roosevelt, Nov. 29, 1915, TR Mss. Also see *Annual Report of the Federal Trade Commission for the Year Ending June 30, 1917* (Washington, 1917), 32; Merchants' Association of New York, *Report of the Committee on the Federal Trade Commission, May 20, 1915* (New York, 1915), 2; Merchants' Assoc. of N. Y., *Urging Immediate Passage of the Webb Bill . . . With Certain Suggested Modifications, January, 1917* (no place, no date), 6-9.

29. PWW, IV, 316. Also Perkins to Tumulty, Sept. 26, 1916, GP Mss; Am. Fair Trade League to Perkins, Dec. 4, 1916, FTC Mss; and resolutions of support in FTC Mss, file 8149-30.

30. Hurley to Wilson, Jan. 6, 1917, WW Mss. For the subsequent history of the F.T.C., see Henry R. Seager and Charles A. Gulick, Jr., *Trust and Corporation Problems* (New York, 1929), chap. XXIII.

Conclusion: The Lost Democracy

1. Paul Mattick, "Marx and Keynes," *Cahiers de L'Institut de Science Économique Appliquée: Études de Marxologie*, No. 5 (Janvier, 1962), 113-212.

2. Karl Marx, *Capital* (Chicago, 1906), I, 14-15.

3. *Ibid.*, 532.

4. *Ibid.*, 787, 838.

5. *Ibid.*, 263, 296, 298, 304, 524-25.

6. Karl Marx, *Capital* (Moscow, 1959), III, 772.

7. Engels, *Anti-Dühring*, 211, 226.

8. F. Engels, *The Origin of the Family, Private Property and the State* (Moscow, 1954), 281-82.

9. I have criticized Weber in greater detail in "A Critique of Max Weber's Philosophy of History," *Ethics*, LXX (1959), 21-36; "Max Weber on America: Theory and Evidence," *History and Theory*, I (1961), 243-60.

10. Max Weber, *Law in Economy and Society* (Cambridge, 1954), 304-05. Also see Max Weber, *The Theory of Social and Economic Organization* (New York, 1947), 278.

11. H. H. Gerth and C. Wright Mills, eds., *From Max Weber: Essays in Sociology* (London, 1948), 215.

12. Max Weber, *The Religion of China* (Glencoe, 1951), 247.

13. *Ibid.*, 249.

14. Thorstein Veblen, *Absentee Ownership* (New York, 1923), 36-37.

INDEX